CONTEMPORARY HOUSING ISSUES IN A GLOBALIZED WORLD

Law, Property and Society

Series Editor:
Robin Paul Malloy

The Law, Property and Society series examines property in terms of its ability to foster democratic forms of governance and to advance social justice. The series explores the legal infrastructure of property in broad terms, encompassing concerns for real, personal, intangible, intellectual and cultural property, as well as looking at property-related financial markets. The series is edited by Robin Paul Malloy, and book proposals are welcome from all interested authors.

Robin Paul Malloy is E.I. White Chair and Distinguished Professor of Law, and the Kauffman Professor of Entrepreneurship and Innovation at Syracuse University College of Law, USA. He is Director of the Center on Property, Citizenship, and Social Entrepreneurism. He is also Professor of Economics (by courtesy appointment) in the Maxwell School of Citizenship and Public Affairs, Syracuse University. Professor Malloy writes extensively on law and market theory and on real estate transactions and development. He has authored eight books (one now in its third edition and another in its second edition) and has edited seven additional books. He has also written more than 30 scholarly articles, and has contributed to 12 other books. His recent books include: *Law and Market Economy* (2000, in English and translated into Spanish and Chinese); *Law in a Market Context* (2004); and *Real Estate Transactions* 4th Edition (with James Charles Smith, 2013).

Contemporary Housing Issues in a Globalized World

Edited by

PADRAIC KENNA
NUI Galway, Ireland

Routledge
Taylor & Francis Group
LONDON AND NEW YORK

First published 2014 by Ashgate Publishing

2 Park Square, Milton Park, Abingdon, Oxfordshire OX14 4RN
52 Vanderbilt Avenue, New York, NY 10017

Routledge is an imprint of the Taylor & Francis Group, an informa business

First issued in paperback 2020

British Library Cataloguing in Publication Data
A catalogue record for this book is available from the British Library

The Library of Congress has cataloged the printed edition as follows:
Kenna, Padraic.
Contemporary housing issues in a globalized world / by Padraic Kenna.
pages cm. – (Law, property and society)
Includes bibliographical references and index.
ISBN 978-1-4724-1537-0 (hardback)
1. Right to housing. 2. Housing–Law and legislation. 3. Squatters–Legal status, laws, etc. 4. Land tenure–Law and legislation. 5. Right to housing–Europe. I. Title.
K3550.K46 2014
344'.063635–dc23

2013023977

ISBN 978-1-4724-1537-0 (hbk)
ISBN 978-0-367-60089-1 (pbk)

Contents

List of Figures and Tables

Figures

Tables

Notes on Contributors

Rachelle Alterman is based at the Technion – Israel Institute of Technology, where she holds the Azrieli Chair in Town Planning. With degrees in planning and in law from Canadian and Israeli universities, she is a leading authority on cross-national comparative analysis of planning laws, land use regulations, property rights and planning practice. She is the Founding President of the International Academic Association on Planning, Law and Property Rights (2006–10) and serves on the editorial boards of leading academic journals. The Association of European Schools of Planning has awarded her Honorary Member status (the fifth person so honoured).

Jane Ball was admitted as a solicitor in 1978 and practised in property law and then in litigation. After starting to lecture in law at Manchester Metropolitan University from 1994, she obtained a doctorate from the University of Sheffield on housing disadvantaged people in France. A specialist in French law and the sociology and economics of housing, she researches areas where there is a mismatch in national disciplines, often the neglected fringes of comparison in English property law. Now a senior lecturer at Newcastle University, she teaches equity, trusts, land law and land use and international security and credit.

Joe Finnerty teaches social policy in the School of Applied Social Studies, University College Cork. His housing research interests include the attitudes and behaviour of private landlords, the evaluation of homelessness policy and changes in the tenure trajectories of low-income households. He is joint coordinator of the homelessness working group of the European Network of Housing Researchers and is Ireland's research advisor to the European Observatory on Homelessness.

Mark Jordan is a research fellow at the University of Southampton and a graduate of NUI Galway. He is part of the TENLAW research project, where he is responsible for researching issues relating to property law, housing law and landlord and tenant law across Scotland and the Republic of Ireland. In addition to his researching responsibilities, he teaches property law on the LLB programme at the University of Southampton. Prior to joining the Law School at Southampton in 2012, he carried out research on human rights issues in Ireland on behalf of a range of NGOs and charitable bodies.

Elizabeth Kamundia completed an LLM in International and Comparative Disability Law and Policy in 2012 at the Centre for Disability Law and Policy, NUI, Galway. Prior to joining NUI Galway, she worked at the Kenya National Commission on Human Rights (KNCHR) as the Human Rights Officer on Disability. She also worked as a researcher with the Committee of Experts on Constitutional Review that helped deliver a new Constitution for Kenya in 2010. She is an advocate of the High Court of Kenya and also holds a Masters in Public International Law from the University of Nairobi. Currently she is working as a consultant with Users and Survivors of Psychiatry – Kenya as well as with the Open Society Initiative for Eastern Africa and the KNCHR on the reform of legal capacity law in Kenya.

Padraic Kenna is a graduate of the School of Law, University of Warwick and holds a PhD from NUI Galway. His most recent publication *Housing Law, Rights and Policy* (Dublin, Clarus Press 2011) provides a comprehensive examination and critical analysis of contemporary housing law and policy. In 2004, he established, with others, the FEANTSA Expert Group on Housing Rights. He is a Member of Housing Rights Watch and the Editorial Advisory Board of both the *International Journal of Law in the Built Environment* and the *Irish Human Rights Law Review*. He is also affiliated to the NUI Galway Centre for Disability Law and Policy, where he is engaged in research, teaching and PhD supervision. Currently, he is developing the new Centre for Housing Law, Rights and Policy at NUI Galway.

Karen Lynch-Shally is a Hardiman PhD Scholar at NUI Galway. Her doctoral thesis is entitled 'Towards a Sustainable European Mortgage System: The Role of Regulation'. This undertakes a comparative analysis of the regulation of mortgage markets, both from an origination and a funding perspective, in the European and international context. The objective of the analysis is to assess the potential for regulation to contribute to a sustainable market model.

Sergio Nasarre-Aznar is Professor of Civil Law at the University Rovira i Virgili and a Deputy Judge in the Court of Tarragona. He has been awarded European Doctor in Law and Masters in Real Estate Economics by the University of Cambridge. In 2008 he was made Corresponding Member of the Spanish Royal Academy of Jurisprudence and Legislation. He is the author of three books on mortgage market and tort law, has edited four more and is the author of over 50 scientific articles published in Spain, Germany, the US, Switzerland, the Netherlands, Portugal, the UK, Ireland and Poland. He has delivered more than 70 lectures in several European countries and has been visiting scholar at the Universities of Barcelona (2005), Bremen (2007), Valladolid (2009, 2010 and 2012), National University of Ireland (2009), Cambridge (2011, 2012 and 2013) and Duke (2011). He has been main researcher of four projects on access to housing (2010, 2011 and 2012) and is a member of the TENLAW project, the 7th Framework Programme of the

EU, the European Network for Housing Research and the Common Core Project of the University of Trento. He has taken part in various legislative committees for Catalonia (2006 trusts, protection of mortgagors' intermediate tenures, 2011, 2012) and across Spain (reform of the Law of Leases 2012 and to draft the Spanish Housing Plan 2013–16). The recipient of several awards, his research interests are mainly property and real estate law, territorial credit, mortgages, the mortgage market, housing, securitization, European private law, trust, mortgage refinancing, real estate and tort law.

Maria Antonieta Nestor is a PhD candidate at the School of Law, Trinity College Dublin. She holds a Bachelor of Civil Law degree from University College Dublin (UCD) and an LLM from the University of California Los Angeles (UCLA). She was the first foreign student to be admitted into the prestigious David J Epstein Programme in Public Interest Law & Policy in August 2008, where she piloted an LLM specialization. She also holds a diploma in journalism, is a trained legal interpreter and translator, and is the co-founder and past co-editor of the *Irish Review of CED Law & Policy*.

Cathal O'Connell is Senior Lecturer in Social Policy at the School of Applied Social Studies, University College Cork. His research and teaching interests centre on the development of Irish social policy, housing policy and social housing management. His recent publications include: *The State and Housing in Ireland* (2007, Nova Press), 'Citizenship and Social Exclusion in Limerick' in N Hourigan (ed), *Understanding Limerick: Social Exclusion and Change* (Cork University Press, 2011) and 'Social Housing Management, Governance and Delivery in Ireland: Ten Years of Reform on Seven Estates' (2010) 25(10) Housing Studies 317–34 (with M Norris). He is currently undertaking Irish Research Council-funded research of the role of young people in housing estate regeneration.

Michelle Oren is a PhD candidate at the Technion-Israel Institute of Technology in the Urban Planning Programme. She holds a Master's degree in Urban and Regional Planning from the Technion and a Bachelor in Political Sciences and Environmental Studies from the University of Haifa. Born in Israel, she spent her childhood years in Bogota, Colombia. In 2012 she worked as an Intern at UN-Habitat in Nairobi for the policy analysis branch. Her chapter is partially based on her PhD thesis. Professor Alterman is her main PhD supervisor and Professor Yaffa Zilbershatz from Bar Ilan University Law School is her co-supervisor.

Vanesa Valiño is a Bachelor of Political Sciences and holds a Masters in Gender Politics from the Universtat Autònoma de Barcelona. During the last six years, she has been the Director of the Observatory of Economic, Social and Cultural Rights, a non-profit association located in Barcelona which aims to promote social rights as fundamental human rights. She has contributed to many publication,s most recently 'Defender y repensar los derechos sociales en tiempos de crisis' (Observatory DESC 2009). She has also written articles related to housing matters such as 'Derecho a la vivienda ynejecuciones hipotecarias. Estrategias contra el sobreendeudamiento de las familias' (2010)

Yaffa Zilbershats is the Deputy President of Bar-Ilan University and previously served as the Dean of the Faculty of Law in Bar-Ilan University. She specializes in international, human rights and constitutional law and has published extensivley on these topics. She earned her LLB and PhD from Bar-Ilan University's Faculty of Law. Her LLM degree in International Legal Studies was received from New York University, where she also served as a Visiting Scholar. She has served on Israeli blue-ribbon committees, including the Committee for the Preparation of Citizenship Legislation, the Rubinstein Committee for reviewing Israeli immigration and citizenship laws, and the Keshev Committee for equality in military and civil service. She currently serves as a member of the Board of Governors of the International Association of Jewish Lawyers and Jurists and as their academic adviser, and as a board member of the Israel Democracy Institute.

Chapter 1
Introduction

Padraic Kenna*

Introduction

Housing addresses the basic need for human shelter and facilitates the essential human requirement for a home. In recent times, housing has also been promoted by global financial institutions as the contemporary repository of household wealth and equity.[1] Yet, this approach to housing has created the greatest global financial crisis for generations. *The Economist* has pointed out that the house price boom that preceded the 2008 financial crisis was remarkable for its scope and scale.[2] However, house prices have begun to rise again in the US, but continued to fall in the peripheral countries of the Eurozone in spring 2013.[3] Indeed, across the world, there is a mixed picture, with house prices falling (the largest annual drop of nine per cent in Spain) and rising in equal numbers. In spring 2013, *The Economist* house-price indicators data showed that since 2007, house prices had fallen by 49 per cent in Ireland, 24 per cent in Spain, 21 per cent in the US, 14 per cent in the Netherlands and Japan, and 11 per cent in Italy and the UK.[4] However, in that period, house prices had increased by 86 per cent in Hong Kong, 24 per cent in Austria and Singapore, 21 per cent in Switzerland, 20 per cent in Canada, 17 per cent in China, 12 per cent in South Africa and 10 per cent in Australia.[5] Consequently, the book focuses somewhat on the situations in

* I wish to thank all the contributors and especially Robin Paul Malloy and Dee Halloran for their valuable assistance in preparing this book.

1 The benefits of home-ownership as a driver of development based on Hernando De Soto, *The Mystery of Capital* (London, Bantam Books 2000) have been promoted by many global development institutions.

2 'Home Truths' *The Economist* (12 January 2013).

3 Initially, the house price fall in Estonia was sharper than any other country, but house prices have now recovered to one-third of the fall experienced between 2005 and 2007. In Latvia, a large part of the mortgage portfolio has been backed by investment loans. See HJ Dübel and M Rothemund, *A New Mortgage Credit Regime for Europe* (Brussels, Centre for European Policy Studies 2013) 8.

4 'Home Truths' *The Economist* (12 January 2013).

5 The highest annual increases to the fourth quarter of 2012 in the Eurozone were Latvia (+9.8 per cent), Estonia (+5.8 per cent) and Malta (+5.4 per cent), with the largest falls in the same period occurring in Spain (-12.8 per cent), Romania (-9.1 per cent) and Slovenia (-8.8 per cent). See Eurostat, *News Release/Euroindicators 55/2013* (11 April 2013).

the two countries (Ireland and Spain) where globalization has had the greatest impact on housing systems.

What then are the key contemporary housing issues in a globalized world? This book brings together a range of topics and approaches originally discussed at the 'Contemporary Housing Issues in a Changing Europe' conference held at National University of Ireland, Galway, in 2012. This was organized by the Centre for Housing Law, Rights and Policy, the European Network of Housing Researchers (Legal Aspects of Housing, Land and Planning Group), FEANTSA (the federation of European organizations working with homeless people) and Housing Rights Watch. The conference, which attracted more than 100 participants from Europe, the US and Israel, provided an opportunity to examine and discuss key contemporary housing issues in the context of the global financial and sovereign debt crisis.

The objective of this book is to build on the findings of the conference and to take up the challenge of developing a new paradigm, working towards the possibility of an alternative future. The book revolves around three constellations of writing by diverse authors, each possessing a clear and developed approach to contemporary housing issues.

The first major theme considers the crisis in mortgage market regulation, the development of mortgage securitization and comparisons between Spain and Ireland, two countries at the epicentre of the global housing market crisis. The second thematic consideration focuses on housing rights within the European human rights architecture, within national constitutions and arising from new international instruments, with their particular relevance for persons with disabilities and developing economies. The third theme incorporates an examination of some responses to the decline and regeneration of inner cities, legal issues around squatting in developed economies, and changes in tenure patterns away from home-ownership.

A Globalized World

Definitions of globalization are diverse and the term itself is hotly contested.[6] Globalization is a generic term used to describe a range of economic, industrial, social, military and cultural changes which have created high levels of interdependence, interaction and integration between different parts of the world,

6 It has been argued that the epithet 'global' was born in 'business management schools' (Harvard, Columbia, Stanford). Specifically, the first text was *The Globalization of Markets* from Theodore Levitt (*Harvard Business Review*, May/June 1983). Later, the English-language economic press expanded the concept and afterwards the think tanks of neoliberalism adopted the concept.

between people and between producers and consumers.[7] Globalization primarily involves the intensification of worldwide social relations.

Technological development and communication are key features of globalization, which has also been variously conceived as action at a distance; time-space compression; accelerating interdependence; a shrinking world; and, among other concepts, global integration, the re-ordering of interregional power relations, consciousness of global conditions and the intensification of interregional connectedness. The local becomes embedded within more expansive sets of interregional relations and networks of power – the global village.[8]

From the information superhighway to the international trade in drugs and arms, to the phenomenal impact of Macworld, Nike and the global media, the subject of globalization has come to concern all and sundry. At the core of most discussions of the issue is the extraordinary explosion of both technology and information, in ways that have considerably reduced the twin concepts of time and space. In particular, information and communications technology (ICT) has emerged as perhaps the most dominant force in the global system of production, albeit with significant ramifications in all other spheres of contemporary human existence.[9]

Giddens regarded globalization as having four dimensions, involving the world capitalist economy, the nation-state systems, the world military order and the international division of labour.[10]

A precise and widely quoted definition of globalization is put forward by Held and others as:

> a process (or set of processes) which embodies a transformation in the spatial organisation of social relations and transactions – assessed in terms of their extensity, intensity, velocity and impact – generating intercontinental or interregional flows and networks of activity, interaction and the exercise of power.[11]

Globalization has been described as an ideological construction, a convenient myth which, in part, helps justify and legitimize the neoliberal global project that

---

7 There is an important distinction between internationalization and globalization; see David Held et al, *Global Transformations, Politics, Economics and Culture* (Cambridge, Polity Press 1999) 52–58.

8 See D Held and A McGrew, 'The Great Globalization Debate: An Introduction' in D Held and A McGrew (eds), *The Global Transformation Reader* (Cambridge, Polity Press 2000).

9 UN Doc. E/CN.4/Sub.2/2000/13. *The Realization of Economic, Social and Cultural Rights: Globalization and its Impact on the Full Enjoyment of Human Rights.* Preliminary report submitted by J Oloka-Onyango and Deepika Udagama, in accordance with Sub-Commission resolution 1999/8, 15 June 2000, at para. 6.

10 Anthony Giddens, *The Consequences of Modernity* (Cambridge, Policy Press 1990).

11 See D Held, A McGrew, D Goldblatt and J Perraton, 'Rethinking Globalization' in Held and McGrew (eds) (n 8) 68.

is the creation of a global free market, and the consolidation of Anglo-American capitalism within the world's major economic regions.[12]

Of course, contemporary globalization may be viewed as no more than a continuation of centuries-old global trade, which hugely intensified after the Industrial Revolution, as described by Marx and Engels in their description of the global nature of capital.[13] Depicting globalization as the *second great transformation*, Howard-Hassmann suggests that globalization is the final assault of capitalism on those areas of the world that previously escaped it, either because of explicit communism or socialist politics, 'or because capitalism had no interest in the region as a source of capital or resources, a source of workers or a market'.[14] It now appears that globalization is forcing onto an unwilling world the conditions of early European capitalism, ignoring the international human rights law that now prohibits such conditions.[15] Indeed, Andreasson claims that the contemporary international vigour to create property rights in land and housing can be viewed as merely one step beyond the former colonial processes of dispossession of property by force.[16]

The primary agents and institutional focus of contemporary economic global practices are widely identified as transnational corporations.[17] But the World Bank, the International Monetary Fund (IMF), the World Trade Organization (WTO), commodity and currency exchanges, and other international organisations, such as the World Economic Forum, comprising leading industrialists and politicians, set the agenda and course for globalized corporations, states and institutions to follow. Indeed, the World Bank has provided the theoretical framework for states to create housing policies which sponsored markets as the primary actors in housing systems.[18]

Sachs describes three overarching effects of the new globalization, a phenomenon which is globally transformative,[19] all of which have a significant

---

12 For an excellent account of the development of neoliberalism, see David Harvey, *A Brief History of Neoliberalism* (New York, OUP 2005).

13 See Karl Marx, *Capital, A Critique of Political Economy. Volume 2* (London, Routledge 1983).

14 RE Howard-Hassmann, 'The Second Great Transformation: Human Rights Leapfrogging in the Era of Globalization' (2005) 27 HRQ 1, 5.

15 ibid 18.

16 See S Andreasson, 'Stand and Deliver: Private Property and the Politics of Global Dispossession' (2006) 54 Political Studies 3.

17 See Joel Bakan, *The Corporation: The Pathological Pursuit of Profit and Power* (London, Constable 2004).

18 See World Bank, *From Plan to Market: World Development Report 1996* (Washington DC, World Bank 1996); World Bank, *The State in a Changing World* (Washington DC, World Bank 1997); World Bank, *Development Report* (Washington DC, World Bank 1997). See also RM Buckley and J Kalarickal, *Thirty Years of World Bank Shelter Lending – What Have We Learned?* (Washington DC, World Bank 2006).

19 Jeffrey Sachs, *The Price of Civilization* (London, Vintage 2012) 93–103.

impact on housing policies. The convergence effect refers to the fact that the new globalization provides the conduit for today's emerging economies to leapfrog technologies. This leads to the second effect – the labour effects. The opening up of China to global trade in 1978 brought millions of low-skilled workers into a globally integrated labour pool. Inevitably, manufacturing jobs moved to China, with increasing unemployment among traditional manufacturing workers, many of whom had mortgages. The third effect – the mobility effect – means that as capital becomes internationally mobile, countries begin to compete for it, cutting corporate tax rates, easing regulations, reducing social spending and generating a 'race to the bottom'. When the 2008 financial crisis struck, it demonstrated a crisis of utterly mismanaged globalization.[20]

Robinson describes the current globalization as the near-culmination of five centuries of capitalism, or the fourth epochal shift in social structures.[21] The first epoch, from 1492 to 1789, was ushered in with the emergence of capitalism from its feudal origins in Europe and its outward conquests of other continents. It was the epoch of mercantilism and primitive accumulation. The second epoch, which lasted until the late nineteenth century, of competitive or classical capitals, was marked by the Industrial Revolution, the rise of the bourgeoisie and the forging of the modern state, brilliantly described by Hobsbawn.[22] The third epoch marked the rise of corporate (monopoly) capitalism, 'the consolidation of a single world market and the nation-state system into which world capitalism became organized'.[23] It was marked by the development of the financial industrial corporation, imperialist wars and the emergence of a socialist alternative to capitalism.

Today, in the fourth epoch of capitalism, globalization is associated with the microchip and information age. Thomas Friedman's iconic text *The Lexus and the Olive Tree* viewed this globalization as a new technological economic system based on the microchip and driven by financial investors.[24] However, this epoch also led to the collapse of twentieth-century attempts at socialism, as well as a 'transition from the nation state phase of world capitalism, with its distinct institutional, organisations, political, and regulatory structures, to a transnational phase'.[25] This emerging transnational phase of capitalism is qualitatively new.

The defining feature of this epoch is the rise of transnational capital, which creates the basis for globalization. The globalization of the production process, orchestrated by global corporations, integrates national circuits of capital into

---

20 ibid 103.

21 W.I Robinson, *A Theory of Global Capitalism* (Baltimore, Johns Hopkins University Press 2004) 4–17.

22 See Eric Hobsbawm, *The Age of Revolution* (New York, Mentor 1962); *The Age of Capital* (London, Sphere 1977); *The Age of Empire* (New York, Pantheon 1987).

23 Robinson (n 21) 4.

24 Thomas Friedman, *The Lexus and the Olive Tree* (New York, Farrar, Straus & Giroux 1999).

25 Robinson (n 21) 5.

global circuits of capital. Foreign direct investment (FDI) represents the emanation of this flow, which has played a critical role in integrating different regions of the world. In 2012, some 44 per cent of global FDI inflows were hosted by only five countries. China attracted the lion's share (US$253 billion or 18 per cent of the total), followed by the US (US$175 billion), Brazil (US$65 billion), the UK (US$63 billion) and France (US$62 billion).[26]

Finance capital has become hegemonic with the use of offshore tax havens as impenetrable shields from public accountability, regulation and taxation, as well as perfectly legal means of concealing ownership.[27] The use of offshore tax havens, where an estimated one-third of global wealth is held and through which half of all global trade passes, has been highlighted by the International Consortium of Investigative Journalists.[28] It is suggested that half a million offshore accounts are held in the British Virgin Islands, and are estimated to facilitate some 40 per cent of global offshore companies. Murphy has identified the perverse effects of this 'feral finance', pointing out that the global stock of financial assets is estimated at $220 trillion (of which $150 trillion is debt of some sort), whereas global GDP is about $63 trillion per annum. Meanwhile, the total flow of financial speculative trades in the world each day was estimated at approximately $4 trillion, or $1 quadrillion per annum.[29]

Robinson identifies a 'transnational capitalist class' arising from this capital globalization, which seeks to capture the commanding heights of state policy-making in key sectors of the economy, especially central banks and finance and foreign ministries.[30] This transforms countries, using national state apparatuses to re-structure and integrate them into the global economy. Rothkopf describes a 'superclass' or global power elite of about 6,000 people, influencing everything from the way currencies are priced worldwide to choosing which political candidates would have sufficient funding for presidential campaigns.[31] This global 'superclass' – the 'vanguard of globalization' – has stepped in to fill the void in global governance, but not in a conspiratorial manner.

Business leaders engage in what is effectively self-regulation. Unelected clusters of the most powerful effectively drive governments' decision-making on global issues. Empowered individuals direct private resources that have become

26 See OECD, *FDI in Figures* (Paris, OECD April 2013). The OECD countries, Luxembourg, Belgium, Ireland, Chile and Hungary enjoyed FDI inflows greater than 10 per cent of GDP in 2012.

27 Nicholas Shaxson, *Treasure Islands* (London, Bodley Head 2011).

28 See the International Consortium of Investigative Journalists website: http://www.icij.org/offshore accessed 24 April 2013.

29 Richard Murphy, *The Courageous State*. (London, Searching Finance 2011) 249.

30 Robinson (n 21) 47–53.

31 David Rothkopf, *Superclass: The Global Power Elite and the World They Are Making* (London, Little, Brown 2008). Rothkopf points out (at 121) that a few thousand people among the corporate elite effectively control perhaps $100 trillion – two-thirds of the world's total assets.

the *sine qua non* of development capital flows. These are all important strands of the connective tissue binding the global community. The superclass confronts issues that many national governments and multilateral organizations cannot or will not address.[32]

Murphy urges politicians to champion a 'courageous state', avoiding political capture by financial capital, and acting in the public interest. He suggests a remedy for the crisis in banking caused by the housing finance crisis:

> A Courageous State must now split banks in two so that no bank involved in the processing of transaction, managing customer deposits or in routine business and household lending, including mortgages, can engage in speculative market trading; and nor can such entities themselves or through related entities rely on bulk money markets for fund, as, for example, Northern Rock did.[33]

Globalization of this epoch represents the near-culmination of the centuries-long process of the extensive enlargement of capitalism. However, many people across the world have benefited from this integration into the global economy. Sachs has suggested in *The End of Poverty* that the effect of globalized industrial development on Bangladesh has been a 66 per cent drop in infant mortality in 30 years and a reduction in numbers in extreme poverty in India and China, respectively, by 200 and 300 million people since 1990.[34] The numbers in the world experiencing 'extreme poverty' (surviving on less than $1.25 per day) has reduced from approximately half to one-quarter of the global population over the past 25 years.

Significantly, Sachs claims that the women working in the 'sweatshops' already 'have a foothold in the modern economy that is a critical measurable step up from the villages of Malawi'.[35] Of course, working conditions can be harsh, but are better than those of subsistence agriculture, especially for women. Perhaps the globalization of production therefore represents, more than anything else, a greater proletarianization of women's work worldwide.

Clapham has pointed out that globalization involves the re-orientation of national governments in a climate where regulation and control are increasingly difficult.[36] The danger of a flight of capital and jobs constrains taxation and public expenditure policies, resulting in reduced expenditure on housing. This has accompanied an emphasis on targeted spending, 'value for money' approaches and the privatization of state-owned housing. Regional economic imbalances arising from policies of flexible labour markets and freedom to locate given to corporations

---

32 ibid 315.

33 Richard Murphy, *The Courageous State* (London, Searching Finance 2011) 253.

34 Jeffrey Sachs, *The End of Poverty* (London, Penguin 2005).

35 ibid 11.

36 David Clapham, 'Housing Policy and the Discourse of Globalization' (2006) 6(1) European Journal of Housing Policy 55.

have resulted in housing shortages in some areas and surpluses in others. The flexible labour market approach increases the risk of episodes of poverty, with housing systems unable to respond adequately. Increased risk in the labour market has been transferred to housing through the deregulated housing finance system. Indeed, the role of planning is increasingly seen as merely supporting the housing market, even an overheated housing market. There is an emphasis on the supply of new housing in areas of economic growth and consequent high demand.[37]

Housing Issues

Kenna has pointed out that globalization has impacted on homelessness across the world, particularly in the creation of millions of migrants; the growth of global corporations linked to housing, home construction and consumption; the globalization of property rights in housing systems; the global spread of housing finance; globalized real estate investment; the re-ordering of cities and slums; and the diminution of state housing responses.[38]

Housing and the built environment are greatly influenced by the current global crisis (both social and economic), with governments on the one hand struggling to reconcile and regulate the forces of international finance, and on the other, to manage, plan and provide a good-quality built environment and housing stock. However, the root of the current financial crisis could be seen as the inadequate development and fortification of the law of the built environment and housing against the vagaries of unregulated global finance. The downgrading of financial and banking regulation in the 1980s unleashed an international flow of housing finance which has inundated housing systems across the world, integrating housing finance with global finance. This lead to mortgage market deregulation and the consequent lowering of lending standards.[39] In Europe this followed the convergence of national currencies into the euro, with a common (and low) interest rate, after 1999.

The World Bank has described the speed at which market-based housing finance has spread around the world: 'Since 2000, the world changed from one in which most of the world's population now lives in countries with a market-based mortgage finance system with generally affordable terms.'[40] Yet, the Bank has acknowledged that 'while market-based housing finance is now available to most middle-income people in the world it is still not available in most countries or for the poorest people'.[41] Many informal housing settlements house renters or

37 ibid.

38 Padraic Kenna, 'Globalization and Housing Rights' (2008) 15(2) Indiana Journal of Global Legal Studies 397.

39 Mark Stephens, 'Mortgage Market Deregulation and its Consequences' (2007) 22(2) Housing Studies 201.

40 Buckley and Kalarickal (n 18) xii.

41 ibid.

squatters who are unable to access housing finance because they have no clear marketable or mortgageable title.[42]

While large-scale informal settlements and individual squatting are prevalent in many developing cities, squatters' rights or adverse possession as a means of acquiring property has been part of European law for many centuries. In this context, the chapter by Jane Ball examines squatting in England and France, both countries with developed property registration systems. She compares individual squatting with the emergence of collective squats. In Europe, collective squats often arose as a form of protest – 'squats of conviction', which act as *foci* for campaigns for political and social change. Historically, individual squatting has been treated in the law of both countries as a valuable means of using land which has been left idle. However, there is also the fear of granting title to such people and various 'moral panics' have been fomented. Indeed, the stereotype of the good squatter – a white farmer who tills the unused land – is being abandoned in law, and recent legislation in both countries seeks to criminalize squatting in residential property. Ball also refers to the large informal settlements of developing cities and to the Constitution of Brazil (1988), where certain squatters of five years can register their title.

Ball uses insider/outsider theory, originally developed by Lindbeck and Snower,[43] to show how entry and exit costs of employment create a barrier to the entry of new employees. In a similar vein, she applies this theory to housing systems, based on her research in three regions of France. She posits that, although different from employment markets, the theory can be used to explain the exclusion of certain people from social housing and owner-occupation. Squatters are *outsiders* in the housing market and social housing system. Although squatting is a response to high transaction costs in accessing the housing market or social housing, squatters are also stigmatized. She suggests that the high transaction costs and outsider/insider approaches ultimately produce housing difficulties for everyone, and the emergence of squatting should be viewed as an early warning of housing system failure. The practical answer to insider/outsider dichotomies is to create a more 'level playing field' for all participants in housing systems.

Elsewhere, Angel has promoted regulated housing markets as the key enablers of housing across the world, although his analysis is more nuanced than most international writers. He defines effective housing systems as comprising five subsystems; finance; property registration; infrastructure; regulation; and social/

---

42 UN Centre for Human Settlements (UNCHS), *Cities in a Globalizing World* (London, Earthscan 2001) 77–87. While this report favours self-build and contrasts the view of housing as a right with housing as a function of ability-to-pay or purchase as a commodity in housing markets, it nevertheless outlines how globalization impacts on housing finance.

43 A Lindbeck and D Snower, *The Insider-Outsider Theory of Employment and Unemployment* (Cambridge, MA, MIT Press 1988).

subsidized housing.[44] Significantly, he suggests that, in order for the enabling market system itself to have potency, there must be an element of social housing or subsidized housing for those who cannot afford to access the market. This comprehensive approach to housing market systems should, ideally, ensure a supply of housing at affordable prices for all.

However, in most OECD countries with enabling market systems, the share of household spending on housing rose during the past decade, partly reflecting increased real house prices. From the mid-1980s until recently, particularly large price increases were observed in Ireland, Spain, the UK and the Netherlands, although prices were stable or even declined in Japan, Switzerland and Germany. This surge in housing prices was accompanied by booming housing investment in several countries, particularly in Spain and Ireland, and also in some Baltic/Nordic countries.[45]

Table 1.1 House price increases across the world: 1980 (or earliest year available) –2008[46]

Very large increases (60 per cent or more)	Moderate to large increases (20 per cent to 90 per cent)	Stable or declining (less than 20 per cent increase)
Australia	Austria	Chile
Belgium	Canada	Germany
Finland	Denmark	Hungary
Ireland	France	Israel
Netherlands	Greece	Japan
New Zealand	Italy	Korea
Norway	Slovenia	Portugal
Spain	Sweden	Switzerland
UK	US	

Nominal prices deflated by the consumer price index.
Source: national sources and OECD Economic Outlook No. 87.

44 Schlomo Angel, *Housing Policy Matters: A Global Analysis* (New York, OUP 2000).

45 See D Andrews, A Caldera Sánchez and Å Johansson, 'Housing Markets and Structural Policies in OECD Countries', *OECD Economics Department Working Papers, No 836* (Paris, OECD Publishing 2011). The OECD is made up of 34 countries: Australia, Austria, Belgium, Canada, Chile, the Czech Republic, Denmark, Estonia, Finland, France, Germany, Greece, Hungary, Iceland, Ireland, Israel, Italy, Japan, Korea, Luxembourg, Mexico, the Netherlands, New Zealand, Norway, Poland, Portugal, the Slovak Republic, Slovenia, Spain, Sweden, Switzerland, Turkey, the UK and the US.

46 ibid 10.

According to the UN Special Rapporteur on adequate housing, market-based housing finance has contributed to a widespread bubble in real estate prices and a decrease in affordability. It has done little to promote access to affordable adequate housing for the poorest. Between 1997 and 2004, average housing prices grew by 149 per cent in Spain, 139 per cent in the UK, 187 per cent in Ireland, 112 per cent in Australia, 65 per cent in the US and 227 per cent in South Africa.[47]

In 2012, the UN Special Rapporteur on adequate housing outlined the globalized prevalence of housing finance policies and their impact on the right to adequate housing for those living in poverty:

> In the late 1970s a dramatic shift occurred in housing policies, starting with North America and Europe, followed later by developing countries in Latin America, Asia, Africa and by formerly planned economies. This shift, supported by predominant economic doctrine, called for the transfer of activities from State control to the private sector and for unrestricted free markets and free trade. This view soon gained hegemony, shaping the policies of States, international financial institutions and development agencies. The effects of this approach on housing policies across the globe have been dramatic and well documented.

A growing consensus was formed, whereby governments renounced their role as suppliers of affordable housing and become facilitators, supporting market demand rather than directly providing outcomes: 'Governments should be encouraged to adopt policies that enable housing markets to work … and avoid distorting housing markets.'[48] This new role implies creating conditions, institutions and regulations aimed at supporting housing finance systems to promote home-ownership under the neoliberal dogma of reliance on private property and market forces. [49]

From the 1980s onwards, housing finance became perceived not only as a tool for promoting access to adequate housing, but also as critical to the development of the financial sector, and gradually became a central pillar of the financial market, expanding the terrain for global capital:[50]

> The deregulation, liberalization and internationalization of finance that started in the 1980s had major implications for housing and urban development. Funds for mortgage lending now derive from national and international capital markets

47 Raquel Rolnik, *Report of the Special Rapporteur on Adequate Housing as a Component of the Right to an Adequate Standard of Living: The Rights to Adequate Housing,* UN Doc A/67/286, 2012, para 12.

48 World Bank, *Housing: Enabling Markets to Work*, World Bank Policy Paper (Washington DC, World Bank 1993) 6.

49 Rolnik (n 47) paras 2–4.

50 ibid para 10.

> and not solely from existing savings and retail finance. These developments have been characterized as the 'financialization' of housing.[51]

This process has been accompanied by the conceptual transformation of adequate housing from a social good into a commodity, and part of a strategy for household wealth accumulation and welfare security.[52]

This 'tsunami of liquidity' is described in the chapter by Vanesa Valiño, where she traces its impact on Spain's housing system and how it created an over-indebtedness among the working class in the absence of any other housing options. Spain has less than one per cent social housing and the rental market is not very well developed. The crash exposed the vulnerable position of home-ownership borrowers, as well as the inconsistencies in the mortgage legislation, which is described in detail in the chapter by Sergio Nasarre-Aznar. Indeed, the state response was less than adequate in protecting borrowers, a different position from that of Ireland, as set out in the chapter by Karen Lynch-Shally. Some limited respite from the courts towards borrowers has been evident, particularly in relation to EU unfair clauses in consumer contracts provisions. Civil society organizations are developing a response in Spain, unlike Ireland, with half a million signatures being collected in one petition. Valiño suggests that the Spanish housing policy needs to be recast along the lines of the recommendations of the UN Special Rapporteur on the rights to adequate housing.

In contrast, the chapter by Joe Finnerty and Cathal O'Connell describes the changing tenure trajectories in contemporary Ireland – a country at the epicentre of the housing crisis. Reflecting the global policy influences of the World Bank and allied institutions, they chart the shift in state policy since the 1980s towards supporting the housing market as the primary vehicle for housing supply. This invokes the conceptual imagery of the 'housing ladder' – a metaphor prevalent in academic and public discourse. The embodiment of owner-occupation as the symbol of permanent security and stability offered a higher-order existence from that of the insecurity of the Irish rented sector. However, despite the dramatic surge in lending on home ownership for the past two decades, Ireland's tenure pattern followed a different pattern from that of Spain. Owner-occupation declined as a proportion of tenure, as unaffordable house prices and improvements in the regulation and standards of private renting took effect. Finnerty and O'Connell also question why there has been so little downward slide on the home ownership 'ladder' in Ireland following the financial crisis. There have been few repossessions, and here state policy has been a critical factor, providing a safety net for poor borrowers unable to repay loans and supporting vulnerable households with mortgage arrears. Indeed, there may also be hidden factors influencing the low rates of repossession. Low-income households who now enter the Irish housing

---

51 Manuel B Aalbers, 'The Financialization of Home and the Mortgage Market Crisis' (2008) 12(2) Competition and Change 148.

52 Rolnik (n 47) para 11.

system will be accommodated within hybrid forms of social/private housing rather than being encouraged into low-cost home-ownership schemes. Clearly, political and legislative action can reduce the worst effects of the crisis.

Re-ordering and Growth of Cities

At a global level, the most significant contemporary housing issue is the rapid growth of urbanization. In the last decade, the urban population in the developing world grew by an average of 1.2 million people per *week*, or about one full *year*'s demographic growth in Europe's urban areas.[53] In the context of housing development, it is expected that by the middle of this century, out of every 10 people on the planet, seven will be living in urban areas. Of course, increasing slums are one feature of this global phenomenon.[54]

A new structural phenomenon has been identified within the world's cities, which are expected to number 358 with a population of more than one million people by 2015.[55] A new constellation of globally networked cities, sometimes referred to as the 'urban archipelago', has been identified for over two decades. These cities may have more relations with other cities than with their hinterlands.[56]

In the globalized cities there are 'mosaics of growing inequality' within the 'global archipelago of interconnected city cores'.[57] The combination of new information technologies and socio-economic re-structuring is reshaping cities and regions, ushering in new urban forms, with deprivation and poor housing locations also distinguished by under-investment in such technology and services.[58]

53 UN-Habitat, *State of the World's Cities 2012/13 Report* (Nairobi, Kenya, UN Habitat 2012).

54 See Mike Davis, *Planet of Slums* (London, Verso 2006).

55 See R Fuchs et al, *Mega-city Growth and the Future* (New York, UN University Press 1994) ch 1.

56 See UNCHS, *Cities in a Globalizing World* (London, Earthscan 2001). M Davis, 'Planet of Slums: Urban Involution and Informal Proletariat' (2004) 26 NLR 5, 8 points out that: 'Urbanists also speculate about the processes weaving together Third World cities into extraordinary new networks, corridors and hierarchies. For example, the Pearl River (Hong Kong–Guangzhou) and the Yangtze River (Shanghai) deltas, along with the Beijing–Tianjin corridor, are rapidly developing into urban-industrial megalopolises comparable to Tokyo–Osaka, the lower Rhine, or New York–Philadelphia. But this may only be the first stage in the emergence of an even larger structure: "a continuous urban corridor stretching from Japan/North Korea to West Java." Shanghai, almost certainly, will then join Tokyo, New York and London as one of the "world cities" controlling the global web of capital and information flows. The price of this new urban order will be increasing inequality within and between cities of different sizes and specializations.'

57 See UNCHS (n 57).

58 See M Castells, *The Informational City: Informational Technology, Economic Restructuring and the Urban-Regional Process* (Oxford, Blackwell 1989).

In many developing cities, high-quality ICT infrastructures are being packaged through entrepreneurial planning, public subsidies and defensive urban design into industrial parks for international firms and 'Euro-American'-style gated residential enclaves for social and economic elites.[59]

Global finance competes with local private and state bodies for land in the new globally networked cities. This has an enormous impact on subsequent housing costs and the affordability of housing, as well as the location and subsidy levels required for social housing.[60] As the United Nations Centre for Human Settlements (UNCHS) has pointed out, 'many cities now acknowledge that the current funding flows and investment capital demands an international urban orientation over and above managing local issues'.[61] States are faced with the outcomes of rising market prices where key workers such as teachers and public servants cannot afford to buy housing. In Europe, political pressure from these organized groups has led to various 'affordable' housing schemes to enable access to the market by state subsidies on mortgages or on land or purchase prices.[62] The effect, of course, has been to buttress the rising markets, as states were drawn into higher and higher levels of subsidies to meet the prices of starter homes rising with the market.

The development of housing townships and projects/gated communities represents a particularly divisive aspect of recent patterns of urbanization. This has led to large tracts of land and civic services being denied to lower-income residents of cities. According to Kothari and Chaudhry:

> In Shanghai, Pow highlights the moral order underpinning the erection of gated communities, which represent the move to create 'civilised' communities away from the uncivilised and stigmatised underclass of rural immigrants. Caldeira in her compelling analysis of Sao Paulo's gated communities notes that once the upper class withdraws into enclaves, an inevitable contraposition between a safe and familiar inside and a threatening and unknown outside surfaces. Perhaps nowhere is this tendency more extreme than in Dubai, a de facto vast gated community founded on overarching commercial interests and built according to its global image, in order to attract 'upper classes' from all over the world. Behind the facade of luxury lies the fate of thousands of Filipino, Indian and Pakistani immigrants unable to gain citizenship (and related rights) and de facto

59 UNCHS (n 57) 11.

60 B Needham, *Land for Social Housing* (Brussels, CECODHAS 2000).

61 UNCHS (n 57) 4.

62 See Sarah Monk and Christine Whitehead, *Making Housing More Affordable: The Role of Intermediate Tenures* (Oxford, Wiley-Blackwell 2010); Kathleen Scanlon and Christine Whitehead, *Social Housing in Europe II: A Review of Policies and Outcomes* (London, LSE Publishing 2008).

> forced to live in camps on the periphery in extremely precarious conditions, working draconian hours, and experiencing totalitarian social control.[63]

In the introduction to the UN-Habitat *State of the World's Cities 2012/13 Report*, Joan Clos, the Executive Director of UN-Habitat, points out that the crisis has impacted on cities in different ways:

> It shows that a lopsided focus on purely financial prosperity has led to growing inequalities between rich and poor, generated serious distortions in the form and functionality of cities, also causing serious damage to the environment – not to mention the unleashing of precarious financial systems that could not be sustained in the long run.[64]

The Report introduces a new tool – the 'City Prosperity Index' – together with a conceptual matrix, the 'Wheel of Urban Prosperity', to assist decision-makers to design clear policy interventions. It advocates a transformative change towards a people-centred, sustainable urban development, where our current understanding of prosperity is revised to include quality of life, infrastructures, equity and environmental sustainability.

In this context, the chapter by Marie Antoineta Nestor critically examines the various legislative, funding and political measures applied to US inner-city under-served communities in the past 60 years. She questions whether the public interest law models developed within these neighbourhoods could be effectively transposed to similar neighbourhoods in Ireland. Contemporary approaches to regeneration of these neighbourhoods have involved developing new legal services aimed at combating poverty and social exclusion. Law centres and community lawyering seek to empower local people and communities, prompting the practice of community economic development. In the US, community lawyers have been central to this regeneration response to the globalized re-ordering of inner cities. Nestor considers how public interest law and regeneration can be connected in this way in Dublin through linking sustainable development with the establishment of a community law centre.

Housing and the Global Financial Crisis

At the beginning of 2007, the Mortgage Bankers Association of America reported increasing default among American over-indebted home-owners. This was but the tip of the iceberg. Beneath the surface was a universal credit crisis in housing finance. In short, mortgage lending had expanded into unsustainable

63 See Miloon Kothari and Shivani Chaudry, *Taking the 'Right to the City' Forward: Obstacle and Promises* (New Delhi, India Habitat International Coalition 2010).

64 UN-Habitat (n 54) iv.

territory, with borrowers unable to repay loans. The explosion in credit had led to two decades of rising house prices. Sachs points out that the fall in house prices in 2006 spelled the end of a couple of decades when the middle classes treated their homes as ATM machines, drawing on the ostensible value of their homes through equity loans.[65]

Many American house purchasers had been attracted by novel arrangements, such as 'teaser' mortgages (below market rates for an initial period), 'ninja' mortgages (borrower having no income, no job and no assets), 'piggyback' mortgages (further lending on an existing mortgage to cover repayments) and 'liar loans' (loans based on unverified statements of income). However nefarious these arrangements may have been, and they resulted in many millions of borrowers losing their homes, they were only part of the crisis. These arrangements were at the base of a global pyramid of 'synthetic' securities traded between financial institutions. Lenders (usually banks) sold off their riskiest mortgages by repackaging them into securities called collateral debt obligations (CDOs), channelling the cash flows from thousands of mortgages into a series of tiered or tranched bonds, with risks and yields attuned to different investor tastes.[66] The top-tier tranches would have first call on the underlying cash flows arising from the mortgage repayments, and would be rated and sold as AAA-rated bonds. The lower tiers, which would have a call on the underlying cash flows, were rated lower, but carried higher yields. These 'securities' were traded around the world. As Soros points out:

> Starting around 2005, securitization became a mania. It was easy and fast to create 'synthetic' securities that mimicked the risks of real securities but did not carry the expense of buying and assembling actual loans. Risky paper could therefore be multiplied well beyond the actual supply in the market. Enterprising investment bankers sliced up CDO and repackaged them into CDOs of CDOs, or CDO^2s. There were even CDO^3s. The highest slices of lower rated CDOs obtained AAA ratings. In this way more AAA liabilities were created than there were AAA assets. Towards the end, synthetic products accounted for more than half the traded volume.[67]

By 2007, these mortgage-backed securities were held by financial institutions and banks around the world. Both public and private-label securitization took place outside the regulated financial system in the 'shadow banking system'. Official regulation never really existed.[68]

---

65 Sachs (n 19) 16.

66 George Soros, *The Crash of 2008 and What it Means* (New York, Public Affairs 2008).

67 ibid xviii.

68 Dübel and Rothemund (n 3) 11.

From 2007, house price falls rendered most US subprime mortgages worthless. The base of the global apex of housing mortgage-related financial derivatives began to crumble. When the true nature of these high-risk, low-value instruments became evident, the financial system panicked.

In the second half of 2008, the US credit crisis began to trigger a global crisis in the financial system that spread to the real economy. Soros points out that this crisis was of an entirely different character compared to previous capitalist crises.[69] It had spread from one segment of the market to others, particularly those which employed newly created structured and synthetic instruments. Both the exposure and the capital base of major global financial institutions were brought into question. Once this crisis began, financial markets unravelled rapidly. It was no longer certain which financial institutions were actually solvent, given the widespread nature of assets held in these now-worthless 'synthetic' instruments. Uncertainties about major losses resulted in a lack of confidence between banks and a 'credit crunch' as the interbanking lending system froze.

From 2007, central banks across the developed world began to inject enormous levels of funds to maintain the global banking system.

The convergence of a credit crunch, failing banks, house price collapses and economic slowdown prompted states to take action in their housing systems:

> The financial crisis starting in 2008, and the important role of mortgage loans not only in the subprime crisis in the United States, but also in some EU markets, has acted recently as a catalysing factor to change the traditional perspective. Mortgages and related asset classes, such as developer loans, are so large in proportion to bank assets that, as the crisis developed, the problems in some EU mortgage markets no longer remained confined to national boundaries. Rather they had EU-wide ramifications, e.g. by affecting investors in other jurisdictions funding banks, or by deteriorating the country's fiscal position as a result of massive support for failing banks.[70]

These housing policy impacts of the international financial crisis differed markedly between and within European and other states.[71] Some states, such as Ireland, undertook to guarantee all the liabilities of banks and thus banking debt became

69 See Soros (n 67) 26. For Soros, this demonstrated the fallibility of neoclassical approaches to economics, based on the supply/demand nexus and the limited techniques and metrics used by economics to analyse a situation that is vastly more complex, and on which they are not independent observers. These techniques distort the underlying information, but take on an existence of their own, further complicating reality and the task of understanding it.

70 Dübel and Rothemund (n 3) 2.

71 See H van der Heijden, K Dol and M Oxley, 'Western European Housing Systems and the Impact of the International Financial Crisis' (2011) 26(3) Journal of Housing and the Built Environment 295.

sovereign debt. The result was the destruction of states' credit ratings and an inability to borrow, requiring intervention from the IMF and the European Central Bank – measures which precipitated programmes of austerity. CECODHAS, the Federation of Social Housing Organizations in Europe, pointed out in 2012 that the deep economic downturn and austerity measures have led to an increase in levels of poverty and housing exclusion across Europe; the numbers on waiting lists for social housing is increasing rapidly in many countries; state budgets dedicated to housing policies have been significantly reduced; mortgage and rent arrears and repossessions are increasing; and in some cases social housing organizations are re-structuring or selling their stock to raise capital.[72]

A European Parliament Report in 2013 detailing how EU Member States responded to the financial crisis noted that states applied different strategies by choosing to finance a specific type (or group) of social expenditure that could provide a 'safety net' for an increasing share of the population experiencing severe economic conditions:[73]

> Despite EU housing markets being characterized by a high share of home-ownership, the deep economic crisis created an exogenous shock for the social housing market with all European countries experiencing a significant increase in poverty rates and housing exclusion ... The EU recognizes social housing as a key instrument in ensuring the right to housing as stated by international law, to meet the requirements of the Treaty and achieve Europe 2020 targets.[74]

Direct state housing provision for low-income households has diminished, and some states are unable to dedicate any resources towards social housing. Homelessness has risen across the EU as the economic and financial crisis has persisted.[75] Similarly, the extent of material deprivation or 'the inability to live a decent life' has increased dramatically in some EU Menber States such as Greece, the Baltic States, Ireland and Spain since 2008.[76]

In this context, the chapter by Sergio Nasarre-Aznar critically examines the weaknesses in mortgage lending practices and the deficient common law system of mortgage lending regulation. He raises even more significant questions in relation to the role and legality of the rating agencies that legitimized the synthetic

72 CECODHAS, *Impact of the Crisis and Austerity Measures on the Social Housing Sector. CECODHAS Housing Europe's Observatory, Research Briefing* (Brussels, CECODHAS 2012).

73 European Parliament, Directorate General for Internal Policies, *Social Housing in the EU* (Brussels, PE 2013) 492.469.

74 ibid 6–7.

75 Nicole Fondeville and Terry Ward, 'Research Note 8/2011, Homelessness During the Crisis' (Social Situation Observatory, November 2011).

76 European Commission, *EU Employment and Social Situation, Quarterly Review* (European Commission, Luxembourg June 2012) 48.

financial products. Major questions are also raised as to the reliability and transparency of the US mortgage titling system – issues which may not be entirely resolved by a house price recovery and redemption of these mortgages. Examining the detrimental impact of the international crisis on the Spanish housing system, he shows how excessive and reckless bank lending and the securitization of mortgages also contributed to the crisis in Spain. He provides a key contemporary legal analysis of the Spanish situation and also outlines valuable initiatives being developed to prevent a repeat of this scenario, and to rescue something from the gross over-supply of housing.

One of the key areas highlighted by Nasarre-Aznar is the difference between recourse and non-recourse across the US and in Spain. The generally accepted view that a mortgage is a 'real right in land created by the owner (mortgagor) entitling the mortgagee to payment of a certain sum out of the land with priority to other creditors on the forced sale of the property'[77] would appear to be at odds with the prevalence of recourse mortgages. In Spain, the recourse to the assets and income of guarantors to the mortgage (which often include extended family members) by the mortgagee in the event of default is creating an enormous social impact.

In her chapter, Karen Lynch-Shally compares the constitutional, legislative and secondary provisions relating to mortgages in Spain and Ireland in the context of the widely differing levels of repossession for arrears. It would appear that such provisions exert a significant influence, with relatively few repossessions in Ireland where the protection for the borrower has been strong. The courts have begun to give legal effect to the consumer codes in Ireland, integrating these into mortgage law, following legislation in 2009 which established a distinct classification of 'housing loans' within mortgage law. However, an unintended repeal of a statutory provision in 2009 provided the primary legal reason for the low level of repossessions in Ireland.

Housing Rights

Globalization has contributed to the widespread proliferation of human rights discourse and information, especially the UN instruments. However, some view the move towards rights-based approaches as contemporaneous with a move towards individualization in social policy, influenced by the growth of consumerism, the development of modernist and postmodernist social theory and the effects of globalization.[78]

---

77 *Real Property Law & Procedure in the European Union* (European University Institute, Florence, 31 May 2005) 85.

78 See Alastair Hudson, 'Equity, Individualisation and Social Justice' in Alastair Hudson et al, *New Perspectives on Property Law, Human Rights and the Home* (London, Cavendish Publishing 2004); Kenna (n 38).

Housing rights are viewed as rooted in human rights and particularly socio-economic rights.[79] These rights are now seen as an integral part of economic, social and cultural rights within the United Nations, European, Inter-American and African human rights instruments. At the level of public international law, the UN Committee on Economic, Social and Cultural Rights (UNCESCR) offers a global supervisory mechanism for the implementation of housing rights, while the European Committee of Social Rights of the Council of Europe (ECSR) is creating valuable contemporary clarifications on the nature and extent of housing rights. Aspects of housing rights are regularly adjudicated upon in courts throughout the world,[80] including in the US,[81] with contemporary South African jurisprudence in this area attracting keen academic interest.[82] Social rights (including housing rights) have formed part of most new constitutions since 1945, not just in Europe, but around the world.[83]

In their chapter, Michelle Oren, Rachelle Alterman and Yaffa Zilbershatz have examined the nature and extent of housing rights across the world within national constitutions. This chapter, based on a comprehensive contemporary survey of 205 national constitutions, reveals three approaches taken by states to incorporate such rights. First, there is a direct or explicit approach along the lines of individual housing rights for certain persons. Second, housing rights can be found embedded within other rights, such as social security, assistance to the needy, etc. Third,

79 Classical human rights discourse is usually confined to public international law largely ignoring housing rights within consumer rights, property rights, family law rights, etc. See S Deutch, 'Are Consumer Rights Human Rights?'(1995) 32(2) *Osgoode Hall Law Journal* 538. For comprehensive overviews of socio-economic rights, see A Eide et al (ed), *Economic, Social and Cultural Rights: A Textbook*, 2nd edn (Dordrecht, Martinus Nijhoff Publishers 2001); M Craven, *The International Covenant on Economic, Social and Cultural Rights* (Oxford, Clarendon Press 2005); MA Baderin and R McCorquodale (eds), *Economic, Social and Cultural Rights in Action* (OUP 2007).

80 See Jessie Hohmann, *The Right to Housing: Law, Concepts, Possibilities* (Oxford, Hart Publishing 2012); Centre on Housing Rights and Evictions, *Litigating Economic, Social and Cultural Rights* (Geneva, COHRE 2003); T Melish, *Protecting Economic, Social and Cultural Rights in the Inter-American Human Rights System* (Connecticut, Yale Law School 2002); A Nolan, 'Litigating Housing Rights: Experiences and Issues' (2006) 13(1) Dublin University Law Journal 145.

81 See B Harris, *Defending the Right to a Home* (Aldershot, Ashgate 2004).

82 See especially *Government of South Africa and others v Grootboom and others* CCT11/00 2001 (1) SA 46 (CC), 4 October 2000, 2000 (11) BCLR 1169 (CC); *Port Elizabeth Municipality v Various Occupiers* 2005 (1) SA 217 (CC). Case No CCT 53/03 *City of Cape Town v Rudolph* 2003 (11) BCLR 1236 (C).

83 See A Ben-Bassat and D Momi, 'Social Rights in the Constitution and in Practice' (2008) 36(1) *Journal of Comparative Economics* 103; JM Woods, 'Justiciable Social Rights as Critique of the Liberal Paradigm' (2003) 38 Texas International Law Journal 763. J Kemeny, *Housing and Social Theory* (London, Routledge 1992) points out that the level of state control over housing markets reflects the balance of political power between labour and capital.

housing rights can be discerned from indirect or implied rights, such as peaceful enjoyment of possessions or privacy rights. The authors suggest that much enrichment of international cross-learning on housing rights could develop in this area of law.

Beneath the level of constitutions, many housing rights are enshrined in both private and public law at the national and local levels, such as regulations on rights of access, building standards, planning, sanitation and associated law and decisions.[84] There are detailed legal regulations and institutionalized regulatory systems on land use, building standards and housing cost controls, all with legally enforceable sanctions for violations, and compensation for breaches. In line with the growth of regulatory systems for over a century, construction and construction product norms that establish minimum quality standards are in place in many states across the world.[85]

Courts across the world have enforced housing rights in areas of security of tenure, respect for home, non-discrimination, decent physical standards and fair procedures in evictions.[86] This regulatory machinery seeks to protect, preserve and promote the physical and mental health and social well-being of people, control nuisances, prevent and control communicable diseases, and regulate adequate sanitation and public health.[87] The use of planning law to achieve integration of social/affordable and private housing, control of land use and quality of infrastructure and amenities is now becoming widely recognized, as a somewhat lateral but practical means of realizing some housing rights.[88] Indeed, some of these measures can go so far as to delimit and deny traditional civil and political rights,

84 UN-Habitat UNHRP Report Series, No 3, *National Housing Rights Legislation*, 3rd edn (HS/638/01E) (UNHRP, Nairobi 2006); UN-Habitat UNHRP Report Series, No 1, *Housing Rights Legislation: Review of International and National Legal Instruments* (HS/638/01E) (UNHRP, Nairobi 2002); Centre on Housing Rights and Evictions, *Sources No 4: Legal Resources for Housing Rights: International and National Standards* (COHRE, Geneva 2000): Scott Leckie (ed), *National Perspectives on Housing Rights* (The Hague, Kluwer Law International 2003). See also, for example, Roger Burridge and David Ormandy, 'Health and Safety at Home: Private and Public Responsibility for Unsatisfactory Housing Conditions' (2007) 34(4) Journal of Law and Society 544.

85 Cass Sunstein, *After the Rights Revolution: Reconceiving the Regulatory State* (Cambridge, MA, Harvard University Press 1990). See also P Cartwright, 'Consumer Protection in Financial Services: Putting the Law in Context' in P Cartwright (ed), *Consumer Protection in Financial Services* (The Hague, Kluwer Law International 1999).

86 See DB Bryson, 'The Role of Courts and a Right to Housing' in Bratt et al, *A Right to Housing* (Philadelphia, Temple University Press 2006).

87 Schlomo Angel, *Housing Policy Matters: A Global Analysis* (New York, OUP 2000) 155–60.

88 Juli Ponce-Sole (ed) *Land Use Law, Housing and Social and Territorial Cohesion* (Denver, Rocky Mountain Institute 2006); Padraic Kenna, *Housing Law, Rights and Policy* (Dublin, Clarus Press 2011).

such as property rights, by extended rights of occupancy for tenants overriding the legal owners' powers to sell.[89]

In the global context of housing being secured primarily through markets, and in terms of owner-occupation, where a loan is required, many states have introduced protections for such housing consumers. Indeed, EU law provides that such contracts cannot contain unfair terms. A new concept – that of the 'vulnerable consumer' – has been introduced into Irish consumer protection and mortgage law, with lenders required to take reasonable steps to accommodate that person. This places a duty of care on lenders so that no inappropriate mortgages are given – a situation which would challenge the legality of many subprime loans.

Minimum Core Obligations and Persons with Disabilities

Housing rights are often associated with the right to basic shelter, invoking a 'minimum core obligation' on states. Article 2(1) of the International Covenant on Economic, Social and Cultural Rights requires states to take steps 'to the maximum of its available resources, with a view to achieving progressively the full realization of the rights recognized'.[90] This includes housing rights. However, without an established measurable baseline of minimum core obligations, it is, in reality, impossible to properly measure any progressive realization. UNCESCR General Comment 3 (1991) established that:

> a minimum core obligation to ensure the satisfaction of, at the very least, minimum essential levels of each of the rights is incumbent upon every State party. Thus, for example, a State party in which any significant number of individuals is deprived of essential foodstuffs, of essential primary health care, of basic shelter and housing, or of the most basic forms of education is, *prima facie*, failing to discharge its obligations under the Covenant. If the Covenant were to be read in such a way as not to establish such a minimum core obligation, it would be largely deprived of its *raison d'être*.[91]

While human rights scholars often claim credit for it, the notion of minimum core state obligations to ensure people's basic existence is shared across the political spectrum. Frederich Hayek argued that substantive equality and distributive (social) justice conflicted with rule of law, but nevertheless accepted that

89 Christopher McCrudden, *Buying Social Justice: Equality, Government Procurement, and Legal Change* (OUP 2007).

90 UN Doc A/6316 (1966) *International Covenant on Economic, Social and Cultural Rights*. UNGA Resolution 2200A (XXI), entered into force 3 January 1976.

91 UN Doc E/1991/23, UN Committee on Economic, Social and Cultural Rights, *General Comment 3, The Nature of States Parties Obligations* (art 2, para 1) 12/14/1990, para 10.

governments could provide a minimum level of support for the 'unfortunate' in society.[92] Similarly, Milton Friedman accepted the need for a guaranteed minimum income, albeit at a low level.[93] Sen and Nussbaum argue for a minimum provision useful for the facilitation of human capabilities, leading to the development of people's lives.[94] A classical Marxist approach recognizes that, for the capitalist system to continue, capitalism must ensure (either through wages or state welfare provision) that workers are able to work, but also that the working class must reproduce itself. A minimum core obligation of the availability of basic necessities is essential for the reproduction of the working class.

Chapman and Russell describe the 'minimum core' as one of the more difficult concepts in human rights, 'bridging the gap, as it does, between lofty goals and available resources'.[95] Across the world, courts struggle to advance a coherent legal approach to making this minimum core a reality.[96] However, contemporary writers such as King suggest that such social rights can only be advanced incrementally by courts – and, indeed, courts have not always proven to be effective guardians of such rights.[97]

Indeed, King proposes state obligations of a 'social minimum' or a claim for resources required for a minimally decent life. This 'social minimum' involves an entitlement to resources to meet a healthy subsistence threshold, meeting basic physical needs of shelter, nutrition, childhood development, health, psychological integrity; a social participation threshold involving education, insurance against economic shocks and resources for minimal social engagement with family and peers; and finally an agency threshold involving education and economic stability to engage in basic life-planning, framing and achieving long-term goals.

---

92 Frederich Hayek, *The Road to Serfdom* (University of Chicago Press 1944) 133: 'There can be no doubt that some minimum of food, shelter, and clothing, sufficient to preserve health and capacity to work, can be assured to everybody.'

93 Milton Friedman (with RD Friedman) *Capitalism and Freedom* (University of Chicago Press 1962) 192.

94 Amartya Sen, *Inequality Re-examined* (Oxford, Clarendon Press 1992); Martha Nussbaum and Amartya Sen (eds), *The Quality of Life* (OUP 1993). See also NC McNaughton, 'Housing, Homelessness and Capabilities' (2010) 27(1) Housing, Theory and Society 23.

95 A Chapman and S Russell (eds), *Core Obligations: Building a Framework for Economic, Social and Cultural Rights* (Antwerp, Intersentia 2002) 8–9. It is variously referred to as minimum core content, core content, essential elements, core obligations and minimum state obligations.

96 *Government of South Africa and others v Grootboom and others* (n 84); *R (on the application of Limbuela) v Secretary of State for the Home Department* [2005] UKHL 66, [2006] 1 AC 396; *Moldovan v Romania* (2005) 44 EHRR 16; *Shantistar Builders v Narayan Khimalal Totame* [1990] 1 SCC 520. See also Colm O'Cinneide, 'A Modest Proposal: Destitution, State Responsibility and the European Convention on Human Rights' (2008) 5 EHRLR 583.

97 Jeff King, *Judging Social Rights* (CUP 2012).

Traditional housing rights indicators based on shelter and physical elements of housing are also being transcended by a focus on housing rights as a means to an end rather than an end in itself. For instance, Article 19 of the UN Convention on the Rights of Persons with Disabilities (UNCRPD) provides for a right in relation to: 'Living independently and being included in the community.' States must take effective and appropriate measures to facilitate full enjoyment by persons with disabilities of this right and their full inclusion and participation in the community.[98] This includes ensuring that persons with disabilities have access to a range of in-home, residential and other community support services, including personal assistance necessary to support living and inclusion in the community, and to prevent isolation or segregation from the community.[99]

Elizabeth Kamundia shows in her chapter that the universal nature of UN human rights instruments can impact differently on countries with different levels of economic resources, despite having legal effect domestically. She traces how Article 19 has become part of Kenyan constitutional law and examines key legislative and policy provisions. The central and supportive role of families for people with disabilities is enormously significant in any discussion of rights in the Kenyan (and African) context. However, the right to independent living can be hampered by poor education and transport facilities, a lack of assistive devices and discrimination. More serious obstacles lie in the structural challenges facing the state in relation to poverty and housing deprivation. The resettlement of large numbers of internally displaced persons, extremely high levels of poverty, acute shortages of habitable dwellings and the prevalence of extensive slums and squatter settlements present major obstacles for human rights realization. Indeed, Kamundia points out that 60–80 per cent of residents in Kenya's largest urban centres live within informal settlements, lacking basic services. Clearly, implementing the right to independent living depends on the effective enjoyment of the right to housing.

The contemporary enjoyment of the right to independent living allied to housing rights is set to become a key element of housing policies and law, since the UNCRPD has now been ratified by 130 states and signed by 155. The Optional Protocol attached to the UNCRPD, whereby individuals can make a complaint to the UN Committee on the Rights of Persons with Disabilities, has already begun to create a global jurisprudence in this area.

Thus, while the minimum core obligation on states is becoming more person-centred, it still requires the devotion of significant resources. The establishment of a globally accepted and enforced minimum core obligation, however, has proved to be elusive to date.

---

98 UN Doc A/RES/61/106.

99 See Report of Inclusion International, *Inclusive Communities = Stronger Communities, Global Report on Article 19: The Right to Live and Be Included in the Community* (London, Inclusion International October 2012).

Globalization Meets Housing Rights

Contemporary debates on housing oscillate between traditional perspectives of freedom of contract and sanctity of property on the one hand, and the realization of housing and human rights on the other. There is a fundamental difference between orthodox economic and human rights approaches to housing across the world today. Indeed, some writers suggest that contemporary mainstream economics is fundamentally contradictory to many human rights, especially economic, social and cultural rights.[100] Mainstream economics and human rights have different language and conceptual frameworks – the former using the language of wants and the latter using the language of rights.

Within the language of wants, ability to pay is the key question, whereas within the language of rights, it is entitlement. If in the first case exclusion and inequality are tolerable, in the second case the only acceptable situation is one characterized by inclusion and equality. In other words, goods and services can be unequally distributed, but rights cannot.[101] The UN Special Rapporteur on Adequate Housing has highlighted this dichotomy in relation to housing:

> Housing finance policies based on credit are inherently discriminatory against lower-income households, and at their best increase housing affordability for upper- and middle-income groups. Housing finance policies often 'redline' the poor, who are required to pay much higher prices for financial services, exposing them to financial risks inherent to global financial markets and indebtedness.[102]

Indeed, housing policies around the world, since the 1970s, have involved states creating conditions, institutions and regulations aimed at supporting globalized housing financial systems promoting home-ownership as the primary tenure, often under the neoliberal paradigm on private property and market forces.[103] Housing has been promoted as a financial asset rather than a home, and the subsequent securitization of housing loans has integrated housing finance into global capital movements, effectively freezing mortgage law development. However, while robust neoliberal economic arguments against housing rights may have historical integrity, they are less than convincing in the context of modern industrialized and urbanized societies. As the UN Special Rapporteur on the right to adequate housing pointed out in 1993, the ideologies of states are reflected in their human settlement policies:

> The arguments against awarding socio-economic rights on the grounds of cost and their impact on the spending priorities of the Legislature and Executive are

100 M.C Branco, *Economics versus Human Rights* (London, Routledge 2009) 4–5.
101 ibid 5.
102 Rolnik (n 47) para 65.
103 ibid para 3. See De Soto (n 1); Buckley and Kalarickal (n 18).

> dwarfed in the face of the large-scale public spending programmes and market intervention measures, which are a permanent feature of modern governance.[104]

Even the OECD accepts the need for state intervention in housing systems:

> Housing warrants attention for several reasons. It is an important element of wealth as well as the single biggest expenditure for a majority of households and, as witnessed by the recent financial and economic crisis, housing market outcomes can have repercussions for the macro economy. A well-functioning housing market supporting geographical mobility is also necessary to ensure efficient labour market outcomes. Housing also deserves attention for social reasons, *inter alia* because adequate housing and their future employment. A wide range of public policies affect the housing market. Such policies are justified on the basis of repairing market failures, pursuing broader economic efficiency goals and a desire to influence the housing opportunities available to citizens. These interventions include fiscal measures (such as subsidies and taxes), direct provision of social housing (i.e. housing let/sold at below-market rents and/or allocated by non-market mechanisms) and regulations aimed at influencing rental markets, as well as the quantity, quality and allocation of dwellings. They also involve public resources being directed to redistribute income by supporting housing consumption (e.g. housing allowances).[105]

Of course, there is no mechanism within markets which can guarantee that rights will be provided or that they will be provided equally.[106] However, this dissonant position has been transcended by states for more than a century and there is a ubiquitous acknowledgement by states that access to housing is a human right. Both neoliberal and social democratic governments across the world accept the market as the primary provider of housing. In both systems, however, state action is acceptable to regulate the excesses of the housing market and to intervene when the market fails (including the provision of social and subsidized housing). Marcuse and Keating point out that the only disagreement between these two dominant global political perspectives is on how serious that failure is at any particular time, and just what governments should do about it.[107] Indeed, such

---

104 UN Doc E/CN.4/Sub.2/1993/15, *1st Report of Mr Sachar Special Rapporteur*, quoting from the 1975 UN Vancouver Declaration on Human Settlements.

105 See Andrews, Caldera Sánchez and Johansson (n 45) 5.

106 But RJ Shiller, *Finance and the Good Society* (Princeton University Press 2012) 12 suggests that the real cure for the ills of financial capitalism lies in improving and democratizing it, where technology works with financial and legal advice and financial education to make it possible for everyone to participate intelligently in the financial system.

107 See P Marcuse and WD Keating, 'The Permanent Housing Crisis: The Failures of Conservatism and the Limitations of Liberalism' in R Bratt et al, *A Right to Housing* (Philadelphia, Temple University Press 2006). For a thorough examination of the arguments

intervention has recently involved the nationalization and state capitalization of banks and financial institutions. All across the world, states have recapitalized banks whose assets were wiped out through the purchase of securitized subprime loans. Social democratic and liberal political systems behaved similarly in the recent financial crisis.

These two dominant political approaches can be contrasted with the archetypal right-to-housing position 'in which government's first obligation is to see that all are decently housed, and the for-profit market is managed and regulated in a way subservient to that goal'.[108] The for-profit market is the default position for neoliberal and social democratic policies, while the default position of the right-to-housing approach is state support for universal decent and affordable housing (but allowing the for-profit market to function where it does not interfere or frustrate that position).

While economic liberals posit that globalization is an economic inevitability, Anderson suggests that lawyers have come late to this globalization debate,[109] although human rights expert Philip Alston asserted in 1997 that 'international lawyers have, in many respects, served as the handmaidens of the changes wrought by globalization'.[110] Concurrently, the development of 'transgovernmentalism' where individual elements of states (or civil servants) interact directly with their counterparts abroad is creating a new order.[111] A new technocratic elite deals with important issues, yet operates not through law or rights, but through sharing information, developing common principles and soft law measures at the subnational level across states.[112] This is the contemporary context within which the application of housing rights to housing systems takes place.

Falk has suggested that a subaltern discourse on human rights encompasses the full panoply of human rights, with the Universal Declaration of Human Rights (UDHR) laying the foundations for superseding the dominant globalization discourse. There is a core demand, from a strictly materialist perspective, within Article 25(1): 'Everyone has the right to a standard of living adequate for the health and well-being of himself and of his family, including food, clothing,

---

in favour of a right to housing from a contemporary American legal perspective, see KD Adams, 'Do We Need a Right to Housing?' (2009) 9(2) Nevada Law Journal 275.

108 Marcuse and Keating (n 109) 139.

109 GW Anderson, *Constitutional Rights after Globalization* (Oxford, Hart Publishing 2005) 3.

110 See Philip Alston, 'The Myopia of the Handmaidens: International Lawyers and Globalization' (1997) 3 *EJIL* 435.

111 See Sol Picciotto, 'Networks in International Economic Integration: Fragmented States and the Dilemmas of Neo-liberalism' (1996) 17 Northwestern Journal of International Law & Business 1014; A Slaughter, 'Governing the Global Economy through Government Networks' in M Byers (ed), *The Role of Law in International Politics* (OUP 2003).

112 For a response to Alston's article, see SV Scott, 'International Lawyers: Handmaidens, Chefs, or Birth Attendants? A Response to Philip Alston' (1998) 9 EJIL 750.

housing and medical care and necessary social services.'[113] Similarly, Article 11 of the International Covenant on Economic, Social and Cultural Rights (1966) (ICESCR) (now adopted by most states in the world) states:

> The States Parties to the present Covenant recognize the right of everyone to an adequate standard of living for himself and his family, including adequate food, clothing and housing, and to the continuous improvement of living conditions. The States Parties will take appropriate steps to ensure the realization of this right, recognizing to this effect the essential importance of international co-operation based on free consent. [114]

There is an obligation on States Parties to recognize, promote, protect, and fulfil the right of everyone to an adequate standard of living, including adequate housing.[115]

Miloon Kothari, UN Special Rapporteur on adequate housing, pointed out in 2003 that while the debate continues at the international level as to whether or not globalization can bring benefits to the world's poor, the fact remains that the deepening inequalities of income and opportunity between and within nations has led to an increase in the number of people without adequate and secure housing:

> It is time to rethink the current global economic and social policies and to recommit ourselves to the human rights principles and standards that offer the only real paradigm for improving the lives of millions of the poor … Every woman, man, youth and child has the human right to a secure home and community in which to live in peace and dignity. This human right has received global recognition and is firmly established in a number of international human rights instruments, most notably in the International Covenant on Economic, Social and Cultural Rights.[116]

Notwithstanding the constraints and difficulties placed upon them, central governments still have an important role to play in reconciling macroeconomic policies with social objectives, keeping in mind the primacy of their human rights obligations. They have the responsibility to make targeted interventions

---

113 R Falk, 'Interpreting the Interaction of Global Markets and Human Rights' in A Brysk (ed) *Globalization and Human Rights* (Berkeley, University of California Press 2002) 61.

114 UN Doc A/6316 (1966) *International Covenant on Economic, Social and Cultural Rights*. UNGA Resolution 2200A (XXI), entered into force 3 January 1976.

115 P Alston and G Quinn, 'The Nature and Scope of States Parties Obligations under the ICESCR' (1987) 9 HRQ 156.

116 Miloon Kothari, *Privatising Human Rights: The Impact of Globalization on Access to Adequate Housing, Water and Sanitation* (UN Special Rapporteur on Adequate Housing. Montevideo, Uruguay, Social Watch 2003) http://unpan1.un.org/intradoc/groups/public/documents/apcity/unpan010131.pdf accessed 27 November 2012).

in order to ensure universal access to public services, including water and sanitation, on a fair and equitable basis; this is fundamental for the fulfilment of the right to adequate housing.[117]

In a similar vein, the UNCESCR has addressed the role of international organizations in protecting housing rights in the age of globalization:

> The Committee calls upon the International Monetary Fund and the World Bank to pay enhanced attention in their activities to respect for economic, social and cultural rights, including through encouraging explicit recognition of these rights, assisting in the identification of country-specific benchmarks to facilitate their promotion, and facilitating the development of appropriate remedies for responding to violations. Social safety nets should be defined by reference to these rights and enhanced attention should be accorded to such methods to protect the poor and vulnerable in the context of structural adjustment programs. Effective social monitoring should be an integral part of the enhanced financial surveillance and monitoring policies accompanying loans and credits for adjustment purposes. Similarly the World Trade Organization (WTO) should devise appropriate methods to facilitate more systematic consideration of the impact upon human rights of particular trade and investment policies. In that regard the Committee urges the Secretary-General to undertake, if possible in collaboration with the WTO, a careful study of the potential impact upon respect for economic, social and cultural rights of the draft Multilateral Agreement on Investment (MAI) being negotiated within the OECD.[118]

While the global model – the 'transmission belt' of international human rights being adopted into national law is widely accepted, it faces major and growing obstacles from the new forms of governance and patterns of law, and particularly from increasing forms of soft law regulation. This classical approach to international human rights law, where states accept, ratify and implement the international human rights norms through national laws and other measures, is based on a globalized liberal legalist approach. It views laws as coherent and autonomous systems of norms 'that operate as an effective tool of social engineering to promote or protect individual freedom'.[119] Anderson points out that while there has been a huge increase in international and national charters of rights, any discussion of states' constitutional authority 'now has to take account of the disciplining effects of the global economy, and the power networks formed by transnational corporations'.[120]

117 ibid.

118 UNCESCR, *Globalization and its Impact on the Enjoyment of Economic, Social and Cultural Rights*. UN Doc. E/1999/22-E/C.12.1998/26; ch VI, s A, para 515.

119 Anderson (n 110) 6.

120 ibid 7.

State and constitutional rights development must now incorporate positive obligations on states to intervene and regulate private actors, national and international corporations. Michelle Oren, Rachelle Alterman and Yaffa Zilbershatz allude to this impact on national constitutions in their chapter, but their analysis reveals that rights are also contained in nuanced ways within such constitutions.

A significant number of the 47 Member States of the Council of Europe[121] have ratified Article 16 of the European Social Charter (ESC), which requires states to ensure that adequate and affordable housing is available for families.[122] Significant jurisprudence on measurable and enforceable standards is being developed by the ECSR, which is the supervisory body for the ESC. In their chapter, Padraic Kenna and Mark Jordan trace this jurisprudence of the ECSR, which is effectively linking Article 16 on the rights of families to social and economic protection, with other articles of the Social Charter on the right to protection from poverty and social exclusion, and a deeper right to adequate housing for all. Key links are made with the developing EU jurisprudence which applies to its 28 Member States.[123] In this context, the historical and now legally binding Charter of Fundamental Rights of the EU has created a 'right to social and housing assistance so as to ensure a decent existence for all those who lack sufficient resources'.[124] This could act as a defining base for housing rights across Europe.

Indeed, the issue of housing rights is specifically identified in a contemporary European Parliament Report:

> Housing plays a crucial role in enhancing social cohesion, with adequate housing long included among the universal rights in more than one hundred national constitutions. Moreover, after the entry into force of the Treaty of Lisbon, the Charter of fundamental rights including the right to housing assistance has become part of the legal basis for EU policies. Although all Member States agree that 'the access to good quality and affordable housing is a fundamental need and right', available statistics indicate that around 3 million people in Europe lack access to decent housing.[125]

Despite all this housing rights development, Branco suggests that contemporary economic policies still deride the implementation of economic, social and cultural

121 The Council of Europe is made up of 47 Member States and overlaps with the EU, but these are separate organizations.

122 Turin, 18 October 1961, Council of Europe, European Treaty Series – No 35; *European Social Charter. (Revised)* Council of Europe, Strasbourg 3 May 1996.

123 The EU 28 States are; Austria, Belgium, Bulgaria , Croatia, the Czech Republic, Cyprus, Denmark, Estonia, Finland, France, Germany, Greece, Hungary, Ireland, Italy, Latvia, Lithuania, Luxembourg, Malta, the Netherlands, Poland, Portugal, Romania, the Slovak Republic, Slovenia, Spain, Sweden and the UK.

124 Charter of Fundamental Rights of the European Union, art 34(3), OJ 2010/C 83/02.

125 European Parliament (n 74) 8.

rights.[126] For instance, no schedule for the full implementation of these rights has been created by the UN or any supervisory body. Indeed, many political figures and scholars claim that these rights are merely policy goals rather than implying and sort of legal responsibility for state institutions. Of course, many socio-economic rights are enforced by courts, such as the right to equality, health and safety, etc. But mainstream contemporary economics discourse has regarded human rights as an institution competing with economic efficiency rather than as an instrument complementing economics in promoting human welfare.[127] For this reason, contemporary mainstream economics discourse constitutes one of the major obstacles to the promotion of human rights in the global era.[128]

Thus, the hegemony of the housing market ideology, with its inherent links to global financial markets, represents a major barrier to the advancement of housing rights. But major crises have been used in the past to develop radical new approaches. Examples include the launch of the current Danish mortgage lending system after the great fire of Copenhagen in 1795, which spurred the need for an organized mortgage credit market to quickly provide funding to build a large number of new buildings, and the German *Pfandbriefe* (covered bond) system, which dates back to 1769 and was heavily influenced by the aftermath of the Seven Years' War. In response to the latest crisis, a number of countries have also taken steps to further strengthen their mortgage market regulations.[129]

In 2009, Raquel Rolnik, the UN Special Rapporteur on adequate housing, pointed out that the crisis 'represents an opportunity for reflection and to consider how to improve housing systems, policies and programmes so as to ensure adequate housing'.[130] Few, however, have used the opportunity to advance the incorporation of housing rights into mortgage systems.

Again in 2012, Rolnik set out the UN housing rights approach to the financial crisis and the course for a rights-based housing policy.[131] She called for a paradigm shift from housing policies based on the financialization of housing to a human rights-based approach. In this context, she made the following recommendations:

> The promotion of access to adequate housing cannot be based solely on financial mechanisms. Broader State policies and interventions should be adopted, including, inter alia, public investments in infrastructure and basic services,

---

126 Branco (n 101) 12.

127 ibid 134.

128 Padraic Kenna, 'Can International Housing Rights Based on Public International Law Really Impact on Contemporary Housing Systems?' in Lorna Fox and James Sweeney (eds), *The Idea of Home in Law: Displacement and Dispossession (*Farnham, Ashgate 2011).

129 International Monetary Fund, *Global Financial Stability Report: Durable Financial Stability: Getting There from Here* (Washington DC, IMF 2011) 115.

130 UN Doc A/HRC/10/7 (2009), para 75.

131 Rolnik (n 47).

> human settlements upgrading and rehabilitation, urban planning and land policies, public financing, land and housing provision, rent regulation and related legal and institutional frameworks … States should refrain from focusing their housing policies on housing finance schemes with predominantly regressive effects, such as mortgage interest rate subsidies or mortgage interest tax exemptions … States should promote a mixture of tenure systems, including a public housing sector that is not tied to liberalized markets and limited-profit rental or regulated rent schemes, in order to prevent social exclusion and segregation. A mixture of tenure solutions is essential for the promotion of access to adequate housing for the various segments of society and in order to shield the housing sector from economic and financial shocks … In their ongoing assessment efforts, States should employ human rights indicators to identify trends that signal progress, stagnation or retrogression in the realization of the right to adequate housing. All indicators should be disaggregated by prohibited ground of discrimination in order to identify patterns of marginalization and discrimination … States should take prompt measures to increase the availability of adequate housing options, particularly for those most affected by sub-prime and predatory mortgage lending. States should prioritize funding and construction of public housing and the promotion of housing assistance in order to address the impact of the economic and financial crises on the most vulnerable … States should increase their expenditure on housing in order to circumvent the adverse impacts of the crises on the housing sector … States should ensure that recovery measures do not further erode social housing programmes and policies.[132]

The clash between neoliberal globalization and the full implementation of housing rights remains unresolved. There remain some critical questions about the effectiveness and role of human rights and their advocacy institutions in the context of globalization. The World Bank has not proposed the incorporation of human or housing rights within its proposals and monitoring of financial institutions focusing on traditional responses to the failure of regulation and supervision.[133] In the context of this dissonance between globalization and human rights, Ghazi points out that:

> One the one side, are the NGOs and human rights activists that, even though they defend human values, have very little idea of the functioning of the international economic and financial system. The second group of scholars, scholars in the field of economics, tend to rally to the dominant ideology and back up the only system that is actually in place, while others criticize this vision … Human rights are still perceived as an obstacle to political dialogue by IFIs [International

132 ibid paras 70–71.

133 See *World Bank Banking Bank Regulation and Supervision Survey 2011* (Washington DC, World Bank), where there were no questions on human or housing rights addressed in the detailed questionnaires to banks.

> Financial Institutions], and as pressure tool[s] or internal interference by states. A mental shift must be made to consider human rights standards and norms as an aspect of internal and international affairs that is here, not for controversy, but for dialogue and common progress.[134]

In April 2013, the UN Special Rapporteur on adequate housing met with the World Bank and she emphasized:

> … that the obligations of States parties to the international human rights treaties should be understood as extending to their membership of the World Bank and their role as Executive Directors, including decisions to support the adoption of operational policies and to approve lending, credit and grant proposals. These obligations include the duty of States parties to the International Covenant on Economic, Social and Cultural Rights to respect the rights recognized in the Covenant and to take steps through international assistance and cooperation, to the maximum of their available resources, with a view to achieving progressively the full realization of these rights.[135]

The Special Rapporteur believes that the World Bank is also uniquely placed to support governments around the world in meeting their international human rights obligations during the process of development and, in particular, to progressively realize economic and social rights in their countries.[136] However, she has also pointed out that:

> From the information gathered during the Special Rapporteur's visit, it appears that there is resistance among Bank staff to the current framework of safeguard policies. Safeguard policies are often perceived by [the] Bank's staff as substantially limiting the Bank's ability to 'attract' State clients and compete with other regional and international financial institutions.[137]

Clearly, the position of housing rights in the globalization debate is weak.

---

134 Bahram Ghazi, *The IMF, the World Bank and the Question of Human Rights* (New York, Ardsley 2005) 311.

135 UN Doc A/HRC/22/46/Add.3. *Report of the Special Rapporteur on adequate housing as a component of the right to an adequate standard of living, and on the right to non -discrimination in this context*, Raquel Rolnik. *Addendum. Mission to the World Bank* (February 2013) para 9.

136 See Independent Evaluation Group (IEG), *Safeguards and Sustainability Policies in a Changing World: An Independent Evaluation of World Bank Group Experience* (Washington DC, World Bank 2010).

137 UN Doc A/HRC/22/46/Add.3. *Report of the Special Rapporteur on adequate housing as a component of the right to an adequate standard of living, and on the right to non -discrimination in this context,* Raquel Rolnik. *Addendum. Mission to the World Bank* (February 2013) para 70.

Conclusion

The global financial system, and indeed many states, have to date failed to grasp the central role of housing in the economy, in society and in people's lives. Housing is rarely seen as the focal point of policies, but regularly as a means of achieving other goals. In social stability, political support, expansion of property ownership or the construction industry, new technologies, consumer demand, expansion of the economy, financial investment, control of unrest or indeed concern for human rights, housing plays a central role.

In the midst of scepticism about housing policies, especially in Europe, we know that the current crisis, based on the collapse of the boom built around reckless lending, touches almost everyone. This tide of international finance has flowed into every city in the world, driving up land prices and creating unaffordable housing for new households. It has stratified housing markets, creating major inequality and life chances for generations to come. In situations of inadequate housing and homelessness, particularly for people with disabilities denied opportunities for independent living, the full development of people and households is obstructed. Where it exists, the market residual model of social housing is failing to meet international housing rights obligations in many countries.

The once-exalted asset-based welfare, where older people would release equity in their homes to pay for their care in old age, is now a dream of another age for many. Housing as a repository of wealth, a nest egg or valuable inheritance is now risky. Negative equity is not just a personal problem, but one which global markets now follow with great interest.

Housing, then, is at the centre of a global social and economic crisis. It is a central issue in the political landscape, as governments struggle to reconcile the imperatives of international finance on the one hand, and housing as a home, a right and a place of development of people, communities and society, on the other. The idea of home is an enormously powerful and evocative concept, bringing to mind ideas of security, belonging, family, warmth, privacy, connectedness, roots and safety. It is a concept that has been widely studied across several disciplines and 'home' appears to have three essential elements: first, the physical structure which provides shelter, security and a fixed location; second, the social relationships within the home and with others in the wider environment of the home – neighbours, relatives and other social networks; third, the atmosphere within the home, which provides warmth, privacy, control, a place for self-expression and the development of self-identity.[138]

But who is charged with advancing the principle of housing as home? The most powerful actors in housing systems are currently financial institutions. It is assumed that these can be regulated in the public interest across the world. Mortgage market deregulation and the consequent lowering of lending standards

138 See Lorna Fox, *Conceptualising Home, Theories, Law and Policies* (Oxford, Hart Publishing 2007).

ultimately generated a subprime lending industry in the US and elsewhere, which contaminated the global financial system. Alongside the new globalized financial institutions, there has also been an ideological shift in public policy and economics towards a neoliberal approach, more redolent of nineteenth-century ideals than contemporary popular expectations.[139] Yet, critics of this debacle are often accused of promoting an ideology. But what is an ideology? Reporting to a Congressional Committee on Oversight and Government Reform considering Financial Market Regulation (October 2008), Alan Greenspan (erstwhile Chairman of the US Federal Reserve from 1987 to 2006), when asked if his ideology was wrong, stated:

> Remember what an ideology is. It is a conceptual framework for the way people deal with reality – everybody has one – you have to – to exist you need an ideology. The question is whether it is accurate or not. What I am saying is – yes – I found a flaw. I don't know how temporary or permanent it is … A flaw in the model I perceive as the critical structure that defines how the world works.[140]

Housing policies are indeed based on ideologies, and the dominant one in recent decades has been that of deference to financial and housing markets. The ideology of housing as a base, a home, a foundation for participation in family, community and society is not yet established in the global narrative of housing. This would recognize that personal status, identity and opportunities are largely shaped by housing circumstances. Equally, person-centred ideologies of housing and home have yet to find their place in legal systems.

Yet, law and housing rights can play an important role in the development of housing systems. These can provide a source of autonomous values which can temper the housing market system and structure it in different ways. This can draw on the reservoir of international jurisprudence, rights and principles to inform and creatively expand the conceptual framework of housing law, rights and policy.

The President of Ireland, Michael D. Higgins, has recently pointed out that:

> Intellectuals are challenged now, I believe, to a moral choice: to drift into, be part of, a consensus that accepts a failed paradigm of life and economy, or to offer, or seek to recover, the possibility of alternative futures.[141]

Nowhere is this more relevant than in housing.

---

139 Kenna (n 38).

140 See *New York Times* http://www.nytimes.com/2008/10/24/business/economy/24panel.html?_r=0 accessed 4 May 2013).

141 President Michael D Higgins, 'The Role of the University at a Time of Intellectual Crisis', speech on receipt of Doctorate of Laws (*Honoris Causa*) from the National University of Ireland. Full text available at http://www.president.ie/speeches/the-role-of-the-university-at-a-time-of-intellectual-crisis accessed 24 April 2013.

Chapter 2

A Legal Perspective of the Origin and the Globalization of the Current Financial Crisis and the Resulting Reforms in Spain[1]

Sergio Nasarre-Aznar

Introduction

This chapter examines the legal factors which were central to the US subprime crisis, the international credit crunch and subsequent global economic developments. The negative impact of the international financial crisis on the Spanish housing system is considered, as well as the limited nature of reforms in the Spanish mortgage and housing markets. It is suggested that deficient regulation in the US mortgage securitization process has been the catalyst for the global crisis; however, its impact has generated significant changes in national mortgage and housing legislation in the affected countries. Some innovative developments are examined, such as increased protection for mortgage consumers and an intermediate tenures project in Catalonia.

From the US Subprime Crisis to the International Credit Crunch and its Legal Context

Background to the Crisis

The devastating impact of the US mortgage crisis, involving massive mortgage defaults, across the world was fundamentally due to international 'mortgage securitization' (see Figure 2.1). This is a financial technique to 'transform' mortgages into securities. It provides funding for a mortgage originator's lending business through the issue of mortgage-backed securities (MBSs) by a special purpose vehicle (SPV). In itself, it is not a detrimental process, since it allows lenders to access greater levels of funding. However, once the original mortgage, which is the collateral base of the security, is defective, the whole process becomes contaminated.

1 This work has been possible thanks to the 'Las tenencias intermedias para facilitar el acceso a la vivienda' research project (Spanish Ministry of Economy and Competitiveness, DER 2012-31409).

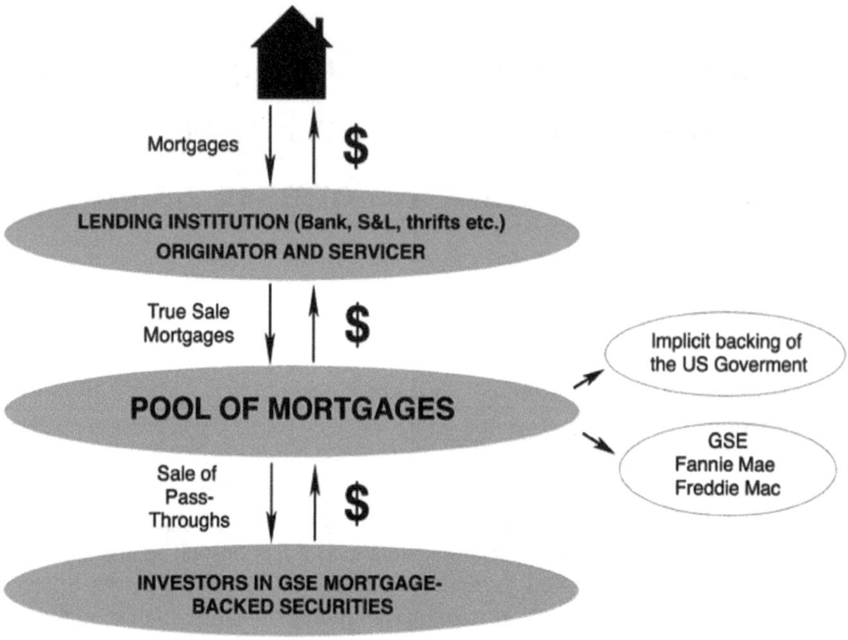

Figure 2.1 Standard US mortgage securitization
Source: own elaboration

The degradation of the quality of securitized mortgages in the US arose from two main sources.[2] First, the general policy of maximizing home-ownership at any cost, even to those households that clearly did not have the resources to repay mortgage loans, created an unsustainable financial subsystem. This situation arose due to borrowers' limited economic capabilities and/or because of the conditions of the mortgages themselves, such as a high loan-to-value ratio (LTV) coupled with a high interest rate. Both Republican and Democrat administrations promoted home-ownership as part of the American Dream. As far back as 1994, President Clinton promoted wider home-ownership: 'More Americans should own their own homes, for reasons that are economic and tangible, and reasons

2 There are others which are also important but which cannot be addressed here, such as the insufficient backing given by the US government to the agencies that issued the MBSs, the lack of a proper body of rules for MBS business in the US and the lack of liability for losses of rating agencies in that jurisdiction. See Sergio Nasarre-Aznar, *Securitisation and Mortgage Bonds. Legal Aspects and Harmonisation in Europe* (Saffron Walden, Gostick Hall 2004) 39. This book also discusses the weaknesses of some international mortgage securitization systems.

that are emotional and intangible, but go to the heart of what it means to harbour, to nourish, to expand the American Dream'.[3] President George W. Bush endorsed this approach and encouraged many ethnic groups to become home-owners.[4] Of course, this generalization of home-ownership necessitated a concurrent expansion of mortgage lending. A lowering of standards was also required in mortgage underwriting, and thus a reduction of quality of mortgages. There was a corresponding increase in the default risk of mortgages, which could not be borne by most lenders. For this reason, government-sponsored enterprises (GSEs),[5] such as Fannie Mae, Freddie Mac and Ginnie Mae, were authorized to buy what were increasingly less sustainable mortgages from lenders in order to transform them into securities, thus generalizing, externalizing and internationalizing this default risk. This process is explained in more detail below.

Second, the moral hazard or conflict of interest inherent in the US model of mortgage securitization was hugely significant. It allowed lenders to pass on any default risk in the repayment of the mortgages through to MBS investors, many of whom were European, international banks and other financial institutions.[6] These institutional investors almost blindly relied on international rating agencies' assessments and the theoretical/implicit backing of the US government to their

3 Speech of Bill Clinton, 42nd President of the United States of America, 'National Partners in Homeownership', before the Association of Realtors (Washington DC, 1994).

4 See the American Dream Downpayment Initiative, which was signed into law on 16 December 2003 and provided 'downpayment, closing costs, and rehabilitation assistance to eligible individuals' (for more details, see http://www.hud.gov/offices/cpd/affordablehousing/programs/home/addi/ accessed 29 October 2012.

5 Mortgage GSEs were created by the US Congress with the aim of improving the flow of credit into certain housing markets while reducing the cost of that same credit.

6 See H Blommestein, A Keskinler and C Lucas, 'The Outlook for the Securitisation Market' (2011) 1 OECD Journal: Financial Market Trends 2 at 3. The authors stated that 'regulation and underwriting standards were seen to be significantly more robust in Europe', that 'there's no doubt that the securitisation asset class in general was tarnished by the fallout from the US subprime crisis' and that 'from mid-2007 to the end of 2010, only 0.95% of all European structured-finance issues defaulted, compared to 7.7% of US structured-finance issues'. See also J Cox, J Faucette and C Valenzuela, 'Why Did the Credit Crisis Spread to Global Markets?' (2010), available at http://blogs.law.uiowa.edu/ebook/uicifd-ebook/part-5-ii-why-did-credit-crisis-spread-global-markets, pt 5, p 3 and 17, which says that 'European banks became involved when they invested in AAA-rated asset-backed securities (i.e. subprime mortgage-backed securities) produced in the United States', that 'Because European banks had heavily invested in U.S.-produced MBS, they were greatly exposed to those assets once they became toxic. By February 2009, European banks, specifically banks in the United Kingdom, had seventy-five percent as much exposure to toxic assets as U.S. banks' and that 'unfortunately, a "perfect storm" of regulatory breakdowns allowed what initially was a mortgage crisis in the United States to morph into a global financial crisis via securitization'.

GSEs.[7] We now know that among these securitized mortgages were those created through the 'predatory lending' of subprime mortgages.[8]

Subprime mortgages are those that do not fulfil the quality standards for repayment for one reason or another. In the US, a variety of these were created in unusual circumstances. These included situations where the LTV surpassed 80 per cent or because these were second mortgages (often described as 'piggy-back mortgages')[9] that were charged on the remaining 20 per cent LTV after an existing mortgage for the first 80 per cent of LTV. Mass default on the mortgages arose when housing prices dropped as mortgagors could not refinance their debts. Even in non-recourse states, mortgagors voluntarily defaulted once their mortgage debt was more than the value of their property.[10] This impacted negatively on MBSs and had an even more detrimental impact on those securities known as 'collateralized debt obligations' (CDOs),[11] where the true risk was almost impossible to properly assess, due to their financial complexity and the remoteness of the underlying collateral. The result was the holding of 'toxic assets by many international financial institutions'.[12] Other structural conflicts of interest in the standard US mortgage securitization process included the lack of incentive for the originator to reveal the true value of a pool of mortgages when they are transferred to the arranger of the issue, and there may indeed

7 See the explicit assertions of N Eric Weiss, 'Fannie Mae's and Freddie Mac's Financial Problems', Congressional Research Service, CRS Report for Congress (10 August 2012) 17 http://www.fas.org/sgp/crs/misc/RL34661.pdf assessed 4 October 2012: 'Fannie Mae and Freddie Mac are GSEs whose charters limit them to buying single family and multifamily home mortgages originated by others. This lack of diversification makes them more exposed to housing and mortgage market problems than other financial institutions such as commercial banks that have other lines of business. The GSEs' charters give them a special relationship with the federal government, sometimes called an implicit guarantee, which has allowed them to borrow at interest rates only slightly above those paid by the federal government'.

8 See '"Malicious Mortgage" Nets 400 Defendants' (19 July 2008), https://www.fbi.gov/news/stories/2008/june/malicious_mortgage061908) accessed 4 October 2012, which relates to mortgage fraud schemes that involved 400 defendants.

9 See Jack Guttenburg, 'Mortgage Crisis Drives Home Value of PMI' *InMan News* (8 April 2008) http://www.inman.com/buyers-sellers/columnists/jackguttentag/mortgage-crisis-drives-home-value-pmi accessed 4 October 2012.

10 Todd J Zywicki and Joseph D Adamson, 'The Law and Economics of Subprime Lending' (2009) 80(1) University of Colorado Law Review 31 and 32. See also Andra C Ghent and M Kudlyak, 'Recourse and Residential Mortgage Default: Evidence from US States', Federal Reserve Bank of Richmond Working Paper No 09-10R (2011) 29.

11 CDOs are asset-backed securities issued over collections of MBSs, i.e., 're-securitized' mortgages.

12 This 'toxicity' meant that, even if the mortgages had not defaulted, the market for them had now disappeared, their value then dropped and the holders (the banks) were obliged to correct their books to show this 'write-down' loss in order to reflect the new real market value of the assets.

have been an incentive to hide its risks.[13] There was also little to incentivize the originator to properly monitor the behaviour of mortgagors in matters such as timely repayment or risky behaviour towards the property, as he or she had already sold the mortgages to the arranger, passing on any risks of default to the MBS investors. While these risks were difficult to avoid, as they are part of a standard mortgage securitization process, they could have been reduced through effective supervision, due diligence and disclosure obligations.

Legal Regulatory Weaknesses

While these two factors are widely accepted as causes of the US financial crisis, there has been little published analysis of the legal factors behind these developments. From a legal perspective, there were at least three causative factors that explain the collapse of the 'house of cards' of the US mortgage market.

First, the lack of a strong regulatory framework for MBSs led to an 'outlaw-like' securitization process. Unlike the highly regulated covered/mortgage bonds, such as *Pfandbrief* in Germany,[14] the situation is different in the US, and indeed all common law countries. These lack a strong and specific regulatory framework, and often there is no clear-cut and dedicated legislation that specifically deals with MBSs.[15] In my opinion, this situation leads to the circumstances shown in Table 2.1, which are evidenced to some extent by the better financial performance of covered bonds, as compared with MBSs, from the start of the credit crunch onwards.[16]

---

13 The one who financially builds up the pool of mortgages to be securitized.

14 See, for more details, Nasarre-Aznar (n 2) 5–13.

15 Traditionally, many authors in the US see the intervention of the state – even with a piece of legislation – in the economy as a mistake, although the fragility of the US banking and financial system has been evident throughout its recent history. See the numbers of insolvent US banks during the twentieth century in Maury Klein, 'The Panic of 2008: Something Old and Something New' in Lawrence E Mitchell and Arthur E Wilmarth, Jr (eds), *The Panic of 2008. Causes, Consequences and Implications of Reform* (Cheltenham, Edward Elgar Publishing 2010) 49. For the situation in the UK, see Nasarre-Aznar (n 2) 24.

16 See the constant ascending outstanding covered bonds from 2003 to 2011 in European Covered Bond Council, *Fact Book*, 7th edn (September 2012) 54. Although with the help of the European Central Bank and European national central banks that provide liquidity to the system (at 21), covered bonds have performed relatively well since 2007 to the point that 'the covered bonds asset class is still the main pillar for real estate financing in Europe' (at 31). Most problems for covered bonds do not arise from their intrinsic standard legal structure, but from the decrease of mortgage lending in some EU countries and the problems with the Eurozone sovereign debt crisis (at 31 and 32), while the transparency to investors remains essential (at 32). This contrasts with MBSs. The outstanding principal balances of MBSs insured or guaranteed by the US agencies has constantly decreased from $7.5 trillion in 2008 to $2.9 trillion in second quarter of 2012 according to the US Federal Reserve: http://www.federalreserve.gov/econresdata/releases/mortoutstand/current.htm#fn5r) accessed 3 March 2013. Moreover, since the crisis, MBSs have faced increasing

Table 2.1 Regulated versus non-regulated mortgage markets

Non-regulated contexts (most MBS contexts)	Regulated contexts (most covered bonds contexts)
More flexibility (unlimited types of MBS structures that may be adapted quickly to the market)	Less flexibility (basically, each national covered bond has its own law; non-legal covered bonds may exist. but are riskier than regulated ones)
Contractual basis (to which extent should exist an obligation to disclose contractual information to third parties)	Legal basis (everything is public: collateralization ratio, role of cover assets monitor, minimum quality of covering mortgages, etc.)
Rights of the stakeholders left to general rules of law	Specific rules for misbehaviour, losses, etc.
More dependence on 'private opinions' such as the rating agencies or government direct sponsorization (e.g. the GSEs, that distort the free (concurrence competition) in the MBS market in the US)	Transparency of the law need (the lowest profile of state intervention) reduces the need for rating agencies.
More complex structures (more difficult to understand by investors and other stakeholders; more intermediation costs)	Simpler and straightforward structures (transparency)

Contract-based securitization differs fundamentally from covered bonds governed by public law regulation. The attributes of public law regulation derive from its public character, where rules are published in official documents. It also offers transparency, in the sense that these rules, regulations and expected outcomes are accessible to everyone, usually without charge (increasingly through the Internet) and often translated into English. The rules can be easily understood, not least by stakeholders. On the other hand, contractual-based securitization is closed. Contractual arrangements only bind the parties and there are no clear rules on the disclosure of specific information to others involved in the transaction,

legal and regulatory restrictions in Europe, such as greater disclosure requirements (see Capital Requirement Directive II, 2009/111/EC, OJ L302, 17 November 2009, P 0097–0119), more onerous capital requirements for securitizations held in trading books (see Capital Requirement Directive III, 2010/76/EU, OJ L329, 14 December 2010, P 0003–0035), more onerous liquidity requirements for residential mortgage-backed securities (RMBSs) than for covered bonds (see Proposal of Capital Requirement Directive IV; European Commission Proposal 20-7-2011, COM(2011) 453 final. For more information on these Directives see http://ec.europa.eu/internal_market/bank/regcapital/index_en.htm accessed 3 March 2013. Capital surcharge under Solvency II Directive (2009/138/EC, OJ L335, 17 December 2009, P 0001–0155) is up to 10 times higher for AAA MBSs than for AAA covered bonds and the European Central Bank requires as collateral at least AA MBSs in comparison of only B- covered bonds (at 208).

such as investors. There is little transparency in contractual-based securitization. Its performance will depend on private arrangements and the 'opinion' of private agents known as 'rating agencies'.[17] This leads to complicated structures and undisclosed procedures. There is a lack of transparency in relation to the description and identification of the actual securitized assets and their relevant features, how they have been transferred, which law is applicable in case of default of the underlying mortgages, etc. This has contributed to the widespread development of the so-called 'blind trust' crisis, where those taking part in a securitization process relied (often without checking due to the complexity and costs) on the statements of the previous stakeholder in the process. Clearly, investors were even further removed from such enquiries.

In contrast, the covered bonds system promotes more responsible lending, as the originator retains the full default risk of the mortgages and is incentivized to minimize risks and consequent mortgage default.[18] Indeed, it has been estimated that the introduction of an effective covered bond system in the US would decrease the mortgage default rate eight times more than the provision of section 941 of the Dodd-Frank Act, which obliges originators to retain a five per cent credit risk of securitized non-qualifying mortgages on their balance sheets.[19]

Second, the lack of a public standardized MBS in the US was fatal. Covered bond legislation in Germany, Spain, France and other European states creates a standardized type of covered bond for each country. Moreover, these regulated covered bonds fulfil the minimum requirements of Article 52.4 of the UCITS Directive and, because of this, they have some benefits across Europe.[20] The situation in the US has provided the opportunity for private institutions, such as rating agencies, to act as private gatekeepers of this market. Using their ratings and simple final 'marks' (A+, B, etc.), they purport to assess the risk of a specific issue of MBS for international investors. This dependence on such private control would not have been possible or, at least, would not have been so relevant within an effective securities public supervision system. Such a system does not exist in the US.[21] Indeed, rating agencies are not required to assess the 'legal risk' of European covered bonds (although rating agencies do rate them), as the law is public and transparent for everybody. Only those

---

17 See below.

18 European Covered Bond Council (n 16) 151.

19 The Dodd-Frank Wall Street Reform and Consumer Protection Act 2010. See Ryan Kreitzer, *Covered Bond Markets: An Analysis of Their Impact on Mortgage Underwriting* (New York, Leonard N Stern School of Business 2012) 46 and 47.

20 Directive 2009/65/EC of the European Parliament and of the Council of 13 July 2009 on the coordination of laws, regulations and administrative provisions relating to undertakings for collective investment in transferable securities (UCITS), OJEU 17 November 2009, L302/32.

21 See Tamar Frankel, 'Regulating the Financial Markets by Examinations' in Mitchell and Wilmarth, Jr (n 15) 219.

securities that comply with legislative requirements can be called 'covered bonds'. There is even a 'denomination protection'. The behaviour of the rating agencies during the boom years has been heavily criticized for their contribution[22] to the financial mortgage bubble. The agencies are culpable, not least through apparently careless ratings of MBSs and CDOs,[23] but also in directly assisting the issuer of these instruments in structuring them in a way which transmogrified subprime loans into Triple A securities. These were, of course, initially attractive for international investors, but were ultimately worthless.[24] Moreover, from 1983 until the introduction of the Dodd-Frank Act in 2010, the rule in s 436(g) of the US Securities Act 1933 prohibited anybody from suing for damages against any of the three biggest rating agencies – Moody's, Standard & Poor's and Fitch Ratings. These were termed Nationally Recognized Statistical Rating Organizations (NRSROs). Such a prohibition or immunity from justice should not be acceptable in states that guaranteed the universal right to access to justice. For instance, in Spain, anybody can sue anybody for any reason, according to Article 24 of the Spanish Constitution. After the abrogation of section 436(g) by the Dodd-Frank Act 2010, it seems clear that rating agencies were considered as experts and were not simply giving their 'opinion',[25] thus losing the protection of the First Amendment of

22 Frank Partnoy, 'Overdependence on Credit Ratings was a Primary Cause of the Crisis' in Mitchell and Wilmarth, Jr (n 15) 116. See also Lawrence J White, 'The Credit Rating Agencies' (2010) 24(2) Journal of Economic Perspectives 218–21: 'The securitization of these subprime mortgages was only able to succeed ... because of the favourable ratings bestowed on the more senior tranches'.

23 Steven L Schwarcz, 'Too Big to Fail?: Recasting the Financial Safety Net' in Mitchell and Wilmarth, Jr (n 15) 96.

24 Mark Anchor Albert 'Ratings Wars. The Lawsuit Filed by Calpers May Be Able to Overcome the Rating Agencies' Traditional First Amendment Defense' *Los Angeles Lawyer* (October 2009) 38. We mentioned above the concept of the 'blind trust' crisis. Paragraph 10 of the introduction of European Regulation 1060/2009, of the European Parliament and of the Council of 16 September 2009, on credit rating agencies (OJ L302/1, 17 November 2009) states that: 'Credit rating agencies are considered to have failed, first, to reflect early enough in their credit ratings the worsening market conditions, and second, to adjust their credit ratings in time following the deepening market crisis. The most appropriate manner in which to correct those failures is by measures relating to conflicts of interest, the quality of the credit ratings, the transparency and internal governance of the credit rating agencies, and the surveillance of the activities of the credit rating agencies. The users of credit ratings should not rely blindly on credit ratings but should take utmost care to perform [their] own analysis and conduct appropriate due diligence at all times regarding their reliance on such credit ratings'.

25 As was considered the case in many cases, such as *Jefferson County Sch Dist v Moody's Investors Servs* 1999 175 F 3d 848, 856 (10th Cir 1999) and *County of Orange v McGraw-Hill Cos* 1999 245 BR 151, 157 (CD Cal 1999).

the US Constitution for their ratings.[26] The *CalPERS* case[27] was an example of an institution that incurred losses of about $1,000 million by relying on the rating agencies' representations. In December 2012, the court held that the defendants did not seem to be protected by the First Amendment.

Third, the deficient regulation of the 'US mortgage securitization market' is a major concern. At the end of the day, the assets which are securitized in a mortgage securitization process are mortgages.[28] The strength of a mortgage, and the securities it backs, depends on a pool of factors. Some of these are directly related to the property charged, such as location, building materials, whether the property is a flat or a house, etc. Similarly, the type and features of the mortgage loan involved, such as the LTV, interest rate, etc., are important. However, some key factors are directly related to the legal configuration of the mortgage itself, such as the way in which it is legally structured within a particular legal environment.

It is useful to outline here the details of the so-called 'US mortgage' – the type of mortgage at the base of the chain of any US mortgage securitization process, although it is difficult to talk about a single type of 'US mortgage'.[29] Traditionally, from a legal perspective, there are two basic types: those states, mainly west of the Mississippi river, which follow the lien theory (the creditor has a security interest, but the title is not transferred to him or her) and those states, mainly east of the Mississippi river, which follow the title theory (in which the mortgage title is transferred to the lender).[30] However, other classifications can be made depending on different criteria, such as the way in which mortgages are formalized (regular mortgages between mortgagee and mortgagor, deeds of trust where there is a trustee between both who holds the mortgage title)[31] and

26 See *New York Times v Sullivan* 376 US 254 (1964).

27 *California Public Employees Retirement Scheme v Moody's Corp et al* CGC-09-49024. See http://dockets.justia.com/docket/california/candce/3:2009cv03628/217999 accessed 17 September 2012.

28 This is true for the US and most countries that allow mortgage securitization, but not, for example, for Spain. See Nasarre-Aznar (n 2) 60–63.

29 Although this expression is the one that is used in response to international investors when they ask for the type of collateral of the MBSs or CDOs they are about to buy, in fact the mortgage pooling is done at the federal level through the agencies, and the rules that govern these mortgages are state or even county-based. Conversely, securitizations organized in Europe are national and it is not common to sell them whilst saying that they are backed by 'European mortgages' as no 'European mortgage' exists.

30 GJ Siedel and Janis K Cheezem, *Real Estate Law*, 4th edn (Boston, MA, South-Western College Publishing 1999) 310.

31 Robert Kratovil, 'Mortgage Law' in Robert H Pease and Homer Virgil Cherrington (eds), *Mortgage Banking* (New York, McGraw-Hill 1953) 24 states that this type can be useful if there are a number of lenders as a trustee acquires mortgage titles (instead of the lenders) who can eventually also foreclose the mortgage instead of the default of the mortgagor.

others (reverse mortgages, equitable mortgages). But, apart from this, mortgages are registered, conveyed and foreclosed in a different way between states. Indeed, this diversification and lack of common regulations at a federal level[32] contributes to the weakness of an efficient securitization process,[33] especially in those aspects relating to investors' protection.

In relation to registration, there is no common land register in the US, but instead many county equivalents, amounting to some 3,000 registers, following a tradition since the seventeenth century. Each county register has its own requirements, fees, procedures, rules, etc. In fact, they have been defined as 'a terribly cumbersome, paper-intensive, error-prone, and therefore costly process for transferring and tracking mortgage rights'.[34] To attempt to make the system more efficient, title insurance companies maintain copies of the records of the county recorders and assume, through their policies, the risks (mistakes, omissions, etc.) that accompany those records, although this system has its own problems.[35] This wholescale inefficiency in the mortgage registration system was the impetus for the main US mortgage market stakeholders – Fannie Mae, Freddie Mac and the Mortgage Bankers Association of America – to create a private land register in 1995. This would operate alongside, but outside of, the rules of the county registers:[36] a device called Mortgage Electronic Registration Systems (MERS).

MERS performs two functions. It is a private land register for those members of the system where they assume the role of 'land registrars', as mortgages are transferred within the system. Significantly, MERS also acts as the mortgagee in each recorded mortgage relationship. Remarkably, it is registered in the county register as the mortgagee, even though it is not the lender. Any other operation

---

32 Grant S Nelson, 'Confronting the Mortgage Meltdown: A Brief for the Federalization of State Mortgage Foreclosure Law' (2010) 37(538) Pepperdine Law Review 606. Various attempts in the last 90 years at different types of initiatives (e.g. the soft law of the American Law Institute with its Restatement (Third) of Property: Mortgages 1997) have been insufficient to achieve a country-wide mortgage. In Europe, doctrinal works have been carried out through the drafting of a Eurohypothec, a common mortgage for Europe (see Agnieszka Dziecrewicz-Tulodziecka (ed), *Basic Guidelines for a Eurohypothec* (Warsaw, Mortgage Credit Foundation 2005). See also Sergio Nasarre-Aznar, 'Eurohypothec: Drafting a Common Mortgage for Europe' (2010) 2(1) Journal of Legal Affairs and Dispute Resolution in Engineering and Construction 50.

33 Nelson (n 32) 594.

34 Phyllis K Slesinger and Daniel McLaughlin, 'Mortgage Electronic Registration System' (1995) 31 (808) Idaho Law Review 808.

35 Christopher L Peterson, 'Foreclosure, Subprime Mortgage Lending, and the Mortgage Electronic Registration System' (2010) 78 University of Cincinnati Law Review 1366. From a European perspective, the problem of data protection should be added to those listed by the author, as it is questionable whether private companies can hold and manage the personal data and details of the titles over land.

36 Instead of focusing on trying to push forward a sort of harmonized system, such as the EULIS initiative in Europe: http://eulis.eu accessed 3 March 2013.

with the mortgage registered in this way is not public and does not alter the county register,[37] but operates within the MERS system. It should be noted that MERS is directly operated by the members involved in each transaction[38] and is a unique system for the whole country. Two-thirds of the mortgages originating in the US are contained within MERS, amounting to approximately 60 million mortgages in 2007.[39] In many ways, the MERS system distorts the character of an ideal land registry system, which should be public, accessible by everybody, controlled by the public administration and controlling the validity of the recorded titles. Indeed, it has created a range of new problems, where, among other issues, it claims to be the mortgagee and also the enforcer of the default arrangements, but not the lender. Of course, this leaves the mortgagor unprotected, since it is clearly inappropriate that the enforcer of the security in the mortgage is not the lender under the mortgage loan arrangement. Several court resolutions have stated that MERS cannot enforce the mortgage as it does not hold the promissory note (technically it does not have a claim),[40] which probably has remained in the hands of the originator of the mortgage.[41] Thus, it may be the case that MERS is contributing to the poor identification of liabilities arising from the predatory lending process.[42] This may be related to the 'robo-signing' scandal, involving the forging of false documents evidencing the transfer of promissory notes to the bank purported to foreclose the mortgage.[43] In December 2011, the Massachusetts Attorney General filed the first major state lawsuit over 'robo-signing' against several major banks and MERS.[44] The Attorney General alleged that these five entities:

> engaged in unfair and deceptive trade practices in violation of Massachusetts law by pervasive use of fraudulent documentation in the foreclosure process, including

---

37 This remains recorded with MERS as 'mortgagee'. This allows the mortgage industry to use MERS to evade paying the fees and taxes related to mortgage transactions. See Peterson (n 35) 1362.

38 This leads to new problems, such the one raised in *Deutsche Bank National Trust Co v Maraj* 2008 NY Slip Op 50176 (U) (NY Sup Ct Kings Co).

39 Peterson (n 35) 1362 and 1373.

40 See National Consumer Law Center, *Foreclosures* (4th edn, Boston, MA, National Consumer Law Center 2010) 143. See also the decision in *Johnson v Home State Bank* 501 US 78, 111, S Ct 2150, 2154, 115 L Ed 2d 66 (1991).

41 In fact, it is MERS itself that alternately presents itself as a mere agent of the mortgagee (when it is sued for fraud, bad practice or violation of consumers' rights) or as a mortgagee (when tries to foreclose a mortgage). See, in this sense, Peterson (n 35) 1376.

42 ibid, 1399.

43 'Mortgage Mess: Who Really Owns Your Mortgage' *Sixty Seconds* (3 April 2011) http://www.cbsnews.com/video/watch/?id=7361596n accessed 19 July 2013.

44 *Commonwealth of Massachusetts v Bank of America et al* (Superior Court Depatment of the Trial Court 11-4363, 1 December 2011) http://www.mass.gov/ago/news-and-updates/press-releases/2011/five-national-banks-sued-by-ag-coakley.html accessed 29 October 2012.

> so-called 'robo-signing', foreclosing without holding the actual mortgage, corrupting [the] Massachusetts land recording system through the use of MERS, and failing to uphold loan modification promises to Massachusetts home-owner.[45]

In relation to this, JP Morgan, Bank of America, Citigroup, Ally Financial and Wells Fargo & Company were accused of faulty foreclosure practices. However, in 2012, a settlement was reached with the Department of Justice, the Department of Housing and Urban Development and 49 states, through which the lenders were given immunity from prosecution for this cause in exchange for direct compensation ($25 billion) to home-owners who were at risk of foreclosure or who had already been foreclosed.

Thus, the system of mortgage transfer in the US is in jeopardy, giving rise to questions concerning the credibility of the whole US mortgage securitization process. This situation creates major risks for US MBS holders. It is remarkable that only now, after 40 years of US mortgage securitization, is there an active discussion in the US on how mortgages can be properly transferred as an essential step in any standard US securitization process. This discussion is taking place at a number of levels: in the report of the Permanent Editorial Board for the Uniform Commercial Code 2011;[46] regarding the differences in the transfer of regular mortgages and deeds of trust;[47] among authors who have evidenced sharp differences among different systems;[48] within the mortgage industry itself;[49] and in the courts, such the decisions in *Ibanez* and *Bevilacqua.*[50]

---

45 'First Major State Lawsuit Filed Over "Robo-Signing"' *CNBC* (1 December 2011) http://www.cnbc.com/id/45511868 accessed 15 March 2013.

46 The Permanent Editorial Board for the Uniform Commercial Code, 'Application of the Uniform Commercial Code to Selected Issues Relating to Mortgage Notes' 14 November 2011. The American Law Institute and the National Conference of Commissioners on Uniform State Laws (14 November 2011) establishes a set of four rules on the basis of the Uniform Commercial Code, but it says that: 'The enforcement of real estate mortgages by foreclosure is primarily the province of a state's real property law.'

47 See National Consumer Law Center (n 40) 145; and *Landmark National Bank v Kesler*, 216 P 3d 158 (which establishes that separating interests of note and deeds of trust can leave the mortgage unenforceable).

48 Nelson (n 32) 591 and 592.

49 See the discussion of the report of the American Securitization Forum, 'Transfer and Assignment of Residential Mortgage Loans in the Secondary Mortgage Market' ASF White Paper Series (16 November 2010).

50 The first case is *US Bank National Association v Antonio Ibanez, Supreme Judicial Court of Massachusetts*, 7 January 2011 (458 Mass 637), in which the Court stated that: 'In Massachusetts, where a note has been assigned but there is no written assignment of the mortgage underlying the note, the assignment of the note does not carry with it the assignment of the mortgage. *Barnes v Boardman* 149 Mass 106, 114 (1889). Rather, the holder of the mortgage holds the mortgage in trust for the purchaser of the note, who has an equitable right to obtain an assignment of the mortgage, which may be accomplished

It is worth mentioning the relevant inefficiencies (delays and losses) of the mortgage enforcement systems in the US that directly affect the capacity for lenders to recover the money they have lent, and therefore the capacity of investors in MBSs to recover the money they have invested in those securities. The average time to process a foreclosure in the US increased from 253 days in 2007 to 674 days in 2011, although the duration is about three years in Florida, Washington and New York.[51] Mortgage foreclosure law differs from one state to another.[52] In 40 per cent of states, it is only possible to start a judicial foreclosure, which is a long, complex, expensive and inefficient system.[53] If the lender finally succeeds in foreclosing, the inefficient auction process involving the sheriff does not facilitate a proper sale of the property based on its market price – a system which causes losses to the lender that may affect the stability of the securitization structure in which that particular mortgage was included. Second, those states in lighter grey in Figure 2.2 are non-recourse states – where the mortgagee is only secured with the charged property and not with the rest of the estate of the mortgagor. The possibility of mortgage default can be up to 81 per cent higher in these compared with recourse states.[54] This has given rise to the phenomenon of the 'strategic defaulter' – those mortgagors who can pay the mortgage, but since their property is worth less than the money they still owe to the lending institution, they simply 'walk away', giving the lender the keys of the property.[55]

by filing an action in court and obtaining an equitable order of assignment.' In the praxis this means that thousands or even millions of mortgages are unenforceable (and therefore the MBSs issued over them depreciated greatly or simply defaulted as they were often structured over closed pools of mortgages) unless mortgagees acquire all those notes or 'forge' them through robo-signing because they did not exist at all. The second case is *Bevilacqua v Rodriguez*, Supreme Judicial Court of Massachusetts, 18 October 2011 (460 Mass 762), which confirmed that the mortgage holder must have a valid assignment of mortgage to foreclose a property.

51 Les Christie, 'Foreclosure Free Ride: 3 Years, No Payments' *CNN Money* (28 December 2011) http://money.cnn.com/2011/12/28/real_estate/foreclosure/index.htm accessed 18 September 2012.

52 Nelson (n 32) 586.

53 Prentiss Cox, 'Foreclosure Reform Amid Mortgage Lending Turmoil: A Public Purpose Approach' (2008) 45 (3) Houston Law Review 699; see also Nelson (n 32) 586.

54 Ghent and Kudlyak (n 10) 29. See also Kreitzer (n 19) 46 and 47.

55 Moreover, there is a plethora of techniques available to the borrower to delay the foreclosure, such as filing for bankruptcy, staying at home during foreclosures, equity skimming, etc. Other arrangements with the lender, such as deeds in lieu, short sales or conciliations, also affect the secondary mortgage market as they usually entail a loss to the lender, which is transferred to the MBS investors if that mortgage was included in a backing pool.

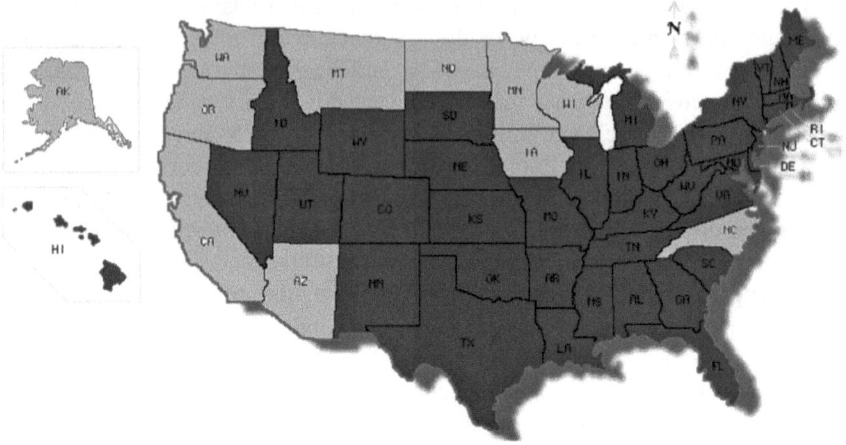

Figure 2.2 Recourse (dark grey) and non-recourse (light grey) states
Source: own elaboration [56]

Thus, it is questionable whether the inefficiencies in 'US mortgages' were already known by investors at the time they bought US MBSs and CDOs, or whether they were being taken into account by rating agencies when they were giving 'Triple A' ratings to those mortgage-collateralized MBSs and CDOs. All this evidences a significant level of distortion[57] of the legal system and generalized reckless practices in the origination, transfer and enforcement of mortgages in the US. This has clearly contributed to the failure of the international financial system and the globalization of the crisis.

From the International Crisis to the Detrimental Impact on the Spanish Housing System

In 2009, global losses in the international banks and other financial institutions arising from US-originated assets were estimated at approximately $2.7 trillion.[58] In Europe, three major British banks lost $31.8 billion, two major Swiss banks

56 Using the data of Ghent and Kudlyak (n 10) 44 and 55.

57 On this concept, see Steven L Schwarcz, 'Distorting Legal Principles' (2010) 35(4) Journal of Corporation Law, available at: http://papers.ssrn.com/sol3/papers.cfm?abstract_id=1532465 accessed 18 September 2012.

58 International Monetary Fund, 'Global Financial Stability Report (GFSR)' (April 2009) 11 http://www.imf.org/external/pubs/ft/gfsr/2009/01/pdf/text.pdf accessed 18 September 2012.

lost $62.3 billion, and $41.1 billion was lost by three major German banks up to December 2008, – all traceable to the US subprime crisis.[59] These losses heavily affected the capital position of the banks, which entered a liquidity crisis. The securitization market dropped dramatically, as did interbank lending, due to the general lack of trust between financial institutions. In some countries, such as Spain, banks almost completely ceased lending to families or businesses, thus virtually halting the economy. It is significant that in 2007, loans (mostly mortgage loans) represented about 65 per cent of the Spanish banks' balance sheets.[60]

Indeed, the Spanish economy and financial system has performed even worse than would be expected during a globalized crisis, particularly when compared to the impact in the majority of EU countries. Although many causes could have contributed to this, it is suggested that the last housing boom/bubble (1995–2007) is one of the most relevant. In a manner similar to the US pattern described above, the promotion of widespread home-ownership at any cost, combined with the speculative or the buy-to-let business approach, has been prevalent in Spain and other European countries. Spanish housing policy, before and during the housing bubble, involved massive construction and enormous levels of mortgage loans, which has now led to an over-indebted society.[61] This was facilitated by ready access to mortgage credit as a result of low interest rates and the liquidity of Spanish banks, which benefited from a good interbank lending system (based on trust among banks), and the massive issuing of Spanish covered bonds and MBSs. In fact, Spanish banks had for many years been the second largest issuer of covered bonds and MBSs after Germany (covered bonds), and the UK (MBSs).[62] Other countries such as Ireland experienced similar policies and a housing market collapse on a similarly large scale.[63]

---

59 Cox, Faucette and Valenzuela (n 6) 18.

60 Ibid.

61 For numbers, see below.

62 See Sergio Nasarre-Aznar, 'Operaciones pasivas. La refinanciación de créditos y préstamos hipotecarios' in Esther Muñiz Espada, Sergio Nasarre-Aznar and Elena Sánchez Jordán (eds), *La reforma del mercado hipotecario* (Madrid, Edisofer 2009) 399–552, but especially 406–12, where the bad performance of Spanish covered bonds when compared to other European covered bonds since the beginning of the crisis is discussed.

63 At least three authoritative reports on the Irish financial crisis have highlighted massive overlending, which overheated the housing market. See Klaus Regling and Max Watson, *A Preliminary Report on the Sources of Ireland's Banking Crisis* (Dublin, Government Publications Office 2010); Commission of Investigation into the Banking Sector in Ireland, *Misjudging Risk: Causes of the Systemic Banking Crisis in Ireland* (March 2011), known as the Nyberg Report; Governor of the Central Bank, *The Irish Banking Crisis. Regulatory and Financial Stability Policy 2003–2008* (Dublin, The Stationery Office 2010). This latter report shows that by 2006, the increase in construction and housing had increased beyond population needs, reflecting speculative purchases that represented 15 per cent of the housing stock that stood vacant. But it also says (at 30) that taxation incentives aimed at the construction sector, e.g. lowering stamp duty five times

However, in Spain, the situation was more severe as a consequence of the unavailability of a *real* alternative housing tenure to home-ownership. For years, the Spanish housing rented sector remained one of the smallest in Europe (see Figure 2.3), which in practice meant that it was of poor quality and relatively expensive.[64] All tax benefits were targeted at home-owners rather than tenants/lessees. There was an inefficient eviction process for rented properties, which compared poorly with an efficient (but very lender-oriented) mortgage enforcement procedure. State housing plans revolved around build-to-sell rather than a renting-what-is-already-built-oriented approach. Market advantages, in the form of structured and funded mortgage facilities, have overshadowed an undeveloped rented market, while Spanish legislation over the past 60 years focused on the needs of banks and home-owners rather than lessors and lessees. The result is that, even today, only 12 per cent of households occupy rented housing and only two per cent occupy social rented housing. Thus, there is still no real (in terms of affordability, quality, stability, etc.) alternative to home-ownership for families, which is an issue in many other European states .[65]

In fact, since the beginning of the financial crash in the last quarter of 2007 (and the subsequent mortgage and housing crisis), Spanish economic stability[66]

---

between 2001 and 2007 to improve the affordability of houses to first-time buyers and special schemes, existed for many types of constructions. Moreover (at 31), the ceiling on the income tax deductibility of mortgage interest for owner-occupiers was increased four times between 2000 and 2008. See also P van den Noord, 'Tax Incentives and House Price Volatility in the Euro Area: Theory and Evidence', OECD Economics Department Working Papers No 356, 2011, 9, which clearly stated that the tax system was subsidizing housing in Ireland and Spain (among others).

64 See a complete discussion in Sergio Nasarre-Aznar and Estela Rivas Nieto, 'La naturaleza jurídico-privada y el tratamiento fiscal de las nuevas sociedades cotizadas de inversión en el mercado inmobiliario (SOCIMI)' en la Ley 11/2009 Estudios Financieros. Revista de Contabilidad y Tributación, 2009 DIC; (321); and D Rae and P van den Noord, 'Ireland's Housing Boom. What Has Driven it and Have Prices Overshot?' OECD Economics Department Working Papers No 492, 6.

65 See a complete discussion of this in Montserrat Pareja Eastway, 'El régimen de tenencia de la vivienda' in Jesús Leal (ed), *La política de vivienda en España* (Madrid, Ed Pablo Iglesias 2010) 101.

66 Which has been recently (2011–12) replicated into a political crisis (e.g. the form of state divided into autonomous regions since 1978 is in question, with Catalonia's current government requesting the independence from the rest of Spain (see http://www.nytimes.com/2012/10/06/world/europe/in-catalonia-spain-artur-mas-threatens-to-secede.html?partner=rss&emc=rss&smid=tw-nytimes&_r=0 accessed 6 October 2012) and serious social unrest (e.g. just in the main city of Spain, Madrid, there have been 983 demonstrations between July and September 2012 (see 'Las manifestaciones pasan factura a Madrid' *LaVanguarida* (27 September 2012) **http://www.lavanguardia.com/local/madrid/20120927/54351933893/las-manifestaciones-pasan-factura-a-madrid.html** accessed 6 July 2013.

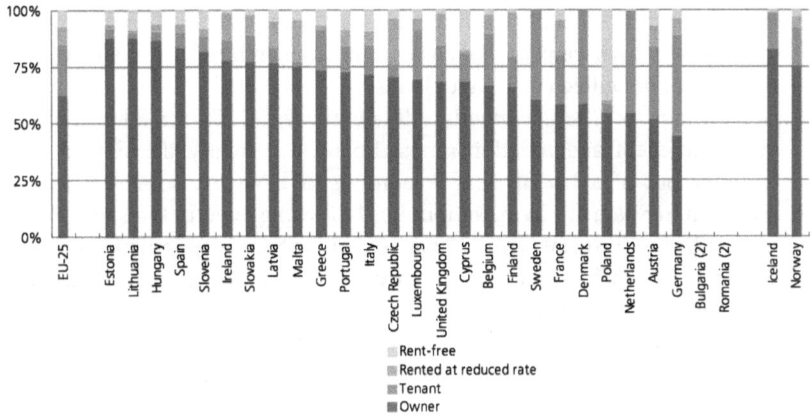

Figure 2.3 Number of dwellings by type of tenure in Europe, 2009
Source: Eurostat.

itself has been in constant danger.[67] This has had an important impact on housing. The following data outlines the current situation of housing in Spain after five years of economic crisis:

1. From 2007 to 2011, there have been 330,000 mortgage foreclosures.[68] Paradoxically, the new census of 2011 reveals that there are 3.5 million empty dwellings.[69]
2. Mortgage funding and house sales are still decreasing – down by 29.3 in 2011 compared to 2010.[70]

67 The massive banking reforms through mergers and acquisitions and nationalization, the current lack of liquidity of Spanish banks that remain untrustworthy in international business, the 'intervention' of the EU in the Spanish economy in July 2012, the creation of a 'bad bank' with thousands of unsold properties at bargain prices, the sovereign rate risk that exceeded 600 basic points in relation to Germany in July 2012 and the cuts in workers' salaries and other social rights are only some examples of the elements of the drama.

68 Consejo General Del Poder Judicial, 'Datos sobe el efecto de la crisis en los órganos judiciales 3T 2011' (Madrid, 2011) www.poderjudicial.es accessed 19 July 2013, under 'Estadística'. However this data does not differentiate between first residences and other dwellings or even between dwellings and other type of properties.

69 See, however, Juan Carlos Martinez, 'En España un 20 per cent de las viviendas están vacías' *El Pais Economia* (8 May 2012) http://economia.elpais.com/economia/2012/01/05/actualidad/1325752378_850215.html accessed 18 September 2012.

70 Statistics can be found at the website of the Ministerio de Fomento http://www.fomento.gob.es/BE2/?nivel=2&orden=34000000 accessed 18 September 2012.

3. Some 5.7 million people were unemployed in July 2012, an unemployment rate of 24.63 per cent.[71] This has a significant influence in the increasing number of defaulted (mortgage) loans.
4. According to *The Economist* (9 February 2012), on the basis of unemployment and inflation ratios, Spain is currently the sixth poorest country out of a list of 92.[72] According to UNICEF, some 2.2 million children in Spain are living in families below the poverty threshold.[73]
5. According to Eurostat, some 37 per cent of the Spanish population between 18 and 35 consider access to a dwelling as one of the most important problems facing Spanish youth[74] and as the main cause of why children are not leaving their parents' house until they are 30 years old.[75] Even then, some 30 per cent still need economic support from their parents or other relatives.[76]

There are at least four legal factors which, in my opinion, contribute to an understanding of the current situation of Spanish housing and mortgage markets, and which bear similarities to factors in the US that caused the crisis.

First, bad banking practices are a major contributory factor. For many years, Spanish banks undertook bad practices by offering inadequate products,[77] including those related to their mortgage loans. Subprime mortgages were also a reality in Spain during the housing bubble. Lenders granted mortgages of even more than 100 per cent LTV, regardless of the capability of the borrower to pay

---

71 According to the Instituto Nacional de Estadistica (INE): http://www.ine.es/jaxi/menu.do?type=pcaxis&path= per cent2Ft22 per cent2Fe308_mnu&file=inebase&L=0 accessed 18 September 2012.

72 'Feeling Gloomy' *The Economist* (9 January 2012) http://www.economist.com/blogs/graphicdetail/2012/01/daily-chart-0 accessed 18 September 2012.

73 UNICEF, 'La infancia en España 2012–2013. El impacto de la crisis en los niños' (May 2012) 8 http://www.unicef.es/sites/www.unicef.es/files/Infancia_2012_2013_final.pdf accessed 17 September 2012.

74 Centro de Investigaciones Sociológicas (CIS), 'Estudi 2835' (27 April 2010) http://www.cis.es accessed 18 September, 2012.

75 Eurostat, 'Youth in Europe. A Statistical Portrait' (2009) 31 http://epp.eurostat.ec.europa.eu/cache/ITY_OFFPUB/KS-78-09-920/EN/KS-78-09-920-EN.PDF accessed 18 September 2012.

76 Fundacion Encuentro, 'Informe España 2011. Una interpretación de su realidad social' (2011) 191 http://www.fund-encuentro.org/ accessed 19 September 2012.

77 As an example, the Spanish Securities Exchange Commission (Comisión Nacional del Mercado de Valores) has established fines for 10 credit institutions for commercializing a kind of security called 'preferred participations' (*participaciones preferentes*) without explaining them properly to their clients, and thus failing to fulfil the Markets in Financial Instruments Directive requirements to obtain a proper consent from them: http://economia.elpais.com/economia/2012/09/13/actualidad/1347528967_278279.html accessed 13 September 2012.

the instalments under the mortgage.[78] The careless examination of the repayment capability of the borrower led, according to the Bank of Spain, to a delinquency rate of housing mortgage loans of 3.22 per cent in mid-2012, up from 1.31 per cent in mid-2008.[79] The risk to banks was usually covered by requiring borrowers to find a friend or a relative to mortgage their own dwelling, or even provide a personal guarantee (*aval*) with their whole estate for the repayment of the mortgage loan. This practice has contributed to the extension of the housing crisis among families of all income levels.[80] Similarly, for years, Spanish banks had sold risky financial products to both small corporations and consumers. These were arranged with corresponding credit default swaps, to stabilize the volatility of the variable interest rate of their mortgage loans (referenced to the Euribor index)[81] or to provide a floor clause within the mortgage loan contract terms. These types of financial products were commercialized just a few months before the biggest drop of the Euribor in its history[82] and some months after the first effects of the credit crunch in Spain.[83] Many of those contracts were worded in an obscure manner for clients. The reference indexes were imposed by the banks (a fixed reference index of around 4.5 per cent), which, in practice, meant that since October 2008, clients have been paying extra over and above their mortgage instalments to the banks on a monthly basis. This is the typical obligation resulting from an interest rate swap or a floor clause, as the Euribor has remained since then lower than those 'agreed' reference indexes.

Moreover, customers/clients found it very difficult to assess the real legal and economic consequences of underwriting those contracts, as neither neutral nor complete information was provided to them. There was no legal requirement to ensure that customers/clients understood all the details of the arrangement, demonstrating the major asymmetry of information between the parties. Banks could have reasonably been expected to have known in advance that the Euribor rate would drop significantly, or were at least more likely to do so than the

78 Since 2002, banks have been legally allowed to securitize Spanish subprime mortgages through the issue of Spanish asset-backed securities (ABSs) (*bonos de titulización de activos*). This meant that Spanish banks were allowed to get rid of problematic mortgages as soon as they were granted and therefore they had no problem in granting them to families and people who were unable to repay them.

79 It is about 25 per cent for mortgage loans granted to builders. See Asociación Hipotececaria Espanola, 'Tasas de dudosidad hipotecaria, Segundo Trimestre 2012' (2012) http://www.ahe.es/bocms/images/bfilecontent/2006/04/26/90.pdf?version=17 accessed 6 October 2012.

80 'Las ejecuciones hipotecarias amenazan ya a las familias de las zonas de rentas altas' *El Mundo* (24 September 2012) http://www.elmundo.es/elmundo/2012/09/24/suvivienda/1348478744.html accessed 9 September 2012.

81 'EURIBOR' (the Euro Interbank Offered Rate) is the money market reference rate for the euro.

82 October 2008.

83 September 2007.

consumers or small businesses with whom they made such arrangements. The courts have reacted to this situation by declaring many thousands of swaps, caps, floor clauses and similar financial derivative agreements void.

It is significant that the transposition of the Markets in Financial Instruments Directive (MiFID)[84] into Spanish law arrived late, in 2008, when all banking activity had already virtually stopped. Although now implemented, its application has been disappointing for non-professional customers. Indeed, non-professional customers can still engage in contracts associated with the vast majority of risky financial products, even where the non-professional customer has not passed the adequacy or convenience test. This, in practice, means that he or she does not know what he or she is contracting, and is bound just by signing that he or she agrees to the contract (even if he or she does not understand it and/or its consequences). Conversely, banks are using these tests as a defence against claims from consumers to demonstrate that they had properly assessed them, and that the customers wished to enter into contracts for these products, even if they did not understand them.[85]

Spanish legislation has allowed and even promoted new forms of risky banking practices, even in the delicate field of housing. In this sense, the reform of the mortgage market in Spain, by Act 41/2007,[86] introduced two new risky

---

84 Directive 2004/39/EC of the European Parliament and of the Council of 21 April 2004 on markets in financial instruments amending Council Directives 85/611/EEC and 93/6/EEC and Directive 2000/12/EC of the European Parliament and of the Council and repealing Council Directive 93/22/EEC (OJEU, 30 April 2004, L145/1).

85 This is a similar criticism noted in C Castronove, 'Information Duties and Precontractual Good Faith' (2009) 4 European Review of Private Law 568 of consumers' protection through long lists of pre-contractual information to be provided by the professional seller before an arrangement (see, as an example, the 20 pieces of pre-contractual information to be provided in distant contracts according to art 6 of Directive 2011/83/EU of the European Parliament and of the Council of 25 October 2011 on consumer rights, amending Council Directive 93/13/EEC and Directive 1999/44/EC of the European Parliament and of the Council and repealing Council Directive 85/577/EEC and Directive 97/7/EC of the European Parliament and of the Council, OJEU 22 November 2011, L304/64). Basically, consumers do not read all this information on a regular basis and, even if they do so, in some cases they may not fully understand it, thus evidencing that there is not necessarily a correlation between more pre-contractual information and more consumer protection. For criticism of this system, see T Sefton Green, *Mistake, Fraud and Duties to Inform in European Contract Law* (Cambridge University Press, 2009) 398. See also research on this in the US in O Ben-Shahar and CE Schneider, 'The Failure of Mandated Disclosure', Chicago Working Paper Series Index (March 2010) 64, where it is shown that the history of compulsory provision of information 'is a history of failure'. See also F Marotta Wurgler, 'Will Increased Disclosure Help? Evaluating the Recommendation of the ALI's "Principles of the Law of Software Contracts"' (2011) 78 (1) University of Chicago Law Review 165.

86 Spanish Act 41/2007, 7 December, which modifies Act 2/1981, 25 March, of regulation of the mortgage market (BOE 8 December 2007, no 294, 50593).

practices that were discouraged by the European Commission White Paper on the Integration of EU Mortgage Credit Markets.[87] The first of the two is related to the tying practices, i.e. banking practices that make it more difficult for the borrower to change his or her lending institution because of the costs or the numerous links with the existing lender. Thus, while Act 41/2007 limited the effects of former Article 2 of Act 2/1994 on subrogation and modification of mortgage loans,[88] from 2007 onwards, as soon as the borrower receives an offer from a new lender, he or she cannot change if the existing lender matches this offer. Significantly, Objective 3.4 of the European Commission White Paper 2007 strongly discourages the establishment of such limitations on borrowers in Europe.[89] Moreover, Article 9 of the Report of the Economic and Monetary Affairs Committee[90] of the European Parliament clearly states that countries should forbid these tying products. Surprisingly, however, Article 18 of the same Report foresees a similar outcome to the one in Spanish Act 41/2007, which is not desirable as it is contrary to the EU principle of freedom of movement of people and is against free competition among lending institutions in Europe, freedom of choice and consumer mobility.

A second paradox arises in the context of the Commission's caution in the White Paper in respect of equity-release products, such as the reverse mortgage. Yet, these type of products are legally backed in Article 18 of the Report of the Economic and Monetary Affairs Committee and the reverse mortgage was introduced for the first time into Spanish law by Additional Disposition 1 of Act 41/2007. As an example of this approach in Spain, Figure 2.4 shows the 'recommended' way in which a person's life can be linked to a single lending institution. First the lender grants a mortgage loan to buy the first family dwelling when the borrower is in his or her mid-twenties; then it grants consumer loans when the borrower has partially repaid the mortgage loan and he or she is between his or her mid-forties

87 White Paper on the Integration of EU Mortgage Credit Markets, COM(2007) 807 final.

88 BOE 4 April 1994, no 80, 10364.

89 Consumer mobility is a clear-cut objective of the White Paper to achieve a true European mortgage market. In this sense, it says (at 5) that: 'Information alone cannot, however, facilitate customer mobility. By increasing switching costs, "tying" practices (e.g. obliging the consumer to open a current account or take out an insurance policy with the same company when purchasing a mortgage credit) effectively bind consumers to a particular financial services provider, thus restricting mobility and weakening competition. Practices such as obliging consumers to transfer their salary to the current account attached to the mortgage credit may have a similar effect. These practices not only have implications for customer mobility but can also reduce price and product competition in the markets for the tied and tying products and discourage the entry of new players, particular those providers specialising in the tied product.'

90 'Home Loans: Better Advice for Borrowers, More Stable Markets for Lenders', press release, Committee of Economic and Monetary Affairs (7 July 2012) http://www.europarl.europa.eu/sides/getDoc.do?pubRef=-//EP//TEXT+IM-PRESS+20120604IPR46265+0+DOC+XML+V0//EN&language=EN accessed 9 September 2012.

and mid-sixties; and finally it grants equity-release products when the borrower retires. This form of continuous dependency on the same financial institution means that it is too onerous or complicated to change the lending institution. From 25 years to death (where the reverse mortgage operates), this process even links the borrower's heirs to the lender, since the heir must decide whether to repay the parent's reverse mortgage (perhaps with another mortgage loan) or allow the family home to be sold or be given to the lender.

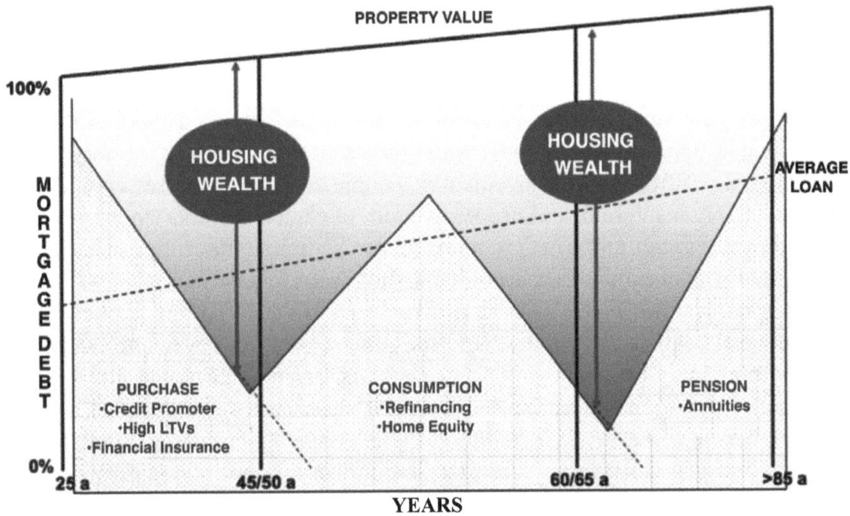

Figure 2.4 'Useful' life of an immovable versus indebtedness (literal translation from the original title)[91]

In relation to mortgage procedural law, the Spanish mortgage enforcement system and insolvency system is one of the most lender-oriented in Europe. The former has not traditionally allowed the borrower as a consumer to raise any defence in relation to abusive clauses (Articles 695 and 698) that may be present in the loan contract, an approach which does not seem reasonable.[92] A request to the European Court of Justice to determine whether the system foreseen in Spanish

91 Santos Gonzalez Sanchez, 'Presente y futuro del negocio hipotecario' a handout of a paper given at the *Curso de crédito hipotecario* conference (Barcelona, Universidad Rovira i Virgili 2008).

92 According to art 83 RDL 1/2007, they are void and can render the whole loan contract ineffective. In this case, the ineffectiveness of the loan contract will affect the mortgage validity that secures that loan contract, thus making it void. This is because Spanish mortgages are legally dependent on the credit they secure (legal accessoriness).

law conflicts with European consumer law[93] has been recently decided (in *Aziz v Catalunya Caixa*),[94] where it has been stated that this situation goes against EU law (Directive 93/13/CEE).[95] thus forcing the Spanish government to reform the law (Act 1/2013, 14th May[96]) and causing the suspension of hundreds of mortgage enforcement procedures. Moreover, the mortgagee can, in the same procedure, take action against the rest of the estate of the consumer after an unsuccessful auction of the mortgaged property (Article 579 LEC), a situation that is not the case in many European countries.[97]

Moreover, the Spanish insolvency legislation does grant any second opportunity to 'start again' for an 'insolvent in good faith'[98] natural-person borrower after an insufficient/unsuccessful insolvency process. In contrast, many other European jurisdictions offer more lenient insolvency consequences for natural-person borrowers or consumers, as is shown is Figure 2.5.[99] A timid reform on this field has not arrived until art. 21 Act 14/2013, 27 September[100], to promote entrepreneurship.

To further demonstrate the lender-oriented nature of Spanish law, it is notable that one of the most relevant problems for the Spanish insolvency procedure is the opacity of the auction of the immovable property. Quite often, only professional auctioneers attend these auctions, which often end without any offer. In this case, the property is assigned to the lender, thus bypassing the historical prohibition of the *pactum commissorium* (Article 1859). This makes it more difficult to achieve the real price of the property, a situation detrimental to the borrower, since he

---

And this is precisely the mechanism that cannot be discussed – because of legal constraints – during a mortgage enforcement procedure, which of course affects the rights of consumers.

93 OJEU 12 November 2011, C 331/7.

94 Case C-415/11.

95 Directive 93/13/CEE of 5 April 1993 on unfair terms in consumer contracts (OJEC L095, 21 April 1993).

96 BOE 15 May 2013, no 116, 36373.

97 See the whole discussion for both aspects in Sergio Nasarre-Aznar, 'Malas prácticas bancarias en la actividad hipotecaria' (2011) 727 Revista Crítica de Derecho Inmobiliario 2721–23.

98 'Bona fide insolvent' is quite a difficult concept, but basically means that such a person has not put himself or herself negligently into insolvency, that he or she has always collaborated with his or her creditors to try to solve his or her case, and that he or she has not hidden goods or has not lied to the judge or to the insolvency trustees.

99 Figures 2.5 and 2.6 are the result of an intensive research task undertaken by more than 30 researchers from around Europe and Japan, led by Dr Otmar Stöcker (VdP), since 2005 on mortgage law in Europe in the so-called 'Runder Tisch'. The latest versions of the maps can be found in M Stocker Otmas and Rolf Sturner, *Flexibilität, Sicherheit und Effizienz der Grundpfandrechte in Europa Band III*, 3 erweiterte Auflage, Band 50 (Berlin, Verban Deutscher Pfandbriefbanken 2012).

100 BOE 28 September 2013, no 233, 78787.

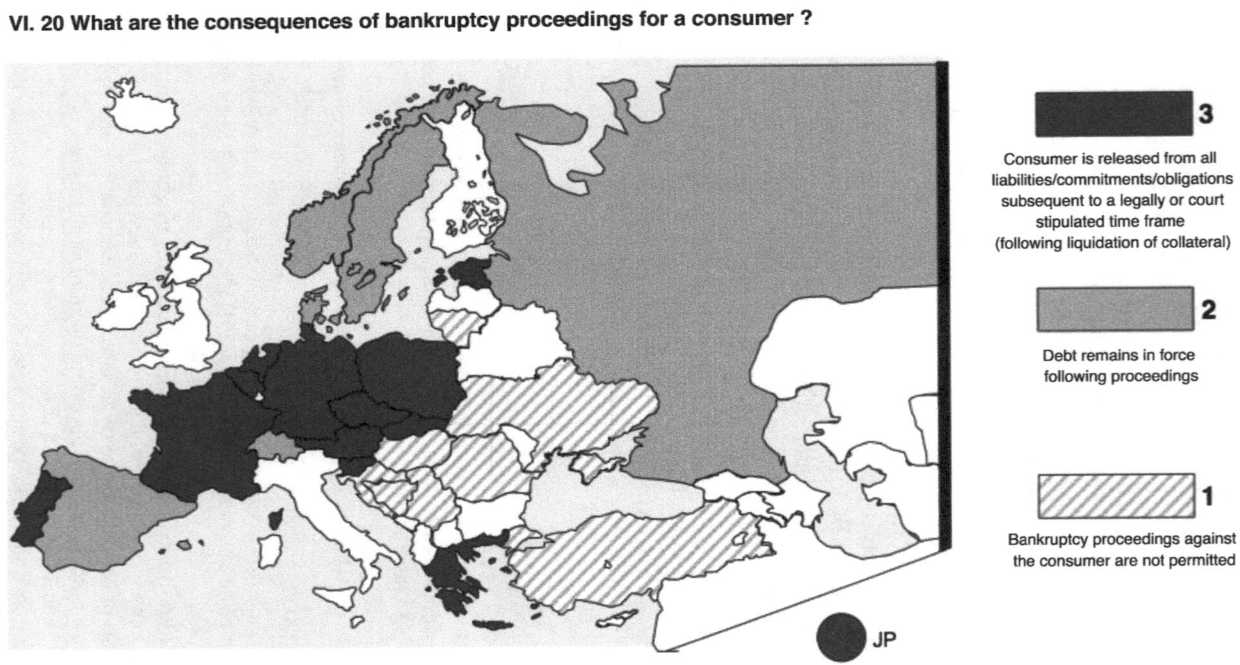

Figure 2.5 The insolvency process against consumers in Europe
Source: Runder Tisch, 2012.[99]

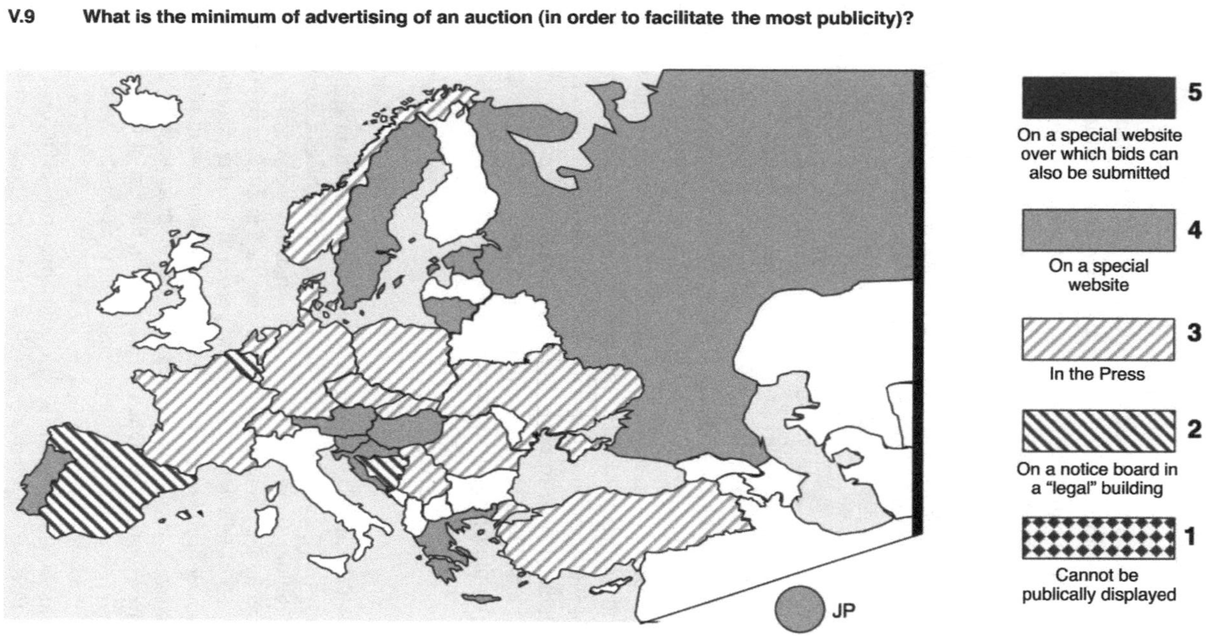

Figure 2.6. Minimum advertising of an auction in order to facilitate maximum publicity
Source: Runder Tisch, 2012.[99]

or she remains a debtor for life[101] for the amount of the loan not covered by the amount obtained by the sale of the house.[102] As shown in Figure 2.6[99], Spain is one of the very few countries in Europe (together with Belgium and Bosnia) which requires that only an announcement on the physical noticeboard of the court where the auction is going to take place is adequate publicity for a mortgaged property auction. Clearly, this is insufficient for an open, transparent international property market. A sort of system of auctions resulting from mortgage enforcements is foreseen in Act 1/2013, although it still needs to be developed through regulations to exist in the praxis.

Finally, Spain still has inadequate regulation of the mortgage securities. Spanish covered bonds (*cédulas hipotecarias*) and MBSs (*bonos de titulización hipotecaria*) are insufficiently regulated under Spanish mortgage market legislation. As this has been developed in depth elsewhere,[103] just two remarks are necessary here. The first is that the security of Spanish covered bonds for investors is unclear and comparatively insufficient, and their performance in cases of insolvency of the issuer is below the standard of the securities in other European jurisdictions. For instance, no separate estate is created in the case of insolvency of the originator/issuer that may allow the continuation of a healthy covered bonds business. The second is that the legal construction of Spanish MBSs is insufficient, from a civil law point of view, to assure that the SPV (issuer) is an insolvency-remoteness entity, and the rights of MBS holders, in case of mismanagement by any stakeholders, are weak and unclear. This lack of legal certainty contributes to the international lack of trust towards Spanish banks and Spanish mortgage-related financial products. Despite this, no reform is foreseen in the short term in this area, although it would be highly desirable.

101 For a number of situations, however, this is more a theoretical than a real situation as the RDL 8/2011, 1 July (BOE 7 July 2011, no 161, 71548), has increased the mortgagor's minimum unforeclosability threshold (i.e. the part of the monthly income of a mortgagor that cannot be foreclosed by the mortgagee). In a standard case in 2012, it has risen from about €642/month (Art 607 LEC) to €962/month. Moreover, it is quite theoretical that a bank will be able to recover the owed amount after a partially unsuccessful auction of the borrower's main residence, as it is likely that he or she has no more valuable goods and will not have any for many years. Therefore, the 'recourse' to the rest of the estate of the borrower acts more as a preventive and deterrent measure than as a real way for the lender to recover the rest of the money.

102 This has led to social movements to push legislative changes in Spain in favour of the introduction of a forced *datio pro soluto*, which, in case they succeed, would convert Spain into a form of 'non-recourse' state. As seen above in the case of the US, this does not seem to be a good solution for any mortgage market.

103 See Nasarre-Aznar (n 2) 58. The problems addressed there were not solved in the reform of Spanish mortgage securities in 2007, as is explained in Nasarre-Aznar (n 62). For a summary, see also Nasarre-Aznar (n 96).

Insufficient Reforms in the Spanish Mortgage and Housing Markets

The Guidelines for a New Situation

In relation to the Spanish situation, a number of appropriate reforms, based on the preceding analysis, can be suggested:

1. Measures should be taken to avoid a repetition of any of the following circumstances that led Spain to the current situation: the easy access to credit regardless of mortgagors' resources or repayment capacity; the absence of any real alternative to home ownership; the promotion of the social value of massive consumption[104] and a pro-lender and weak mortgage securities legislation. All of these contributed decisively to the creation of the mortgage and housing bubble in Spain.
2. The choices for families should not be either over-indebtedness due to home-ownership or the lack of stability that results from renting a house in Spain. Yet, even today, access to home-ownership automatically involves over-indebtedness, since salaries in recent years have not increased at the same rate as house prices. In June 2012, five years after the collapse of the mortgage and housing market in Spain and internationally, house prices remain as high as in 2005, one year before the peak of the housing bubble. Even in the rental sphere, there are few signs of improvement. The Spanish government has recently passed Act 4/2013, 4th June[105] to reform the Spanish law on urban leases (*Ley de arrendamientos urbanos*: LAU). This reform brings even less stability to tenants. For example, there is a reduction in the protection period from five to three years, the legal right of pre-emption for the tenant is removed and referenced prices during the protection period is removed. Clearly, this will not increase the attractiveness of renting as a type of housing tenure for families.
3. Mortgagors, and consumers in general, should be able to calculate, from the very beginning of a mortgage agreement, the costs of the mortgage they are about to sign. Equally, mortgagors should be aware of the risks that this might entail. Spain lacks specific protective legislation for mortgagors (as consumers), and these consumers are even explicitly excluded from regular consumer protection laws.[106] The rules foreseen

104 See Jim Kemeny, The Myth of Homeownership. Private vs Public Choices in Housing Tenure (London, Routledge & Kegan Paul 1981) 62 and 63.

105 BOE 5 June 2013, no 134, 42244.

106 See, as examples, Act 22/2007, 11 July, on distance financial contracts (BOE 12 July 2007, no 166, 29985); or Act 47/2007, 19 December (BOE 20 December 2007, no 304, 52335) on the transposition of the MiFID Directive. Even the Spanish legislator did not take advantage of the possibility given in EU Directive 2008/48/CE of the European

in Order EHA/2899/2011[107] to avoid future bad banking practices do not appear sufficient to avoid future bad banking practice and do not add anything extra to the current situation. Indeed, there are no specific legal consequences for misbehaviour by lenders in the marketing and pre-contractual phases, such as the failure to properly assess the capability of the debtor to repay the offered mortgage or the failure to disclose sufficient information to the debtor so that he or she is able understand the cost and the legal and economic consequences of the legal documentation he or she is about to sign. Nor are there any legal consequences from this upon the loan contract. There is a simple administrative fine in Article 14, but this does not in any way lead to the possible invalidity of the loan contract or any type of contractual or torts liability on the lender. Moreover, the rules in this Order do not create greater obligations for those who take part in the standard process of granting a mortgage loan. For instance, there is no compulsion on a notary public to check for the validity of all type of pre-formatted and pre-included clauses in the loan contract, or to forbid excessively onerous mortgage loans. Indeed, the functioning of the Latin notarial system in Spain is now being questioned.[108] Notary publics in Spain still claim that it is not their duty to assess the position of the parties, although legislation provides that they have to 'inform' or to 'warn' them. But there is no requirement to ensure that they understand the legal and economic consequences of underwriting a mortgage loan. Nor, it is claimed, is it their duty to control the legality of any abusive clauses incorporated into the public deeds unless they had previously been declared void by a judge. This would appear to be a reasonable request, according to Article 83 RDL 1/2007, which provides that if an abusive clause in a contract with consumers is void, this fact must be declared by any person, especially by notaries, which should prevent the registration of that mortgage loan with that clause.

Parliament and of the Council, of 23 April 2008 on credit agreements for consumers and repealing Council Directive 87/102/EEC (OJEU, 22 May 2008, L 133/66) to extend its scope to mortgage consumers, when it implemented this Directive through Act 16/2011, 24 June (art 3a); BOE 25 June 2011, no 151, 68179.

107 BOE 29 October 2011, no 261, 113242.

108 See, as an example, U Schmid Christoph et al, 'Conveyancing Services Market', ZERP, Study COMP/2006/D3/003 (University of Bremen, December 2007) 77 which establishes that: 'As shown above, most of this regulation, particularly on *numerus clausus*, fixed fees and reserved rights is unacceptable when considered in the light of European competition and internal market law.' Moreover, the STS 16 December 2009 (RJ 2010/702) revealed that lending institutions used to include void clauses in mortgage contracts that had not been properly controlled by notary publics.

In addition to this, in order to resolve previous banking practices, the RDL 6/2012[109] was passed on 9 March 2012. However, its efficacy is very limited. First, the 'good banking practices code' which is proposed as the basic tool for protection of mortgagors is merely voluntary. Second, there are a large number of requirements to be fulfilled by mortgagors in order to qualify for specific solutions to address mortgage default or arrears, such as acquittances, postponement of payments, reduction of interest rates, *datio pro soluto*, etc. Some of these requirements are extremely onerous to achieve, such as the one that states that the whole family of the mortgagor must be unemployed and the loan should not have more guarantees. There is also a limitation to properties within a certain maximum value for the mortgaged property, depending on the size of the city where it is located. The aforementioned Act 1/2013 has recently relaxed the requirements to achieve by debtors and families in need to benefit from RDL 6/2012 but it is still uncertain if this time they will be the adequate to help those that really deserve these special rules.

As a consequence of all this, new and stronger rules are still required to create a comprehensive form of mortgagors' protection, both in relation to the current consequences of reckless past lending and to avoid the negative effects of another housing bubble.

Forthcoming Measures

There are essentially two types of forthcoming measures that are being introduced into the Catalan legal system, thus they will only apply to Catalonia once passed into law. One group of provisions will deal with the necessity to really strengthen the protection of mortgage consumers. Another group of provisions will deal with the fact that new types of housing tenures are needed to augment the housing market, and to adapt it to the economic capabilities of each family, instead of making families to choose between full ownership and renting.

More protection for mortgage consumers

Devolution rules in relation to mortgages are unclear in the decentralized regions of Spain. Despite this, the Catalan legislator has drafted a Law Project to reform the Catalan Consumer Code (CCC) in July 2012,[110] which addresses the main issues in relation to protection of the mortgagor.[111] This reform is inspired in the Proposal for a Directive of the European Parliament and of the Council on credit agreements relating to residential property of March 2011[112] and goes beyond any

109 BOE 10 March 2012, no 60, 22492.

110 DOGC 30 July 2012, no 364, 34. Although the Catalan Parliament is to be dissolved because of the calling of an election, it is foreseeable that this draft will continue to be processed after the elections. If it is passed, it will be in force only in Catalonia.

111 I was, in fact, personally involved in the drafting of its first version in September 2011.

112 Brussels, 31 March 2011, COM(2011) 142 final.

measures taken until now for the whole of Spain (including many aspects of Act 1/2013). The relevant issues are as follows:

(a) A clear legal limitation (new Article 251-6 CCC) on the rate of interest charged on arrears to be limited to no more than 2.5 times the legal interest rate of money (which is fixed on an annual basis by the Spanish government), regardless of what the parties have arranged in the mortgage contract. Indeed, it is currently usual to find interest rates on arrears of more than 20 per cent in mortgage loan contracts.

(b) The obligation on the professional lender to check the economic capacity of the borrower (consumer) to repay the mortgage loan he or she is offering to him or her. If the lender discovers the unsuitability of that mortgage for a particular borrower, he or she should warn the borrower about its unsuitability (new Article 263-2.3 CCC). Unfortunately, the Catalan reform does not foresee the same strong results as are foreseen in Article 14.2 of the Directive Proposal (at least in its first version of 31 March 2011[113]) in the event of the contravention of this obligation. Under Catalan law, the borrower will be allowed to contract such a mortgage anyway, while in the Directive Proposal, there is a clear prohibition on the lender from granting it. However, the Directive Proposal fails to state the consequences for the lender who grants that inadequate mortgage to the borrower. The natural consequence in many legal jurisdictions would be the voidability of that mortgage loan, which entails a difficult situation for the borrower, who will then be obliged to return an amount of money he or she no longer has. This is not the only case in which the Catalan proposal could have further protected the mortgagor. The defining of the notarial role in the new Article 123-10 CPCC is another. On the one hand, this increases notarial duties in relation to the provision of information to the mortgage consumer in a way in which it can be understandable,[114] while on the other hand, it limits the notarial control to those clauses in mortgage contracts that have been previously declared void by a judge. Instead, it could have expanded the notary's duty to those clauses which are clearly abusive (regardless of

113 But no longer in its version resulting of its adoption by the European Parliament on 10 September 2013 (T7-0341/2013). Its art. 18.5 states that: "Member States shall ensure that: (a) the creditor only makes the credit available to the consumer where the result of the creditworthiness assessment indicates that the obligations resulting from the credit agreement are likely to be met in the manner required under that agreement" while art. 14.2 of the Project at 31 March 2011 stated that: "Member States shall ensure the following: (a) Where the assessment of the consumer's creditworthiness results in a negative prospect for his ability to repay the credit over the lifetime of the credit agreement, the creditor refuses credit", which at least seems a more expedited wording.

114 This is essential because simply providing long lists of information is not enough, especially for financial products. See the discussion above about the dubious efficacy of the 'long lists' system to protect consumers that is normally used in European Directives.

whether they have been previously declared void by a judge) in Article 83 RDL 1/2007.

(c) Pre-contractual clear information for mortgagors is required in the marketing phase of the contractual path (new Articles 262-3 and 262-4 CPCC). For example, when the law is passed, the following sentence (or something similar) will be compulsory in each advertisement for a mortgage product: 'Contracting this mortgage may cause you to lose your dwelling and a part of your personal estate.' After the marketing phase, but before the contract is signed, the offer by the professional lender should be incorporated and given to the mortgagor in a pre-formatted form, which should be the same for every professional lender. This application form should be formatted in such a way that it discloses the grounds for the final price of the mortgage loan (i.e. to which extent swaps, caps, floors, insurances and other linked financial products influence the final interest rate of the mortgage loan and its other conditions). Only then will the mortgage borrower have the sufficient information to be able to compare this particular offer with other offers from the same or another professional lender – this is what is needed by every consumer.

New Forms of Housing Tenure – The Catalan Intermediate Tenures

Justification

The measures described above would improve the current situation and would avoid repeating the mistakes of the last 15 years in relation to housing and the mortgage markets. However, they do not, in fact, create anything new, and there is really a need for imaginative measures to overcome the current situation and to re-start both markets.

Intermediate tenures can play an important role here. The Directive Proposal 2011, as was mentioned previously, will no longer allow lending institutions to grant subprime mortgages, which would mean, in practice, that the maximum LTV would, in a best-case scenario, amount to no more than 80 per cent. If this is passed in this or in a similar way[115], it will bring a completely new set of rules to play in the Spanish mortgage market, as it would essentially mean that lending institutions would only be allowed to fund 80 per cent of the value of the house. The other 20 per cent should be paid by the buyer upfront. Numerically, this would mean that for a flat valued at €150,000,[116] the mortgagor would have to pay

115 As said, this seems to have been somehow softened by its version of 10 September 2013, although member states should control anyhow that no more careless lending is undertaken by lending institutions.

116 This is nearly the medium price for a 80m^2 dwelling in Spain according to fotocase.es http://www.fotocasa.es/indice-inmobiliario__fotocasa.aspx accessed 19 October 2012.

€30,000 upfront in cash, quite a large amount for many. In effect, this might mean that many families will never be able to become home-owners[117].

One significant initiative[118] that is being developed in Catalonia[119] is the regulation of intermediate tenures,[120] based on the success of the shared-ownership model in the UK,[121] and the work of housing associations there in developing social housing on this basis. The UK shared-ownership model is based on the device of the leasehold, an approach conceived under common law that is unknown in many civil law jurisdictions.[122]

That is why, under Catalan law, the proposal is to differentiate between 'shared ownership' (*propietat compartida*) and 'temporal ownership' (*propietat temporal*). The using of the word 'ownership' is crucial to differentiate these two forms of tenure from limited real rights – traditionally not an attractive option for either consumers or financers to access a dwelling. This proposal clearly points out that they are two new alternative ways to the 'traditional ownership'[123] (*propietat*) of achieving all faculties of the full ownership – step by step in shared ownership and time-framed in temporal ownership.

This approach is conceived, in fact, as a middle way between ownership and renting, and is intended to create a real third housing market, which will lead to a viable alternative for families to achieve a type of housing tenure which is

117 The only remaining option being to rent, and it has already addressed the issues in relation to this type of tenancy in Spain.

118 By the Housing Research Group of University Rovira i Virgili, Tarragona, Spain http://www.urv.cat/grups_recerca/housing/english/RGAH/Welcome.html accessed 19 July 2013.

119 The proposal is currently under consideration in the Catalan Codification Commission in order to introduce the intermediate tenures into the Catalan Civil Code.

120 As mentioned in note 1, this work belongs to a Project of the Spanish Ministry of Economy and Competitiveness to expand the intermediate tenures to the rest of Spain.

121 See a complete study on economic aspects of intermediate tenures in Sarah Monk and Christine Whitehead, *Making Housing More Affordable: The Role of Intermediate Tenures* (Oxford, Wiley-Blackwell 2010).

122 Although as Jane Ball in 'Fragmentando la propiedad para la asequibilidad: la shared ownership o 'nuevas' tenencias en Inglaterra y Francia' in Sergio Nasarre-Aznar (ed), *El acceso a la vivienda en un context de crisis* (Madrid, Edisofer 2011) 173 states, 'there might exist similar institutions in Continental Europe, such as the emphyteusis or the usufruct. However, they do not achieve the grade of "utility" or "usability" as the leasehold, as they are not ownership-like institutions but only rights in *re aliena*, which are quite limited in their scope'.

123 This 'traditional ownership' date from the French Revolution and entails all rights of use and disposal (*usus, fructus et abusus*) in relation to a thing. It is present both in the Spanish Civil Code (art 348 CC) and in the Catalan Civil Code (art 541-1 CCC). Both are constitutionally palliated (i.e. those faculties within the ownership are limited) by their social function (e.g. someone cannot destroy their own thing if this affects another's fundamental rights, and nobody is allowed to exploit a property if, in doing so, it affects another's fundamental rights).

Table 2.2 Goals to achieve the Catalan intermediate tenures

Ideal goals of housing policies according to the current situation	Shared ownership	Temporal ownership
To reduce the vacant housing stock and to reactivate the housing and mortgage market	Allows the sale of portion of ownership of dwellings instead of complete title of dwellings (that are not being sold today anyway)	Allows the sale of dwellings for periods of time, adapted to the needs of each family
To reduce the financial illiquidity of financial institutions	Loans of smaller amounts: this will depend on the percentage of the acquired share of the property	Loans of smaller amounts: this will depend on how long the buyer has the property
To prevent families from becoming over-indebted	To grant smaller and more sustainable mortgage loans. Investment in housing will be more needs-based, relying somewhat on savings rather than borrowing	
To create a favourable context for responsible lending and borrowing	Progressive acquisition of home-ownership (staircasing)	Real necessity to buy a dwelling based on time limits. This type of tenure clearly goes against speculative operations
To allow flexibility of approaches in access to a dwelling	A continuum in the form of housing tenure can be achieved; thus, there is one for each type of family need	
To develop stable but flexible tenure	When there is more need for a stable tenure (ex. retirement), the full ownership has been already acquired. In the meantime, there is a clear and progressive investment in one's house	During the tenure, the buyer becomes the true owner of the house. Once the time expires, it returns ex lege to the original owner
In the current context of social housing, today's conjuncture does not allow too onerous intervention in social housing by the public administration	The public administration can limit its intervention to the part of rent of the shared ownership	The public administration can sell real estate and dwellings to families that can be recovered at a certain point in time to be reused (and given to another family in need), refurbished (if it is deteriorated) or rebuilt (if it is in derelict)

affordable (avoiding over-indebtedness), stable (allowing families to become established, unlike the aforementioned reform of the Spanish law of leases) and flexible (not necessarily tying families to a piece of land for 30 or more years). Intermediate tenures would help to reduce the vacant housing stock, alleviate the need for liquidity for Spanish lending institutions and, ultimately, help families to access to a sustainable and stable home. Table 2.2 shows how this can be achieved through the developing Catalan shared and temporal ownership approach.

*Shared Ownership (*propietat compartida*)*

The shared ownership approach provides the buyer (the shared owner) with a share of the property, while the other share is owned by the seller (the original owner), both coexisting. In other words:

> i. The buyer is the (shared) owner of (a part of) the property from the outset. In this sense, this approach differs from others, such as the rental with purchase option (which usually only entails a delay in the purchase for about three years) or rights to build.
> ii. The shared owner pays the (shared) seller of the property a rent for the portion of the legal element of the property that the former does not currently own. This, in combination to his or her owned share, entitles him or her to use the whole property in an exclusive way.
> iii. This means that shared owners have all the rights related to home-ownership: the exclusive use and enjoyment of the whole property, and the ability to dispose of the share he or she owns, both *inter vivos* and *mortis causa.* As a consequence of this, the shared owner pays all taxes relating to the use and ownership of the house (e.g. utility bills, taxes on home-ownership). He or she can attend the condominium government body and can take part in its decisions.
> iv. The shared owner can mortgage his or her share on the property, even for funding his or her acquisition. Of course, a mortgage on 20 per cent of the property (based on the norm under the English shared ownership scheme of five per cent funded by the buyer from his or her own resources, 20 per cent as the first share of acquisition and 75 per cent held by the seller/lessor) is less onerous for the buyer and for the credit institution than a mortgage to fund the acquisition of the whole property.
> v. The shared owner has the right to progressively acquire more shares of the ownership of the property (staircase up). In social housing, the scheme would also offer the possibility 'to staircase down', i.e., the shared owner can reduce his/her share of the property in accordance to his housing and economic needs.

Thus, the shared ownership approach has been designed to give those in need of housing and those that cannot buy a property in the private home-ownership market the possibility to own (step by step) a house without becoming over-indebted. The shared owners (buyers) are granted all powers necessary to act as full owners of the property, although with certain limitations to protect the interests of the seller (who is retaining, in our example, 75 per cent of the property), and the eventual financer of the acquisition. Of course, the buyer in a shared-ownership scheme cannot alter the substance of the property, and he or she must use it for the agreed purpose (e.g. residence in case of social housing) and cannot alter its structural elements.

*Temporal Ownership (*propietat temporal*)*

There is also temporal ownership, where a new owner acquires the ownership from an original owner of a property, but only for a certain and determined period of time. During this time, he or she has all the powers on the property (use, enjoyment, disposal *inter vivos* and *mortis causa* and charge – e.g. with a mortgage to acquire the temporal ownership), as he or she is considered a 'temporal owner'. For this same reason, the temporal owner will be responsible for all expenses related to the property.

This approach differs substantially from the current system, where a property is acquired 'forever' (i.e. eternally) under Spanish and Catalan laws. The introduction of 'temporal ownership' will allow the purchase of a property for a specified number of years. This entails important stability for the buyer and significantly increases its affordability. After this specified number of years, the ownership of the property will revert automatically and without cost to the original owner (the seller), unless extensions are agreed. The original owner is entitled to be compensated for all depreciation of the property caused by the negligent or wilful misconduct of the temporary owner.

This temporal ownership approach may provide a solution to a variety of situations, given that its duration may be decades or hundreds of years in length. Moreover, it is foreseen that it can be used in combination with shared ownership, thus increasing the fragmentation and the affordability of the available housing stock in the same way as the leasehold is used in combination with shared ownership in the UK.

Conclusions

It is now widely accepted that the current global financial, economic, mortgage and housing crisis started in the US in 2007. The origins of the US crisis can also be explained as a consequence of severe deficiencies in the legal architecture and institutions. It is difficult to understand how a market of several trillion US dollars could effectively operate without a specific piece of legislation covering the rights and obligations of the parties, or how mortgages could be effectively recorded and verified through more than 3,000 land registers, or how these could have been properly and efficiently transferred fulfilling traditional rules of common law, or how they could be properly enforced in non-recourse states, or in those states with only judicial enforcement procedures. Only in this context can we understand the misbehaviour of the rating agencies, the existence of structural problems in a standard US mortgage securitization process, or the creation of MERS. The US crisis spread to Europe and to the rest of the world due to the international mortgage securitization of US subprime mortgages through MBSs and CDOs. This created a 'lack of trust' crisis among credit and investment institutions globally, from which many countries have not yet recovered. Some countries, such as Spain, are in an even deeper crisis due to a variety of factors, but fundamentally due to the high dependence of their economy in recent years on housing construction.

Spain's current situation is a result of a range of factors that have led to a housing bubble and its subsequent bursting. Among these are the widespread existence of mortgage loans, now acting in detriment to other more affordable types of housing tenure, the inadequate regulation of the mortgage and banking operations, the lack of sufficient protection for mortgagors and bad banking practices. The measures undertaken in reaction to the crisis by the Spanish government to date have been insufficient. However, new measures involving increased protection for mortgagors are being considered by Catalan legislators, which deal with some bad banking practices and abuses, and also with the lack of sufficient and effective pre-contractual information. There are also some innovative approaches being developed, which seek to create a third type of housing market (in addition to the two classic ones: home-ownership and renting) and which have the potential to reinvigorate the housing and the mortgage market systems in Spain. These are the so-called 'intermediate tenures', which in Catalonia are being adopted in the forms of shared and temporal ownership. Clearly, in the face of the global and local economic collapse which relied on many outdated and inadequate legal structures and regulatory mechanisms, new and innovative legal approaches are now required more than ever in relation to housing.

Chapter 3
Comparing Mortgage Law in Ireland and Spain

Karen Lynch-Shally

Introduction

There are striking similarities between Ireland and Spain. Both experienced sustained and significant house price inflation and, in the reversal of house price trends since 2007, were amongst those countries which experienced the highest consistent house price falls in Europe.[1] The extension of credit in an inflationary context, based on inexpensive capital from increasingly integrated global and national capital markets, created a major house price bubble. This was followed by massive unemployment of 14 per cent in Ireland and 25 per cent of the workforce in Spain, which was triggered by the bursting of the housing bubble.[2] This, and the ensuing global recession, has led to an indebtedness crisis amongst national mortgage consumers. It is manifested in a repossessions crisis in Spain. However, in Ireland, the level of repossessions is low, although mortgage arrears are high. The question arises as to whether this difference in repossession rates is linked to differences in the national legal framework applicable to mortgage consumers. In Ireland and Spain, the rights and protections of mortgage consumers are contained in a variety of constitutional provisions and primary and secondary legislation. This chapter identifies the nature and scope of existing frameworks in both markets. It also examines the comparative status of the mortgage consumer under contemporary national provisions.

---

1 HJ Dübel and M Rothemund, *A New Mortgage Credit Regime for Europe*, Centre for European Policy Studies (CEPS) Special Report (Brussels, CEPS, June 2011) 8. Although Latvia suffered an even sharper house price to income correction than Ireland, there has been a recovery in Latvian house prices, which increased by 9.8 per cent in Q4 2012 compared to the same quarter in 2011.

2 *Irish Mortgage Arrears Analysis* (Dublin, Davy Research, August 2012) 18, 19 and 41. The report cites employment as the key variable driving mortgage arrears in Spain. The scale of post 2007, house price deflation in Ireland raises questions as to the dynamic between negative equity and arrears. The report identifies high Loan to Value Ratios (LTV's) within sample data of mortgage arrears from the Central Bank of Ireland (CBI), but ultimately asserts that negative equity 'has not been a clear trigger for arrears behaviour'.

The National Mortgage Market Profile

In 2009, the populations of Ireland and Spain were 4.45 million and 45.82 million, respectively.[3] In Ireland, 73.7 per cent of householders were owner-occupiers, of which 32.9 per cent had an outstanding loan or mortgage.[4] Some 26.3 per cent of households were in rental tenure, 11.3 per cent were tenants with rent at market price and the remaining 15 per cent had rent at a reduced rate or free.[5] In Spain, the ownership rate was 83.2 per cent, of which 34.5 per cent had a mortgage or outstanding loan.[6] The proportion of the households in rental tenure was 16.8 per cent, of which 8.2 per cent were tenants with rent at market price.[7] The volume of outstanding residential mortgage loans was €147.65 billion in Ireland and €678.87 billion in Spain, while the mortgage debt to GDP ratios were 90.3 per cent and 64.6 per cent, respectively.[8]

This situation was the result of a major expansion in national mortgage markets in the preceding decade. In 1999, the volume of outstanding residential mortgage loans was €26.18 billion and represented 26.5 per cent of GDP in Ireland, compared to €154.55 billion and 23.9 per cent of GDP in Spain.[9] The expansion in mortgage lending paralleled significant and sustained house price inflation in both markets. In an analysis of house price cycles in 18 OECD markets from 1970 to 2005, Ireland registered an increase in *real* house prices of 242.7 per cent and Spain an increase of 114.2 per cent in the upswing to the mid-2000s.[10]

---

3 *Europe in Figures – Eurostat Yearbook 2012 edition* (Belgium, Eurostat 2012). Population: Ireland 4,450,030; Spain 45,828,172.

4 ibid. In parallel with house price inflation, ownership tenure had been in decline in Ireland. In 2004, the percentage of owners was 81.8 per cent; by 2010, this figure had fallen to 73.4 per cent. Although the percentage of owners with a mortgage has remained relatively stable (35.3 per cent in 2004 and 34.6 per cent in 2010), the decrease in the percentage of owners without a mortgage or loan (from 46.5 per cent in 2004 to 38.8 per cent by 2010) points to increased leverage amongst consumers. In contrast, the figures for Spain show less variation, although the Eurostat dataset commences at a later period. The rates of ownership in 2007 and 2011 were 83.6 per cent and 82.7 per cent, respectively. The percentage of owners without an outstanding mortgage or loan was 50.4 per cent in 2007 and 49.8 per cent in 2011. A similar percentage of owners with a mortgage or loan were recorded in 2007 (33.2 per cent) and 2011 (32.9 per cent).

5 *Europe in Figures – Eurostat Yearbook 2012 edition* (n 3).

6 ibid.

7 ibid.

8 *Hypostat 2009* (Brussels, European Mortgage Federation (EMF), November 2010) 70 and 82: Ireland €147.654 billion; Spain €678.872 billion.

9 ibid: Ireland €26.186 billion; Spain €154.556 billion.

10 N Girouard, M Kennedy, P van den Noord and C Andre, 'Recent House Price Developments: The Role of Fundamentals', OECD Economics Department Working Paper, No 475, 2006, 8. The term 'real house prices' refers to the ratio of actual house prices to the Consumer Price Index (CPI). Of the 18 OECD states analysed, Ireland recorded the most significant increase in percentage terms. The percentage for Ireland is for the period

However, from 2007 onwards, there was a reversal of house price trends, with Irish prices dropping by 51 per cent by February 2013.[11] Figures from the official Spanish House Price Index assert that national house prices are now 27.1 per cent below their peak in nominal terms.[12] Expressed as a percentage of nominal GDP, household debt in Ireland was 116.6 per cent compared with Spain at 83.8 per cent by the end of 2011.[13] In March 2013, in Ireland, some 11.9 per cent (94,488) of private residential mortgage accounts for principal dwelling houses were in arrears in excess of 90 days.[14] However, notwithstanding such a high arrears rate, the banks disposed of only 178 properties during the last quarter of 2012, and at that point a total of 903 properties were in the banks' possession.[15] In contrast, the arrears rate cited for Spain was 3.07 per cent, but there have been in excess of 400,000 repossessions in Spain since the beginning of the crisis.[16]

This prompts the question, why is the rate of repossessions so low in Ireland ?. In order to fully consider this situation, I will examine mortgage law and consumer protection in both countries, including constitutional law, case law, primary legislation and secondary legislation.

National Constitutions

Both Ireland and Spain have written constitutions, adopted in 1937 and 1978, respectively.[17] These documents contain provisions which are of relevance to an

---

1992–2005, while the previous increases in the period under review were 53.9 per cent (1970–81) and 27.7 per cent (1987–90). In Spain, the percentage quoted related to the period from 1996 to 2004 and was preceded by deflation in the 1991–96 (-18.3 per cent) and 1978–86 (-32.2 per cent) periods, and a significant increase of 134.8 per cent in the period from 1986 to 1991.

11 *Residential Property Price Index* (Dublin, Central Statistics Office (CSO), February 2013).

12 *Housing Price Index* (Madrid, *Instituto Nacional Estadística*, March 2013).

13 *Irish Mortgage Arrears Analysis* (Dublin, Davy Research, August 2012). The Irish figures are for Q1 2012.

14 *Residential Mortgage Arrears and Repossessions Statistics*, Q1 2013 (Dublin, Central Bank of Ireland, March 2013).

15 ibid. In total, 134 properties were taken into possession during Q4 2012. Of these, 38 were on the basis of a court order and the remaining 96 were either voluntarily surrendered or abandoned.

16 *Datos sobre el efecto de la crisis en los organos judiciales 1T 2013*, Consejo General del Poder Judicial España, (Madrid, 2013). In the period from Q1 2008 to Q4 2012, there have been 415,117 mortgage foreclosures in Spain, although the data does not indicate what proportion of orders relate to principal private dwellings. *Irish Mortgage Arrears Analysis* (Dublin, Davy Research, August 2012) 41. The arrears figure cited in the report is based on data from the *Banco De Espana* for Q1 2012.

17 The 1937 Irish Constitution, *Bunreacht na hEireann*, replaced the previous 1922 Irish Constitution.

assessment of the protections available to mortgage consumers. The Articles may be distinguished both by subject matter and the nature of any right conferred on the mortgage consumer.

Constitution of Ireland – Bunreacht na hEireann

Private property A mortgage is a 'real right in land created by the owner (mortgagor) entitling the mortgagee to payment of a certain sum out of the land with priority to other creditors on the forced sale of the property'.[18] A mortgage is a real property right, and as a result, constitutional provisions which recognise and protect property rights are pertinent. The Irish Constitution (*Bunreacht na hEireann*) contains two Articles which refer to two property rights.[19] The contemporary judicial view is that the provisions 'mutually inform' each other, so both have to be taken into account by the courts when assessing the constitutional protection of property rights.[20] The first reference is contained in Article 40.3, 'Personal Rights', and it provides;

> 1° The State guarantees in its laws to respect, and, as far as practicable, by its laws to defend and vindicate the personal rights of the citizen.
> 2° The State shall, in particular, by its laws protect as best it may from unjust attack and, in the case of injustice done, vindicate the life, person, good name, and property rights of every citizen.

The second reference contained in Article 43, 'Private Property', states:

> 1.1° The State acknowledges that man, in virtue of his rational being, has the natural right, antecedent to positive law, to the private ownership of external goods.
> 2° The State accordingly guarantees to pass no law attempting to abolish the right of private ownership or the general right to transfer, bequeath, and inherit property.
> 2.1° The State recognises, however, that the exercise of the rights mentioned in the foregoing provisions of this Article ought, in civil society, to be regulated by the principles of social justice.

18 *Real Property Law & Procedure in the European Union* (Florence, European University Institute, May 2005) 85.

19 *Report of the Constitution Review Group* (Dublin, The Stationery Office 1996). Commissioned by the Government of Ireland, the report recommended the replacement of the existing provisions with a single article which would expressly protect the right to property subject to limitations imposed on the grounds of social justice or public policy. Consumer protection was identified as a basis for the imposition of limitations on the right.

20 GW Hogan and GF Whyte, *JM Kelly: The Irish Constitution*, 4th edn (Dublin, LexisNexis 2004) 1978.

2° The State, accordingly, may as occasion requires delimit by law the exercise of the said rights with a view to reconciling their exercise with the exigencies of the common good.

The cumulative effect of the provision is that the state guarantees to protect and vindicate the private property rights of Irish citizens, including the right to own and transfer property. This secures the right to home-ownership and the use of a mortgage to secure the loan. However, the constitutional protections conferred are not absolute, but are limited by the principles of social justice. Although the state is precluded from passing a law the effect of which would be to abolish the right of private ownership or the general right to transfer property, it is empowered to limit the exercise of such rights where in the interests of the common good it is necessary to do so.

Inviolability of the dwelling Constitutional provisions are also relevant in the context of enforcement of the security by the creditor due to the existence of a provision asserting the inviolability of the dwelling.

Article 40.5, 'Personal Rights', of the Irish Constitution states that:

> 'The dwelling[21] of every citizen is inviolable and shall not be forcibly entered save in accordance with law.'

The provision broadly guarantees that entry into the home may take place only with the consent of the individual or in accordance with the law. The provision assures that enforcement of the mortgage security by the lender must comply with mortgage law.

The provisions concerning private property and the inviolability of the dwelling are contained in the Social and Fundamental Rights section of the Irish Constitution. Article 40.3.1[22] imposes a duty on the state to prevent an infringement of the personal rights contained therein, whilst Articles 40.5 and 43 contain an express guarantee of rights subject only to limitation on the grounds specified.

Directive principles of social policy These provisions in the Irish Constitution are merely intended to guide the development of national legislation. Article 45, 'Directive Principles of Social Policy', states:

> The principles of social policy set forth in this Article are intended for the general guidance of the Oireachtas. The application of those principles in the making of laws shall be the care of the Oireachtas exclusively, and shall not be cognisable by any Court under any of the provisions of this Constitution.

21 *DPP v Corrigan* [1986] IR 290, 296, Blayney J: 'Dwelling in this section means a house or part of a house.'

22 Hogan and Whyte (n 20) 1296; *ESB v Gormley* [1985] ILRM 494.

In the current context, Article 45 (2)(iv) is of particular relevance:

> 2. The State shall, in particular, direct its policy towards securing:
> – iv. That in what pertains to the control of credit the constant and predominant aim shall be the welfare of the people as a whole.

This suggests that the framing of legislation in the context of mortgage finance must be examined in the context of *collective welfare.* Hogan and Whyte identify early legislative recognition of this constitutional provision by its inclusion in s 6(1) of the Central Bank Act 1942.[23] The provision asserts that in addition to the powers, duties and functions specifically conferred by law, the Central Bank had the general function and duty of ensuring that in the control of credit, the constant and predominant aim shall be the welfare of the people as a whole.

Spanish Constitution – Constitución Española

The Spanish Constitution also contains provisions of relevance to a discussion of residential mortgages.

Private property The Spanish Constitution contains a singular provision which addresses the constitutional right to private property.[24] Article 33 states:

> (1) The right to private property and inheritance is recognized.
> (2) The social function of these rights shall determine the limits of their content in accordance with the law.
> (3) No one may be deprived of his or her property and rights, except on justified grounds of public utility or social interest and with a proper compensation in accordance with the law.

Article 33 acknowledges the right of ownership.[25] It provides that the scope of the right should be determined by the legislator with reference to its social function, an open concept which encompasses both individual and collective benefit.[26] Although the precise scope and content of the guarantee is not fixed, it preserves the 'institution of private ownership' and prevents the legislator from suppressing ownership or restricting its scope to the extent that the acknowledgment becomes

---

23 Hogan and Whyte (n 20) 2086.

24 Chapter 2 of the Spanish Constitution is entitled 'Rights and Freedoms' and is subdivided into Division 1 – Fundamental Rights and Public Freedoms (arts 15–29 inclusive) and Division 2 – Rights and Duties of Citizens (arts 30–38 inclusive).

25 TC 2.12.1983 (RTC 111). The acknowledgment of the right of ownership is from an individual and institutional standpoint.

26 TC 26.3.1987 (RTC), TC 17.3.1994 (RTC 89). Function of property has an individual and collective dimension, i.e. satisfaction of owners interests and common good.

devoid of any meaning.[27] The right of expropriation reserved to the legislator in s.s (3) limits the right of ownership in safeguarding social or public interests. However, it guarantees that this is the sole context in which the owner can be deprived of his/her rights and that he/she must be compensated.

Inviolability of the dwelling The Spanish Constitution also asserts the inviolability of the dwelling. Article 18.2 provides:

> The home is inviolable. No entry or search may be made without the consent of the householder or a legal warrant, except in cases of flagrante delicto.

The substance of the provision is similar to the Irish equivalent, in that it guarantees that entry into the home may take place only with the consent of the individual or in accordance with the law.

Article 53(1) of the Spanish Constitution addresses the nature of the rights conferred in articles 33 and 18(2). It states;

> The rights and freedoms recognized in Chapter 2 of the present Part are binding on all public authorities. Only by an act which in any case must respect their essential content could the exercise of such rights and freedoms be regulated, which shall be protected in accordance with the provisions of Article 161(1)(a).

Article 53(1) thus asserts the binding nature of the rights conferred in the aforementioned Articles. It stipulates that the exercise of the rights can only be regulated by law, which must in any event respect the essential content of the right. Article 161(1)(a) asserts the jurisdiction of the Constitutional Court to hear applications concerning the constitutionality of legislation.

Principles governing economic and social policy Chapter 3 of the Spanish Constitution is entitled 'Principles Governing Economic and Social Policy'.[28] Two of the Articles within the chapter, Articles 47 and 51, are of particular significance in the current context. Article 47 addresses constitutional housing rights. It states:.

> All Spaniards have the right to enjoy decent and adequate housing. The public authorities shall promote the necessary conditions and establish appropriate standards in order to make this right effective, regulating land use in accordance with the general interest in order to prevent speculation. The community shall have a share in the benefits accruing from the town-planning policies of public bodies.

---

27 JF Angosto Saez, 'The Constitutional Concept of Ownership' in S Van Erp and A Vaquer Aloy (eds), *Introduction to Spanish Patrimonial Law* (Granada, Comares 2006) 263.

28 Chapter 3 comprises arts 39–52 inclusive.

Article 51 is directly relevant to the current examination as it identifies the protection of consumers and users as an impetus to the development of economic and social policy:

> (1) The public authorities shall guarantee the protection of consumers and users and shall, by means of effective measures, safeguard their safety, health and legitimate economic interests.
> (2) The public authorities shall promote the information and education of consumers and users, foster their organizations, and hear them on those matters affecting their members, under the terms established by law.
> (3) Within the framework of the provisions of the foregoing paragraphs, the law shall regulate domestic trade and the system of licensing commercial products.

The use of the word 'right' in Article 47 would appear to infer a binding obligation. However, in common with the corresponding Irish provisions, these 'principles' are intended to guide the development of legislation and policy, and do not confer directly enforceable rights. This is confirmed by Article 53(3) which states:

> Recognition, respect and protection of the principles recognized in Chapter 3 shall guide legislation, judicial practice and actions by the public authorities. They may only be invoked before the ordinary courts in accordance with the legal provisions implementing them.

Irish Mortgage Law

The contemporary Irish mortgage has evolved through a combination of common law supplemented by equitable principles and statute law. The original common law mortgage entailed a conveyance of the fee simple to the lender, subject to the condition that the estate would be re-conveyed to the borrower, provided that the debt was repaid by the legal date of redemption, otherwise the land was forfeit, although the borrower remained liable for the debt. The harshness of the outcome at common law in the event that a borrower did not repay the mortgage by the due date and the land was forfeited led to the intervention of the Court of Chancery through the development of the equity of redemption. A corpus of case law prescribes the rights and duties of borrowers and lenders from this time and until 2009, the statutory framework for mortgagors and mortgagees was contained in the Conveyancing Acts 1881–1911.[29]

Prior to 2009, the requirements for the creation of a legal mortgage were determined by whether the land in question was registered or unregistered. The former is land the title to which is registered in the Land Registry according to the

29 P Kenna, *Housing Law, Rights & Policy* (Dublin, Clarus Press 2011) 441.

statutory framework contained in the Registration of Title Act 1964,[30] as amended by the Registration of Deeds and Title Act 2006 and the Land and Conveyancing Law Reform Act 2009. Unregistered land is land subject to the registration system established under the Registration of Deeds (Ireland) Act 1707, which was applicable to legal or equitable interests in land, arising from wills, deeds, and conveyances.[31] Memorials of deeds relating to a transaction in land were registered in the Registry of Deeds and although registration was not compulsory, there was an incentive to do so as registered deeds took priority over unregistered deeds.[32] The statutory framework for mortgages created after 1 December 2009 is contained in Part 10 of the Land and Conveyancing Law Reform Act 2009.[33]

Spanish Mortgage Law

Spain is a civil law jurisdiction. The hypothec (*la hipoteca*) performs the same function in Spanish law as the common law legal mortgage in Ireland. The hypothec is regulated by title XV of the Spanish Civil Code and the Ley Hipotecaria 1946 (LH).[34] It is a real right which charges the immoveables or immoveable property of the debtor to guarantee payment of a credit.[35] In Spanish law, the hypothec is not fully constituted until it is registered in the Land Registry.[36] Only public documents can be registered, and accordingly the hypothec is always created by a public document, such as a notarial public deed.[37] Upon registration, the hypothec is given a ranking, which determines its priority relative to other charges on the land. The Spanish hypothec is an accessory mortgage. This means that it may only be created to secure a credit, and its continued existence is dependent on the existence of the secured claim.[38] The mortgagor is entitled to possession of the property and is free to dispose of it, in which context the hypothec will 'follow the

30 Section 31 of the Registration of Title Act 1964 provides that the register is conclusive evidence of ownership and any rights and burdens affecting the land.

31 M. Donnelly, The Law of Credit and Security, (London, Thomson-Reuters, 2011), 400.

32 See JCW Wylie, *Irish Land Law*, 4th edn (Dublin, Bloomsbury Professional 2010) chapters 13 and 22.

33 Land and Conveyancing Law Reform Act (Commencement) Order 2009 (SI 356/2009).

34 *Spanish Civil Code* (Madrid, Ministerio de Justicia 2009). Title XV, Chapter one, 'Provisions common to pledges and mortgages', arts 1857–62, Chapter three, 'Mortgages', arts 1874–80. RCL 1946/886 Ley Hipotecario of 8 February 1946.

35 Article 1874 CC, art 106 LH. Under art 107 LH, a *hipoteca* can be created over any real right which can be transferred. It is possible in Spanish law to have a hypothec over certain moveables, although this is not relevant in the current context.

36 Article 1875 CC; arts 106 and 145 LH.

37 Article 1216 CC: 'Public instruments are those authorised by a Notary Public or competent public employee, with the solemnities required by the law.'

38 Articles 1857(1), 1860 and 1876 CC.

property', which continues to guarantee performance of the secured obligation.[39] The creditor has the right to protect their claim by making an application to the courts in the context where the actions of the debtor may result in a depreciation of the value of the property.[40]

In the context of default, the creditor is entitled to seek enforcement of the security, i.e. *acción hipotecaria*.[41] Most frequently enforcement is via the summary judicial procedure regulated by the Civil Procedure Act.[42] However, it is also possible for the sale to occur on an extra-judicial basis if it is provided for in the document creating the hypothec.[43] A recent case of the Court of Justice of the European Union (CJEU) has implications for Spanish mortgage law. In *Aziz v CaixaCatalunya*,[44] the court held that the restricted scope of defence against an action for enforcement, permitted under current Spanish law, is inconsistent with the objectives of the EU Unfair Contract Terms Directive, since the declaratory proceedings before which broader challenges may be raised do not have the power to stay the Spanish enforcement proceedings.[45] This imputes a change to existing Spanish enforcement law.

Irish Primary Legislation

Land and Conveyancing Law Reform Act 2009 (LCLRA) – Part 10

There are two aspects of the LCLRA which are significant in the present context. The first is its impact on mortgage law in regard to the creation of a legal mortgage. A legal mortgage may now only be created by a charge by deed, irrespective of whether the land in question is registered or unregistered, thus removing the prior distinction.[46] The mechanisms which existed prior to 2009 for creating an

---

39 Articles 1857(3) and 1859.

40 Article 117 LH.

41 Article 129 LH.

42 Law 1/2000 of 7 January on Civil Procedure. Book III, Title IV, arts 681 et seq.

43 Article 129 LH provides that this procedure is premised on art 1858 CC and will be conducted by a notary in conformance with the formalities of the Mortgage Regulations, Decree of 14 February 1947 (BOE 106 of 16 April 1947).

44 C – 415-11 Judgment of the Court, 14 March 2013.

45 Council Directive 93/13/EEC of 5 April 1993 on unfair terms in consumer contracts. Under Spanish law, art 695 (LEC) permits a challenge to enforcement proceedings only on the following grounds: (a) extinguishment of the security or secured obligation, (b) an error in determining the amount due, or (c) the existence of another guarantee or mortgage registered before the security subject to the proceedings. Article 698 (LEC) provides that challenges on any other grounds shall be settled in subsequent proceedings without having the effect of staying or terminating the judicial enforcement proceedings. The court held that payment of damages was insufficient in the circumstances to compensate for the loss of a home.

46 Section 89(1).

equitable mortgage are unaffected by the statute.[47] The law of equity provides that an attempt to use one of the pre-LCLRA mechanisms for the creation of a legal mortgage, where monies have been advanced on the assumption that it would be so created, would give rise to an equitable mortgage.[48]

The second significant aspect of the LCLRA is the establishment of a new and differential treatment of housing loan mortgages as compared with other mortgages. Housing loans are defined as:

> (a) an agreement for the provision of credit to a person on the security of a mortgage of a freehold or leasehold estate or interest in land:
> – (i) for the purpose of enabling the person to have a house constructed on the land as the principal residence of that person or that person's dependants, or
> – (ii) for the purpose of enabling the person to improve a house that is already used as the principal residence of that person or that person's dependants, or
> – (iii) for the purpose of enabling the person to buy a house that is already constructed on the land for use as the principal residence of that person or that person's dependants, or
> b) an agreement for refinancing credit provided to a person for a purpose specified in paragraph (a)(i), (ii) or (iii), or
> (c) an agreement for the provision of credit to a person on the security of a mortgage of a freehold or leasehold estate or interest in land on which a house is constructed where the house is to be used, or to continue to be used, as the principal residence of the person or the person's dependants, or
> (d) an agreement for the provision of credit to a person on the security of a mortgage of a freehold or leasehold estate or interest in land on which a house is, or is to be, constructed where the person to whom the credit is provided is a consumer.[49]

The LCLRA confirms that the new 'mortgage by charge' will confer the same security rights and remedies as the previous mortgage by conveyance or

47 Section 89(6) of the LCLRA states that 'nothing in this section affects the creation of equitable mortgages of land'. Prior to the introduction of the LCLRA, an equitable mortgage was created in three contexts: where the mortgagor only has an equitable interest in the land at the time the mortgage is created, where the parties have a specifically enforceable agreement to create a mortgage, although this has not occurred, and where there is a deposit of title deeds. The Registration of Deeds and Titles Act 2006 abolishes the latter possibility in the context of registered land as land certificates are no longer issued and existing certificates ceased to have force and effect as of 1 January 2010.

48 JCW Wylie, *Irish Land Law* (4th edn, Dublin, Bloomsbury Professional 2010) 767.

49 Section 2 of the Consumer Credit Act 1995, as amended by pt 12, sch 3 of the Central Bank and Financial Services Authority of Ireland Act 2004.

assignment.[50] The significance of this provision is that existing Irish mortgage law has continued applicability, subject to any reform introduced within the LCLRA itself. The most significant change within the statute arises from the distinction between the statutory rights, duties and powers of the parties of 'housing loans' as compared with other mortgages.[51]

The LCLRA provides that a mortgagor can now redeem a 'housing loan' without having to redeem any other mortgage with the mortgagee, whether in respect of the same or another property.[52] A general power of leasing is conferred on the mortgagor and contractual restrictions on the sale or transfer by the mortgagor of their interest in the property are prohibited.[53]

Section 97 of the LCLRA provides that a mortgagee cannot take possession of the property without a court order unless the mortgagor 'consents in writing to such taking not more than 7 days prior to such taking'.[54] The exercise of a mortgagee's inherent common law power of sale similarly necessitates a court order, unless the mortgagor consents in writing to the exercise of the power no more than seven days prior to the sale.[55] The LCLRA provides that the Circuit Court has exclusive jurisdiction to deal with orders for possession or sale in the context of housing loans, whereas for all other mortgages, jurisdiction lies with the High Court.[56] The mortgagee is under a statutory obligation to obtain the best price which can reasonably be obtained when selling the property.[57]

The High Court decision in *Start Mortgages v Gunn*[58] highlighted a potential lacuna in the law. The drafters of the LCLRA repealed the statutory right to apply for an order of possession under s 62(7) of the Registration of Title Act 1964 without replacing it with a similar provision. Dunne J asserted that where in the

50 Section 90.

51 Section 96(3). In relation to other mortgages, the provisions take effect subject to the mortgage unless the provision provides otherwise.

52 Section 92 altering s 17 of the Conveyancing Act 1881.

53 Sections 94 and 112.

54 Section 97. Under s 98, an emergency possession order may besought 'where a mortgagee has reasonable grounds for believing that the mortgagor has abandoned the mortgaged property and urgent steps are necessary to prevent deterioration of, or damage to, the property or entry on it by trespassers or other unauthorised persons'. Under a possession order pursuant to s 98, the mortgagee is not strictly liable to account to the mortgagor.

55 M Donnelly, *The Law of Credit and Security* (London, Thomson-Reuters 2011). This may not be varied by contract for housing loan mortgages and Donnelly suggests that, due to the practical difficulties associated with the seven days prior to sale pre-requisite, it is probable that lenders will seek a court order in all cases in which contractual variation is prohibited.

56 Section 101(5). An application for an emergency possession under s 98 may be made to the District Court or any other court 'already seised of any application or proceedings relating to the mortgaged property'.

57 Section 103.

58 *Start Mortgages v Gunn* [2011] IEHC 275.

context of registered land, the statutory right had not been incorporated into the mortgage contract, unless the principal monies had become due and a demand had been made prior to the repeal (1 December 2009), the statutory right of possession for default had not accrued or been acquired. The result is that only where the mortgage was in arrears and a demand for all outstanding monies had been made by the mortgagee by the specified date could a possession order be sought. It should be noted here that this situation arose from what appears to have been an oversight in the drafting of the LCLRA and not through any political or judicial activism. In *EBS v Gillespie*,[59] Laffoy J confirmed the legislative gap. Draft legislation to reinstate the necessary provisions is currently being debated in the Irish Parliament.[60]

Consumer Credit Act 1995

In Ireland, the Consumer Credit Act 1995 (CCA), which provides a statutory framework for certain types of consumer credit, contains provisions which are relevant to mortgage consumers.[61] Part IX of the Act applies to 'housing loans' made by a mortgage lender. The provisions of the Act are thus applicable where the loan falls within the scope of the definition of 'housing loan' as contained in the statute. The CCA regulates the content and format of information and warnings which must be contained in the credit agreement.[62] It confers a statutory right to early redemption on the mortgagor, whilst prohibiting the imposition of any fees,

59 *EBS v Gillespie* [2012] IEHC 243 [25]: 'In order to establish that its claim for possession came within s. 62(7) prior to 1st December, 2009, the plaintiff has to establish compliance with the two requirements expressly set out in the sub-section, namely (a) that repayment of the principal monies secured by the Charge had become due by that date; and (b) that the plaintiff was the registered owner of the Charge. Apart from those two requirements, the Court must be satisfied that it would have been proper to afford the plaintiff the statutory remedy of an order for possession against the defendant to enforce the right acquired. Having regard to the observations of Geoghegan J. in *Bank of Ireland v. Smyth* quoted earlier, I consider the Court would have to be satisfied not only that the application was made *bona fide* with a view to realising the plaintiff's security, but also that the power of sale had arisen and was exercisable by virtue of the terms of the agreement between the plaintiff and the defendant contained in the Charge.'

60 Land and Conveyancing Law Reform Bill 2013.

61 Consumer Credit Act 1995 (Commencement) Order 1996 (SI 121/1996). In Ireland, consumer credit which is not subject to the Consumer Credit Act is governed by the European Communities (Consumer Credit Agreements) Regulations 2010 (SI 281/2010).

62 The Consumer Credit Act 1995 transposed Directive 87/102/EEC on Consumer Credit. Mortgage and housing loans were excluded from the scope of the Directive; however, Irish consumer law included housing loans within the remit of the domestic legislation. The level of consumer protection in Ireland thus exceeds other EU Member States. Section 129 mandates the provision of particular information on the front page of the credit agreement. A template is contained in pt II of the Third Schedule of the Act.

save in the context of fixed-rate agreements.[63] It imposes limitations on the ability of lenders to levy charges in respect of valuation reports and legal costs associated with the investigation of title.[64] It also prohibits linking practices and imposes a statutory obligation on the lender to arrange mortgage protection insurance for all housing loans.[65] Breach of the provisions of the CCA in a housing loan context results in administrative sanctions for the lender.[66]

Spanish Primary Legislation

Royal Decree Law 27/2012

Royal Decree Law 27/2012 of 15 November was an emergency measure introduced in response to incidents of suicide amongst distressed mortgagors facing eviction.[67] The law imposes a two-year moratorium on the execution of an eviction order arising from enforcement proceedings by the creditor, where it relates to the residence of vulnerable debtors.[68] The moratorium relates only to loans granted for the purpose of and secured on the debtors' primary residence.[69] There are twin eligibility requirements to access relief under the law. The debtor must be classified as 'vulnerable', a term defined with reference to the size and composition of the household, the employment and income status of the debtor and the capacity of members of the family unit to work.[70] In addition, the debtor must fulfil specified economic criteria.[71] The focus of the economic criteria is on aggregate household income and the proportion of income required to sustain the

---

63 Section 121.

64 Sections 123 and 125. The lender is required to provide a copy of any valuation report to the applicant in all cases.

65 Sections 126 and 127. There are limited exceptions to the obligation to arrange mortgage protection insurance (MPI), such as where the house is not intended for use as the principal private residence of the borrower.

66 Section 13, but see the judgment of Laffoy J in *Stepstone Mortgage Funding v Fitzell* [2012] IEHC 142 below, which explores the effect on possession proceedings of non-compliance by the lender with mandatory statutory provisions.

67 Royal Decree Law 27/2012 of 15 November (BOE 276 of 16 November 2012). On 9 November 2012, 53-year-old Amaia Egana jumped from her fourth-storey window in the Basque Country as officials arrived to evict her from her home. Hers was the second eviction-related suicide in Spain in a matter of weeks. Public demonstrations followed and international media coverage ensued, and Spanish Prime Minister Mariano Rajoy announced hours after Egana's death: 'I hope that on Monday we'll be able to talk about a temporary suspension of evictions for the most vulnerable families.'

68 Article 1(1). The law applies both to judicial and out-of-court enforcement commenced prior to the entry into force of the law, i.e. 16 December 2012.

69 Article 1(3)(d). The residence must be the only home owned by the debtor and the loan in question must have been advanced for its purchase.

70 Article 1(2)(a)–(g).

71 Article 1(1) and (3).

mortgage obligation.[72] The law stipulates that there must have been a detrimental change in economic circumstances in the four years preceding the application.[73] This is assessed with reference to an increase in the mortgage debt burden relative to income.[74] The application may be made by the debtor at any time prior to the execution of the eviction order and the documentation required to support the application is identified in Article 2.

In addition, the law contains a proposal for a collaborative scheme between the government and the financial sector to provide social housing on a rental basis.[75] The proposal envisages the use of the unoccupied housing stock held by credit institutions to offer access to those vulnerable debtors who fall within the scope of the law but who have already been evicted from their homes.

Royal Decree Law 6/2012

Royal Decree Law 6/2012 of 9 March was introduced to address the plight of mortgagors who were struggling to sustain their mortgage obligations.[76] It applies a primary residence requirement and thus addresses those whose homes are at risk in the context of default.[77] The loan must have been advanced for the purchase of and secured on the debtors' primary residence, and must be in existence at the date that the Law came into force, ie 11 March 2012.[78] There are twin eligibility requirements to access relief under the scheme. First, the debtor must fall within the exclusion threshold, the criteria for which are identified in Article 3.[79] As with other Spanish statutes, the emphasis is on individuals who have lost their income due to the deterioration in macroeconomic conditions and who are lacking any other means to support their mortgage obligations. In addition, the purchase price of the property must not exceed the value outlined in Article 5, which is determined with reference to the population of the municipality in question.[80] The measures

---

72 Article 1(3)(a)–(d).

73 Article 1(3)(b) and (c).

74 Article 1(4)(a). The amount of loan instalments must have increased by 150 per cent relative to net income, resulting in a mortgage payment greater than 50 per cent of net income.

75 Additional provision.

76 Royal Decree Law 6/2012 of 9 March (BOE 60 of 10 March 2012).

77 Article 3(1)(d).

78 Article 2.

79 ibid. With two exceptions, the provisions of the law are applicable only to debtors within the exclusion threshold. These exceptions are art 12, the extra-judicial enforcement procedure which is generally applicable to debtors, and art 13, pursuant to which debtors who have been evicted due to judicial or extra-judicial enforcement from 1 January 2012 onwards are eligible for aid to tenants under the terms established in arts 38 and 39 of Royal Decree 2066/2008 of 12 December, regulating the Housing and Rehabilitation Plan 2009–12.

80 Article 5(2). The monetary limitations in respect of which the Code is applicable are as follows: for municipalities with up to 100,000 inhabitants, the purchase price cannot exceed €120,000; between 100,001 and 500,000 inhabitants, the threshold is €150,000; and

contained in the Law are not mandatory and are applicable only to those lenders who voluntarily subscribe to the Code of Good Practice.[81]

There are two main mechanisms through which the Law attempts to offer relief to debtors. The first is the inclusion of provisions to prevent an escalation of the mortgagors' indebtedness. The Law imposes a cap on the financial penalties which can be levied on a debtor in default.[82] The procedure for out-of-court mortgage foreclosure and auction is also amended to minimize expenses and prevent the underselling of assets.[83] The purpose of these amendments is to minimize the amount payable by the mortgagor in the context of enforcement.

The second mechanism is a framework, in the form of a *Code of Good Practice*, contained in an Annex to the Law, which addresses the viability and sustainability of loans. The Code provides three options for debtors, dependent on their situation. First, a debtor within the exclusion threshold may request and obtain a re-structuring of their mortgage debt so as to achieve medium- to long-term sustainability. The statute provides income-based parameters which determine the viability of re-structuring arrangements. Secondly, where a restructuring of existing debt is not viable, the debtor may request a rebate on the outstanding principal amount.[84] Thirdly, the Code details measures to replace mortgage foreclosure where neither of the foregoing options is successfull. The measure which is referred to as *dación* comprises delivery of the mortgaged asset to the mortgagee institution, which is obliged to accept it in settlement of both the secured debt and any related personal liability.[85] This is in contrast to the legal status of Spain as a recourse jurisdiction in which the debtor remains personally liable for mortgage debt, which is not discharged by the realization of the housing asset.[86] When applying for *dación*, the debtor may request to remain in the house as a tenant for a period of two years, with a rent equivalent to three per cent of the total amount of the debt at the time of *dación*.[87]

---

for municipalities with between 500,001 and 1,000,000 inhabitants or integrated townships in metropolitan areas with over 1,000,000 inhabitants, the upper limit is €180,000. The maximum purchase price of €200,000 is reserved for municipalities with populations in excess of 1,000,000 inhabitants. For assessments pursuant to the decree, the statute provides that population figures can be verified in the Municipal Register.

81 Article 5(1).

82 Article 4. A cap of 2.5 per cent of the outstanding principal of the loan is the maximum additional interest payable in respect of loans covered by the Royal Decree.

83 Article 12.

84 Annex, Code of Good Practice for the Viable Restructuring of Debts Secured by Mortgages on the Residence, s 2.

85 ibid s 3(a) and (b).

86 1911 CC.

87 Section 3(c). According to s 3(e), the option of *dación* is not available where the property has already been listed for auction or where the property has other encumbrances.

Royal Decree Law 8/2011

Royal Decree Law (RDL) 8/2011 of 1 July was enacted in response to the plight of mortgage debtors who contracted at the height of the inflationary trend in the Spanish property market and who have lost their homes due to their inability to sustain their contractual obligations.[88] It focuses on the issue of preservation of income and introduces reforms to minimize the residual debt obligation in the context of sale of the residence. The objective of the statute is to protect low-income families and to ensure that 'foreclosures are conducted without causing abusive situations or underselling of affected assets'. The legislation acknowledges the policy dilemma inherent in its intervention. The social and public policy objectives underlying the responsive provisions are juxtaposed with the desire to maintain 'the fundamental elements of collateral for loans and, with them, the safety and soundness of our mortgage'.[89]

Essentially, the legislation amends articles in the Civil Law Procedure Act (LEC) 1/2000 of 7 January, which govern two aspects of the enforcement process, the first of which is the auction of the mortgaged property. It amends Articles 670(4) and 671 LEC, thereby increasing the minimum threshold for the adjudication of the asset to the creditor, where the property has failed to meet its reserve or where there are no bidders.[90] The deposit required by potential bidders has been reduced from 30 per cent to 20 per cent of the appraised value in an attempt to promote greater participation and competition by bidders.[91] The objective of the amendment is to ensure that the borrower will receive adequate compensation for the property, which will allow him/her to cancel or minimize the remaining debt.

The second aspect of the enforcement process which is subject to amendment is the attachment of wages and pensions, where the auction of the mortgaged asset is insufficient to cover the related credit. RDL 8/2011 increases the unforecloseability threshold to 150 per cent of the minimum wage. It stipulates that the threshold increases by an additional 30 per cent in respect of each member of the household who does not receive an income, salary or pension in excess of the minimum wage.[92] The measures are designed to protect what is deemed to be a basic minimum income for those families who had lost their primary residence as a result of 'difficult economic circumstances'.

88 Royal Decree Law 8/2011 (BOE 161 of 7 July 2011).

89 Royal Decree Law 8/2011 of 1 July 2011 (BOE of 7 July 2011) preamble.

90 Chapter 1, s 2, arts 2.2 and 3, amending arts 670(4) and 671 of the Civil Law Procedure Act (LEC) 1/2000, of 7 January. The property can be awarded for no less than 60 per cent of its appraised value.

91 Chapter 1, s 2, art 2.1, amending arts 669(1) and 671 LEC.

92 Chapter 1, s 2, art 1, amending art 607(1) LEC. The household for the purposes of RDL 8/2011 is defined as 'spouse or domestic partners, ascendants, descendants of the first degree' who live with the owner-occupier of the forecloseable dwelling. Where the income of these household members exceeds the minimum wage, they will be attachable on an incremental basis according to the provisions of art 607(2) LEC.

Sustainable Economy Law 2/2011

Article 29 of the Sustainable Economy Law (SEL) 2/2011 of 4 March outlines principle-based parameters for the implementation of measures to promote responsible lending and consumer protection in financial services.[93] It is framework legislation and Article 29(2) requires the Minister for Finance to adopt rules to ensure an appropriate level of consumer protection in respect of consumer interaction with credit institutions, including 'measures relating to the transparency of the financial conditions of loans, mortgages and consumer credit'. Significantly, the article imposes a statutory obligation on credit institutions to assess the creditworthiness of borrowers, the first time that such an obligation has been imposed in Spain.[94] Article 29 was implemented through Order EHA 2899/2011, which also consolidated pre-existing provision regarding transparency and consumer protection in financial services.[95]

Law 2/2009

The statutory framework for the protection of consumers who source loans from non-credit institutions is contained in Law 2/2009 of 31 March.[96] Prior to its enactment, non-credit institutions were unregulated, so the existence of the law is of itself an enhancement of consumer protection. The consumer, as defined in Article 1(b), encompasses both natural and legal persons who are acting in a field which is outside their trade, business or profession. The provisions of the Law are mandatory and the rights conferred on consumers cannot be waived.[97] The Law requires lenders to comply with the transparency regime in respect of general and personalized pre-contractual information contained in Order EHA2899/2011.[98] This establishes a universally applicable minimum threshold of information to be provided to consumers, irrespective of the classification of mortgage lender.

---

93 Sustainable Economy Law 2/2011 of 4 March (BOE 55 of 5 March2011).

94 Article 29(1).

95 Order of 5 May 1994 and Circular 5/1994 contained the prior transparency regime for the financial condition of mortgage loans. These have been repealed and replaced by Order EHA2899/2011 and Circular 5/2012.

96 Law 2/2009 of 31 March (BOE 79 of 1 April 2009); *Study on the Role and Regulation of Non-Credit Institutions in EU Mortgage Markets* (London Economics for EU Commission, 19 September 2008). The report identifies six types of credit institution in Spain: banks, official credit institutions, savings banks, credit cooperatives, financial credit entities and electronic money institutions. A non-credit institution is a lender which is not included in this classification.

97 Article 2 of Order EHA/2899/2011, which contains the provisions applicable to credit institutions, permits clients acting 'within the scope of their business or profession' to waive all or part of the provisions of the order, except as provided in Title III, Chapter II of the Rules on Loans and Mortgages.

98 The first transparency regime on the financial condition of mortgage loans was contained in Order 5 May 1994 and Circular 5/1994. This has been repealed and replaced by Order EHA/2899/2011 and the related Circular 5/2012.

The notary has a broadly similar role as under the regime applicable to credit institutions and is prohibited from authorizing loans that do not comply with the Law.[99] Amongst the duties of notaries are the obligations to inform the customer of the scope of the obligations assumed and to check for inconsistencies in the pre-contractual information, binding offer and contract.[100]

Despite this convergence in the regimes applicable to the different classifications of lender, there are also differences. Some of these can be attributed to the lack of regulatory competence by the *Banco de Espana* and the corresponding need to increase the protection afforded to consumers. This is exemplified by the imposition of additional disclosure and transparency requirements in relation not only to products, services and costs but also to the lending entity itself.[101] Article 3 requires companies, prior to the commencement of activity, to be listed in the register of the autonomous community in which the company is registered. Foreign companies who do not have a registered office in the Spanish territories must be inscribed in the State Register at the National Consumer Institute (INC).[102] Companies are under a statutory obligation to provide 'truthful and verifiable information' to the public authorities and those responsible for maintaining the records.[103] A pre-requisite to registration is that the entity must obtain civil liability insurance or a bank guarantee to cover the liability they might incur vis-à-vis the consumer in the supply of intermediation services or lending activity.[104]

The Law confers standing on the INC to apply for an injunction against conduct by the lender which adversely affects the collective consumer interest.[105] Significantly, there are no obligations imposed in respect of responsible lending and the responsible lending provisions of Order EHA/2899/2011 are inapplicable. Law 2/2009 pre-dates the introduction of the statutory obligation in Spanish law, so it is unsurprising that it is not contained in Law 2/2009 as enacted. However, the failure to amend the law to incorporate such an obligation would appear to be a policy choice.[106]

---

99 Article 18. The duty under this article extends to registrars who are prohibited from registering a non-compliant contract. Where a notary discovers an inconsistency, he/she is required to inform the consumer of the differences and his/her right to cancel the transaction.

100 Article 18.

101 Articles 4 and 5.

102 Article 3(2).

103 Article 3(5).

104 Article 7.

105 Article 11. The standing extends to any other consumer association or user who meets the requirements of Royal Decree 1/2007 or of regional consumer protection legislation where applicable. An injunction may be sought to compel cessation of ongoing conduct or to prohibit reoccurrence of prior conduct.

106 *Study on the Role and Regulation of Non-Credit Institutions in EU Mortgage Markets*, Report for the EU Commission (London Economics, September 2008). In the report, it was asserted on the basis of information provided by the Spanish Public Treasury

Breach of the obligations imposed by the Law is addressed by Royal Decree 1/2007 of 16 November.[107] Of particular note is the impact of failure by the lender to meet the requirements in respect of pre-contractual information. Article 14(3) specifies that such a failure may lead to the invalidity of the contract.

Irish Secondary Legislation

Consumer Protection Code 2012

The Consumer Protection Code 2012 (CPC) has been applicable as of 1 January 2012. The CPC defines a 'mortgage' as a loan secured by a property, and provisions in respect of mortgage credit refers to all such credit sought or obtained by personal consumers, whether in respect of a principal private residence or investment property.[108] The CPC contains an expansive definition of consumer, but the provisions in respect of 'mortgage credit' are addressed to personal consumers', a subset which accords with the more traditional statutory definition of 'a natural person acting outside his or her business, trade or profession'.[109] It also introduces the concept of the 'vulnerable consumer' as a subset of the personal consumer. This is defined as a natural person who due either to incapacity or individual circumstances requires assistance in making decisions.[110] An obligation is imposed on the lender to ensure that where a personal consumer has been identified as a vulnerable consumer, he/she is provided with 'such reasonable arrangements and or assistance that may be necessary to facilitate him or her in his or her dealings with the regulated entity'.[111] The CPC is applicable to the 'regulated activities of

---

and the Spanish Mortgage Association that any lending in the Spanish market by non-credit institutions is marginal.

107 Title IV, book I. Breach of the registration obligation contained in Art 3 is cited as a very serious offence, resulting in the imposition of sanctions by the National Consumer Institute, pursuant to Arts 51 and 52 of the revised text.

108 *Consumer Protection Code 2012 Guidance* (Dublin, Central Bank of Ireland, December 2011) 3 and 4.

109 ibid 73.

110 ibid 75. The definition of 'vulnerable consumer' contained in the Code is: 'a natural person who: (a) has the capacity to make his or her own decisions but who, because of individual circumstances, may require assistance to do so (for example hearing impaired or visually impaired persons); and or (b) has limited capacity to make his or her own decisions and who requires assistance to do so (for example, persons with intellectual disabilities or mental health difficulties)'. A guidance document which accompanied the Code provides further detail on the categories of vulnerable consumer, identifying those who are capable of making decisions but whose 'particular life stage or circumstances should be taken into account when assessing suitability'. The examples of vulnerability listed are 'age, poor credit history, low income, serious illness bereaved etc'.

111 Provision 3.1.

regulated entities operating in the State' and in a mortgage context, this includes all lenders, irrespective of classification.[112]

The CPC regulates the provision of pre-contractual information to mortgage consumers both in respect of the lender and the mortgage products, specifying the content, format, presentation and timing of information and warnings to be provided.[113] The CPC also imposes disclosure requirements to increase transparency regarding the existence, basis and quantum of charges and the commercial arrangements between mortgage intermediaries and product producers.[114] It imposes restrictions and prohibitions on market practices, as in the context of product bundling, which is prohibited, unless there is demonstrable financial benefit for the consumer.[115] Similarly the CPC regulates product tying, contingent sales and consolidation of charges.[116] The CPC identifies the post-sale information requirements[117] and regulates the manner and extent of contact that the lender can have with consumers who are existing or potential customers.[118]

Chapter 5 of the CPC imposes a substantive obligation on the lender to assess the suitability of the products offered to consumers, and an assessment of affordability is a central component.[119] The provisions address the issues of affordability, sustainability and suitability, which are central to the current indebtedness issue affecting Irish mortgage consumers. The CPC stipulates the minimum requirements in the assessment of product suitability and mandates a written statement of suitability to be provided to the consumer.[120] There is a requirement to maintain consumer records such that any material change is noted, and the regulated entity is prohibited from supplying products or services to a consumer who has refused to provide the information required to make a suitability assessment.[121] It is mandatory to take account of assessments of affordability when

112 *Consumer Protection Code 2012 Guidance* (n 107) 3 and 4. Retail credit firms and home reversion firms became subject to the Code following the introduction of legislation governing their authorization.

113 Provisions 4.7–4.20 (provisions regarding regulatory status, the regulated entity and its regulated activities), 4.23–4.29 (provision of information for credit including mortgages) and 4.41–4.45 (provision of information in context of lifetime mortgages and lifetime reversion agreements).

114 Provisions 4.54–4.56 (information on charges) and 4.57–4.61 (remuneration for mortgage intermediaries).

115 Provision 3.19.

116 Provisions 3.17–3.23.

117 Provisions 6.5–6.12 (credit) and 6.18–6.19 (information on charges).

118 Provisions 3.37–3.45 (telephone contact and personal visits).

119 Provisions 5.1–5.8 (knowing the consumer) and 5.9–5.15 (assessing the affordability of credit).

120 Provisions 5.16–5.18 (assessing suitability) and 5.19–5.23 (statement of suitability).

121 Provisions 5.3 and 5.4. The 2006 Code required only that the refusal was noted on the consumer's record.

deciding whether a personal consumer is likely to be able to comply with the terms of the credit agreement.[122] However this does not amount to a prohibition on the provision of credit in the context of a negative assessment of affordability.

The CPC states that its provisions 'are binding on *regulated entities* and must, at all times, be complied with when providing financial services'.[123] The Central Bank has the power to administer sanctions for contravention of the CPC, pursuant to Part IIIC of the Central Bank Act 1942.[124]

Code of Conduct on Mortgage Arrears 2010

The CPC addresses the policies, practices and procedures surrounding the ongoing provision of mortgage credit. In contrast, the Code of Conduct on Mortgage Arrears (CCMA) addresses the context in which the borrower is having or anticipates having difficulty in meeting his/her repayment obligations under the mortgage contract.[125] The current CCMA is applicable as of 1 January 2011, it applies to 'the mortgage loan of a borrower which is secured by their primary residence' and is applicable to all lenders, except credit unions.[126]

It imposes a statutory obligation on the lender to engage with the borrower in an attempt to put in place arrangements to resolve the arrears problem.[127] The centrepiece of the CCMA is a five-step Mortgage Arrears Resolution Process (MARP), which comprises; communication with the borrower, financial information, assessment, resolution and appeals.[128] Where a borrower is cooperating with the lender, the CCMA imposes a 12-month moratorium on the commencement of enforcement proceedings.[129] Notwithstanding the commencement of legal action, it requires lenders to attempt to maintain contact with the borrower or his/her representative.[130] In the event that agreement can be reached and an alternative arrangement can be put in place before an order for possession is granted, the lender is obliged to suspend proceedings for the period that the borrower adheres to the terms of the alternative repayment arrangement.[131] Where a borrower is engaged in the process, the CCMA prohibits the imposition

122 Provision 5.13.

123 The current legislative basis for the Code: s 117 of the Central Bank Act 1989; ss 23 and 37 of the Investment Intermediaries Act 1995; s 8(h) of the Consumer Credit Act 1995; and s 61 of the Insurance Act 1989.

124 As inserted by s.10 Central Bank and Financial Services Authority of Ireland Act 2004.

125 Chapters 1 and 2.

126 Chapters 1, 2 and 3. It is not necessary to be in occupation of the property if it is the sole property owned by the borrower.

127 Chapter 3, s 46.

128 Chapter 3.

129 Chapter 3, s 47.

130 Chapter 3, s 50.

131 Chapter 3, s 50.

of fees, charges and surcharges on the arrears to prevent an escalation of the borrower's indebtedness.[132]

The CCMA clearly delineates the time periods which do or do not constitute a portion of the 12-month moratorium.[133] It also addresses organizational aspects of the arrears process, such as personnel and contact points, staff training and systems requirements.[134] The CCMA mandates the scope and content of information to be provided to borrowers.[135] In common with the CPC, it requires that processes and justification of options are documented and that the lender is required to be able to demonstrate compliance with the Code.[136] It also imposes prohibitions on practices and regulates the number of unsolicited communications which a lender can initiate outside of those required by the CCMA or other regulation.[137] The underlying objective of the statute is to prevent the loss of homes by facilitating the rehabilitation of viable loans; however, there is no suggestion that every loan is viable. Sections 39 and 40 outline the requirements where the MARP process results in a finding that the loan is not viable.

In common with the CPC, the statutory basis for the CCMA is s 117 of the Central Bank Act. Ostensibly, breach of the provisions of either of the Codes incurs administrative sanction, but, significantly, does not affect the validity of the loan contract. However, the question of whether the provisions of the CCMA are implied contractual terms has arisen in possession proceedings. Recent case law appears to indicate a change in judicial approach to the impact of these statutory codes.

In *Stepstone Mortgage Funding v Fitzell*, Laffoy J in the High Court refused an order for repossession on the basis that the provisions of the CCMA had not been complied with:

> I find it impossible to agree with the proposition that, in proceedings for possession of a primary residence by way of enforcement of a mortgage or charge to which the current code applies, which comes before the court for hearing after the current code came into force, the plaintiff does not have to demonstrate to the Court compliance with the Current Code.[138]

She also opined that 'some development of the jurisprudence in this area in the future may be anticipated'. In a recent High Court decision, *Irish Life and Permanent PLC v Malcolm Duff and Susan Duff*, Hogan J, following the reasoning

132 Chapter 3, s 9.
133 Chapter 3, s 47.
134 Chapter 3, ss 1–4 and 11.
135 Chapter 3, ss 10–14.
136 Chapter 3, ss 52–56.
137 Chapter 3, ss 21 and 35.
138 [2012] IEHC 142 at 8, para 5.5.

of Laffoy J in *Stepstone*, refused an order for possession on the basis of non-compliance by the lender with the provisions of the Code.[139]

It would appear that the Codes have become part of mortgage law with significant implications for consumer protection.

Spanish Secondary Legislation

Order EHA2899/2011

Order EHA2899/2011 of 28 October is the statutory framework for banking services offered or supplied by credit institutions.[140] In Spanish consumer legislation, the term 'consumer' usually refers to 'natural or legal persons'. However, Article 19 asserts the applicability of the rules on loans and mortgages to those undertaken with a 'customer as an *individual*' after the entry into force of the Order.[141]

The provisions for mortgage consumers are contained in Title III, which has a dual orientation. Chapter I addresses the statutory duty to assess creditworthiness of a borrower prior to the conclusion of a credit or loan agreement as a component of responsible lending. It is a new development in Spanish mortgage protection provisions and one which is currently only applicable to credit institutions. The credit institutions are responsible for the development of internal procedures to assess the client's ability to meet the obligations under the agreement.[142] The procedures must be reviewed periodically, and whilst the credit institutions are free to develop the procedures internally, the Order stipulates the minimum requirements of these procedures.[143] Article 18(4) provides that the existence of insurance in respect of the loan should not alter the requirement for a positive assessment of the client's creditworthiness and repayment capacity. Where credit is refused on the basis of credit history and income status, this should be disclosed to the client.[144]

139 [2013] IEHC 43. The possession order related both to registered and unregistered land. The court held that in respect of the registered land, the lender had not 'accrued' the right to demand possession prior to 1 December 2009, and due to the repeal of s 62(7) of the Registration of Title Act 1964 under the LCLRA, the court had no jurisdiction to grant an order. In respect of the unregistered land, although the court had jurisdiction to grant possession, it held that the bank had not complied with the requirement in the Code of Conduct on Mortgage Arrears not to seek an order for possession until 'every reasonable effort has been made to agree an alternative repayment schedule'. It also held that the defendants could not be classified as non-cooperating borrowers.

140 Order EHA/2899/2011 of 28 October (BOE 261 of 29 October 2011).

141 Article 19(1).

142 Article 18.

143 Article 18(1) and (2).

144 Article 18(5).

Chapter II is entitled 'rules on loans and mortgages' and contains the current transparency regime applicable to housing and mortgage loans.[145] There are a number of new requirements under the regime. It mandates the provision of general (FIPRE), and personalized (FIPER) information sheets and the development by the *Banco de España* of a 'Mortgage Loan Access Guide' to assist consumers in making a decision.[146] The Order introduces a specific transparency regime for reverse mortgages, which stipulates the provision of an independent advisory service alongside delivery of the binding offer.[147] In respect of interest rates, there is an effort to enhance the visibility of floor and ceiling clauses, as the requirement to include such clauses in the contractual documentation is replaced by a requirement to include them in an annex to the FIPER.[148] The Order also regulates the components and calculation of the annual percentage rate (APR).[149]

Breach of the provisions of the Order does not affect the validity of a notarized and registered contract.[150] However, under Article 30(3), a notary may refuse to authorize a contract which does not comply with the provisions of the law.

Conclusion

There are significant parallels between Ireland and Spain, both in pre-2007 developments in housing and mortgage markets and the subsequent indebtedness crisis amongst mortgage consumers. The challenge facing both jurisdictions is twofold. First, there is a need to address the social and economic difficulties arising from the inflationary pre-crisis period. Second, there is a requirement to establish parameters for future lending to address the practices, policies and procedures which gave rise to the crisis. In response to these requirements, measures have been introduced in both countries to assist distressed mortgagors and to amend the protocols for loan origination. Notwithstanding the commonality of objectives, there are differences in the form and effect of these national provisions.

In Ireland, distressed mortgage loans are now addressed through a single statutory CCMA. In contrast, there have been a total of four laws introduced

145 Chapter II has six sections: general provisions, pre-contractual information, provisions on interest rates and reference indices, contractual documentation, the Annual Percentage Rate (APR) and its calculation and reverse mortgages.

146 Articles 20(1), 21(1) and 22(2). Annex I and II of the Order contain templates of the FIPRE and FIPER, respectively.

147 Article 32. Annexes III and IV provide templates for the FIPRE and FIPER in the context of a reverse mortgage, which also has its own specific mortgage access guide.

148 Article 25.

149 Article 31 and Annex V.

150 Law 26/1988 of 29 July (BOE 182 of 30 July 1988) contains the sanctions for breach of the provisions of the Order.

in Spain to address the issue of distressed mortgagors.[151] Notwithstanding the multiple statutes, the Spanish mortgage consumer is not in a better position than his/her Irish counterpart. Only Royal Decree Law 6/2012 addresses the issue of over-indebted mortgagors in a pre-enforcement context.[152] In the relevant statutes, both jurisdictions target loans in which the residence of the borrower is at risk in the context of default and offer re-structuring options. Despite these parallels, there are significant distinctions in the scope of applicability of provisions. The Irish CCMA is a permanent framework for addressing distressed loans and is of mandatory applicability to all lenders. In contrast, the Spanish Law is applicable only to loans which existed on 11 March 2012, participation by lenders is on a voluntary basis and it imposes eligibility requirements.[153] If a debtor cannot satisfy the eligibility requirements or can, but his/her lender is not participating in the scheme, there is no substantive relief available pre-enforcement.

The recent development in Irish mortgage law, whereby the Irish High Court has refused orders for repossession in the context of non-compliance by lenders with the Code, has undoubtedly strengthened the Code as an instrument of consumer protection. The contrast between the low repossession rate alongside high mortgage arrears in Ireland and the low arrears and high repossession rate in Spain could not be greater. However, the question is whether the low repossession rate in Ireland to date is attributable to the efficacy of the Code in facilitating re-structuring or the inadvertent *lacuna* in the law relating to repossession of registered land, created by the LCLRA.

The other legislative focus is on the protocols for current and future loan origination. Both Ireland and Spain have introduced provisions which impose information-based requirements and responsible lending obligations. The efficacy of these measures is difficult to assess in what is currently a conservative credit market. However, there are some observations which can be made. The Irish CPC is applicable to all lenders, and thus there is no distinction in terms of the protection conferred on consumers. In contrast, there is a differential treatment of consumers in Spain based on the classification of lender. There are distinct statutory frameworks applicable to credit and non-credit institutions, and only

151 In addition to the current laws, Royal Decree 1975/2008 of 28 November (BOE 290 of 2 December 2008) contained a temporary and partial moratorium on the payment of mortgage loans. Although it was extended in Royal Decree 97/2009 of 6 February (BOE 33 of 7 February 2009), the moratorium came to an end on 28 February 2011.

152 Royal Decree Law 8/2011 is aimed at post enforcement income and debt aspects, and Royal Decree Law 27/2012 imposes a temporary moratorium on the execution of an eviction order.

153 In practice, the cumulative pre-requisites for eligibility, in particular the ceiling on loan values and the requirement for not only the household but also the mortgage guarantor to be devoid of payment capacity, have precluded its applicability to the vast majority of mortgagors. See V Valiño, ch 4 in this volume. The author asserts that the failure of the RDL 6/2012 to offer widespread relief can be inferred from the introduction of urgent new measures to address the worsening crisis amongst borrowers less than seven months later.

credit institutions are currently subject to responsible lending obligations.[154] It is notable that under the statutory responsible lending obligation, neither country currently imposes an express prohibition on lending in the context of a negative assessment of creditworthiness.[155]

The new 'vulnerable consumer' in Irish law may offer additional protection in this context, as it increases the obligation on lenders to substantiate that the decision to offer credit was appropriate, with reference to factors such as age, low, income and poor credit history. It is arguable that the existence of this type of provision in a pre-crisis context may have prevented some of the inappropriate lending decisions that occurred.

154 It is unclear why the obligation has not been imposed, although notably the sanctions for non-compliance by non-credit institutions with the information-based requirements is more punitive than for credit institutions, potentially invalidating the contract.

155 If the Draft EU Directive on Credit Agreements relating to Residential Property COM (2011) 142 remains in its present format, it will necessitate the imposition of this prohibition pursuant to Art 14. It will also require the equalization of the responsible lending obligations in Spain under Art 2.

Chapter 4

Mortgage Foreclosure and Housing Rights in Spain: Crisis or General Deception?

Vanesa Valiño

Introduction

This chapter highlights the contemporary housing situation in Spain, one of the countries experiencing the worst outcomes of the global financial and housing crisis. With more than 500 daily evictions, almost 400,000 foreclosures since the beginning of the economic crisis in 2007 and at least five known suicides by home-owners who could not meet their mortgage payments, the situation can only be described as catastrophic. The severity of the problem is due not only to the flood of evictions, but also to the fact that the majority of people affected by mortgage foreclosures not only lose their homes but end up in debt for life. Second, apart from documenting the devastating mortgage losses and demonstrating the detrimental impact on home-owners affected by this problem, this chapter also demonstrates the links between the current housing crisis and certain political policies. These policies were implemented by public and private parties obsessed with the possibility of earning indiscriminate profits. To date, however, they have not accepted responsibility for the consequences of this in the current economic crisis. Third, the chapter outlines the gap in Spanish mortgage laws in terms of effective judicial protection and the right to a home, which is affecting so many home-owners, and also the lack of second-chance policies for over-indebted individuals. Fourth, it aims to identify the controversy which surrounds the current legislation and condemns thousands of families to social exclusion, as well as studying the various responses from institutions and the victims themselves.

The Origin of the Problem: Urban Planning in Spain

Urban planning in Spain has been characterized by envisaging the construction of homes and infrastructures as investment goods, a source of business, instead of fixed assets linked to public needs. This business, the real estate business, is based, above all, on the ability to add considerable value to land prices for the mere sake of being developable, an approach which explains the indiscriminate proliferation of homes, motorways and high-speed trains that has taken place in recent decades.[1] The continual rezoning of land outside areas included in urban and territorial planning without taking into account basic environmental factors, the construction of new homes above the average disposable income without addressing population growth, along with the destruction of real estate patrimony are all common factors in the history of Spanish urbanism starting in the Franco era, prolonged during the democratic transition and still visible today. All this has been facilitated by the existence of two large and powerful business groups that have close ties to public administrations at local, regional and national levels.

These two business groups – construction companies and banks – have become very well established since Franco's time and are very interested in urban growth.[2] Indeed, a significant part of the land reclassification operations driven by local authorities have been linked to raising funds to make up for a financial system that disregards the economic needs of local authorities,[3] speculative processes and corruption,[4] instead of resolving housing issues.

In order to encourage growth in the financial and real estate sector and urban growth, the housing policy during the last 60 years has promoted access to private home-ownership. Tax relief on property investment and different measures, such as easy access to loans, has situated private home-ownership as the main dwelling tenancy preference. This has had a negative effect on other more affordable means, such as renting, leasing, collective ownership or surface rights. In fact, the current prominence of private ownership in housing systems contrasts greatly with the general trend for rented property, which was characteristic in the housing industry up until the 1950s.[5] Hence, the general residential needs of the public

---

1 Spain is currently the EU country with the most housing per inhabitant. Whilst China claims first place, Spain has the second highest worldwide percentage of high-speed trains per km^2, exceeding Japan and Germany. It also has the highest rate of secondary residences and vacant housing in Europe. See José Manuel Naredo, 'The Spanish Property Model and its Implications' in Jordi Borja and Mireia Belil (eds), *Cities: An Impossible Equation* (Barcelona, Icaria Ed 2012).

2 See Naredo (n 1).

3 Local governments only receive 15 per cent of public income and are contending with a very high percentage of public services. During the real estate boom, much of the gap between income and expenditure was covered by incomes derived from urbanism. These incomes were considered normal, when in fact they were extraordinary and should have been administered with more caution, allowing for the subsequent crisis in the housing industry. See Jamie Buron, 'The Challenges of Local Governments and Housing Policies', Province of Barcelona, 2012.

4 Urban corruption in the local councils is one of the main reasons why Spain continues to appear in the global Corruption Perceptions Index. In 2012, according to the Global Corruption Report created by the NGO International Transparency, Spain occupied thirtieth place out of a total of 180 countries along with Cyprus, Estonia and Botswana.

5 The building and housing census of 1950 indicated that more than half of Spanish housing stock was rented, and this percentage reached levels of almost 90 per cent in large cities such as Madrid (94 per cent), Barcelona (95 per cent), Seville (90 per cent) and Bilbao

have been dependent on banks and leading real estate companies. Even public housing (official protection housing – Viviendas de Protección Oficial (VPO)) has been offered mainly as private ownership. This initiative was aimed at stimulating the construction industry in times of recession in order to reactivate the economy and generate employment, but failed to take into consideration whether prices would be affordable for impoverished people.

At present, there is no public homes supply available – the percentage of social rental housing is below one per cent of the total stock, compared to a European average of between 20 and 30 per cent. Nor is the rental market in the private sector sufficiently large – at less than 10 per cent – when the EU average is between 30 and 50 per cent. Intervention schemes have not been applied to the Spanish housing market in order to prevent speculation.

The Over-indebtedness of the Working Class During the Construction Boom

The central role of the real estate market became dangerously large during the construction boom that took place between 1997 and 2007. These years were characterized by a marked increase in liquidity at the international level and an excellent return on investment property. This 'tsunami of liquidity' meant indiscriminate access to credit for the construction sector, which accounted for almost 70 per cent of credit loans, and also to the working class as a gateway to home-ownership.[6]

The generalization of credit allowed Spain to become the European Union (EU) member with the most motorways and high-speed trains per square metre, and a leader in cement consumption. The housing stock, meanwhile, grew by 25 per cent so that the Spanish state, with 25.5 million homes, had one of the highest ratios of housing per capita in the EU. Many of these properties, however, were built on developments far from city centres or in run-down tourist sites along the coast and responded to the speculative process instead of genuine residential demands.[7]

Thus, despite the significant increase in the housing stock available and although the real value of wages did not grow during the 10 years of the housing bubble, house prices tripled. The housing bubble led to various abuses and

---

(88 per cent). This situation has since reversed dramatically. Today there is an excess of housing available, which is predominantly privately owned. See José Manuel Naredo, *By an Opposition that Opposes* (Barcelona, Anagram 2001).

6 Ada Colau and and Adrià Alemany, *Mortgaged Lives: From the Housing Bubble to Rights to a Home* (Barcelona, Angle Editorial 2012) is fundamental on this aspect.

7 The supply growth was consistently above the level of houses required to meet the demand for new households. Between 1997 and 2007, 390,000 new households were created each year. However, 6.6 million homes were constructed during this time, a figure higher than those built in France, Italy and Germany. In total, it is estimated that between empty housing and second homes, 35 per cent of the housing stock is not utilized.

discrimination against non-EU immigrants interested in renting a home, growth of substandard housing and overcrowding. However, the most widespread abusive practice during the housing boom was the over-indebtedness of the working class. In this way, the remarkable increase in housing prices was largely concealed by generalizing the over-indebtedness, which increased from 55 per cent to 130 per cent of households' disposable incomes during the decade 1997–2007.[8]

During these years, loans of up to 120 per cent of the value of property were given, with payments that could be returned over timeframes of 30, 40 and even 50 years. Many of the conditions were agreed through misleading advertisements which did not take into account scenarios forecasted by financial experts, such as interest rate increases or the bursting of the real estate bubble, which led to the devaluation of property. Moreover, a significant percentage of the mortgage loans included complex investment products that were causing significant economic losses to mortgage debtors.

The repertoire of abusive practices is vast. The granting of 'growing mortgages' starts off with affordable instalments that can later be tripled in a short period of time; the obligatory inclusion of additional products of questionable value in mortgages such as unemployment insurance with small print specifying that the policy would only be effective when the person had previously held a permanent contract, establishment of cross-guarantors, through which family and friends as well as strangers agreed to meet not only their own mortgage payments but also those of others in the event of default, and the inclusion of 'ground clauses' that did not protect the buyer against interest rate increases and at the same time prevented him/her from benefiting from drops in interest rates.

Meanwhile, access to rental housing was not without its complications. A shortage of available rental property, many not meeting the minimum conditions of habitability, was compounded by the imposition of conditions that were difficult to fulfil, such as the requirement of deposits of six months' to one year's rent, indefinite work contracts and equally exorbitant rents. Immigrants in particular experienced multiple discrimination based on their nationality, skin colour, lack of long-term employment contracts, etc. These obstacles were reinforced by legislation governing urban renting, which enables indiscriminate increases in rental contracts every five years and provides insufficient protection to tenants, along with an endlessly repeated message that states that renting equated to throwing away money. In turn, since pensions and social welfare payments cannot guarantee decent living conditions for adults, resolving the housing issue has become a basic necessity of life.

While accessing housing caused over-indebtedness amongst large sections of the population, the working class were particularly affected. Racial discrimination and the absence of family networks in the case of foreigners, and a tendency to

8 From 1997 to 2007, the average mortgage increased from €50,786 to €149,007, and the average mortgage timeframe increased from 19 to 28 years. Meanwhile, the number of mortgages formalized annually was around 822,000. See Colau and Alemany (n 6).

be employed in temporary positions in the service and construction sectors all represented major obstacles in trying to access rented accommodation. This was not the case, however, when applying for a mortgage.

The Bursting of the Housing Bubble and Inconsistencies in Mortgage Legislation

At the end of 2007, the US suffered a subprime mortgage crisis. The consequences of this crisis were noted quickly in Spain. Rising interest rates and the international credit crunch severely affected the real estate business, a strategic sector in terms of employment.[9] Growing unemployment in the context of over-indebtedness quickly resulted in increasing difficulties in meeting mortgage payments. Unemployment has risen from eight per cent in 2007 to 25 per cent in 2012,[10] particularly affecting young people and immigrants. Therefore, from 2008 to 2013, there has been an unprecedented increase in the number of foreclosures. According to the General Council of the Spanish Judicial Authority, a total of 397,651 procedures have been initiated from 2007 to the first half of 2012, and the rate of foreclosures initiated during the first half of 2012 was more than 500 a day.[11] Unfortunately, there are no official figures regarding the number of procedures that relate to normal housing as the figures available do not distinguish between second homes or business premises.

However, we must remember that foreclosure processes affect not only the individual but also the entire family unit. Furthermore, a single foreclosure process can involve more than one home. Many financial institutes foresaw potential difficulties in repayments of high-risk mortgages and demanded guarantees, and often the home of a close relative, particularly those of parents, was used as equity. The Platform for People Affected by Mortgages estimates that the problems of

9 During the peak years of the bubble, the volume of the real estate sector accounted for 18 per cent of GDP (30 per cent taking into account the indirect economic activities which proliferated under the umbrella of construction) and employed 13 per cent of the population, well above the 6.7 per cent in Germany and 8 per cent levels in the UK, See Colau and Alemany (n 6) 35.

10 The number of unemployed people in the third quarter of 2012 reached 4.7 million people and the autonomous communities Andalusia and Catalonia have been the most affected. In more than 1.4 million households, all household members are unemployed (National Institute for Employment, 2012). Meanwhile, the Organization for Economic Cooperation and Development (OECD) has forecast an increase in the Spanish unemployment rate to 26.9 per cent in 2013.

11 Foreclosures rose from 25,943 in 2007 to 58,686 in 2008, 93,319 in 2009, 93,636 in 2010, 77,854 in 2011 and 48,213 in the first six months of 2012. Meanwhile, during the first half of 2012, 94,502 dispossession orders were issued, which means that each day in Spain, 512 evictions take place. Supreme Judicial Council, 'Report on the Impact of the Crisis on the Judiciary Authorities' (Q2, 2012).

foreclosure affect two million people in Spain directly and indirectly. As a result, various organizations have reported the emergence of new phenomena in housing, such as subletting rooms by entire families, the occupation of abandoned buildings by excluded population groups and a significant increase in homelessness.[12]

However, in the case of Spain, the issues concerning people with unaffordable mortgages are not only to do with the loss of housing. The prevailing legislation is based on the principle of universal liability and does not permit the cancellation of the debt with the handing over of the home. The debt is associated entirely with the owner and not with the property, and the mortgagor must respond with his/her property as well as current and future salaries.

Moreover, foreclosure legislation does not allow judges to have access to important facts, such as whether the contract includes unfair terms or the reasons why the home-owner is not meeting mortgage payments. Finally, unlike other European countries, no process exists to resolve situations of personal indebtedness, such as 'second-chance policies'[13] which allow individuals to overcome their insolvency. The lack of this opportunity implies that those affected can remain on debtors' lists for life and are impeded from carrying out necessary functions, such as renting a home, having access to credit and applying for a government job, not to mention the stigma attached.

Far from helping to avoid the disintegration of families with mortgages, Spanish legislation shows complete juridical injustice towards insolvent people. The Insolvency Act 22/2003, passed on 9 July at a time of economic growth and absolute majority of the Popular Party (PP), was aimed theoretically at covering both corporate entities and physical persons. In practice, it allows companies to settle debts and start over. However, the same does not hold for insolvent families. Article 55 states that once the bankruptcy process has commenced, all financial activities are put on hold, except when the creditors have access to a security right, as is the case with property loans. At the same time, Article 56 states that only activities linked to the professional activity will be put on hold, which, according to the traditional understanding that the law has adopted, would exclude the individual's home.[14]

---

12 Marta Plujà i Calderon, *With a Roof But No Home: Effects of Substandard Housing on the Lives of People* (Barcelona, Caritas 2011).

13 Second-chance policies refer to those mechanisms or institutions such as the Commission for Indebtedness in France or the English Insolvency Agency. The goal of these organizations is to help 'honest' people who have been affected. Through financial reorganization and payment plans, they can once again benefit from equality in legal transactions. It is as much about debt relief as overcoming the restrictions associated with payment defaults. Ultimately these processes help to avoid social exclusion by allowing people to overcome their debts and promote economic growth.

14 Luis Gonzaga Serrano, 'Administrative Economic Law Reflections on Bankruptcy and Second Chances' (presentation given by the Minister for Tourism and Commerce, Madrid, 28 September 2011).

Moreover, the Civil Law Procedure Act (LEC) 1/2000 of 7 January restricts rather than facilitates the exercise of the right to effective legal protection throughout the foreclosure process. Article 695 limits its claims to cases whereby the loan has already been cleared or where the bank has made a miscalculation, hence preventing judges from examining the circumstances that led to the insolvency of the family. They are also unable to assess the level of information available to the victims when they took out their mortgages and whether unfair terms existed in their contracts.

Another controversial aspect of the same Act is the reference to the auction of the property as mortgage collateral. Article 671 establishes that in cases of unsuccessful auctions, the creditor may claim the right to the property for 60 per cent of its appraised value. With the outbreak of the economic crisis, there has been a substantial drop in bidding, meaning that the financial institutions can reclaim the property at 60 per cent of the valuation price and demand payment of the remaining 40 per cent, plus interest and legal costs by the mortgage owner or its guarantors. This means that families not only lose their homes, but are also indebted for life to financial institutions, which, in turn, can refinance the sale of the same property at a higher price than that at which it was repossessed.

Meanwhile, the free legal aid regulation establishes revenue-based scales which, *a priori*, often exclude the indebted households, based on the fact that they are considered property owners. Article 3.1 recognizes the right to free legal aid for those individuals whose resources and income do not exceed two times the minimum wage. This figure is calculated annually based on general concepts of the family unit and equates to a maximum monthly income of €1,054.48 per household. In many cases the average income of families with mortgages exceeds this figure. However, almost the entire household income is dedicated to mortgage repayments and, as a result, many people with obvious cases of bankruptcy are excluded from access to free legal aid.

Institutional Responses to the Problem of Foreclosures

The plight of thousands of people unable to pay mortgage fees and the corresponding debts associated with the handing back of property, as organized by the Platform of People Affected by Mortgages, has generated much public debate. To date, the central government has shown more concern for guaranteeing the solvency of the financial institutions than considering the implementation of measures to help avoid foreclosures and assist people with unaffordable mortgages. Nor is it addressing the gap between the huge amount of existing empty housing stock and the growing number of homeless people.[15] Unlike the rapid transfusion of funds

15 According to information conducted by the National Institute of Statistics 2012 Census, there are six million empty homes (20 per cent of the total). This percentage exceeds the average of the most advanced countries of the EU, which is between 2.5 and 5

injected into the financial sector, the measures aimed at resolving family issues have been very few and of limited scope.[16]

The main measure that the Socialist Party government implemented to help solve insolvency within the family unit was a moratorium on the payment of a portion of the mortgage payment, approved in late 2008. Known as the Moratorium of the Official Credit Institute (ICO), and with a designated budget of €6 billion, it allowed unemployed people to postpone up to €500 on their monthly mortgage payments. However, the requirements necessary to benefit from this measure did not cover most of the affected population. First, the moratorium only applied to mortgages that did not exceed €170,000. This figure may have been representative of the general housing price in Spain as a whole. However, this was not the case in large cities such as Madrid, Barcelona, Valencia and Murcia, where during the construction boom an apartment seldom cost less than €200,000. In addition, the moratorium could only be applied when there was no default on any of the mortgage payments. Finally, even when the individual met the necessary requirements, it was entirely up to the bank whether it accepted the moratorium or not. Hence, while the government forecasted helping 500,000 families, from the time it was implemented in March 2009 until it finished in late 2010, only 13,665 individuals benefited from the measure. A total of €78 million, just one per cent of the appropriated funds, ended up being assigned to the cause.[17]

Subsequently, the persistent augmentation of the problem led to the approval of the Royal Legislative Decree 8/2011 of 1 July in order to provide support to mortgage borrowers, and two basic changes were implemented. On the one hand, the appraisal value price with which financial entities could acquire property at auctions was increased from 50 per cent to at least 60 per cent. As such, if an auction was unsuccessful, as has often been the case since the onset of the crisis, the creditor now has to pay 60 per cent of the evaluation price of the property instead of 50 per cent and follow up on remaining payments, legal costs and any existing interest charges. On the other hand, there was a slight increase in the volume of controlled rental properties for people who had lost their homes through foreclosure. In short, it is a legislative reform aimed at alleviating the financial sentence which hangs over mortgage debtors, but due to its limitations, hardly any changes in the living conditions of the people affected are visible.

The amendment of the Insolvency Act 22/2003 with Law 38/2011 on 10 October was another missed opportunity by the Socialist government to tackle the problem of over-indebtedness and put into place a second-chance policy.

---

per cent. Meanwhile, financial institutions estimate that the stock of unsold new homes is between 800,000 and one million.

16 In 2008, due to the financial crisis, the government created the Fund for Orderly Bank Restructuring (FROB), which was basically oriented to rescue the financial sector with a budget of €9 billion.

17 Javier Gómez Guinda, *Financing of Public Housing Policy* (Official Credit Institute (ICO) 2011).

Despite the large number of insolvencies that existed due to the crisis, the reform of the Bankruptcy Act was not used to adapt the bankruptcy procedure to assisting the problematic over-indebtedness of mortgagors. The only agreement that was reached was the possible adaptation of future second-start measures.[18]

On the other hand, since its coming into power in December 2011, the Partido Popular has not suitably addressed the problematic issue of thousands of people being affected by foreclosures. The answers have been prioritized at all times to serve the interests of financial institutions and have only ever tried to partially resolve the most extreme cases.

The first measure, the 'Code of Good Banking Practice' approved to protect mortgage owners in March 2012 by Royal Decree-Law 6/2012, was announced with much song and dance as an innovative proposal in curtailing the financial drainage associated with mortgages. This law, theoretically aimed at resolving mortgage over-indebtedness by facilitating mortgage renegotiation and in extreme cases the cessation of payments, establishes overly restrictive conditions.

Again, as in the ICO Moratorium adopted by the Socialist government, the limitations – the mortgage ceiling, the lack of application when the mortgage guarantor had payment capacity and the maximum income criteria of the mortgagor[19] – meant the exclusion of the vast majority of people affected by the repercussions of the housing bubble. The clearest signs of the limited impact of this measure were, first, the positive response by the financial institutes, which all demonstrated their immediate approval, and, second, the necessity to adopt new urgent measures only seven months after its introduction.

In fact, the last reaction of the government, the Royal Decree Law 27/2012 of 15 November, an urgent measure introduced to increase protection for mortgagors, responds to the situation of social alarm created through the media attention surrounding several suicides in less than a month by people who were due to be evicted from their homes.[20] Hence, the decree, presented as a draft law, aimed at promoting a two-year moratorium in cases of evictions rather

18 'This report shall include the possible adoption of other measures, both substantive and procedural, through appropriate initiatives, which complete economic and social protection of consumers and families. For this purpose, out-of-court dispute resolution options such as notary, registration, mediation, or other types may be proposed.' Single Additional Provision, Law 38/2011, Bankruptcy Reform, 10 October.

19 The price of housing for eligibility cannot exceed €200,000 in big cities and €120,000 in smaller urban areas.

20 It is difficult to estimate with certainty the number of people who have taken their lives because of their inability to meet the payment of housing. In any case, to show the extent of the problem, it is sufficient to talk about the cases of 54-year-old José Miguel Domingo, a resident of Granada, who hanged himself on 25 October 2012 a few hours before being evicted; 53-year-old GB Manuel, who that same day jumped from a balcony in his home in Valencia after a member of the judicial commission came to evict him; and 53-year-old Egaña Amaia, from Barakaldo, Euskadi, who threw herself from the window of her fourth-floor home on 9 November when the judicial commission was going to evict her.

than trying to renegotiate the outstanding debt. A social housing scheme was also set up for people evicted from their homes following the non-payment of mortgages. The creation of the fund is based on the government working closely with the credit institutions.

Once again, the requirements needed in order to benefit from the moratorium on evictions are difficult to meet. The family income cannot be more than €1,597, half of which must be applied to mortgage payments, and certain inconsistent social requirements also apply, such as families with children below the age of three being included. However, families with two or more children above four years of age or single mothers with one child are excluded. In addition, the moratorium is only effective when the financial institute takes ownership of the home. The limited impact of the measure has been recognized by the government, whose initial calculations forecasted assistance for 600,000 families, while in practice the figure has been less than 120,000. In addition, following the criteria of the European Commission, the law does not stipulate any changes in the foreclosure process, nor does it take into account the hundreds of thousands of people who have lost their homes and continue to be in debt, nor does it establish changes for the future. It doesn't even specify whether default interest is suspended during the two-year delay in repayments.

Along with the moratorium, the law stipulates the creation of a social fund for rental property at affordable prices for people who have lost their homes. According to the limited information available, the government´s intention is that the financial institutions will provide the use of unoccupied property as social housing. However, it is not known what methods will be used to promote the social rental of the thousands of empty apartments currently controlled by the financial entities. So far, the numerous attempts by public authorities to reach an amicable agreement with the banks have been ignored.

Generally speaking, the public authorities seem more concerned with reviving the vital signs of the financial and real estate business than with meeting public housing needs.[21] Proof of this is the new legislative reforms applied to property rentals, as well as the new operation to rescue banking through 'bad banking solutions'. For example, the reform of the rental market means that eviction can now take place in just 10 days, hence the term 'express eviction', while it neglects the reasons as to why the rent is not being paid. Overall, the changes in rental legislation are aimed at suppressing basic tenant rights, such as protection against indiscriminate price increases, and at the same time promote investment funds in the rental market.[22] Meanwhile, the public bailout of toxic financial assets held

---

21 Meanwhile, the Autonomous Regions and municipalities pressurized by the collectives of people affected also put forward different symbolic responses, such as resolutions and declarations in favour of the ceding of payment, as well as mediation services and legal advice for people affected.

22 Vanesa Valiño and Caterina Rilo, 'The Vulnerability of Tenants Implies No Real Way Out of the Housing Crisis: Notes on the Proposed Reform of the Rental Market'

by the nationalized banks ('bad banks') does not anticipate the possibility of providing a government social housing stock. Instead, the objective of the bad bank is to stop real estate prices from falling and favours the purchase of property by large investment funds.[23] The clearest sign yet of the government's desire to promote the real estate business at all costs is the announcement that in November 2013, it will offer residence permits to immigrants who purchase properties for more than €160,000.

Institutional Responses in the Judicial Field

Along with the local governments, the judicial courts are one of the areas hardest hit by the avalanche of foreclosure proceedings. Judges and lawyers who have come into close contact with the problem have made numerous public declarations through progressive judges' and magistrates' organizations, such as democratic judges and affiliated bar associations. These declarations defend the need to reform the mortgage legislation in order to stop mortgage owners with unaffordable loans from ending up in debt for life once they lose their homes.

For the time being, while we wait for suitable legislative reform, different measures have been initiated to defend the interests of mortgage-owning families. In September 2010, the Judge Magistrate of the Court of First Instance No. 2 in Sabadell, Guillem Soler, raised a question of unconstitutionality concerning the foreclosure process and possible infringement of rights to effective legal protection, as well as the right of an individual to adequate housing. The appeal challenged the debtor's ability to defend why he/she was not meeting the mortgage payments and demonstrated the general inability of the judge to assess the conditions pertaining to the mortgage. The matter was dismissed by the Constitutional Court in July 2011, alleging, amongst other things, that the foreclosure procedure was a legislative matter rather than a judicial one.[24]

In an attempt to dissolve the mortgage debt when the mortgagor hands over the home, some judges have opted for an alternative interpretation of the Civil Procedure Code. In order to avoid banks repossessing the property for 60 per cent

---

(DESC Observatory, 2012).

23 In fact, what is presented as mere asset management involves creating the largest Spanish real estate of all times, the 'Asset Management Company for the Restructuring of the Banking Sector' (SAREB), which is estimated to own 89,000 finished homes covering 13,000 km^2 of land. Both SAREB and the banks will offer the property through public financial support and state guarantees on loans given to private investors. See the communication published by the DESC Observatory along with other social organizations: 'Evictions and Bad Banking: A Historic Opportunity' (November 2012).

24 Guillem Soler, 'Possible Elements of Unconstitutionality in the Foreclosure Process' (Observatorio DESC, Conference on 'Foreclosure and Housing Rights: Legal Strategies Against Insolvency of Families', Barcelona, September 2009).

of the valuation price and pursuing the remaining 40 per cent of the debt by seizing current and future assets, more and more verdicts are favouring the repossession price being equal to the official valuation price of the property that was originally accepted by the mortgage bank. In addition, some of the sentences passed allude to the necessity of taking into account factors such as the impact of unemployment on families and the responsibility of the banking sector in the current crisis.[25]

Finally, another foreclosure appeal has been opened by the Magistrate of the Mercantile Court No. 3 in Barcelona, Fernández Sejio, who presented a preliminary ruling to the European Court of Justice for a possible violation of consumer rights caused by EU regulations.[26] The magistrate presented the following issues before the Luxemburg Tribunal:

a. Judges do not know what conditions apply to mortgage contracts and is this not a potential violation of consumer rights.
b. It is disproportionate that banks can demand early termination of long-term loans (in the case in question, the loan period was 33 years) for failing to meet payments during a very limited period of time.
c. Is the application of penalty interest rates (in this particular case, higher than 18 per cent) not an unjust measure which would be considered a violation of consumer rights in other sectors?
d. To what extent does the inclusion of variable interest rates imply that the mortgagor cannot negotiate the repayment amounts with their banks before eviction takes place?

In November 2013, the considerations of the Attorney General of the European Court of Justice will be made public, thus implying that the Spanish eviction legislation violates EU consumer protection rights by containing unfair terms. While waiting for judicial resolution, several courts have taken advantage of the situation by imposing delays on current foreclosure cases.

The Response of Society and the People Affected

Since the bursting of the housing bubble in 2007, many groups have highlighted the co-responsibility of general banks, savings banks, notaries, valuation agencies, real estate agencies and public administrations for the over-indebtedness of households. The need for a social audit has been defended in order to demonstrate the various degrees of responsibility for the current crisis, to restore the self-

25 To consult sample judicial decisions, see www.observatoridesc.org/es/sentencias-dacion-hipoteca.

26 Case C-415/11 concerning Directive 93/13/EEC of the Council of 5 April 1993 about unfair terms in consumer contracts.

esteem of over-indebted families and to investigate where the millions of euros generated in the real estate boom have gone.

A second claim, also in the same order, is to stop aid and guarantees designed to recapitalize banks using public money. The management of these grants, more than €250 billion between funds and guarantees, lacks transparency and the monetary authorities have not taken a single step in trying to launch a new financial order that will avoid the negative factors which caused the detonation of the crisis. Neither the increased availability of money nor larger banking entities means more and improved control of the banking system. On the contrary, the bulk of the resources should be devoted to supporting vulnerable groups, such as people affected by high rates of unemployment and people struggling to pay for their homes.

Given the institutional neglect of the thousands of people with unaffordable mortgages, in 2009 the Platform of People Affected by Mortgages (PAH) was set up.[27] Apart from providing a meeting point and collective advice for the mortgagees, its main objectives are to promote the retroactive payment in kind for those affected by foreclosure procedures affecting their only home, and to delay evictions until alternative housing is guaranteed. To highlight social support and the need for essential changes in direction of support policies within the banking sector, the PAH and the two largest unions, along with neighbourhood and social organizations such as DESC Observatory, started a Popular Legislative Initiative (ILP) in April 2012 for payment in kind, social renting and protection for people being evicted. The demands of the ILP include that the handing over of property constitutes the cancellation of a mortgage, the suspension of evictions driven by financial institutions and the possibility that people affected can remain in their homes under social rental schemes. This citizen participation programme is not very strong yet, as the 500,000 signatures collected so far will not warrant a change in the current legislation. However, the million signatures that they expect to acquire will serve to demonstrate a social rejection of policies whose concern for rescuing financial institutions is condemning thousands of families to poverty.

In short, the social organizations and the victims have proposed that operations to save banks using public money be redirected towards the creation of public housing rental stock for people in need of homes. They have also vindicated the need for a change in the housing policy. As United Nations Special Housing Rapporteur Raquel Rolnick states in her annual reports,[28] a thorough review of the housing policy that has been adopted in Spain throughout the last few years is fundamental. We need to consider the housing policy as a public service designed to ensure a proper human right instead of bringing out urgent decrees to cover only the most extreme cases.

---

27 Colau and Alemany (n 6).

28 See Report of the United Nations Special Housing Rapporteur Raquel Rolnick, A/HRC/10/7, of 4 February 2009 on the economic crisis, and Report A/67/286 of 10 August 2012 on financing housing policy.

Chapter 5
Housing Rights in Europe: The Council of Europe Leads the Way

Padraic Kenna and Mark Jordan

Introduction

In global terms, housing is Europe[1] is widely regarded as among the best developed and with the highest standards. Yet, among the population of the European Union (EU) Member States, which numbers some 500 million, approximately six per cent suffered from severe housing deprivation in 2009, while some 30 million people suffered from both lack of space and poor housing conditions. The most frequent problems were noise from the neighbourhood (22.2 per cent), overcrowding (17.8 per cent) and pollution, crime or other environmental problems (16.5 per cent). In addition, 12.2 per cent of people in the EU lived in households affected by high housing costs.[2] Direct state housing provision for low-income households continues to diminish and some states are unable to dedicate any resources

1 It is important to differentiate between the European Union with its 28 Member States and the Council of Europe. The 28 EU Member States are Austria, **Belgium**, Bulgaria, Croatia, Cyprus, the Czech Republic, Denmark, Estonia, Finland, France, Germany, Greece, Hungary, Ireland, Italy, Latvia, Lithuania, Luxembourg, Malta, the Netherlands, Poland, Portugal, Romania, Slovakia, Slovenia, Spain, Sweden and the UK. The Council of Europe includes all 28 EU Member States and 20 more, including the Russian Federation, Georgia, Azerbeijan, etc. See Council of Europe, 'About the Council of Europe' http://www.coe.int/T/e/Com/about_coe accessed 31 July 2013, which gives a brief summary of the Council, its history and its aims.

2 See A Rybkowska and M Schneider, *Statistics in Focus, Population and Social Conditions* (Eurostat 2011) In 2008, the EU adopted the Regulation establishing common rules for the decennial provision of comprehensive data on population and housing, establishing a common set of housing topics to be collated by Member States. Regulation EC 763/2008, 13 August 2008, OJ L218/14. See also Regulation (EC) No 315/2006 of 22 February 2006 implementing Regulation (EC) No 1177/2003 of the European Parliament and of the Council concerning Community statistics on income and living conditions (EU-SILC) as regards the list of target secondary variables relating to housing conditions. 'Severe deprivation' is defined the percentage of the population living in a dwelling which is considered to be overcrowded and with at least one of the following three housing situations: (1) a leaking roof, or damp walls, floors, foundations, or rot in window frames or floor; (2) neither a bath, nor a shower, nor an indoor flushing toilet; or (3) too dark.

towards social housing. Homelessness has risen across the EU as the economic and financial crisis has persisted.[3] Similarly, the extent of material deprivation or 'the inability to live a decent life' has increased dramatically in some EU Member States such as Greece, the Baltic States, Ireland and Spain since 2008.[4]

In 2010, the European Commission launched the 'Europe 2020 Strategy', primarily to encourage economic growth out of the contemporary crisis and prepare the EU economy for the next decade. The Strategy contained an EU poverty target, which is defined as follows: 'promoting social inclusion, in particular through the reduction of poverty, by aiming to lift at least 20 million people out of the risk of poverty and exclusion'.[5] However, it is noticeable that the concept of a 'Social Europe' or a major commitment to social cohesion no longer appears in official documents. Meanwhile, the European Parliament has stated that 'homelessness continues to affect people in all EU Member States and is an unacceptable violation of human rights'.[6] It is becoming clear that as the EU abandons much of its commitment to social cohesion and a 'Social Europe', those who are excluded from markets will rely more on social and economic rights to achieve access to the resources which lead to a 'decent existence'.

Housing rights are growing in significance in the context of homelessness, poor-quality housing, access and affordability problems, and social segregation across Europe. The right to adequate housing has been accepted by all European states (both EU and non-EU) under the international instruments of the United Nations and the Council of Europe. States guarantee to secure for certain categories of people in their jurisdictions a minimum standard of adequate housing and the prevention and reduction of homelessness.[7]

To date, EU law has not focused directly on housing or indeed housing rights. Instead, the Council of Europe has led the way. The Council, which was established in 1949 and now has 47 Member States, promotes housing rights through the

---

3 See European Commission, *Research Note 8/2011, Homelessness During the Crisis* (Brussels, Employment, Social Affairs and Inclusion, European Commission 2011).

4 European Commission, *EU Employment and Social Situation, Quarterly Review* (Brussels, European Commission, June 2012) 48. See also Padraic Kenna, 'Globalization and Housing Rights' (2008) 15(2) Indiana Journal of Global Legal Studies 397.

5 For an evaluation of the open method of coordination in the field of social inclusion and consideration of the new 'Europe 2020' strategy, see H Frazer, E Marlier and I Nicaise , *A Social Inclusion Roadmap for Europe 2020* (Antwerp, Garant 2010).

6 See Declaration of the European Parliament of 16 December 2010 on an EU homelessness strategy, EP T7-0499/2010.

7 In a significant development in December 2010, some 391 Members of the European Parliament signed a written declaration stating that homelessness is an unacceptable violation of fundamental human rights and calling on the Council of Ministers to end street homelessness by 2015. See Declaration of the European Parliament of 16 December 2010 on an EU homelessness strategy, P7_TA-PROV(2010)0499.

European Social Charter and the Revised Charter,[8] and in an oblique way through its European Convention for the Protection of Human Rights and Fundamental Freedoms (ECHR).[9] Through its novel Collective Complaints system, it enables international and some national non-governmental organizations (NGOs) to submit complaints concerning Member States which are not satisfactorily applying their adopted Charter provisions. This process is leading to the development of a new jurisprudence on defining the elements of housing rights in a wider European context.

Significantly, with the adoption of the now-binding Charter of Fundamental Rights of the Lisbon Treaty, on matters of interpretation of EU law, the jurisprudence of the Council of Europe with regard to rights to social and housing assurance will be a source of law. Of course, this may result in a parallel and inconsistent housing rights jurisprudence between EU and Council of Europe Member States, but in any case, there is now a new synergy developing in this area.

The Council of Europe and Housing Rights

The European Social Charter is a Council of Europe treaty which guarantees social and economic human rights.[10] It was adopted in 1961 and was revised in

8 Turin, 18 October 1961, Council of Europe, European Treaty Series – No 35; *European Social Charter (Revised)*, Council of Europe, Strasbourg, 3 May 1996. The binding nature at the national level of the Charters depends on whether a dualist or monist legal system pertains, but many dualist states have incorporated the Charter (or parts of it) into national law. A total of 43 states have ratified the Charter (either the 1961 Charter or its revised version). Albania, Andorra, Armenia, Austria, Azerbaijan, Belgium, Bosnia and Herzegovina, Bulgaria, Croatia, Cyprus, the Czech Republic, Denmark, Estonia, Finland, France, Georgia, Germany, Greece, Hungary, Iceland, Ireland, Italy, Latvia, Lithuania, Luxembourg, Malta, Moldova, Montenegro, the Netherlands, Norway, Poland, Portugal, Romania, the Russian Federation, Serbia, the Slovak Republic, Slovenia, Spain, Sweden, the Former Yugoslav Republic of Macedonia, Turkey, the UK and Ukraine have signed and ratified the Social Charter or the Revised Charter. The four states which have signed but not yet ratified the Charter are Lichtenstein, Monaco, San Marino and Switzerland.

9 The Commissioner for Human Rights of the Council of Europe, Mr Thomas Hammarberg, clarified the legal protection of housing rights, obstacles and gaps in their implementation, with recommendations on how these rights are to be realized. See *Housing Rights: The Duty to Ensure Housing for All*, CommDH/IssuePaper (2008) 1 Strasbourg, 25 April 2008 https://wcd.coe.int/ViewDoc.jsp?id=1292391&Site=CommDH accessed 20 April 2013.

10 The Treaty of London (1949), which established the Council of Europe, had as its foundation the aim of greater unity among the signatory states. Article 1(b) of the Treaty sets out that 'greater unity will be pursued through the organs of the Council by discussion of questions of common concern and by agreements and common action in economic, social, cultural, scientific, legal and administrative matters and in the maintenance and further realisation of human rights and fundamental freedoms'. In this manner, the Treaty of

1996.[11] The Revised Charter (RESC) came into force in 1999 and is gradually replacing the initial 1961 Charter. The revisions, which began during the 1990s, were designed to revitalize the Charter by re-designing the reporting system and adding a number of new social and economic rights including the express right to housing set out in Article 31 of the RESC. In 1995, the Council adopted a Protocol to the Charter that provides for a collective complaint mechanism as an additional compliance procedure.[12] States have discretion over which provisions of the Charter they agree to; however, once a state ratifies and signs the Charter, it has committed itself to the effective realization of a number of human rights. To date, the RESC has been signed by all 47 Member States of the Council of Europe, 43 of which have ratified the Charter, although only 15 have accepted the appurtenant collective complaint supervisory procedure which was introduced with the Revisions of 1996. The rights enshrined within the Charter include the right to housing, health, education, employment, legal and social protection, free movement of persons and freedom from discrimination.

States which sign and ratify the European Social Charter and RESC, with its 31 Articles on socio-economic rights, accept as the aim of their policies, to be pursued by all appropriate means, both national and international in character, the attainment of conditions in which the rights and principles within the Charters may be effectively realized without discrimination.[13] The Charters establish housing obligations in relation to physically and mentally disabled persons,[14] children and young persons,[15] and rights to social, legal and economic protection for families,

---

London put in place the foundation for both the European Convention for the Protection of Human Rights and Fundamental Freedoms 1950 and the European Social Charter of 1961.

11 See the Council of Europe website http://www.coe.int/T/DGHL/Monitoring/SocialCharter accessed 21 April 2013.

12 Additional Protocol to the European Social Charter Providing for a System of Collective Complaints, ETS No 158; 34 ILM (1995) 1453; and Basic Documents, at 451.

13 Part V of art E of the Charter states: 'The enjoyment of the rights set forth in this Charter shall be secured without discrimination on any ground such as race, colour, sex, language, religion, political or other opinion, national extraction or social origin, health, association with a national minority, birth or other status.' States Parties have to accept at least six of the nine articles of the 'hard core' provisions of the Charter (arts 1 (right to work), 5 (freedom of association), 6 (collective bargaining), 7 (right of children and young persons to protection), 12 (right to social security), 13 (right to social and medical assistance), 16 (right of the family to social, legal and economic protection), 19 (right of migrant workers and their families to protection) and 20 (right to equal opportunities and equal treatment in matters of employment and occupation without discrimination on the grounds of sex), and select an additional number of articles or numbered paragraphs to be bound by. The total number of articles or numbered paragraphs by which every state is bound is not less than 16 articles or 63 numbered paragraphs.

14 Article 15.

15 Article 17.

including a state obligation to provide family housing.[16] The Social Charters grant migrant workers an explicit right to be treated equally in relation to access to housing.[17] Article 23 sets out the right of elderly persons to provision of housing suited to their needs and their state of health.[18] Article 30 obliges ratifying states to ensure the exercise of the rights to protection against poverty and social exclusion within the framework of an overall and coordinated approach. The significant references to rights to adequate housing are set out in Article 31(1):

> With a view to ensuring the effective exercise of the right to housing, the Parties undertake to take measures designed:
>
> 1. to promote access to housing of an adequate standard;
> 2. to prevent and reduce homelessness with a view to its gradual elimination;
> 3. to make the price of housing accessible to those without adequate resources.[19]

Monitoring and the Collective Complaints System

The ECSR monitors states' compliance with the Charter through regular reports from states and the Collective Complaints system.[20] It ascertains whether there

---

16 Article 16 on the right of the family to social, legal and economic protection states: 'With a view to ensuring the necessary conditions for the full development of the family, which is a fundamental unit of society, the Contracting Parties undertake to promote the economic, legal and social protection of family life by such means as social and family benefits, fiscal arrangements, provision of family housing, benefits for the newly married, and other appropriate means.'

17 Article 19.

18 Article 23.

19 States which ratified art 31(1) on 26 March 2013 were Andorra, Finland, France, Italy, Latvia, Lithuania, the Netherlands, Norway, Portugal, Slovenia, Sweden, Turkey and Ukraine. See http://www.coe.int/t/dghl/monitoring/socialcharter/Presentation/ProvisionTableRevMarch2013_en.pdf accessed 19 August 2013.

20 The mission of the ECSR is to judge that States Parties are in conformity in law and in practice with the provisions of the European Social Charter. In respect of national reports, the Committee adopts conclusions and in respect of collective complaints, it adopts decisions. The Committee is composed of 15 independent, impartial experts, elected by the Council of the Europe Committee of Ministers for a six-year term of office, which is renewable once. The ECSR issues a set of questions to states in preparation of periodic monitoring reports and in relation to Article 31(1), the following questions are raised: 'Please describe the obligatory standards that apply in relation to housing quality. Please provide information on the extent to which sub-standard dwellings exist. Please indicate what measures are taken to improve housing standards, especially in public-owned housing stock. Please describe the means by which compliance with housing standards is ensured in practice.' See R Brillat, 'The Supervisory Machinery of ECS: Recent Developments and their Impact' in G De Búrca and B De

has been satisfactory application of the Charter by reviewing the materials submitted by the signatory states in regular monitoring reports. These are conducted through regular monitoring cycles of adopted articles, and Conclusions are issued by the ECSR setting out the results of its examination. This process has been supplemented since 1996 by the Collective Complaints system.

The Council of Europe Additional Protocol of 1995[21] providing for a system of Collective Complaints laid the foundations for an additional supervisory mechanism which sought to improve the effective enforcement of the social and economic rights guaranteed by the Charter.[22] Article 1 of the Protocol specifies that organizations of employers or trade unions and accredited international and some NGOs only can submit Complaints to the ECSR. The complaint file must contain details concerning the complainant organization, an indication concerning the provisions of the Charter that have allegedly been violated and the subject matter of the complaint. In this respect, some evidence must be presented to support the alleged violation.[23] Once the ECSR has determined admissibility, it will proceed to examine the merits of the complaint in light of the arguments made by the concerned parties.

Based on these procedures, the ECSR can conclude that there has been an unsatisfactory application of the Charter. The ECSR 'shall draw up a report in which it shall describe the steps taken by it to examine the complaint and present its conclusions as to whether or not the Contracting Party [state] concerned has

---

Witte (eds), *Social Rights in Europe*. (Oxford, OUP 2005); R Churchill and U Khaliq, 'The Collective Complaints System of the European Social Charter – An Effective Mechanism for Ensuring Compliance with Economic and Social Rights?' (2004) 15 European Journal of International Law 417; H Cullen, 'The Collective Complaints System of the European Social Charter: Interpretative Methods of the European Committee of Social Rights' (2009) 9(1) Human Rights Law Review 61–93. Significant housing-related Collective Complaints include *Autism-Europe v France* (n 27); *ERRC v Greece* (n 22); *ERRC v Italy* (n 34); *ERRC v Bulgaria* (n 20); and Complaint 51/2008 *European Roma Rights Centre (ERRC) v France*. For summaries of the decisions on the merits of collective complaints registered between 1998 and 2010, see http://www.coe.int/t/dghl/monitoring/socialcharter/ComplaintSummaries/CCSummariesMerits2012_en.pdf accessed 21 April 2013.

21 Additional Protocol to the European Social Charter Providing for a System of Collective Complaints, ETS No 158.

22 See Complaint No 1/1998, where the ECSR considered that the object of the system of collective complaints, 'which is different in nature from the procedure of examining national reports, is to allow the Committee to make a legal assessment of the situation of a State in the light of the information supplied by the complaint and the adversarial procedure to which it gives rise' ([10]).

23 It would appear that the evidentiary requirements are not extensive at the admissibility stage; see Complaint No 5/1999. However, Complaints have been declared inadmissible at the subsequent merits stage due to a lack of evidence; see Complaint No 2/1999. See also Churchill and Khaliq (n 49) 456.

ensured the satisfactory application of the provision of the Charter referred to in the complaint'.[24] This report shall be transmitted to the Committee of Ministers of the Council of Europe, the organisation which lodged the complaint and the state concerned. It must be transmitted to the Parliamentary Assembly of the Council of Europe and published within four weeks after being sent to the Committee of Ministers.[25]

The Committee of Ministers of the Council of Europe 'shall adopt by a majority of two-thirds of those voting, a recommendation addressed to the Contracting Party [state] concerned'.[26] The state concerned 'shall provide information on the measures it has taken to give effect to the Committee of Ministers' recommendation, in the next report which it submits'.[27] In this way, the complaint by an NGO can ultimately result in the Committee of Ministers examining the measures taken by a state which has unsatisfactorily applied some rights of the Charter.

In terms of the success of complaints, only four were held to be inadmissable between 1998 and 2010;[28] as such, the majority of complaints proceed to the merits stage. To date, at the merits stage there have been 13 complaints where there has been a finding of non-violation of the Charter[29] and eight complaints where there has been a partial violation,[30] and in the remainder there have been findings of an unsatisfactory application of the Charter. As such, it is clear that the majority of Collective Complaints have revealed a violation of the Charter, a situation which perhaps would not have been revealed via the cyclical reporting procedure alone. In this way, the Collective Complaints procedure represents a robust mechanism of examining state obligations under the RESC. It can be argued that the Collective Complaints procedure has revitalized the Charter by, for example, allowing greater specification in supervision by the ECSR and increased participation.[31] However,

24 Additional Protocol to the European Social Charter Providing for a System of Collective Complaints, ETS No 158, art 8.

25 ibid.

26 ibid art 9.

27 ibid art 10.

28 These are Complaint No 3/1999, Complaint No 28/2004, Complaint No 29/2005 and Complaint No 36/2006.

29 These are Complaint No 2/1999, Complaint No 11/2001, Complaint No 23/2003, Complaint No 14/2003, Complaint No 19/2003, Complaint No 20/2003, Complaint No 25/2004, Complaint No 26/2004, Complaint No 37/2006, Complaint No 42/2007, Complaint No 40/2007, Complaint No 43/2007 and Complaint No 50/2008.

30 These are Complaint No 6/1999, Complaint No 9/2000, Complaint No 12/2002, Complaint No 16/2003, Complaint No 22/2003, Complaint No 24/2004, Complaint No 30/2005 and Complaint No 45/2007.

31 See Brillat (n 49) 34, where it was set out that the ECSR, as a result of the Charter, has assumed a quasi-judicial function.

the mechanism is not without its detractors.[32] Robust criticism has been levied at the discretion left to ratifying states over whether or not to accept the Collective Complaints procedure. This discretion has resulted in only 14 of the 47 Member States of the Council of Europe ratifying the Collective Complaints Protocol and, as such, has limited the remit of the mechanism accordingly.[33] Nevertheless, to date (26 September, 2013) already 101 Collective complaints were lodged, the trend towards increasing popularity of the complaint procedure is apparent.[34] With regard to the spread of complaints the housing-related complaints, Article 31 (15 complaints) and Article 16 (18 complaints) are the most litigated provisions of the Charter after Article E (20 complaints).

Indeed, it has been argued that the system 'provides an opportunity for non-governmental bodies to try to persuade the ECSR towards the progressive development of standards'.[35] When viewed in light of the functional overlap which exists between provisions within the Charter, this characteristic of the Collective Complaints procedure could present significant challenges to the legitimacy of the Charter, as states could be caught by obligations arising from provisions which they have not accented.

The European Committee of Social Rights (ECSR) (described below), which monitors the application of the Charter by states, has clarified the meaning of the term 'adequate' housing within Article 31(1) in a number of Conclusions and within a number of Decisions on Collective Complaints. In this context, it is significant that the ESCR has held in *ERRC v Bulgaria*[36] that Articles 16 and 31 of the Charter overlap. This is important because to date only 13 countries have accepted the provisions of Article 31 and as a result the overlap has played a key role in helping to protect the right to housing by using Article 16, which has been more widely accepted:

> The Committee considers that, as many other provisions of the Charter, Articles 16 and 31, though different in personal and material scope, partially overlap with respect to several aspects of the right to housing. In this respect, the notions of adequate housing and forced eviction are identical under Articles 16 and 31.

32 See Churchill and Khaliq (n 51) 456 for a detailed analysis of the Collective Complaints procedure.

33 These states are Belgium, Croatia, Cyprus, the Czech Republic, Finland, France, Greece, Iceland, Ireland, Italy, the Netherlands, Norway, Portugal and Sweden. See http://conventions.coe.int/Treaty/Commun/ChercheSig.asp?NT=158&CM=8&DF=&CL=ENG.

34 At time of writing, the final complaint published on the Council of Europe website is Complaint No 82/2012 *Comité européen d'action spécialisée pour l'Enfant et la Famille dans leur milieu de vie (EUROCEF) v France.*

35 See Churchill and Khaliq (n 49) 450, where the authors identify that 'the collective complaints system importantly, however, provides an opportunity for non-governmental bodies to try to persuade the ECSR towards the progressive development of standards'.

36 Complaint No 31/2005 *European Roma Rights Centre (ERRC) v Bulgaria* [17].

Thus, the interpretation of the obligations of Article 16 of the Charter on the rights of families to social, legal and economic protection encompasses a right to adequate housing.[37]

Article 16 in its very wording of the Charter (the English version, which clarifies the French version) provides for the right to housing of families as an element of the right of the family to social, legal and economic protection. The Committee has already given an interpretation of the notion of the right to housing under Article 16. It summarized this interpretation in its decision on the *ERRC v Greece* complaint as follows:

> The Committee recalls its previous case law to the effect that in order to satisfy Article 16 states must promote the provision of an adequate supply of housing for families, take the needs of families into account in housing policies and ensure that existing housing be of an adequate standard and include essential services (such as heating and electricity). The Committee has stated that adequate housing refers not only to a dwelling which must not be sub-standard and must have essential amenities, but also to a dwelling of suitable size considering the composition of the family in residence. Furthermore the obligation to promote and provide housing extends to security from unlawful eviction.[38]

The jurisprudence of the ECSR in relation to Article 16 is, of course, relevant to the application of these standards of adequacy only to families.[39] In relation to the definition of 'family', the ECSR has pointed out that the protection afforded in this provision covers single-parent families. The definition may also be enlarged

---

37 Council of Europe states which ratified art 16 on 26 March 2013 are: Austria, Azerbaijan, Belgium, Bosnia and Herzegovina, Bulgaria, Croatia, the Czech Republic, Denmark, Estonia, Finland, France, Germany, Greece, Hungary, Iceland, Ireland, Italy, Latvia, Lithuania, Luxembourg, Malta, Moldova, Montenegro, the Netherlands, Norway, Poland, Portugal, Romania, the Russian Federation, Serbia, Slovakia, Slovenia, Spain, Sweden, Turkey, Ukraine and the UK. See http://www.coe.int/t/dghl/monitoring/socialcharter/Presentation/ProvisionTableRevMarch2013_en.pdf accessed 12 March 2013.

38 Complaint No 15/2003 *European Roma Rights Centre (ERRC) v Greece* [16].

39 However, it was established in Complaint No 47/2008 *DCI v The Netherlands* that States Parties must make sure that evictions are justified and are carried out in conditions that respect the dignity of the persons concerned, and must make alternative accommodation available. In this case, the ECSR held that 'since in the case of unlawfully present persons no alternative accommodation may be required by States, eviction from shelter should be banned as it would place the persons concerned, particularly children, in a situation of extreme helplessness which is contrary to the respect for their human dignity'. Therefore: 'On the basis of the above, the Committee concludes that States Parties are required, under Article 31§2 of the Revised Charter, to provide adequate shelter to children unlawfully present in their territory for as long as they are in their jurisdiction. Any other solution would run counter to the respect for their human dignity and would not take due account of the particularly vulnerable situation of children' ([64]).

by reference to the decisions of the European Court of Human Rights (ECtHR) in relation to Article 8, which states that 'Everyone has the right to respect for his private and family life, his home and his correspondence':[40]

> Since 'family' can mean different things in different places and at different times, the Charter refers to the definitions used in national law. No distinction is made between the various models of family and, in keeping with the case law of the European Court of Human Rights in relation to Article 8 of the Convention; the scope of Article 16 is not restricted to family based on marriage. Consequently, every constellation defined as 'family' by national law falls under the protection of Article 16. States enjoy a margin of appreciation to choose the means in their endeavour to ensure the social, legal and economic protection of the various types of families that can be found in the population.[41]

Thus, some 39[42] ratifying states have accepted the obligations of ensuring that existing and new housing for families must be of an adequate standard under the Articles 16 and 31 of the Charter, and this definition has wider implications than just the standard of the dwelling. It is important to examine how the ECSR has treated this definition in detail to clarify the obligations of these 39 states.[43] For example, in *Autism-Europe v France*, the ECSR stated that:

> The Committee recalls, as stated in its decision relative to Complaint No.1/1998 (*International Commission of Jurist v. Portugal*, § 32), that the implementation of the Charter requires the State Parties to take not merely legal action but also practical action to give full effect to the rights recognised in the Charter. When the achievement of one of the rights in question is exceptionally complex and particularly expensive to resolve, a State Party must take measures that

40 The ECtHR has interpreted family as including those with close family ties, although there is no pre-determined model of a family or family life. It includes any stable relationship, be it married, unmarried, engaged or de facto, between parents and children, same-sex couples, siblings, grandparents and grandchildren. See *Schalk and Kopf v Austria* (Application No 31041/04), Judgment 24 June 2010, where the ECtHR held that a same-sex couple living in a stable de facto relationship fell within the notion of 'family life'. See also *Kozak v Poland* (Application No 13102/02), Judgment 2 March 2010; *Keegan v Ireland* (1994) 18 EHRR 342; *Marckx v Belgium* (1979) 2 EHRR 330. In *Kroon and others v The Netherlands* (Application No 18535/91), Judgment 27 October 1994, the ECtHR held that the notion of 'family life' in art 8 was not solely confined to marriage-based relationships and might encompass other de facto 'family ties', such as where parties are living together outside marriage.

41 Conclusions 2006, Statement of Interpretation on Article 16, 13.

42 28 countries ratified Article 16 of RESC and 10 countries ratified Article 16 of ESC and 1 country (Andorra) didn't ratified Article 16, but ratified Article 31.

43 See *Digest of the Case Law of the European Committee of Social Rights*, Council of Europe (September 2008). Conclusions of the ECSR are available at: http://hudoc.esc.coe.int/esc2008/query.asp?language=en accessed 3 March 2013.

> allow it to achieve the objectives of the Charter within a reasonable time, with measurable progress and to an extent consistent with the maximum use of available resources. States Parties must be particularly mindful of the impact that their choices will have for groups with heightened vulnerabilities as well as for others persons affected including, especially, their families on whom falls the heaviest burden in the event of institutional shortcomings.[44]

In *Autism Europe v France*, the ECSR established that the measures taken to implement the Charter Articles must meet three criteria: (i) a reasonable timeframe; (ii) a measurable progress; and (iii) a financing consistent with the maximum use of available resources.[45] In *FEANTSA v France*, the ECSR pointed out that the implementation of the rights to housing must be monitored as well as their impact. Reasonable deadlines must be set and Article 31 must be considered in the light of other international housing rights instruments such as the International Covenant on Economic, Social and Cultural Rights (ICECSR) and the ECHR as well, particularly Article 8[46]:

> The Committee notes that in several areas the Government fails to supply relevant statistical information or does not compare identified needs with the resources made available and results achieved. Regular checks do not appear to be carried out on the effectiveness of the policies applied. In the absence of any commitment to or means of measuring the practical impact of measures taken, the rights specified in the Charter are likely to remain ineffective. In connection with timetabling – with which other regulatory bodies of international instruments are also very concerned – it is essential for reasonable deadlines to be set that take account not only of administrative constraints but also of the needs of groups that fall into the urgent category. At all events, achievement of the goals that the authorities have set themselves cannot be deferred indefinitely. The authorities must also pay particular attention to the impact of their policy choices on the most vulnerable groups, in this case individuals and families suffering exclusion and poverty (*Autisme Europe v France*, Complaint No 13/2002, decision on the merits of 4 November 2003, §53).
> *On the interpretation of Article 31 in the light of other international instruments*
> The Committee considers that Article 31 must be considered in the light of relevant international instruments that served as inspiration for its authors or in conjunction with which it needs to be applied.[47]

---

44 Complaint No 13/2002 *Autism-Europe v France* [53].

45 ibid.

46 Complaint No. 33/2006 (paras. 68–69): 'The Committee is particularly concerned that its interpretation of Article 31 is fully in line with the European Court of Human Rights' interpretation of the relevant provisions of the Convention'.

47 Complaint No 39/2006 *FEANTSA v France* [61]–[64].

Again, in *FEANTSA v France*, the ECSR also pointed out that the obligation of states in realizing the rights in the Charter must be practical and effective:

> The Committee agrees that the actual wording of Article 31 of the Charter cannot be interpreted as imposing on states an obligation of 'results'. However, it notes that the rights recognised in the Social Charter must take a practical and effective, rather than purely theoretical, form (*International Commission of Jurists v Portugal*, Complaint No. 1/1998, decision on the merits of 9 September 1999, §32). This means that, for the situation to be compatible with the treaty, states party must:
> a. adopt the necessary legal, financial and operational means of ensuring steady progress towards achieving the goals laid down by the Charter;
> b. maintain meaningful statistics on needs, resources and results;
> c. undertake regular reviews of the impact of the strategies adopted;
> d. establish a timetable and not defer indefinitely the deadline for achieving the objectives of each stage;
> e. pay close attention to the impact of the policies adopted on each of the categories of persons concerned, particularly the most vulnerable.[48]

The ECSR has set out detailed housing obligations arising from the Charter in relation to the definition and scope of the term 'adequacy' of housing.

Definition and Material Scope

States must guarantee to everyone the right to adequate housing.[49] They should promote access to housing in particular to the different groups of vulnerable persons, such as low-income persons, unemployed persons, single-parent households, young persons and persons with disabilities, including those with mental health problems.[50]

The definition of adequate housing must be applied not only to new constructions, but also gradually to the existing housing stock. It must also be applied to housing available for rent as well as to owner-occupied housing.[51]

---

48 ibid [55]–[56].

49 Conclusions 2003, France, 221. Of course, this does not require that states directly provide housing for all. However, states must ensure that there is a sufficient supply of adequate and affordable housing to meet the varying needs. Sufficient social housing or housing allowances must be provided for those unable to access adequate and affordable housing in the purchase or rental markets. See M Mikkola, *Social Human Rights in Europe* (Helsinki, Legisactio Oy 2010) 348.

50 Conclusions 2003, Italy, 342.

51 Conclusions 2003, France, 221; *FEANTSA v France* (n 29) [77].

Habitability and Standards

In *ERRC v Italy*,[52] the ECSR emphasized the obligations of adequacy under Article 31(1), which means a dwelling that is structurally secure, safe from a sanitary and health perspective (i.e. possesses all basic amenities, such as water, heating, waste disposal, sanitation facilities and electricity), not overcrowded and with secure tenure supported by law. There are overlaps here with the minimum standards established under the Articles 2, 3 and 8 of the European Convention on Human Rights, where the protection of life, prevention of inhuman and degrading treatment, and respect for home and family life have established minimalist benchmarks.[53]

The notion of 'adequate housing' must be defined in law. It means:

> 1. a dwelling which is safe from a sanitary and health point of view, i.e. that possesses all basic amenities, such as water, heating, waste disposal, sanitation facilities, electricity, etc and where specific dangers such as the presence of lead or asbestos are under control;[54]
> 2. a dwelling which is not over-crowded, that the size of the dwelling must be suitable in light of the number of persons and the composition of the household in residence;
> 3. a dwelling with secure tenure supported by the law. This issue is covered by Article 31§2.[55]

In *FEANTSA v France*, the ECSR pointed out that it attaches great importance to General Comments 4 and 7 of the UN Committee on Economic, Social and Cultural Rights.[56] Thus, the obligations established under the General Comments (outlined above) will apply to the evaluation of compliance with Article 31 and Article 16 of the Charter.

Suitability

Suitability is often related to size, surroundings, size, location, etc., as well as cultural factors, and the standards of General Comment 4 will be applicable. The

---

52 Complaint No 27/2004 *European Roma Rights Centre (ERRC) v Italy*.

53 See, for example, *Öneryıldız v Turkey* (2004) 39 EHRR 12; *Moldovan v Romania* (2005) 44 EHRR 16; *Lopez Ostra v Spain* (1991) 14 EHRR 319; *Geurra v Italy* (1998) EHRR 357; *Moreno-Gomez v Spain* (2005) 41 EHRR 40.

54 In 2007 the ECSR requested further information from Italy on levels of asbestos: 'In order to decide whether the situation is in conformity with the Revised Charter, the Committee asks for detailed information in the next report on the measures taken as well as their effectiveness. It also reiterates its request for information on the control of exposure to lead and asbestos.' See Conclusions 2007, Italy, Vol 2.

55 Conclusions 2003, France, 221.

56 *FEANTSA v France* (n 29) [67].

Committee emphasized cultural adequacy in the Complaint No. 61/2010 (paras. 49-50): 'The Committee held that social housing offered to Roma should be, as far as possible, culturally suited to them. Re-housing of Roma families in apartment blocks has often prevented family and casual gatherings, given that their means of existence as a community and bonds of solidarity are broken. Moreover, they are also faced with hostile attitudes of neighbours in apartment blocks'.

Effectiveness and Enforcement

It is incumbent on the public authorities to ensure that housing is adequate through different measures such as, in particular, an inventory of the housing stock, injunctions against owners who disregard obligations, urban development rules and maintenance obligations for landlords. Public authorities must also act to limit the interruption of essential services such as water, electricity and telecommunications.[57]

Even if under domestic law, local or regional authorities, trade unions or professional organizations are responsible for exercising a particular function, States Parties to the Charter are responsible, under their international obligations, to ensure that such responsibilities are properly exercised. Thus, ultimate responsibility for policy implementation, involving at a minimum the supervision and regulation of local action, lies with the government, which must be able to show that both local authorities and itself have taken practical steps to ensure that local action is effective.[58] Indeed, in *COHRE v Croatia*,[59] it was stated that:

> In respect of the adequacy of the housing and tenure provided to families who have returned or wish to return to Croatia, the Committee holds that the complainant organisation has not produced sufficient evidence to establish that the quality of housing provided under the housing programme does not fulfil Article 16.

In every European country, there is a building regulatory system encompassing the building regulations and the building control system. Building regulations set minimum quality requirements to ensure that buildings are safe, healthy, energy-efficient and accessible to everyone who lives and works in and around them. Building control aims to guarantee the application and enforcement of these minimum requirements. The purpose and the subjects covered by the building regulations are identical in EU Member States. However, there are many differences

57 Conclusions 2003, France, 224.

58 *ERRC v Italy* (n 34) [26]; *FEANTSA v France* (n 33) [79].

59 Complaint No 52/2008 *COHRE v Croatia*, Decision on the Merits, 22 June 2010 [76]. This Complaint under Article 16 related to the failure to provide adequate restitution or compensation to ethnic Serbs who were arbitrarily expelled from their homes during the conflict in former Yugoslavia.

between countries regarding who sets the building regulations, how the technical building regulations are organized and formulated, what the role of national standards comprises and how building regulations apply to existing buildings.[60]

The effectiveness of the right to adequate housing requires its legal protection through adequate procedural safeguards. Occupiers must have access to affordable and impartial legal and non-legal remedies.[61] Any appeal procedure must be effective.[62] The ECSR held that insufficient progress as regards the eradication of substandard housing and the lack of proper amenities of a large number of households constitutes a violation of Article 31(1) of the RESC.[63]

Temporary Accommodation

The adequacy of emergency housing or shelters has also been examined by the ECSR. In *ERRC v Bulgaria*, the ECSR again emphasized that the temporary supply of shelter cannot be considered as adequate and that individuals should be provided with adequate housing within a reasonable period.[64] In *France v FEANTSA*, the ESCR held that:

> As regards living conditions in sheltering facilities, the Committee believes these should be such as to enable living in keeping with human dignity, and that support should be routinely offered to help the persons within the facilities to attain the greatest possible degree of independence. It also recalls that the temporary provision of accommodation, even decent accommodation, cannot be considered a satisfactory solution, and people living under such conditions must be offered housing of an adequate standard within a reasonable time.[65]

The ECSR considered that it would be positive if the conversion of homeless shelters into around-the-clock structures became a general practice, and that any offer of accommodation in them should lead in the short or medium term to an independent housing solution.[66]

---

60 See JB Pedro, F Meijer and H Visscher, 'Comparison of Tasks and Responsibilities in the Building Control Systems of European Union Countries' in *Proceedings of COBRA 2008* (London, RICS 2008) 1339–55; F Meijer, H Visscher and L Sheridan, *Building Regulations in Europe, Parts I & 2: A Comparison of the Systems of Building Control in Eight European Countries* (Delft, Delft University Press 2002).

61 Conclusions 2003, France, 224.

62 *FEANTSA v France* (n 29) [80]–[81].

63 ibid [81].

64 ibid [34].

65 ibid [108].

66 ibid [109].

A Functional Overlap between the Articles

The ECSR has, during the Collective Complaints procedure, consistently set out that the overlap between provisions of the RESC is a key functional aspect of the Charter. In practice the ECSR will interpret ESC rights separately from one another, and non-ratification of one ESC right will not prevent related obligations arising under another right. In *FIDH v Belgium*,[67] the Belgian government, during the submissions on the merits, directly challenged this principle of overlap with regard to Articles 16 and 31 of the RESC.

As such, the operation of this overlap has been cast in the spotlight. In *Mental Disability Advocacy Centre (MDAC) v Bulgaria*,[68] a complaint was registered which related to Article 17(2) (the right of children and young persons to social, legal and economic protection) and Article E (non-discrimination) of the RESC. It was alleged that children living in homes for mentally disabled children in Bulgaria received no education. The government argued that the case related to Article 15(1) of the RESC, since it covered the right of persons with disabilities, an article that Bulgaria had not accepted, but not the right of children and young people to social, legal and economic protection provided for by Article 17(2), as the MDAC maintained. The ECSR addressed the argument that the complaint was founded on a provision which the government had not accepted, i.e. Article 15, by setting out that:

> The Charter was conceived as a whole and all its provisions complement each other and overlap in part. It is impossible to draw watertight divisions between the material scope of each article or paragraph. It therefore falls to the Committee to ensure at the same time that obligations are not imposed on States stemming from provisions they did not intend to accept and that the essential core of accepted provisions is not amputated as a result of the fact it may contain obligations which may also result from unaccepted provisions.[69]

From *MDAC v Bulgaria*, it is quite clear that an overlap exists between provisions of the RESC and that the Committee has discretion over the parameters of this

---

67 Complaint No 62/2010 *International Federation of Human Rights (FIDH) v Belgium*.

68 Complaint No 41/2007 *Mental Disability Advocacy Center (MDAC) v Bulgaria*.

69 See ibid, decision on admissibility, 27 June 2007, §9, where the Committee of Social Ministers set out that: 'The Charter was conceived as a whole and all its provisions complement each other and overlap in part. It is impossible to draw watertight divisions between the material scope of each article or paragraph. It therefore falls to the Committee to ensure at the same time that obligations are not imposed on States stemming from provisions they did not intend to accept and that the essential core of accepted provisions is not amputated as a result of the fact it may contain obligations which may also result from unaccepted provisions.'

overlap. The ECSR administers this discretion in the light of competing concerns of granting efficacy to the provisions of the Charter while also ensuring that the legitimacy of the Charter is not harmed in the process. In light of the progressive nature of the Collective Complaints procedure, this overlap can present significant challenges for the ECSR.[70] However, in this respect, the ECSR must administer the discretion identified in *MDAC v Bulgaria* with care. The danger is that an unprincipled discretion in considering the overlap between provisions of the Charter would serve to delegitimize the Charter, as obligations could be imposed on states from provisions which they had no intention of accepting and could reduce respect for economic and social rights. The fundamental challenge for the ECSR is maintaining the legitimacy of the Charter in a dynamic and progressive legal environment.

International Federation of Human Rights (FIDH) v Belgium

The extent of the overlap between Articles 16 and 31 was recently contested in *FIDH v Belgium.*[71]. This complaint concerned an alleged violation of rights related to housing for travellers under the Charter. In particular, issues concerning the insufficiency of stopping places, non-recognition of caravans as a home, lack of respect for the required conditions when carrying out evictions, lack of a global and coordinated policy to combat the poverty and social exclusion of travellers, among other issues. The complaint concerned Article 16 and Article 30 of the RESC as well Article E, the non-discrimination clause.

The overlap between Article 16 and Article 31 regarding the right to housing was central to the complaint. While the Belgian government accepted the overlap as was set out in the *ERRC v Greece* complaint, it challenged the parameters of this overlap. In particular, it challenged the assertion that the *ERRC v France* complaint must also apply to Belgium.

---

70 See P Alston, *Assessing the Strengths and Weaknesses of the European Charter's Supervisory System*, Center for Human Rights and Global Justice, Working Paper, Economic, Social and Cultural Rights Series (NYU School of Law, No 6, 2005), 4–5, where it was noted 'the bottom line, however, is that the collective complaints system represents an important development in the procedure and one which has the potential to transform the effectiveness of the ESC system as a whole. Because the procedure also has the potential to convince governments that complaints systems in relation to these rights represent a step too far, it is important for the ECSR to tread carefully and to ensure that its case law is strongly reasoned and consistent.'

71 Complaint No. 62/2010.

In *ERRC v France*, a breach of Article 30[72] was established via a breach of Article 31.[73] The Belgian government went on to submit that 'this makes it clear that the violation of Article 30 is the result of the finding of a violation of Article 31 of the Charter. Such a reasoning can in no way apply to Belgium, as the FIDH maintains, for the simple reason that Belgium has not ratified Article 31 of the Charter'. At the admissibility stage, the ECSR drew attention to the decision in *MDAC v Bulgaria* and at the merits stage the Committee re-affirmed the principle of overlap.[74] The Belgian government's argument – that complaints detailing violations of Article 30 arising from Article 31 do not transfer to a complaint alleging a breach of Article 30 due to a breach in Article 16 where the respondent state has not accepted or ratified Article 31 – lay down a direct challenge to the ECSR's discretion regarding the overlap between provisions of the Charter.

In order to address this argument, it is necessary to begin by noting that the concept of adequate housing was central to the *ERRC v France* complaint. From *ERRC v Greece*, it is clear that concepts of adequate housing are the same under Article 31 as Article 16. Therefore, a breach of Article 30 arising from inadequate housing cannot be limited to subsequent complaints relating to Article 16 or Article 31. As such, the rationale of the Belgian government's argument is at variance with the principle of overlap as outlined in *ERRC v Greece*.

The fact that Belgium was caught by obligations arising from provisions which it had not expressly accepted could at first glance risk delegitimizing the Charter. However as set out above, this is not the case. Rather the ECSR will interpret ESC rights separately from one another, and non-ratification of one ESC right will not prevent related obligations arising under another right.. The link between housing as between Articles 16, 31 and 30 arises at first instance in the common wording set out in those provisions, i.e. housing is expressly set out in the three articles. In the decision on the merits, delivered in 2012, the Committee found the Belgium to have violated the right to housing and in doing so reaffirmed the principle of overlap between Articles 16 and 31.[75]

72 Article 30 of the RESC: 'With a view to ensuring the effective exercise of the right to protection against poverty and social exclusion, the Parties undertake: (a) to take measures within the framework of an overall and co-ordinated approach to promote the effective access of persons who live or risk living in a situation of social exclusion or poverty, as well as their families, to, in particular, employment, housing, training, education, culture and social and medical assistance; (b) to review these measures with a view to their adaptation if necessary.'

73 See *ERRC v France* (n 49). With regard to the alleged violation of art 30 of the Revised Charter, para 95 reads: 'The Committee considers that it is clear from its conclusions under Article 31 that the housing policy for Travellers is inadequate. It accordingly finds that France has failed to adopt a co-ordinated approach to promoting effective access to housing for persons who live or risk living in a situation of social exclusion'.

74 Complaint No 62/2010, paras 43–46.

75 Complaint No. 62/2010, [44–47].

Potential Future Developments on this Treatment of Overlapping Rights

The overlap between Articles 16 and 31 of the RESC has allowed for the cross-article transfer of key concepts, including the definition of adequate housing. This interaction is indicative of a more general principle of overlap which is a key functional aspect of the RESC. The cross-article transfer arising from this functional overlap presents interesting possibilities when cast against the progressive and dynamic nature of the Collective Complaints procedure. In particular, the relationship between the right to housing as stated in Articles 31 and 16, and the wider right to protection against poverty and social exclusion enshrined in Article 30 may present opportunities for examining the concept of adequate housing through the prism of social inclusion and participation.

With respect to Article 30, the Committee has set out 'that governments must adopt an overall and coordinated approach, which must comprise an analytical framework, and take measures promoting access to social rights, in particular employment, housing, training, education, culture and social and medical assistance for persons in, or at risk of finding themselves in, a situation of poverty or social exclusion'. As such, in characterizing the signatory states' obligations under Article 30, the Committee have consistently set out that Article 30 has a direct link with the right to housing.[76] In *ERRC v France*, it endorsed an inclusivity-centric interpretation of Article 30 after setting out that living in a situation of social exclusion violates the dignity of human beings.[77] It further advocated monitoring mechanisms involving all relevant actors, including civil society and persons affected by exclusion.[78]

Indeed, the right to adequate housing is interdependent with other human rights. The UN Committee on Economic, Social and Cultural Rights has set out that the right to participate in public decision-making is indispensible if the right to adequate housing is to be realized and maintained by all groups in society.[79] Indeed, the right to participate has been cast as intrinsically linked with human dignity. In practice, participation is a multifaceted concept. Arnstein has identified that there are significant gradations of citizen participation ranging from citizen

76 Conclusions 2009, art 30, Italy, 37.

77 *ERRC v France* (n 49) [93].

78 'With a view to ensuring the effective exercise of the right to protection against social exclusion, Article 30 requires States Parties to adopt an overall and co-ordinated approach, which should consist of an analytical framework, a set of priorities and measures to prevent and remove obstacles to access to fundamental rights. There should also be monitoring mechanisms involving all relevant actors, including civil society and persons affected by exclusion. This approach must link and integrate policies in a consistent way': Conclusions 2003, art 30, France, 214.

79 'The right to adequate housing cannot be viewed in isolation from other human rights … the right to participate in public decision-making – is indispensable if the right to adequate housing is to be realized and maintained by all groups in society': UN Committee on Economic, Social and Cultural Rights, General Comment No 4.

power, which includes citizen control, delegated power and participation, to tokenism, which includes placation, consultation and informing, and non-participation, which includes therapy and manipulation.[80] While meaningful participation can break a deadlock, leading to better policy and implementation decisions and fostering education for all involved, it has also been argued that ill-conceived participation models can be time-consuming and costly and can actually lead to worse policy decisions.[81] It is the dynamic nature of the Collective Complaint mechanism, allowing advocates to frame the parameters of the dispute, which presents the avenue for novel arguments concerning the indivisibility of human rights to be put before the ESC. However, advocates must bear in mind that this is not a general overlap rather in practice the ECSR will interpret ESC rights separately from one another, and non-ratification of one ESC right will not prevent related obligations arising under another right.

Housing Rights in the EU: The Charter of Fundamental Rights

While the 1957 Treaty of Rome and subsequent EU treaties do not specifically refer to housing at all, much EU social policy, particularly the drive toward a single market in goods and services, environmental sustainability and the standardization of products, has a bearing on housing rights and housing policy. Following from freedom of movement, equality and citizenship treaty and regulation provisions, individuals have been able to rely on their status as 'citizens of the Union' to obtain access to social benefits in other Member States, such as minimum subsistence and maternity benefits.[82] Unfair contract terms in housing contracts are prohibited across Europe under the 1993 Unfair Terms in Consumer Contracts Directive.[83]

---

80 Sherry R Arnstein, 'A Ladder of Citizen Participation' (1969) 35(4) Journal of the American Institute of Planners 216–24. Arnstein also identifies significant challenges regarding achieving genuine levels of participation; these include racism, paternalism and resistance to power re-distribution. Further difficulties relate to the: 'Inadequacies of the poor community's political socio-economic infrastructure and knowledge base, plus difficulties of organising a representative and accountable citizens' group in the face of futility, alienation, and distrust'.

81 RA Irvin and J Stansbury, 'Citizen Participation in Decision Making: Is it Worth the Effort?' (2004) 64(1) Public Administration Review 55. See also R Hearne, *Public Private Partnerships in Ireland* (Manchester, Manchester University Press 2011).

82 Case C-184/99 *Rudy Grzelcyck v Centre public d'aide sociale d'Ottignies-Louvain-la-Neuve* [2001] ECR I-6193; Case C-85/96 *Martinez-Sala* [1998] ECR I-2681; Case C-274/96 *Bickel and Franz* [1998] ECR I-7637. See further H de Waele, 'EU Citizenship: Revisiting its Meaning, Place and Potential' (2010) 12 *European Journal of Migration and Law* 319–36.

83 See Report from the Commission on the Implementation of Council Directive 93/13/EEC of 5 April 1993 on Unfair Terms in Consumer Contracts, COM (2000) 248 final (27 April 2000).

Since the Maastricht Treaty, subsequent EU treaties have referred to the jurisprudence of the ECHR, although in reality, with its minimalist standards, this correlates with a very low 'floor' for housing rights. Article 19 of the Treaty on European Union (TFEU) reiterates that the EU has competence to legislate to combat discrimination on grounds of sex, race or ethnic origin, religion belief, disability, age or sexual orientation.[84] Articles 151 and 153 of the TFEU commit the EU to combat social exclusion, but not through harmonized legislative measures. Yet, as Craig and De Búrca point out:

> Despite the declaration that in Article 2 that the EU is founded on, inter alia, the value of respect for human rights, and the stipulation in Article 3 that the EU's aim is to promote its values, the EU still requires specific competence under a provision of the Treaties if it is to take concrete action. The Treaties still do not provide the EU with 'any general power to enact rules on human rights'.[85]

In the 1990s, to avoid a 'race to the bottom' or competition between states to lower wages and taxes, and in the absence of EU institutional competence (outside labour legislation) to introduce minimum standards in areas of social policy, the EU developed an alternative approach based on 'fundamental social rights'.[86] This culminated in the EU Charter of Fundamental Rights (EUCFR), adopted at Nice in 2000, but not as enforceable law. However, the Charter of Fundamental Rights of the European Union has now been incorporated into the Treaty of Lisbon[87] and enjoys full legislative force within the Treaty of Lisbon under Article 6:[88]

> 1. The Union recognises the rights, freedoms and principles set out in the Charter of Fundamental Rights of the European Union of 7 December 2000, as adapted at Strasbourg, on 12 December 2007, which shall have the same legal value as the Treaties.
> The provisions of the Charter shall not extend in any way the competences of the Union as defined in the Treaties.
> The rights, freedoms and principles in the Charter shall be interpreted in accordance with the general provisions in Title VII of the Charter governing its

---

84 OJ C83/01, 2010.

85 P Craig and G De Búrca, *EU Law: Cases and Materials* (5th edn, Oxford, OUP 2011) 392.

86 See TK Hervey and J Kenner (eds), *Economic and Social Rights under the Charter of Fundamental Rights of the European Union* (Oxford, Hart Publishing 2003).

87 Charter of Fundamental Rights of the European Union [2010] OJ C83/02. See also Consolidated Versions of the Treaty on European Union and the Treaty on the Functioning of the European Union Charter of Fundamental Rights of the European Union [2010] OJ C83/13, 30 March.

88 Poland and the UK originally opted out of the Charter, but Poland has made some newer arrangements.

> interpretation and application and with due regard to the explanations referred to in the Charter, that set out the sources of those provisions.
> 2. The Union shall accede to the European Convention for the Protection of Human Rights and Fundamental Freedoms. Such accession shall not affect the Union's competences as defined in the Treaties.
> 3. Fundamental rights, as guaranteed by the European Convention for the Protection of Human Rights and Fundamental Freedoms and as they result from the constitutional traditions common to the Member States, shall constitute general principles of the Union's law.

Article 51(1) of the Charter stipulates that:

> the provisions of this Charter are addressed to the institutions, bodies, offices and agencies of the Union with due regard for the principle of subsidiarity and to the Member States only when they are implementing Union law. They shall therefore respect the rights, observe the principles and promote the application thereof in accordance with their respective powers and respecting the limits of the powers of the Union as conferred on it in the Treaties.

While there is not a specific right to housing in the Charter, Article 34(3) on social security and social assistance states:

> In order to combat social exclusion and poverty, the Union recognises and respects the right to social and housing assistance so as to ensure a decent existence for all those who lack sufficient resources, in accordance with the rules laid down by Union law and national laws and practices.[89]

The wording of Article 34(3) of the Charter is distinctive, in that it states that a specific *right* to social and housing assistance is *recognized and respected*.[90] Contrast this with Article 34(1) in relation to social security, which merely states that the EU recognizes and respects the *entitlement* to social security benefits and social services providing protection in cases involving maternity, illness, industrial accidents, dependency or old age.[91]

---

89 Charter of Fundamental Rights of the European Union (n 89) art 34(3).

90 De Waele points out that art 34(2) is of stellar importance as it proclaims that 'everyone residing and moving legally within the European Union is entitled to social security benefits and social advantages in accordance with Union law and national laws and practices'. He points out that 'Everyone, i.e. excluding none – Pandora's box might never appear more open, and it seems incredible that the Member States managed to agree on the inclusion of this phrase'. See de Waele (n 84) 319, 333.

91 See J Tooze, 'Social Security and Social Assistance', in Hervey and Kenner (n 88).

The Explanations to the Charter[92]

There is considerable guidance on the interpretation of each Charter article to be given by the courts and EU Member States. Article 52(7) of the Charter states that:

> The explanations drawn up as a way of providing guidance in the interpretation of this Charter shall be given due regard by the courts of the Union and of the Member States.[93]

These explanations state that paragraph 34(3) of the Charter:

> draws on Article 13 of the European Social Charter and Articles 30 and 31 of the revised Social Charter and point 10 of the Community Charter. The Union must respect it in the context of policies based on Article 153 of the Treaty on the Functioning of the European Union.[94]

Thus, the interpretation of the content of Article 34(3) can be drawn from the jurisprudence of the ECSR, which evaluates and clarifies the obligations contained in Articles 30 and 31 of the RESC.[95] The ECSR has held that Article 30 requires States Parties to adopt an overall and coordinated approach, which should consist of an analytical framework, a set of priorities and measures to prevent and remove obstacles to access fundamental social rights. There should also be monitoring mechanisms involving all relevant actors, including civil society and persons affected by poverty and exclusion.[96]

In relation to Article 31, the ECSR pointed out in *FEANTSA v France* that the obligation of states in realizing the housing rights must be practical and effective.

---

92 Article 52(7) of the Charter states that: 'The explanations drawn up as a way of providing guidance in the interpretation of this Charter shall be given due regard by the courts of the Union and of the Member States.' These explanations relating to the Charter of Fundamental Rights ([2007] OJ C303/02) have been updated under the responsibility of the Praesidium of the European Convention, in the light of the drafting adjustments made to the text of the Charter by that Convention (notably to arts 51 and 52) and of further developments of EU law. However: 'Although they do not as such have the status of law, they are a valuable tool of interpretation intended to clarify the provisions of the Charter.'

93 Explanations relating to the Charter of Fundamental Rights ([2007] OJ C303/02).

94 Indeed, most of the articles of the Charter are worded identically or are clearly based on rights set out in other instruments, such as the ECHR, and the explanations specifically refer to the direct connection, and the corresponding wealth of jurisprudence already developed through the originating article.

95 For a consideration of the obligations on states in relation to the European Social Charter and the Revised Charter, see http://www.coe.int/t/dghl/monitoring/socialcharter/ecsr/ecsrdefault_EN.asp accessed 4 March 2013. See also Mikkola (n 31).

96 Statement of Interpretation on Article 30; see in particular ECSR Conclusions 2003, France, 214. See ECSR (2008) Digest of Case Law 167–69.

In *ERRC v Italy*, the ECSR emphasized the obligations of adequacy under Article 31(1). In *ERRC v Bulgaria*, the ECSR again emphasized that the temporary supply of shelter cannot be considered as adequate and that individuals should be provided with adequate housing within a reasonable period.[97]

The explanations relating to Article 34(3) also state that the EU must respect the EUCFR in the context of social inclusion policies based on Article 153 of the TFEU. Thus, the framing and adoption of social inclusion policies, many of which are prepared jointly between EU agencies and Member States, should contain details of how the right to social and housing assistance as set out in the Charter is being addressed.

Although Article 34(3) may not lead to regulations and directives on social and housing assistance, the institutions and agencies of the EU, as well as the Member States 'implementing' EU law, must recognize and respect the rights contained therein, clarification for which is available from the jurisprudence of the ECSR. It is also clear that the housing-related jurisprudence of the ECtHR and the ECSR will become an integral element of the interpretation of state obligations under the EUCFR when they are implementing EU law.[98] Yet, it may be in the arbitrage between EU law provisions and national laws which contain an element of EU law that the hitherto hidden power of the Charter will emerge. While Article 51(2) of the Charter states that it does not extend the field of application of EU law, there are a host of areas (e.g. consumer protection and financial regulation) where EU law applies and which affect housing rights. Indeed, the institutions, bodies, offices and agencies[99] of the EU include, among others, the European Central Bank and the European Commission,[100] which are regularly putting forward measures which impact on housing and housing rights.

A range of measures have been undertaken by the Commission to ensure that the EU as a body complies with Charter obligations. The Strategy for the effective implementation of the Charter by the Commission[101] states that there is

---

97 *ERRC v Bulgaria* (n 20) [34].

98 See *Housing Rights: The Duty to Ensure Housing for All* (n 9).

99 See Regulation (EC) No 58/2003 of 19 December 2002 laying down the statute for executive agencies to be entrusted with certain tasks in the management of Community programmes.

100 For details of EU institutions and agencies, see http://europa.eu/institutions/index_en.htm accessed 31 July 2013.

101 See Communication from the Commission, Strategy for the effective implementation of the Charter of Fundamental Rights by the European Union, COM (2010) Final, Brussels, 19 October 2010. See also Communication from the Commission Impact Assessment Guidelines, SEC(2009) 92 of 15 January 2009; Report on the practical operation of the methodology for a systematic and rigorous monitoring of compliance with the Charter of fundamental rights, COM(2009) 205 Final of 29 April 2009; Report of the European Parliament Committee on Civil Liberties, Justice and Home Affairs, on the situation of fundamental rights in the European Union (2009) – effective implementation after the entry into force of the Treaty of Lisbon (2009/2161(INI)), A7-0344/2010; Council

now a member of the Commission with specific responsibility for the promotion of justice, fundamental rights and citizenship, and the members of the European Commission promised, in a solemn undertaking before the Court of Justice, to uphold the Charter. The Strategy also states:

> The objective of the Commission's policy following the entry into force of the Lisbon Treaty is to make the fundamental rights provided for in the Charter as effective as possible. The Union must be exemplary in this respect. The Charter is not a text setting out abstract values, it is an instrument to enable people to enjoy the rights enshrined within it when they are in a situation governed by Union law. This is why the Commission will focus its efforts on the effective implementation of the Charter.[102]

The Commission routinely checks its legislative proposals and the acts it adopts to ensure that they are compatible with the Charter. The Strategy states that fundamental rights may, under certain conditions, be subject to limitations, but these must be provided for in law, respect the essence of the said rights, observe the principle of proportionality, be necessary and effectively meet objectives.[103] A fundamental rights checklist is used by the Commission, as set out in the Strategy.[104]

The Commission Report on the Application of the EU Charter of Fundamental Rights (2010)[105] states that there is an urgent need to better inform people as to when the rights of the Charter apply and on 'how to enforce them in practice if they are violated'. Indeed, the Report states that the Commission has the power to start infringement proceedings against a Member State which violates the Charter in implementing EU law. It states that: 'The individual can also complain to the Commission, which has the power to start infringement proceedings against a Member State which violates the Charter in implementing EU law.'[106]

In any case, the Charter has already impacted on EU law in a number of significant cases, such as *Test-Achats ASBL v Belgium*,[107] where the European Court of Justice invalidated Article 5(2) of EU Directive 2004/113/EC of 13 December 2004 implementing the principle of equal treatment between women and men in the access to and supply of goods and services, on the grounds of its incompatibility with the EUCFR. Thus, it is clear that any provision of EU law can

of the European Union, Draft Council conclusions on the role of the Council of the European Union in ensuring the effective implementation of the Charter of Fundamental Rights of the European Union, 6387/11, Brussels, 11 February 2011.

102 COM (2010) Final, Brussels, 19 October 2010, 3.

103 ibid 4.

104 ibid 5.

105 COM (2011) 160 Final, Brussels, 30 March 2011.

106 ibid 7.

107 Case C-236/09 *Test-Achats ASBL v Belgium* (March 2011).

be held to be invalid if it breaches any of the rights in the EUCFR, such as the right to social and housing assistance so as to ensure a decent existence.

Conclusion

It is a time of great potential for housing rights advocates in Europe – or perhaps there will two Europes. One set of 28 EU Member States will rely on the EUCFR, while these and a further 20 states will base their housing rights on the Council of Europe. As we have seen, there is significant development of the jurisprudence within the Council of Europe and the potential for direct complaints to the monitoring body – the ECSR will enhance its effectiveness. Clearly, at the EU level, the EUCFR with its 'right to social and housing assistance so as to ensure a decent existence for all those who lack sufficient resources'[108] is poised to become a key influence in the balance of power between the competing free market or social Europe ideologies. Of course, the interactivity between the jurisprudence of the ECSR and the interpretation of Article 34(3) of the EUCFR gives an added impetus to the development and interpretation of housing rights. However, many housing advocates in Europe have yet to embrace these approaches through test cases and references to the Court of Justice of the European Union. In any case, the housing rights embedded within EU law will emerge in a variety of cases, and perhaps in ways which we may not yet have envisaged.

108 Charter of Fundamental Rights of the European Union [2010] OJ C83/02, art 34(3).

Chapter 6

Housing Rights in Constitutional Legislation: A Conceptual Classification

Michelle Oren, Rachelle Alterman and Yaffa Zilbershats

Introduction

Housing rights are conditions granted by statutes, or entitlements by law, that rest on the understanding of a need for housing. They imply certain duties and obligations either taken by the state or other entities and individuals.[1] Much has been written about housing rights in the international human rights context.[2] However, little comparative work has been published at the national level, particularly in relation to any classification or categorization of the status of housing rights in national constitutions.[3]

At the international level, housing rights are embedded in the Universal Declaration of Human Rights[4] at Article 25(1) and in the International Covenant

1 Peter King, 'Housing as a Freedom Right' (2003) 18(5) Housing Studies 661.

2 Scott Leckie, *From Human Needs to Housing Rights: An Analysis of the Right to Adequate Housing Under International Human Rights Law* (London, International Institute for Environment and Development 1992); Scott Leckie, 'The Justiciability of Housing Rights' in Fons Coomans and Fried van Hoof (eds.), *The Right to Complain about Economic, Social and Cultural Rights: Proceedings of the Expert Meeting on the Adoption of an Optional Protocol to the International Covenant on Economic, Social and Cultural Rights* (Utrecht, 25–28 January 1995) 24–30; Scott Leckie, 'The Human Right to Adequate Housing' in A Eide, C Krause, A Rosas and M Scheinin (eds.), *Economic, Social and Cultural Rights: A Textbook* (2nd edn, The Hague, Martinus Nijhoff Publishers 2000); Centre on Housing Rights and Evictions (COHRE), *Legal Resources for Housing Rights: International and National Standards* (Geneva, COHRE 2003); Padraic Kenna, 'International Instruments on Housing Rights' (2010) 2(1) Journal of Legal Affairs and Dispute Resolution in Engineering and Construction 11–20; Padraic Kenna, *Housing Law, Rights and Policy* (Dublin, Clarus Press 2011) Ch. 8.

3 Although the UN – Habitat Reports – UN-Habitat UNHRP Report Series, No 3, *National Housing Rights Legislation* (3rd edn) (HS/638/01E) (UNHRP, Nairobi, 2006); UN-Habitat UNHRP Report Series, No 1, *Housing Rights Legislation: Review of International and National Legal Instruments* (HS/638/01E) (UNHRP, Nairobi, 2002) provide an overview many new constitutions have emerged since that research was undertaken.

4 UN Doc A/810, The Universal Declaration of Human Rights (1948), (UDHR) UNGA Resolution 2200A (XX1). Adopted and proclaimed by General Assembly Resolution

on Economic, Social and Cultural Rights (ICESCR) at Article 11(1).[5] In the European context, housing provisions are anchored in the Council of Europe's European Social Charter (ESC) (Part I, principle 31), Articles 15(3), 16, 19(4), 30 and 31 (1961, revised 1996).[6] Article 13 of the European Convention on the Legal Status of Migrant Workers (1977) also provides for housing rights for this particular social group[7]. In addition, some rights established under the European Convention on Human Rights and Fundamental Freedoms (ECHR) (1950) have indirect implications for housing rights.[8]

These international instruments have influenced domestic laws in different ways and to different degrees. However, the right to housing and other forms of housing rights were legislated in some national constitutions decades before they were debated in the international sphere. Mexico (1917), South Korea (1948), Costa Rica (1950) and possibly a number of other national constitutions that are no longer in force already had a right to housing before the creation of the ICESCR. By the 1990s, the right to housing and other forms of constitutional housing rights already existed in over 24 national constitutions (which are still in force). Indeed,

---

217A (III) of 10 December 1948, stipulates in Article 25 that: 'Everyone has the right to a standard of living adequate for the health and wellbeing of himself [herself] and of his [her] family, including food, clothing, housing and medical care and necessary social services, and the right to security in the event of unemployment, sickness, disability, widowhood, old age or other lack of livelihood in circumstances beyond his [her] control.'

5 UN Doc A/6316, International Covenant on Economic, Social and Cultural Rights (1966), (ICESCR) UNGA Resolution 2200A (XXI) (entered into force 3 January 1976) states in Article 11(1): 'The State parties to the ... [ICESCR] recognize the right of everyone to an adequate standard of living for himself [herself] and for his [her] family, including adequate food, clothing and housing, and to the continuous improvement of living conditions. The States Parties will take appropriate steps to ensure the realization of this right, recognizing to this effect the essential importance of international co-operation based on free consent.'

6 Turin, 18 October 1961, Council of Europe, European Treaty Series – No 35; *European Social Charter. (Revised)*, Council of Europe, Strasbourg, 3 May 1996. Article 15 relates to the right of persons with disabilities to independence, social integration and participation in the life of the community; art 16 relates to the right of the family to social, legal and economic protection; art 19(4) relates to the right of migrant workers and their families to protection and assistance; art 30 relates to the right to protection against poverty and social exclusion. Article 31 states that everyone has the right to housing: 'With a view to ensuring the effective exercise of the right to housing, the Parties undertake to take measures designed: (1) to promote access to housing of an adequate standard; (2) to prevent and reduce homelessness with a view to its gradual elimination; (3) to make the price of housing accessible to those without adequate resources.

7 Council of Europe, European Convention on the Legal Status of Migrant Workers, Strasbourg, 24 November 1977, art 13.

8 Council of Europe, Convention for the Protection of Human Rights and Fundamental Freedoms, Rome, 4 November 1950.

it was only in the 1990s, according to Leckie,[9] that the right to housing began to gain importance within the international sphere, leading to its official recognition as an international human right. General Comment 4 of the ICESCR on the human right to adequate housing (1991)[10] accentuated the central importance of housing for the enjoyment of all other economic, social and cultural rights as 'the right to live somewhere in security, peace and dignity'. The UN Special Rapporteur on the Right to Adequate Housing suggested at the UN Commission of Human Rights in 1995 that all states proceeding with the elaboration of new, revised or amended national constitutions should give due attention to including housing rights provisions in these texts.[11]

With the beginning of the twenty-first century came a better understanding of the way in which international human rights norms affect national and local-level law. In several cases, constitutional or legislative texts were modeled after international standards, principles and norms.

This chapter focuses on housing rights at the level of national constitutions. It presents an overview of the current state of the right to housing within national constitutions, and a classification of constitutional housing rights. The classification, which is based on a survey of 205 national constitutions (including non-sovereign states),[12] reveals three major forms by which countries have chosen to incorporate housing into their constitutions:

1. explicit (direct) right to housing;
2. embedded rights, that is, rights included in articles referring to housing as a component of some other right;
3. indirect or implied rights.

Certain constitutions include up to 10 articles (e.g. Ecuador, 2008) on housing, and a single national constitution may contain all three forms of housing rights or any combination of them.

9 S Leckie, *National Perspectives on Housing Rights* (The Hague, Martinus Nijhoff Publishers 2003) ix.

10 See UN Doc E/C.12/1771/4, UNCESCR, *General Comment 4. The Human Right to Adequate Housing*.

11 UN Doc E/CN.4/Sub.2/1995/12, *The Realization of Economic, Social and Cultural Rights, The Right to Adequate Housing*, final report submitted by Mr. Rajindar Sachar, Special Rapporteur, para 164.

12 All constitutions were collected from governmental sites. The constitutions presented in this chapter are official translations to English.

Table 6.1 Conceptual classification of constitutional housing rights

Direct rights	Embedded rights	Indirect rights (examples)
• Right to housing, stand-alone • Partial list of social rights	• Responsibilities of the state • Workers' rights • Property rights (explicit) • Children/youth rights • Elder rights • Planning and urban politics • Adequate standard of living • Responsibilities of regional and local authorities • Human dignity • Fiscal policy • Inclusion and equality • Indigenous rights • Social security • Disability rights • Mandatory Report on the implementation of the right to housing • Right to challenge court decisions • Agricultural policy • Rural politics • Homelessness • Access to basic domestic services • Family rights	• Property rights • Freedom of residence • Right to privacy • Right to life • Right to be free from cruel or degrading treatment

Direct Housing Rights within Constitutions

Direct rights refer to constitutional articles that explicitly mention 'the right to housing' either as a dedicated (stand-alone) article or among a list of social rights.

The Right to Housing as a Stand-alone Article

Incorporating the right to housing as a stand-alone article in a constitution is probably the strongest expression of recognition of housing as a national issue. While some countries merely recognize the right, others specify the measures and responsibilities in greater detail. In a five-level scale, the following formats were found:

- Every person/citizen has a right to housing.
- Public authorities shall promote the necessary conditions/policy to ensure the right to housing.
- Every person/citizen has a right to housing. The state must take specified measures for the realization of that right.
- Everyone has the right to a specific standard of housing. The state must take listed measures for its implementation, including a national plan, finance and specialized institutions or funds. The parties involved are listed (municipalities, private sector, etc.).

Partial List of Social Rights

Some national constitutions explicitly provide for 'the right to housing' among a list of other rights. Thus, the right to housing appears in a single article with a myriad of other social rights, such as education, social security as rights, food, work, maternity protection and assistance to the needy, leisure, decent standards of sanitation and access to safe water sources. The Constitution of Kenya (2010) provides an example of this approach:

> **Constitution of Kenya (2010)**
> Chapter four. The Bill of Rights.
> Part 2. Rights and Fundamental Freedoms.
>
> 43(1) Every person has the right –
> (a) to the highest attainable standard of health, which includes the right to health care services, including reproductive health care;
> (b) to accessible and adequate housing, and to reasonable standards of sanitation;
> (c) to be free from hunger, and to have adequate food of acceptable quality;
> (d) to clean and safe water in adequate quantities.

The Embedded Form of Constitutional Housing Rights

The most widespread form of housing rights in national constitutions occurs in articles that, while explicitly mentioning housing, list those rights as a component of some other general right.

Responsibilities of the State

Laws of state responsibility are the principles governing the what, when and how a state is held responsible to provide its citizens with an agreed-upon good (right, duty or other). This group of articles is usually included under the chapter of the 'State' or 'Duties of the State'. The content of the housing-related responsibilities varies between constitutions and may include:

- granting the government exclusive jurisdiction over housing policies;
- adopting measures for the delivery of housing and the distribution of public estates;
- supplementing private initiative and responsibility by fulfilling the housing needs of citizens;
- promoting housing construction programmes and the improvement of living conditions;
- satisfying the housing needs of citizens, combating homelessness, promoting low-income housing and supporting home-ownership;
- creating opportunities for citizens to obtain decent housing;
- providing the basic necessities of life including housing;
- permitting the greatest number of home-owner families and undertaking to see that every farm-owner provides his workers with comfortable homes;
- pursuing a policy establishing rights to housing;
- legislating against abuses in tenancy matters, particularly unfair rents, and challenging unlawful leases.

Workers' Rights

Workers' rights and claims regulate labour relations between workers and employers, such as workers' pay, benefits and safe working conditions. In this context, housing-related articles include:

- establishing a minimum wage/income that meets housing needs;
- specifying which enterprises must provide housing for their workers;
- establishing specific entities to support the finance of workers' housing projects;
- establishing a national housing fund for workers and cooperative construction societies;
- providing an exclusive housing right to agricultural workers and peasants.

Property Rights

While property rights are a classic example of indirect rights, there are cases in which housing is explicitly mentioned in a property-related article. Housing-related articles include those which:

- oblige the state to provide housing for citizens with limited income;
- protect rights to acquire and own housing;
- protect from arbitrary deprivation of housing;
- compensate owners for expropriated land for purposes such as housing;
- protect against forced evictions and the demolition of poor dwellers' housing.

Children's Rights

These rights give special protection and care to the young, including their right to association with both biological parents and human identity, as well as the fulfillment of basic needs for food, universal state-paid education, health care, criminal laws appropriate for the age and development of the child, and shelter. The Constitution of Honduras (1982) provides an example of this approach:

> **Constitution of Honduras** (1982)
> Chapter iv.
> Rights of children.
> Article 123. Every child shall enjoy the benefits of the social security and education. Have the right to grow and develop in good health, for which must be provided, both to him and his mother, special care from the prenatal period, taking right to enjoy food, housing, education, recreation, sports and adequate medical services.

Elder Rights

Factors such as rapid increases in the elderly population and age, as well as ageism, have led to the advent of elders' law. Benefits to the elderly include social security, pensions and access to nursing homes, the delivery of housing suited to their needs and their state of health or of adequate support for adapting their housing. The Constitution of Angola (2010) provides an example:

> **Constitution of Angola** (2010)
> Chapter III Economic, Social and Cultural Rights and Duties.
> Article 82. (The elderly)
> 1. The elderly shall have the right to economic security, housing and a family and community life that respects their personal autonomy and prevents and overcomes isolation or social marginalization.

2. Policies for the elderly shall include economic, social and cultural measures that offer elderly people opportunities for personal fulfillment through active participation in community life.

Planning and Urban Politics

Planning and urban politics are the technical and political processes concerned with the control of the use of land and design of the urban environment, including transportation networks. The role of planning is to ensure the orderly development of human settlements and communities. Housing rights are found in various formats here, including the following:

- providing that urban development, housing, infrastructure and transport be under the regulatory control of the state;
- enabling citizens to claim ownership over previously unclaimed property used for living purposes;
- providing that programmes of urban land reform and housing be undertaken by both the state and the private sector;
- providing that housing plans be determined by laws aimed at ensuring sufficient affordable housing and state control of real estate for public housing;
- providing for legislation to regulate citizens' rights to undertake construction of housing and to protect the interests of landlords and tenants.

Adequate Standard of Living

The right to an adequate standard of living is understood to establish a minimum entitlement to food, clothing and housing at a subsistence level. The Constitution of Armenia (2005) provides an example of this approach:

> **Constitution of Armenia** (1995 revised in 2005)
> Chapter 2. Fundamental Human and Civil Rights and Freedoms.
> Article 31.
> Every citizen is entitled to an adequate standard of living for himself or herself and his or her family, to adequate housing, as well as to the improvement of living conditions. The state shall provide the essential means to enable the exercise of these rights.

The Responsibilities of Regional and Local Authorities

Regional and local authorities are recognized as a form of public administration by many national constitutions, and in most contexts, they exist as the lower tiers of administration within a given state, as entities distinct from national or federal authorities. Some constitutions enumerate the duties and responsibilities of regional and local jurisdictions, including housing affairs. In Venezuela, Article

178 of the Constitution of Venezuela (1999) establishes that municipal authorities shall govern all affairs of 'local living' such as rental politics with criteria of equality and justice, while protecting social interest and improving the living conditions of the community, including social housing. Article 184 establishes that the law will create open and flexible mechanisms to enable the decentralization of power from provinces and municipalities to capable local communities and organized neighbourhood groups so that they can administer their own services in several fields, including housing and the maintenance of urban areas.

Human Dignity

Dignity is intimately linked to humanity, freedom and equality. Humans are born with dignity as an inherent quality that is neither deserved nor capable of being confiscated. This commitment to dignity has been endorsed in the vast majority of codified constitutions, with some constitutions explicitly listing housing as a component of this right. The Constitution of Belgium provides an example of this approach:

> **Constitution of Belgium** (1994)
> Title II. On Belgians and their rights
> Article 23.
> Everyone has the right to lead a life consistent with human dignity. To that end, the laws, decrees or rules established under article 134 guarantee, taking into account the corresponding obligations, economic, social and cultural rights of which they determine the conditions for their implementation. These rights include, in particular,
> … (3) The right to adequate housing.

Fiscal Policy

Fiscal policy is the means by which a government adjusts its levels of spending in order to monitor and influence a nation's economy. Housing is one of the policy areas where significant levels of spending may be involved, and constitutions explicitly mention housing in articles defining the fiscal policy of the state. The Constitution of the Islamic Republic of Iran provides an example:

> **Constitution of the Islamic Republic of Iran** (1979)
> Chapter IV. Economy and Financial Affairs.
> Article 43. The economy of the Islamic Republic of Iran, with its objectives of achieving the economic independence of the society, uprooting poverty and deprivation and fulfilling human needs in the process of development while preserving human liberty, is based on the following criteria:

(1) The provision of basic necessities for all citizens: housing, food, clothing, hygiene, medical treatment, education and the necessary facilities for the establishment of a family.

Inclusion and Equality

Inclusion and equality involve eliminating discrimination, and enabling equal opportunity by providing access to housing or protection against exclusion. Housing is explicitly mentioned in such articles in the following forms:

- the delivery of a national development plan, composed by housing among other things, will be guided by these principles, including non-discrimination;
- the uplift of economically and socially backward groups (landless, squatters and victims of conflict including women) and marginalized populations by making provisions that include housing.

Indigenous Rights

Indigenous rights involve the recognition of the specific conditions of those defined as the original settlers of a land that has been conquered or colonized. Such rights include the right to physical survival and integrity, the preservation of land, religion, language and other elements of cultural heritage, including housing. This can be seen in the Constitution of Guatemala (1985):

Constitution of Guatemala (1985)
Title II. Human rights.
Chapter II. Social rights.
Section III. Indigenous communities.
Article 67. Protection of Indigenous Agricultural Lands and Cooperatives.
The lands of the cooperatives, native communities, or any other forms of communal possession or collective of agrarian ownership, as well as the family heritage and popular housing, will enjoy the special protection of the State, preferential credit and technical assistance, which may guarantee their ownership and development in order to insure [sic] an improved quality of life to all inhabitants.

Social Security

Social security is defined as government action programmes intended to promote welfare for the population at large as well as potentially vulnerable segments of the population, such as children, the elderly, the sick and the unemployed. It is provided through assistance measures that guarantee access to sufficient resources for food and shelter, and to promote health and well-being. The Constitution of Argentina (1994) provides an example:

Constitution of Argentina (1994)
First Part.
Chapter I. Declarations, rights and guarantees.
Section 14bis. Labor in its several forms shall be protected by law, which shall ensure to workers: dignified and equitable working conditions; limited working hours; paid rest and vacations; fair remuneration; …
The State shall grant the benefits of social security, which shall be of an integral nature and may not be waived. In particular, the laws shall establish: compulsory social insurance, which shall be in charge of national or provincial entities with financial and economic autonomy, administered by the interested parties with State participation, with no overlapping of contributions; adjustable retirements and pensions; full family protection; protection of homestead; family allowances and access to a worthy housing.

Disability Rights

Disability covers impairments, activity limitations and participation restrictions. These rights are meant to secure equal opportunities and equal rights for people with disabilities, including accessibility and safety in transportation, architecture and the physical environment, freedom from abuse, neglect and violations of patients' rights, and equal opportunities in independent living, employment, education and housing. Housing in the context of disabled people's rights appears in the constitutions of Ecuador:

Ecuador Constitution (2008)
Section 6: Persons with disabilities
Article 47. The State shall guarantee disability prevention policies and, along with society and the family, it shall ensure equal opportunities for persons with disabilities and their social integration.
Persons with disabilities are recognized the following rights: …
6. Adequate housing, with facilities for access and the conditions needed to address their disability and to achieve the highest possible degree of autonomy in their daily life. Persons with disabilities who cannot be cared for by their relatives during the day or who have no permanent place to live shall have welcoming centers for their shelter

Mandatory Report on the Implementation of the Right to Housing

The South Africa Constitution (1996) declares the functions of the South African Human Rights Commission. Chapter 9, section 184 states that each year, the South African Human Rights Commission must require the relevant organs of the state to provide the Commission with information on the measures that they have taken towards the realization of the rights in the Bill of Rights concerning housing among other subjects.

Right to Challenge Court Decisions

The Ukrainian Constitution (1996) states that human and citizens' rights and freedoms (including the right to housing enumerated in Articles 47 and 48 of the Constitution) are protected by the court (Article 55). Everyone in Ukraine has the right to appeal for the protection of his or her rights to the Authorized Human Rights Representative of the Verkhovna Rada of Ukraine. After exhausting all domestic legal remedies, everyone has the right to appeal for the protection of his or her rights and freedoms to the relevant international judicial institutions or to the relevant bodies of international organizations of which Ukraine is a member or participant.

Agricultural Policy

Agricultural policy describes a set of laws relating to domestic agriculture and imports of foreign agricultural products. Governments usually implement agricultural policies with the goal of achieving a specific outcome in the domestic agricultural product markets, such as a guaranteed supply level, price stability, land use or employment. Article 187 of the Brazilian Constitution (1988) establishes that an agricultural policy shall be planned and implemented pursuant to law, with regular participation in that process by the production sector – involving both rural producers and workers – as well as by the marketing, warehousing and transportation sectors, considering housing for the rural worker among other subjects.

Rural Politics

Rural politics focus on the key issues affecting rural areas today, such as water pollution, forestry, the greening of agricultural policy, as well as mainstream agricultural policy. Article 28 of the Democratic Republic of Korea's Constitution (1998) provides that the state should undertake the building of production facilities of the cooperative farms and modern houses in the countryside at its expense, with the purpose of increasing the role of the countryside and eliminating the city/country divide.

Homelessness

Homelessness is defined as the condition of people who are often unable to acquire and maintain regular, safe, secure and adequate housing or night-time residence. The legal definition of 'homeless' varies from country to country and among institutions in the same country or region. Article 21(4) of the Greek Constitution (2001) addresses homelessness by stating that providing housing to those who are homeless or live in inadequate housing conditions shall be the subject of special attention by the state.

Access to Basic Domestic Services

In modern times, access to and delivery of basic needs includes obtaining water, food, health services and shelter in adequate quantity and quality to ensure survival and to satisfy their right to 'life with dignity'. Article 20 of the Bolivian Constitution (2009) guarantees access to basic domestic services in a universal and equitable manner, including potable water, sewage, electricity, domestic gas, postal and telecommunications. Services must be accountable, accessible, continuous, of sufficient quality, efficient and effective, with equitable and necessary coverage rates, and with participation and social control.

Family Rights

Human rights law upholds the positive right of all peoples to marry and have a family. It bolsters the family unit by specifying state obligations to keep families together and to reunify them when they have become separated, for example, as a result of a refugee crises. It insists on maternity rights for mothers to allow time and space for the bond to develop between mother and child. It also prescribes detailed standards for the treatment of children who lack parental care and require state intervention, and the delivery of foster care or adoption. Article 59 of the Constitution of Paraguay (1992) protects family property, recognized as an institution of a social interest. Family property consists of the family house or estate and its furniture and working tools, which cannot be subjected to any attachment.

Indirect or Implied Constitutional Housing Rights

Indirect forms of protection do not include an explicit mentioning of housing, so in order to turn constitutional language into operative law, the courts and the parliaments would need to interpret general constitutional language as concrete protection.

Property Rights

Property rights grant the peaceful enjoyment of material possessions such as dwellings and land while protecting owners from their deprivation. According to Youngs,[13] property must be subject to the state's power to impose taxes, enforce court decisions and intervene wherever the balance between the public interest and the applicant's right to peaceful possession is disrupted. Forms of state intervention include deprivation, limitation, expropriation or compulsory purchase and compensation.

---

13 R Youngs, *English, French and German: Comparative Law* (2nd edn, London, Cavendish Publishing 2007) 302–04.

Some countries have no constitutional protection of housing rights, but do hold a strong protection of private property. The Constitution of the US, for example, protects property rights mainly through the Fifth Amendment's 'Takings or Just Compensation' clause: 'nor shall private property be taken for public use without just compensation'. America's 'Founders' understood clearly that private property is the foundation not only of prosperity and basic fairness, but also of individual liberty itself.[14] Hartman[15] refers to this as the American anti-safety-net political climate, because housing is viewed primarily as property and a commercial asset.

In contrast, the Dutch Constitution (1983) includes a housing right (Article 22), but it does not include a general right to property, although it includes the prohibition of unlawful expropriation (Article 14). The reason for this, which has been defended by successive governments, is that property rights are so fundamental to Dutch society that it is redundant to explicitly mention them.[16]

Housing and property rights also intersect in the event of 'repossession', that is, the right of refugees and displaced persons to repossess property they have lost in conflict situations through abandonment and subsequent reallocation. Repossession is considered sustainable if the displaced persons can return to their pre-conflict homes, and in many cases this has been elaborated in peace treaties ending hostilities. The reference to 'home' has often been defined as return and repossession of the actual property lost during the conflict. The term 'home' here may be wider than the term 'housing'. The Constitution of Bosnia and Herzegovina (1995) provides an example of this approach:

> **Bosnia and Herzegovina** (1995)
> Article II. Human Rights and Fundamental Freedoms.
> Paragraph 5. Refugees and Displaced Persons:
> All refugees and displaced persons have the right freely to return to their homes of origin. They have the right, in accordance with Annex 7 to the General Framework Agreement, to have restored to them property of which they were deprived in the course of hostilities since 1991 and to be compensated for any

---

14 See E Ziegler and J Laitos, 'Property Rights, Housing, and the American Constitution: The Social Benefits of Property Rights Protection, Government Interventions, and the European Court on Human Rights, Hutten-Czapska Decision' (2011) 21(25) *Indiana International & Comparative Law Review* 2011.

15 C Hartman, 'The Case for a Right to Housing in the United States' in Leckie (n 11) 230–31.

16 As a corollary to these property rights, it is significant that independent housing associations were incorporated into the Dutch housing laws over 100 years ago, making the Dutch housing policy rather unique. See K Olds, 'The Role of Courts in Making the Right to Housing a Reality Throughout Europe: Lessons from France and the Netherlands' 28 Wisconsin International Law Journal (2010) 170–99.

> such property that cannot be restored to them. Any commitments or statements relating to such property made under duress are null and void.

Two subjects that deserve their own chapters are takings and evictions. Recently, much literature has been dedicated to evictions, including many reports by the UN on forced evictions. Takings (expropriations/eminent domain) and compensation are frequently mentioned in constitutions, in most cases as an integral part of the right to property.[17] Although housing may not be mentioned in these clauses, expropriation issues necessarily have a direct bearing on housing.

Freedom of Residence

Freedom of residence is a component of freedom of movement. It guarantees the liberty to choose where to live within the territory of a state and it often provides legal protection from discrimination in housing. Most national constitutions have incorporated this freedom. In the EU, a right of citizens of the EU to move and reside freely within the Member States has been established in the treaty law of the EU since 1992. Article 21(1) of the Treaty on the Functioning of the European Union states that: 'Every citizen of the Union shall have the right to move and reside freely within the territory of the Member States, subject to the limitations and conditions laid down in this Treaty and by the measures adopted to give it effect.'[18]

Areas in which conflict is taking place frequently find themselves restricting and even violating this freedom. In apartheid South Africa, freedom of residence was systematically violated by the apartheid regime, which used legislation to heavily restrict the free movement of black South Africans to and from urban areas.

In situations of internal displacement, the right to freedom of movement and freedom of residence are temporarily restricted. Such was the case in Zimbabwe in 2005, where, despite the constitutional freedom provided, the Government of Zimbabwe embarked on *Operation Restore Order* with little or no warning. The movement, which began in Harare, rapidly evolved into a nationwide demolition and eviction campaign carried out by the police and the army. While purporting to target illegal dwellings and structures and to clamp down on alleged illicit activities, it resulted in the destruction of homes, business premises and vending sites. It is estimated that 700,000 people in cities across the country lost their homes.[19] Yet, the Constitution of Zimbabwe (1979) provided:

---

17 R Alterman, *Takings International: A Comparative Perspective on Land Use Regulations and Compensation Rights* (Chicago, ABA Press 2012).

18 Consolidated versions of the Treaty on European Union and the Treaty on the Functioning of the European Union [2010] OJ C83/47, 30.March.

19 See Internal Displacement Monitoring Centre (IDMC)/Norwegian Refugee Council, 'Training on the Protection of IDPs' http://www.internal-displacement.org/8025708F004BE3B1/(httpInfoFiles)/86B7E7913E385A9EC125711500473D9B/$file/Protection%20from%20module%20handout%20prevention.pdf accessed 24 April 2013.

Constitution of Zimbabwe (1979)
Chapter III. The Declaration of Rights.
Section 22. Protection of freedom of movement.
(1) No person is deprived of his freedom of movement, that is to say, the right to move freely throughout Zimbabwe, the right to reside in any part of Zimbabwe, the right to enter and to leave Zimbabwe and immunity from expulsion from Zimbabwe.

Right to Privacy

Privacy rights are embedded in personality rights and include the protection of privacy, marriage and family life, home and correspondence. The right to privacy states that no interference with this right by a public authority is permitted. The right may be limited in accordance with the law and as necessary in a democratic society, in the interests of national security, public safety or the economic well-being of the country for the prevention of disorder or crime, for the protection of health or morals, or for the protection of the rights and freedoms of others.[20] Privacy and housing rights come within the ambit of family rights, since home is where private life and family life develop. Where members of a family are at risk, such as in situations of unsanitary living conditions, the state may interfere with privacy in order to implement social welfare policies and may provide public housing/shelter.[21]

Housing and privacy are also relevant in the context of inviolability of the home, which is the right to respect for the physical area of a home and the quiet enjoyment of it. State interference may include nuisance, emissions, smells or other disruptions. The state must take positive steps to protect rights even in the area of relationships between individuals.[22] The right to privacy is found in most constitutions worldwide. An example can be found in the recent Constitution of Kyrgyzstan (2010):

Constitution of Kyrgyzstan (2010)
Chapter II. Human rights and freedoms.
Article 30.
1. Everyone shall have the right of the inviolability of housing as well as other objects to which he/she has proprietary or other right. No one may penetrate housing or other objects against the will of a person who uses them.

20 Youngs (n 15) 222.
21 ibid 224–25.
22 ibid 227.

Right to Life

The essential right to life means that a human being has the right not to be killed by another human being. In the context of housing, the right to life applies to regions with extreme weather conditions where a lack of emergency shelter could pose risks to life and personal security. This component of the right to life was identified by the International Human Rights Committee while dealing with Canada. The Committee concluded that homelessness could lead to serious health problems and death.[23]

Finland, where the coldest winter days can be as low as −40°C (−40°F), provides an example of an attempt to incorporate a specific right to shelter into the clause on the right to life. Section 7 of Chapter II of the Constitution of Finland (2000) was originally meant to include shelter, but when the clauses were re-ordered in the final draft, a clause on subsistence and care was transferred to the section of economic and social rights.[24] The Constitution of Finland provides that:

> **Constitution of Finland** (2000)
> Chapter II. Basic Rights and Liberties.
> Section 7 The right to life, personal liberty and integrity.
> (1) Everyone has the right to life, personal liberty, integrity and security.
> (2) No one shall be sentenced to death, tortured or otherwise treated in a manner violating human dignity.

The Right to be Free from Cruel, Inhuman or Degrading Treatment

The right to be free from cruel, inhuman or degrading treatment defines the minimal conditions that a person should be allowed, in order to preserve his or her human character in places where liberty is deprived, such as in prisons. This right relates to housing by defining the minimal needs in terms of shelter necessary to preserve human dignity.

For example, Haiti's Constitution (1987) requires the Government of Haiti to protect the rights of individuals deprived of their liberty. Yet, prisons and detention centres in Haiti have been reported to be overcrowded, poorly maintained and unsanitary, periodically lacking in food and water, as well as basic medical services and medical isolation units for contagious patients. In certain cases, especially following a cholera outbreak, the conditions have resulted in an arbitrary deprivation of life:[25]

---

23 UN Doc CCPR/C/79/Add.105, Concluding Observations on Canada, 7 April 1999.

24 M Scheinin, 'Protection of the Right to Housing in Finland' in Leckie (n 11) 245.

25 P Avril, *Justice versus Politics in Haiti (2001–2004)* (Boca Raton, Universal Publishers 2007); Institute for Justice and Democracy in Haiti, 'Criminal Justice: Submission to the UN Universal Periodic Review' (IJDJ 2011) http://ijdh.org/wordpress/wp-content/uploads/2011/03/UPR-Prisons-SR-English-Final.pdf accessed 24 April 2013.

Constitution of Haiti 1987
Chapter II. Basic Rights.
Section J. ARTICLE 44-1:
Prisons must be operated in accordance with standards reflecting respect for human dignity according to the law on this subject.

Conclusion

Examination of the various constitutions shows the complexity of housing rights. These are not always presented in distinct clauses, but at times are embedded in other rights. The findings presented in this chapter could serve as a guide for legislators seeking to constitutionalize housing rights. These findings shed light on the comparative variations in housing rights across the world's constitutions and reveal the many categories and nuances of these rights.

The broad range of expression of housing rights in the constitutions of nations around the world should enrich the discussion within each jurisdiction.[26] It is hoped that this survey of approaches will allow cross-learning from one jurisdiction to another, not only in new legislation but also in the ongoing interpretations by the courts – those that permit the incorporation of approaches from foreign court opinions.[27]

26 See R Lefler, 'A Comparison of Comparison: Use of Foreign Case Law as Persuasive Authority by the United States Supreme Court, the Supreme Court of Canada, and the High Court of Australia' (2002) 11 Southern California Interdisciplinary Law Journal 165.

27 An example of such use was seen in 2011 following the legislation of a right to housing in Kenya's new Constitution (2010). Two court decisions taken by the High Court of Kenya on domestic housing matters quoted extensively from the South African constitutional authorities *Satrose Ayuma and others v The Registered Trustees of the Kenya Railway Staff Benefits Scheme and others* (High Court Petition No 65 of 2010); and *Susan Waithera and others v The Town Clerk, Nairobi City Council and others* (High Court Petition No 66 of 2010). See also *Government of the Republic of South Africa v Grootboomand Others* (2001) (1) SA 46 CC; *Modderklip Boerdery v President Van Die Rsa en Andere* (2003) (6) BC LR 638(T).

Chapter 7
Independent Living for People with Disabilities in Kenya: Charting the Way Forward

Elizabeth Kamundia

Introduction

This chapter explores the concept of independent living and living in the community from the perspective of a developing country – Kenya. It begins by defining independent living, identifying its key elements and examining its historical and theoretical underpinnings. Second, it provides a rationale for exploring the right to independent living from the perspective of a developing country. It notes that although a significant amount of literature exists on the meaning of independent living with regard to developed countries, little has been written from the perspective of developing countries. Third, it considers measures taken by the government of Kenya towards providing support to persons with disabilities, noting that no single measure is taken specifically with the aim of enabling persons with disabilities to live independently. Fourth, it examines what Kenya reported under Article 19 to the Committee on the Rights of Persons with Disabilities (CRPD Committee) and then concludes with some recommendations for future action.

This chapter argues that independent living is as relevant for developing countries as for developed countries. Indeed, it is significant that the notion of independent living does exist in Africa, although it has been expressed through different concepts. In Africa, emphasis has been placed on habilitation and rehabilitation aimed at enabling persons with disabilities achieving independence. The effect of this in Kenya has been a narrow focus on persons with physical and sensory disabilities, to the exclusion of those with intellectual disabilities, psychosocial disabilities and multiple disabilities.[1]

---

1 See, for example, the Kenya Society for the Mentally Handicapped website, which features a story of a person with intellectual disabilities who was tied, chained and locked up for 35 years. Due to this, he developed muscular atrophy, and lost the use of his legs to date. See http://www.ksmh.org/ksmh-at-work/interventions/rescues accessed 15 March 2013. For more information on the lives of people with intellectual and mental disabilities

Defining Independent Living and Identifying its Key Elements

Article 19 of the UN Convention on the Rights of Persons with Disabilities (CRPD)[2] provides that persons with disabilities have the right to live independently in the community:

> States Parties to the present Convention recognize the equal right of all persons with disabilities to live in the community, with choices equal to others, and shall take effective and appropriate measures to facilitate full enjoyment by persons with disabilities of this right and their full inclusion and participation in the community, including by ensuring that:
> (a) Persons with disabilities have the opportunity to choose their place of residence and where and with whom they live on an equal basis with others and are not obliged to live in a particular living arrangement;
> (b) Persons with disabilities have access to a range of in-home, residential and other community support services, including personal assistance necessary to support living and inclusion in the community, and to prevent isolation or segregation from the community;
> (c) Community services and facilities for the general population are available on an equal basis to persons with disabilities and are responsive to their needs.[3]

Community living (also known as independent living)[4] refers to persons with disabilities being able to live in their local communities as equal citizens, with the support that they need in order to participate in everyday life.[5] Independent living is about having the autonomy and independence to make decisions and having control over the choices and shape of one's life. Where support, such as care in the home and personal assistance, is needed to live in the community, this should be made available as part of the obligations of the state.[6]

The core elements of independent living are self-determination, choice, autonomy, equal access, living in community and inclusion and participation. These elements are universal and are not context-specific. Indeed, independent

---

in Kenya, see the website of the Kenya Association of the Intellectually Handicapped at http://kaihid.org accessed 2 August 2013.

2 UN Convention on the Rights of Persons with Disabilities adopted on 13 December 2006 during the sixty-first session of the UNGA Resolution A/RES/61/106, signed by 155 states and entered into force 3 May 2008.

3 UN Doc A/RES/61/106.

4 European Coalition for Community Living, *Focus on Article 19 of the UN Convention on the Rights of Persons with Disabilities* (Focus Report 2009).

5 European Coalition for Community Living, *Creating Successful Campaigns for Community Living: An Advocacy Manual for Disability Organisations and Service Providers* (London, European Coalition for Community Living 2008).

6 UNICEF *It's About Ability: An Explanation of the Convention on the Rights of Persons with Disabilities* (New York, UNICEF 2009).

living 'has been regarded as a concept rather than an issue requiring specific legal definition'.[7] Seen in this light, it is the philosophy underpinning the struggle by people with disabilities to achieve self-determination, choice, autonomy, equal access, community inclusion and participation. Article 19 also extends the traditional right of liberty. Kayess and French equate Article 19 with the right of persons with disability to live in and be a part of the community.[8]

Article 19 is a clear demonstration of how the CRPD blurs the line traditionally established in human rights between the traditional civil and political rights and economic, social and cultural rights.[9] Indeed, it is difficult to separate the civil and political aspects and the social, economic and cultural aspects within the right to independent living.[10]

Historical and Theoretical Underpinnings of Article 19

Independent living is a civil rights movement of people with disabilities, which grew in the US at the end of the 1960s as a protest against clinical living conditions in institutions. This led to the Independent Living Movement, which views disability primarily as a social and political problem. It adopted the approach of highlighting issues and developing strategies along the lines of the black civil rights and the feminist movements. These key issues for people with disabilities are the articulation of one's own needs, self-determination, assistance geared to the consumer and participation in politics and administration.[11]

Theoretically, the right to independent living is grounded in the social model of disability,[12] which distinguishes between the impairments that people have and the oppression which they experience. Most importantly, it defines 'disability' as the social oppression, not the form of impairment.[13] This model is reflected in the CRPD, which recognizes that disability is an evolving concept and that it results from the interaction between persons with impairments and attitudinal and environmental barriers that hinder their full and effective participation in society on an equal basis with others.

7 Camilla Parker and Luke Clements, 'The UN Convention on the Rights of Persons with Disabilities: A New Right to Independent Living?' (2008) 4 EHRLR 509.

8 Rosemary Kayess and Phillip French, 'Out of Darkness into Light? Introducing the Convention on the Rights of Persons with Disabilities' (2008) 8(1) Human Rights Law Review 1.

9 ibid.

10 Gerard Quinn, 'Reflecting Strategically about the UN Convention on the Rights of Persons with Disabilities' (Interights Guest Speaker Series, London, December 2011).

11 Ingolf Osterwitz, The Concept of Independent Living – A New Perspective in Rehabilitation' (HELIOS European Workshop, Venice, October 1994).

12 Parker and Clements (n 7).

13 Mike Oliver, *The Politics of Disablement* (London, Macmillan 1990) 22.

Article 19 and Developing Countries

Article 19 of the CRPD is one of the articles that illustrated a clear divide between the negotiating standpoints of the developing and developed countries.[14] The issue presents itself differently in the Global North and in the South.[15] The critical issue in the Global North is institutionalization. As Parker and Clements argue, 'in many parts of Europe the predominant provision for disabled people (children as well as adults) continues to be institutionalisation (often for life)'.[16]

The critical issue in the Global South is the absence of the required support services to enable independence and facilitate participation in society.[17] Further, in most countries of the Global South, mutual caring and support in the community is a norm, and it is often felt that there is no need for disabled persons to live physically and financially apart from their families. The emphasis is on one becoming a contributing member of the family rather than on managing one's own household alone. Thus, the concept of independent living associated with developed countries is not always relevant in developing countries. As a result, during the negotiations on the CRPD, the Global South placed great emphasis on support to families taking care of persons with disabilities. Further, states from the Global South emphasized the *promotion* of supportive assistance rather than an *obligation to provide* such assistance.

In Kenya (and in most African states), institutionalization is not the key issue. The Kenyan context is one in which persons with disabilities live with their families, but without state-funded individualized support services, in the background of a cultural context of a (largely) communal way of life.[18] Hence, in Kenya, access to housing is not perceived as being key to the implementation of Article 19. Indeed, the State Report to the CRPD Committee makes no mention of the right to housing when reporting on measures taken towards implementing the

---

14 A developing country, also called a less-developed country (LDC), is a nation with a low living standard, under-developed industrial base and a low UNDP Human Development Index (HDI) relative to other countries. There is no universal, agreed-upon criterion for what makes a country developing versus developed and which countries fit these two categories, although there are general reference points, such as the size of a nation's GDP compared to other nations. Kenya was ranked 145th in the 2012 HDI.

15 The Global South refers to the countries of the rest of the world, most of which are located in the Southern Hemisphere. It includes both countries with medium human development (88 countries with an HDI less than 0.8 and greater than 0.5) and low human development (32 countries with an HDI of less than 0.5). For a more detailed discussion on cultural relativism and universal human rights, see Jack Donnelly, 'Cultural Relativism and Universal Human Rights' (1984) 6 Human Rights Quarterly 400.

16 Parker and Clements (n 7).

17 Inge Komardjaja, 'Independent Living and Self-determination of Women with Physical Disabilities in Bandung, Indonesia' (2004) 24 Disability Studies Quarterly 1.

18 While generally institutionalization is not the predominant provision for persons with disabilities in Kenya, it is with regard to persons with psychosocial disabilities.

right of persons with disabilities to live independently in the community. Indeed, the concept of independent living does exist in Kenya, except that it has been expressed through different concepts. In Kenya (and in most of Africa), emphasis has been placed on habilitation and rehabilitation aimed at enabling persons with disabilities to achieve independence.

Interlinks within the Convention

In order to understand the full import of Article 19, one must be cognizant of the links that exist throughout the Convention.[19] Article 19 has been classified alongside other autonomy and dignity articles, i.e. Articles, 12, 17, 18 and 22 (legal capacity, liberty of movement and nationality, personal integrity and privacy, respectively).[20] It is also closely linked to participation rights, enshrined in Articles 9, 13, 20, 21, 24, 25, 26, 27 and 29 (accessibility, access to justice, employment, health, education, personal mobility, habilitation, participation in private and public life, and freedom of expression, respectively).[21] While independent living is closely linked to the above rights, it is more than the sum of these rights, Article 12, on legal capacity, is a particularly key to independent living. [22] International disability rights experts Gerard Quinn and Michael Stein have stated the following with regard to the right to legal capacity:

> This right acknowledges that people with disabilities have an innate capacity to decide their destinies for themselves – where to live, who to live with, what education or employment to pursue – and to have those choices respected. And if there is to be an intervention on the part of the State, the primary impulse should be to support a residuum of capacity, and to intervene to support people to make decisions for themselves, with appropriate safeguards.[23]

Defining Independent Living

According to the UK Office for Disability Issues:

19 Report of the United Nations High Commissioner for Human Rights, 'On Progress in the Implementation of the Recommendations Contained in the Study on the Human Rights of Persons with Disabilities', UN Doc A/HRC/4/75, para 19.

20 Eilionoir Flynn, 'UN Convention on the Rights of Persons with Disabilities' (9th Irish Human Rights Commission & Law Society Conference, Dublin, October 2011).

21 ibid.

22 Commissioner for Human Rights, 'The Right of People with Disabilities to Live Independently and Be Included in the Community', COMM, Issue Paper (2012) 3.

23 Focus Report 2009 (n 4).

> Independent living does not mean doing things for yourself, or living on your own. Instead, it means having choice and control over the assistance and/or equipment needed to go about your daily life and having equal access to housing, transport and mobility, health, employment and education and training opportunities.[24]

Clearly, these issues are relevant to people with disabilities living both in developed and developing countries.

Prior to the CRPD, no other human rights instrument contained an explicit right for all persons with disabilities to live in the community as equal citizens.[25] The right to independent living as defined by the CRPD is not a new right, but, rather, a creative interpretation of existing rights that has been specially tailored to apply to the context of persons with disabilities. In particular, the UN *Standard Rules on the Equalization of Opportunities for Persons with Disabilities* 1993[26] already provided that 'persons with disabilities are members of the society and have the right to remain within their local communities. They should receive the support they need within ordinary structures of education, health, employment and social services'. The UN Committee on the Rights of the Child *General Comment 7* (2006) stated that young children should never be institutionalized solely on the grounds of disability.[27] It added that it is a priority to ensure that they have equal opportunities to participate fully in education and community life, including by the removal of barriers that impede the realization of their rights. Further, young disabled children are entitled to appropriate specialist assistance, including support for their parents (or other caregivers).

Article 19 of the CRPD requires that States Parties recognize the equal rights of persons with disabilities to live in the community with choices equal to others, and to facilitate the full inclusion and participation of persons with disabilities in the community. Community living (also known as independent living in some jurisdictions) refers to persons with disabilities being able to live in their local communities as equal citizens, with the support that they need to participate in everyday life. It is about persons with disabilities participating in the life activities that matter to all of us, including education, health care, occupation, leisure, social support, civic engagement and housing.[28]

Article 19 applies to all people with disabilities, regardless of their support needs. It has been demonstrated that people who were deemed too 'disabled' to

---

24 Office for Disability Issues, *Independent Living: A Cross-government Strategy about Independent Living for Disabled People* (London, February 2008).

25 ibid.

26 UN Doc A/RES/48/96.

27 UN Committee on the Rights of the Child, General Comment 7, (2005) UN Doc CRC/C/GC/7/Rev.1.

28 Camilla Parker, 'Article 19 – Living Independently and Being Included in the Community: Realizing the Right to Community Living' (4th International Summer School, Galway, June 2012).

benefit from community inclusion thrive in an environment where they are valued, where their autonomy is nurtured and where they are given choices.[29] In applying the social model of disability to Article 19, people with high support needs are not excluded from society 'because of any inherent feature or condition of the person him or herself, but by the social and physical environment in which they live'.[30] Community living emphasizes that whatever support and assistance that may be given should be based on the will and preferences of the person with disabilities.

The UN Committee on the Rights of Persons with Disabilities, which monitors the implementation of the CRPD, has already begun to clarify the nature of state obligations arising from ratification, recently examining reports from Spain,[31] Tunisia,[32] Peru,[33] Argentina,[34] China[35] and Hungary.[36] Three key conclusions arise from the Committee Reports. First, the Committee has interpreted Article 19 as placing choice and autonomy at the centre of the right to live independently and be included in the community. Second, the States Parties are required to make available adequate funding in order for the right to be effectively vindicated.[37] Third, reasonable accommodation is crucial for the inclusion of persons with disabilities in their local communities.

The Situation in Kenya

The Constitution of Kenya, 2010

Kenya ratified the CRPD on 19 May 2008. A new Constitution for Kenya was adopted on 27 August 2010, and Article 2(6) states that: 'Any treaty or convention ratified by Kenya shall form part of the law of Kenya under this Constitution.' Hence, the CRPD is now an integral part of Kenyan constitutional law.

The Constitution of Kenya provides for social economic rights, including the right to the highest attainable standard of health, to adequate food, to safe water, to social security and to education. Article 43(1)(b) provides for the right to housing:

---

29 ibid.

30 ibid.

31 Committee on the Rights of Persons with Disabilities, 6th Session (19–23 September 2011) UN Doc CRPD/C/ESP/CO/1.

32 UN Doc CRPD/C/TUN/CO/1.

33 UN Doc CRPD/C/PER/CO/1.

34 UN Doc CRPD/C/ARG/CO/1.

35 UN Doc CRPD/C/CHN/CO/1.

36 UN Doc CRPD/C/HUN/CO/1.

37 See Gerard Quinn and Suzanne Doyle, *Getting a Life – Living Independently and Being Included in the Community – A Legal Study of the Current Use and Future Potential of the EU Structural Funds to Contribute to the Achievement of Article 19 of the United Nations Convention on the Rights of Persons with Disabilities* (UNHR, Regional Office for Europe 2012).

'every person has the right to accessible and adequate housing, and to reasonable standards of sanitation'. Article 21(2), (3) and (4) of the Constitution allows for the progressive realization of the economic and social rights, and requires particular attention to be paid to vulnerable persons, including persons with disabilities.

Interpreting the new Constitution, the High Court of Kenya sitting in Embu in *Sangor Osman* in November 2011 adopted the iconic (but limited) precedent of the South African case of *Grootboom*,[38] as well as other international human rights standards, in a landmark decision. The case involved over 1,000 residents of Garissa town in the north-east of the country who had been evicted by government agents in 2010. The Court found that their eviction was unconstitutional. Further, it upheld the principle of indivisibility of all human rights and proceeded to order the government to provide shelter and other basic amenities to the same standard as existed before the eviction took place. In rendering its decision, the Court articulated that the obligation to take requisite measures did not mean that states should do more than its available resources permitted. However, it drew inspiration from the provisions of the South African Constitution, which obliged the 'state to devise and implement a coherent, co-coordinated programme' that would ensure that the realizations of the rights as guaranteed in the Constitution were not jeopardized.

Legislation

Kenya has enacted six legislative measures relating to housing. The Building Societies Act 1956, the Housing Act 1953 and the Sectional Properties Act 1987 provide the legal bases for financing and ownership arrangements for housing. The Building Societies Act 1956 provides for the formation and registration of building societies, while the Sectional Properties Act 1987 provides for the division of buildings into units to be owned by individual proprietors, and common properties to be owned by proprietors of the units as tenants in common. The Housing Act 1953 provides for public financing for home development as it establishes the National Housing Corporation (NHC), a parastatal organization which is charged with providing loans from public funds for the construction of private dwellings. The Housing Act 1953 does not provide for any tangible right to housing, sanitation or water. The only provision that somehow 'resembles' (and very weakly at that) a right to adequate housing is the proviso in s 23 that:

> Whenever it appears to the Minister, and after a local inquiry in public by an officer appointed by the Minister for that purpose at which the local authority and other parties interested shall be entitled to be heard, that the provision made in the area of any local authority for the needs of persons ordinarily employed within that area for normal requirements is inadequate or unsuitable, the Minister

38 *Government of the Republic of South Africa and others v Grootboom and others* 2000 (11) BCLR 1169 (CC).

> may, by written notice, require that local authority, within such time as may be stated in the notice, to make such provision for the housing of such persons as the Minister may specify.

The Rent Restriction Act 1959 sets limits on arbitrary increases of rent,[39] penalties for accepting excessive rent[40] and restrictions on distress for rent.[41] The Act also establishes a tribunal,[42] which is mandated with, among other functions, the right to investigate complaints made against a tenant or a landlord, and consequently to make such orders as it may deem necessary. The Landlords and Tenants Act 1965 makes provision with respect to certain premises for the protection of tenants of such premises from eviction or exploitation. Both of these regulate relations between landlords and tenants. An associated law requires employers to subsidize their employees' housing costs.

The Persons with Disabilities Act 2003 provides for the rights and rehabilitation of persons with disabilities, the achievement of the equalization of opportunities for persons with disabilities and the establishment of the National Council for Persons with Disabilities. The Act touches on housing in two regards. First, one of the members of the National Council for Persons with Disabilities is a representative from the Ministry of Housing. Second, one of the functions of the Council under s 7 of the Act is to consult with the government in relation to the provision of suitable and affordable housing for persons with disabilities. In the absence of data, it is difficult to say whether the Council has taken any steps under this mandate and, if so, how effectively this has been done.

Policy Documents

There are several policy documents that touch on housing in Kenya. These include Vision 2030,[43] Kenya's National Land Policy 2009,[44] the Draft National Policy on Human Rights 2010[45] and Kenya's National Housing Policy.[46] The National Housing Policy specifically identifies the poor, women, children in difficult

---

39 Rent Restriction Act 1959, s 9.

40 ibid s 10.

41 ibid s 16.

42 ibid s 4.

43 The National Economic and Social Council of Kenya (NESC), *Kenya Vision 2030: The Popular Version* (2007). Vision 2030 is the Kenyan government's key development blueprint on which specific government policies are based.

44 Republic of Kenya, Ministry of Lands, *Sessional Paper No 3 of 2009 on Land Policy* (Nairobi, 2009).

45 Republic of Kenya, Ministry of Justice, National Cohesion and Constitutional Affairs & Kenya National Commission on Human Rights, *Draft National Policy on Human Rights, 2010)* (2010).

46 Republic of Kenya, Ministry of Housing, *Sessional Paper No 3 of 2004 on National Housing Policy for Kenya* (Nairobi, 2004).

circumstances, persons with disabilities, internally displaced persons and the elderly as groups of persons requiring priority consideration in gaining access to adequate housing and related resources.[47]

The National Housing Policy outlines several objectives in order to improve the housing situation of the identified vulnerable or disadvantaged groups. It provides that the state must facilitate greater access to housing finance to vulnerable groups and take steps to assist economically vulnerable groups in housing improvement and/or production. More specifically, it mandates the state to facilitate the development of credit institutions that can provide shelter financing to persons with disabilities, among other marginalized groups. The policy also urges the state to upgrade slums and informal settlements, and to develop dwellings that are friendly to persons with disabilities. This is critical, taking into account the fact that the majority of persons with disabilities in urban areas live in informal settlements.[48]

While the National Housing Policy does not specifically identify housing discrimination as an issue, it implicitly recognizes that certain groups of people have historically suffered direct and indirect forms of housing discrimination. Consequently, it provides that the state must give these vulnerable or disadvantaged groups priority consideration in accessing adequate housing.[49] While the National Housing Policy makes reference to the progressive realization of the right to adequate housing, this has not been accompanied by comprehensive programmes, strategies and allocation of resources.

The Situation of Persons with Disabilities in Kenya with Regard to Article 19

According to the 2009 Population and Housing Census report, Kenya has a total population of 38,610,097 people, 4.6 per cent of whom are persons with disabilities.[50] However, the 4.6 per cent disability prevalence figure is disputable on several grounds. First, the World Report on Disability (2011) estimates that including children, over a billion people (or about 15 per cent of the world's population) live with a disability.[51] Second, there is a symbiotic relationship

47 Hakijamii, *Assessment of the Realization of the Right to Housing in Kenya 2009–2010: Taking Stock of What is and What Ought to Be* (January 2011).

48 Committee on the Rights of Persons with Disabilities, 'Future Sessions, Consideration of Reports'; National Report: Kenya's Initial Report Submitted under Article 35(1) of the United Nations Convention on the Rights of Persons with Disabilities – 31st August 2011.

49 Hakijamii (n 47).

50 Kenya National Bureau of Statistics and Population and Housing Census http://www.knbs.or.ke/censuspopulation.php accessed 29 June 2013.

51 World Health Organization and the World Bank, *World Report on Disability* (Malta, WHO 2011).

between poverty and disability. Hence, the current high levels of poverty in the country are likely to result in a greater proportion of the population being persons with disabilities. Third, there is a problem with the instruments used to identify persons with disabilities, so that mild to moderate impairments frequently go undetected.[52] Hence, the actual number of persons with disabilities in Kenya is likely to be over five million people, most of whom live with their families, but without the necessary support to ensure their participation and inclusion in the community. Consequently, the issue of exclusion is important because it affects a significant sector of the society whose inclusion and participation Article 19 of the CRPD seeks to ensure.

The legal position of persons with disabilities in Kenya has radically improved since the early 2000s. Kenya enacted the Persons with Disabilities Act 2003, which provided, for the first time, a right to non-discrimination on grounds of disability. In 2008, Kenya ratified the CRPD, which became part of Kenyan law with the promulgation of the Constitution of Kenya 2010.[53] However, despite these positive changes in the law, 'the lives of people with disabilities in Kenya are marked by experiences of discrimination, prejudice and inequality'.[54]

Several Kenyan studies demonstrate that for the majority of persons with disabilities in Kenya, Article 19 remains unfulfilled. For instance, investigations carried out for the UN Universal Periodic Review found that approximately 74 per cent of people with disabilities interviewed reported that they were denied the right to make decisions on issues affecting their own lives. They described how they had been forced into situations against their will because they had been judged incapable of making decisions on their own.[55]

---

52 University of Nairobi, *A Final Report of the University Disability Mainstreaming Committee* (February 2011).

53 Equal Rights Trust and Kenya Human Rights Commission, *In the Spirit of Harambee: Addressing Discrimination and Inequality in Kenya* (London, February 2012).

54 African Union of the Blind, Kenya Union of the Blind and Centre for Disability Rights Education and Advocacy, *State of Disabled Peoples Rights in Kenya* (Kenya, 2007). In preparing this report, the authors interviewed 95 persons with various forms of disability in three different regions of Kenya with the aim of identifying the barriers they faced and understanding the human rights situation of disabled people. A total of 86 per cent of respondents stated that they had experienced unequal treatment, while 80 per cent reported experiencing isolation, segregation and lack of support for their needs, and 74 per cent felt they had been denied the right to make decisions regarding their own lives. The report identified three types of barrier preventing people with disabilities from participating in life on an equal basis: abuse and violence, discriminatory attitudes and limited access. A total of 56.8 per cent of participants in the study reported that they had experienced abuse and violence in the community or society at large, while almost three-quarters (74.7 per cent) of interviewees had experienced discriminatory attitudes in society.

55 Kenya UPR Stakeholders Coalition, Univeral Periodic Review, 'Annual Progress Report 22nd September 2010 – 21st September 2011' (Nairobi, Kenya, September 2011).

The majority of persons with disabilities in Kenya live with their families, and the primary responsibility for providing the necessary support is situated within the family.[56] In a study of people with disabilities in Kenya conducted by Ingstad and Grut in 2007, they note that: 'Individual independence can be a solution when the family is non-supportive, but we have seen that those who manage almost as a rule have a supportive family to rely on.'[57]

In spite of the central role of families, a 2012 report carried out by the Equal Rights Trust (ERT) and Kenya Human Rights Commission states that:

> ERT's interviews with persons with different forms of disability found that prejudice, stigma and discriminatory attitudes towards disability prevailed within families, and that the discriminatory treatment which persons with disabilities experienced in the home often had far-reaching consequences for their ability to participate equally in other areas of life.[58]

Thus, it is clear that although the majority of persons with disabilities live with their families and are physically located in the community, this does not necessarily translate into their participation and inclusion in the community on equal terms with others.

The right to live independently is further hampered by poor education (and the poor self-image and self-motivation that follow), which hinder market entry at a level that is genuinely commensurate with an individual's abilities.[59] Furthermore, a lack of equally effective and accessible transport facilities hinders not merely labour market mobility but also ordinary social intercourse.[60] Lack of access to the assistive devices needed to enable active and equal participation in life presents a particular problem for many of those with physical and sensory disabilities, which, in combination with direct discrimination against them, acts as a barrier

---

56 See Open Society's blog: 'Only a fraction of the people in Kenya in need of support services end up in Mathari (Kenya's only psychiatric facility), thankfully. But most of the rest are isolated at home without the support they need' http://blog.soros.org/2011/03/the-other-side-of-kenyas-terrible-secret accessed 25 February 2013.

57 Benedicte Ingstad and Lisbet Grut, 'See Me But Do Not Forget Me; People with Disabilities in Kenya' (SINTEF Health Research, Oslo, Norway, 2007) 52.

58 Equal Rights Trust and Kenya Human Rights Commission (n 53).

59 UN Committee on Economic Social and Cultural Rights, *Concluding Observations on Kenya*, UN Doc E/C.12/KEN/CO/1, 2008, paras 16, 34. The UNCESCR in its concluding observations on the Government of Kenya's 2007 report drew attention to the fact that many persons with disabilities remained unemployed and had limited access to education.

60 Gerard Quinn, 'The International Covenant on Civil and Political Rights and Disability: A Conceptual Framework' in Theresia Degener and Yolan Koster-Dreese (eds), *Human Rights and Disabled Persons: Essays and Relevant Human Rights Instruments* (Dordrecht, Martinus Nijhoff Publishers 1995).

to independent living.[61] Other problems affecting persons with intellectual and mental disabilities include the under-provision of specialist facilities and services and a lack of facilitation for augmentative and alternative communication (AAC). All these issues profoundly affect the right to live in the community.

While the majority of persons with disabilities in Kenya live with their families, institutionalization does occur in the context of mental health care and, to some extent, the provision of education in separate settings for children with disabilities. In the context of mental health care in Kenya, the only formalized support comes in the form of institutionalization in psychiatric hospitals. Community-based mental health-care services in Kenya are limited[62] and lack adequate funding to reach a wider proportion of the population affected. Kenya has little provision for mental health; the government only spends 0.01 per cent of its health budget on it.[63] Persons with psychosocial disabilities either live in their homes without support (without meaningful engagement in the community) or as homeless people, particularly in urban areas. Otherwise, they are institutionalized in psychiatric hospitals, usually Mathare Mental Hospital – the main referral hospital in Kenya with regard to mental healthcare (in Kenya, referral hospitals are the highest level of health institutions).

Institutionalization in Kenya to a significant extent also occurs in the provision of education for learners with disabilities in separate settings.[64] Learners with disabilities largely access education in boarding schools, away from their families and their communities from primary-school level upwards, largely due to a lack of choice. Learners without disabilities also attend boarding schools, but usually from secondary-school level upwards. Primary-level education is state-funded; hence, non-disabled learners attending boarding schools at primary-school level do so out of choice (usually to get to a better school), which is not the case for learners with disabilities. The latter are often barred from mainstream education and can only access education in separate settings, usually far away from their community. This lack of choice is also evident at secondary-school level – although less so, in the sense that the better-quality public secondary schools for all students tend to

61 Equal Rights Trust and Kenya Human Rights Commission (n 53). The report further notes that: 'In many parts of the country, access to assistive devices and specialist services for persons with physical and sensory disabilities is low, creating substantial problems across all areas of life.'

62 Elizabeth Kamundia, 'Choice, Support and Inclusion: Implementing Article 19 of the Convention on the Rights of Persons with Disabilities in Kenya' (LLM thesis, National University of Ireland, Galway 2012).

63 Mind Freedom Kenya, 'Report on Mental Health in Kenya' (Nairobi, Kenya, October 2008).

64 Public education in Kenya is based on an 8-4-4 system, with eight years of primary education followed by four years of secondary school and four years of college or university. Kenya Education System Overview http://education.stateuniversity.com/pages/772/Kenya-EDUCATIONAL-SYSTEM-OVERVIEW.html accessed 2 July 2013.

be boarding schools. The implication of this is that children with disabilities are denied the choice to exercise their right to education within the community.[65]

It is important to note that the level of participation and involvement in community life depends on how adequately a person's support needs are addressed. The needs of persons with high support needs are often not met, leading to a greater incidence of exclusion from society. This distinction has been expressed in terms of the 'double invisibility' of some persons with disabilities.[66]

The Situation of Persons with Disabilities in Kenya with Regard to the Right to Housing

Persons with disabilities are among the groups identified as vulnerable or disadvantaged by General Comment 4 of the UN Committee on Economic and Social Rights.[67] Hence, policy and legal frameworks for housing must take into account the special housing needs of persons with disabilities. This is not the case in reality in Kenya. The Standard Media Group reported on the difficulties that Keziah Mwelu, a woman with physical disabilities, faced with regard to housing:

> The switches, cooking slabs, kitchen sinks, kitchen cabinets and taps are too high for her and she has to ask for assistance when using them. The washrooms too, are not disability compliant – there are no support rails and neither is there enough space to maneuver about. It gets worse when renting a house and the entire ground floor is taken, nobody is willing to give up their house for this disabled person who cannot get themselves to say, the fourth floor.[68]

Persons with intellectual disabilities and those with psychosocial disabilities also face difficulties accessing housing, primarily because most of them are unemployed.[69] This significantly impacts their capacity to choose where and with whom to live, and, indeed, their capacity to have choice and control over their lives generally.

The overall housing situation is a major factor in the implementation of Article 19. In this context, it is important to highlight some general issues with regard to

65 Kamundia (n 62).

66 Gerard Quinn and Theresia Degener, 'The Current Use and Future Potential of United Nations Human Rights Instruments in the Context of Disability' (United Nations, 2002, HR/PUB/02/1, 23): 'Some groups of people with disabilities are more invisible than others ... People with intellectual disabilities find it difficult in many societies to make progress – or at least as much progress as other groups with disabilities.'

67 Committee on Economic, Social and Cultural Rights, 'General Comment No 4: The Right to Adequate Housing' UN Doc E/1992/23, annex III at 114 (1991).

68 Nloki Chege, 'Home and Away: Building for the Disabled' *Standard Digital* (Nairobi, 7 July 2011).

69 Kamundia (n 62).

the right to housing in Kenya in order to really comprehend the dilemmas arising with regard to a specific group – persons with disabilities.

Kenya is currently grappling with the issue of resettling internally displaced persons who were displaced as a result of the post-election violence of 2008. Persons with disabilities, of course, are among the internally displaced persons. Kenya experiences high levels of poverty. According to the UN Human Development Reports, Kenya is rated as being of medium human development, ranking in the lower quarter of 182 countries. Some 50 per cent of the population live below the poverty line.[70] Poverty in urban areas involves an acute shortage of habitable dwellings, inadequate infrastructure, basic amenities and services, overcrowding, extensive slums and squatter settlements.[71] Some 60–80 per cent of residents in Kenya's largest urban centres, Kisumu, Mombasa and Nairobi, live in informal settlements. These informal settlements are crowded, with poor-quality housing, and lack basic services such as access roads, education facilities and sanitation facilities, and also suffer from chronic insecurity.[72] This is further compounded by the endemic cases of forced evictions, most of whose victims are the poor and marginalized groups.

Conditions of poverty have a direct bearing on the realization of the right to housing, particularly in the Kenyan context, where housing developments and provision remain in the hands of the private sector. The result is that quality low-cost housing remains unavailable for the majority of low-income urban dwellers, among whom persons with disabilities are disproportionately over-represented.

Kenya's complex ethnic diversity has also presented challenges with regard to discrimination in housing. There have been occasional media reports of individuals denied opportunities to rent on the basis of ethnicity and race. Kenya lacks an adequate legal framework specific to discrimination in housing which leaves victims with little recourse. This is compounded in the context of persons with disabilities, due to the fact that they face additional barriers in accessing justice. Work on the realization of the right to housing is also hampered by the lack of data and statistics, particularly with regard to economic and social rights.

In this context, Article 19(c) of the CRPD requires the Kenyan state to ensure that 'community services and facilities for the general population are available on an equal basis to persons with disabilities and are responsive to their needs'. The services referred to by Article 19(c) include housing, but the level of general housing services in Kenya, particularly in urban areas, is poor. The difficulty in this regard is clear – how does one access the right to housing if there are no affordable

70 In terms of its population living under $1.25 and $2.00 a day, it ranks at 70.7 per cent and 80.0 per cent respectively.

71 Kamau Esther Njeri, 'They Are No Longer Policy Goals But Rights: Justiciability of Housing and Water Rights for Slum Dwellers in Kenya in the Wake of the New Constitution' http://www.kituochasheria.or.ke/index2.php?option=com_docman&task=doc_view&gid=74&Itemid=92 accessed 15 October 2012.

72 Hakijamii (n 47).

houses? How does one exercise choice of where and with whom to live if one's resources are limited? Most importantly, in circumstances where public services are limited for everyone, what does this mean for persons with disabilities? At the very minimum, it means they should be able to avail themselves of services at a level commensurate with others, but this is not saying very much where there are no services to speak of for everyone. This demonstrates the difficulties inherent in implementing Article 19 in a resource-scarce setting.

Some Recommendations on Implementing Article 19

To facilitate the right to independent living, it is necessary to remove the barriers that hinder its realization. In the context of Kenya, these barriers stem from a combination of various factors, including stigma, inaccessibility of places, services and social structures, and lack of support within the community.[73] The right to housing is adversely affected by the high levels of poverty currently being experienced in the country, which negatively impact on the fulfilment of social and economic rights generally. In order to address these and other barriers, and move along the implementation of both the right to live independently in the community and the right to adequate housing, the following recommendations are pertinent.

The government should set aside more funds for the Kenya Slum Upgrading Project,[74] which seeks to improve housing in the informal settlements. Further, a special tax should be imposed on unused land to go towards the purchase of land for upgrading urban settlements.[75] This is particularly pertinent where the vast majority of persons with disabilities in urban areas live in informal settlements. The upgraded shelter should be accessible to persons with disabilities, in line with Article 43(1)(b) of the Constitution.

The government should review all existing legislation and policies that touch on housing to bring them into line with the constitutional recognition of the right to accessible and adequate housing. Specifically, there is need to ensure that the most vulnerable individuals are protected through the prohibition of discrimination in housing.[76] Discrimination here must be understood in line with the CRPD, wherein the denial of reasonable accommodation is deemed to be discrimination.

The implementation of the National Housing Policy would go a long way towards ensuring that persons with disabilities can access housing in Kenya. While independent living in the community does not mean merely having a house in which to live and includes many other factors, access to housing is key to the enjoyment

73 Commissioner for Human Rights (n 22).

74 See UN Habitat, 'Kenya Slum Upgrading Project' http://www.unhabitat.org/content.asp?cid=668&catid=206&typeid=13 accessed 17 August 2013.

75 Nairobi Peoples' Settlement Network, 'The Peoples' Budget: Priorities for Action in Nairobi Peoples' Settlements 2007/08' (Ufungamano House, 18 April 2007).

76 Hakijamii (n 47).

of this right. Following *Grootboom*,[77] the measures taken to operationalize the National Housing Policy should be comprehensive, coordinated, reasonably implemented, balanced, targeted and flexible, and make appropriate provision for attention to those whose needs are most urgent and whose ability to enjoy all rights is most in peril. Persons with disabilities in Kenya certainly fall within this group. These measures should include adequate budgetary allocation towards housing.

The government should engage constructively with the private sector in Kenya with regard to the provision of accessible and adequate housing. The Economic and Social Rights Centre (Hakijamii), a non-governmental organization (NGO) that monitors economic, social and cultural rights in Kenya, asserts that:

> Future work on the right to housing must track developments in the private sector not just to highlight violations but to provide policy advice on how the private sector can be better regulated and incentivized to contribute better to the housing rights particularly among the poorest and most vulnerable.[78]

The government should also involve NGOs working on the right to housing, as well as disabled peoples' organizations (DPOs). These NGOs and DPOs should take the lead in assisting the government to set up specific policy and legislative frameworks on accessible and adequate housing.[79] Together, these organizations can help the government in areas where it may be lacking in skills, resources or knowledge, particularly with regard to highlighting housing issues that affect persons with disabilities. Indeed, Article 4(3) of the CRPD requires that persons with disabilities be consulted in all decision-making processes affecting them.

The need for accurate data on disability and the right to housing cannot be emphasized sufficiently strongly. There should be widespread awareness-raising on the rights of persons with disabilities. Private developers would certainly benefit from such knowledge and may be more compelled to design universally accessible houses as a result. Failing this, there may be some merit in examining how the law may be used to ensure that large-scale developments contain units which are accessible to persons with disabilities. Awareness-raising, targeted at persons with disabilities and their families, also has a major role to play in enhancing choice and control within the lives of persons with disabilities in Kenya.

While commending the Cash Transfer Programme for Persons with Severe Disabilities[80] which currently exists in Kenya, the state should upscale the provision of financial support to families and to persons with disabilities

---

77 *Government of the Republic of South Africa and others v Grootboom and others* (n 38).

78 Hakijamii (n 47) 35.

79 ibid.

80 Republic of Kenya, *National Plan of Action for Orphans and Vulnerable Children 2005/6–2009/10* (Nairobi, Department of Children's Services, Ministry of Gender, Children and Social Development 2008).

progressively. In line with the principle of progressive realization, the support provided should be adequate to ensure that families can access adequate housing, among other social economic rights.

In order to address the instances where institutionalization occurs in the country, the state should address mental health care in the country as well as enable inclusive education. With regard to mental health care, the state should embody the paradigm shift of the CRPD, switching from institutionalization towards a community-based mental health-care system. This may be one of the ways of addressing the fact that families sometimes abandon their members with mental health conditions, leaving them in mental hospitals, and such people become long-term inmates in psychiatric institutions. It may also lead to reduced homelessness among persons with mental health conditions. There is also a need to examine the provision of safe houses for persons with psychosocial disabilities transitioning from institutionalization back to the community.

With regard to education, the state should progressively reduce the numbers of students with disabilities accessing education in separate settings and should relocate them, together with the requisite resources to mainstream schools.

It is widely acknowledged that there is a link between Article 19 and Article 12 of the CRPD on legal capacity.[81] The legal requirement to ensure that one should be of sound mind in order to enter into contracts exists in Kenyan law. Persons with disabilities do not, at least by law, enjoy legal capacity on a par with others. The effect this has on access to housing for persons with disabilities, particularly those with intellectual and psychosocial disabilities, should be explored.

Finally, the state should provide state-funded centres for community living. This is particularly pertinent to the implementation of Article 19(b) of the CRPD.

Conclusion

The answer to the key question 'is the right to housing of relevance to the right of people with disabilities in Kenya to live independently?' is yes. First, it is obvious that according to the social model of disability in which this chapter is grounded and upon which the CRPD is predicated, disability is to be understood as resulting from the interaction of impairments with an inaccessible environment. With regard to Article 19, accessible housing would result to increased choice, control and independence among persons with disabilities in the country.

Second, Article 19(c) requires equal access to services, and this must be understood to include housing. Additionally, the National Housing Policy provides that the state must give these vulnerable or disadvantaged groups priority consideration in accessing adequate housing,[82] and this includes persons with disabilities. Third, Article 19 is about exercising choice of where and with whom to

81 Focus Report 2009 (n 4) 21.

82 Hakijamii (n 47).

live. The fact that persons with disabilities are disproportionately over-represented among the homeless imperils their inclusion in the community. Indeed, fulfilling the right to adequate housing is critical for persons with disabilities (particularly persons with psychosocial disabilities whose families tend to abandon them in mental health facilities), who may not for the time being be in a position to access employment in the competitive labour market.

Clearly, there are significant links between the right to live independently in the community and the right to adequate housing. It may be that the key to implementing Article 19 is the full realization of the right to housing for all.

Chapter 8

Public Interest Law and Regeneration: The Case of Ballymun Community Law Centre – Connecting the Dots through Community Economic Development

Maria Antonieta Nestor

Introduction

The development of public interest law in the US in recent years, particularly in the field of community economic development (CED), offers a platform for comparison through which to assess the evolution of public interest law within the CED field in Ireland. While the origins of CED grew amidst the social, economic and political changes brought by the War on Poverty of the Kennedy and Johnson administrations in the US during the 1960s, in Ireland its origins differ. Given the dearth of research in the public interest law arena, little is known about the everyday impact of public interest law within Irish society. Moreover, developments in other jurisdictions seem not to be present in the Irish public interest law landscape. Although this chapter does not provide detailed evaluations and country comparisons, suffice it to say that in the US, the involvement of public interest lawyers in urban revitalization efforts such as regeneration and urban renewal became the main catalyst for the rise of CED law/lawyering,[1] an area of law that since the 1990s has become a 'significant new area of public interest law',[2] contributing to the narrowing of the gap in accessing civil justice and civil legal aid as well as helping to create sustainable communities.

In Ireland, although the development of CED (particularly CED law and lawyering) has been influenced by the community law centre movement and the search for alternative options to the statutory civil legal aid scheme, urban revitalization efforts such as regeneration of affordable housing have also meant that the revitalization of low-income communities is taking centre stage in 'our

1 It is important to highlight that CED as a movement and as a concept can be traced much further back – its roots and genesis can be found within the pre-Civil Rights era.

2 Brian Glick and Matthew Rossman, 'Neighborhood Legal Services as House Counsel to Community-Based Efforts to Achieve Economic Justice' (1997) 23 NYU Rev L & Soc Change 105, 110.

version' of CED law and lawyering. This chapter therefore aims at finding how CED law and lawyering is practised in Ireland by examining the case of the Ballymun Community Law Centre and by arguing that public interest law and regeneration efforts can be connected through the further development of CED.

Definitions

When we speak of CED, three different definitions need to be understood, namely CED, CED law and CED lawyering. In short, CED is addressed at the local (although nowadays calls to expand the definition of 'local' are starting to emerge as different types of communities such as immigrants and others are also using CED).[3] It has a specific geographical focus, makes the community the recipients of development and makes that development accountable to the community it serves. CED law in turn embraces the efforts made by that local community at developing jobs, housing, combating drug abuse and the creation of businesses for low-income people among others – efforts which are on many occasions supported by non-profit organizations and community groups. CED lawyering therefore acts as a facilitator by using different legal tools and approaches, all of which are geared towards the socio-economic improvement and empowerment of the community.[4]

Public Interest Law and CED in the US: A Brief Overview

CED in the US developed out of a social movement[5] that tried to 'revitalize low-income communities' and in which affordable housing development played a central role.[6] The goal of having a 'decent home and a suitable living environment for every American family' was put on a statutory footing as far back as 1949 with the enactment of the Housing Act of 1949.[7] Since then, efforts to develop and

3 Wiliam H Simon, 'Introduction: Lawyers and Community Economic Development' (2007) 95 Cal L Rev 1821. See also Carmen Huertas-Noble, 'Promoting Working-Owned Cooperatives as a CED Empowerment Strategy: A Case Study of *Colors* and Lawyering in Support of Participatory Decision Making and Meaningful Social Change' (2010) 17 Clinical L Rev 255, 262–64.

4 For detailed definitions, see Maria A Nestor, 'CED Lawyering in Ireland: An Overview' (2011) 1(1) Ir Rev CED Law & Pol 6.

5 The community economic development movement originated in the 1960s, but it has its roots in the early 1900s, when Booker T Washington and WEB DuBois looked at African-American emancipation. See Roger A Clay, Jr and Susan R Jones, 'What is Community Economic Development?' in Roger A Clay Jr and Susan R Jones (eds), *Building Healthy Communities: A Guide to Community Economic Development for Advocates, Lawyers, and Policy Makers* (Chicago, American Bar Association 2009) 5.

6 Clay, Jr and Jones (eds) (n 5).

7 42 USCA §1441.

redevelop communities have shaped the evolution of CED as a whole,[8] making it into the composite of legal, social and community development that it is today.

While market-based anti-poverty mechanisms or techniques such as the channelling of capital via tax financing and investment options (Low-Income Housing Tax Credits,[9] New Markets Tax Credits[10] or the creation of Empowerment Zones,[11] for example) have played more of a role in the practice of CED law in the US, public interest lawyers in Ireland, in contrast, have focused more on innovative tools to gain access to justice such as efforts and initiatives that provide legal (and non-legal) services to the poor[12] – which in turn facilitate the building and empowering of communities – rather than on market-based techniques.[13]

---

8 Note, however, that the practice of CED law and lawyering came about much later in the 1980s with the realization that poverty lawyers were part of the problem of client disempowerment rather than the solution to it. See, for example, Scott L Cummings, 'Community Economic Development as Progressive Politics: Towards a Grass Root Movement for Social Justice' (2002) 54 Stanford Law Review 400–93; and Daniel S Shah, 'Lawyering for Empowerment: Community Development and Social Change' [1999] 6 Clinical L Rev 217, 231.

9 Low-Income Housing Tax Credit (LIHTC) started in 1986 during the Reagan administration under the Tax Reform Act of 1986 (100 Stat 2085, 26 USCA §§47, 1042). It seeks to leverage investment by obtaining funding from the private market. It has been successful in building housing units, whose numbers are well over one million. However, how effective the LIHTC has been is hard to tell. For more information about it, see, for example, Bill Lockyer, 'Annual Report 2011: Report on the Allocation of Federal and State Low Income Housing Tax Credits in California' (California Tax Credit Allocation Committee, April 2012) 1 www.treasurer.ca.gov/ctcac/2011/annualreport.pdf accessed 18 January 2013.

10 In 2000, the Clinton administration started the use of New Markets Tax Credits (NMTCs), which were set under the Community Renewal Tax Relief Act of 2000 (Pub L 106–554, §1(a)(7) [HR.5662], 21 December 2000, 114 Stat 2763, 2763A–587) in order to stimulate business development. In short, the NMTCs were designed to give a jump-start to low-income communities by encouraging investment. For more information, see Rapoza Associates, 'The New Markets Tax Credit: Progress Report 2012' (New Markets Tax Credit Coalition, June 2012) 1, 5. The Act can be accessed at www.hud.gov/offices/cpd/economicdevelopment/lawsandregs/laws/actof2000.pdf accessed 18 January 2013.

11 Empowerment Zones (EZs) were created by the Clinton administration as a way of following some of the themes of the 'War on Poverty' of President Johnson and reverting back to the Model Cities Programs. The EZs provided a number of federal benefits over a 10-year period. Some of the benefits included in them were an increase of grants for social services and economic development, the waiver of certain regulatory matters and tax benefits among others. For more information on EZs, see William H Simon, 'The Community Economic Development Movement' [2002] Wis L Rev 377–436, 389.

12 For example, community legal education on housing law and policy or consumer law and group work enabling women to have a voice.

13 Market-based techniques such the use of tax incentives have been used in regeneration efforts and other types of development in Ireland, but public interest lawyers seem not to appear on the landscape. For example, when the regeneration of Dolphin's

The tackling of urban poverty and the creation of a better urban economy in Ireland has meant that the government has played much more of a role in funding the development of social housing regeneration schemes[14] when compared to the US, giving the Irish public interest lawyer a certain advantage and disadvantage when it comes to regeneration efforts.[15] The advantage in Ireland is based on the government reaching out to community groups, non-governmental organizations (NGOs) and service providers with the aim of engendering collaborative efforts in order to achieve specific regeneration goals, whereas in the US, there has been much more private market intervention. By the same token, this approach has created a disadvantage for Irish public interest lawyers as it has made them indifferent when private market intervention in regeneration efforts is concerned. Anecdotal evidence shows that when PPPs[16] were used in regeneration efforts, local communities were at a great disadvantage as there were no lawyers representing community interests.[17]

Regeneration efforts in Ireland and the involvement of public interest law are best exemplified by the regeneration efforts of Ballymun and most recently Limerick, as it is possible to find that because of regeneration, access to legal aid services has become part of the development/regeneration agenda rather than existing in isolation. This change of approach that placed legal aid services within a regeneration framework did not look at access to justice and the provision of

---

Barn via a public-private partnership (PPP) took place, there were no lawyers representing the community interests and, to date, there is no record of lawyers representing community interests in relation to social housing regeneration under PPP schemes: email correspondence from Dr Rory Hearne to the author (February 2012). For an account of the type of policies and legislation in relation to fiscal incentives, see Brendan Williams, 'Fiscal Incentives and Urban Regeneration in Dublin' (University College Dublin 2006) Working Papers Series, Planning and Environmental Policies Research Series.

14 Regeneration of social housing in Ireland has taken place under different schemes and under an array of government department. Data from 2006 indicate that there were 18 separate schemes administered by five different government departments and agencies. These schemes can be divided into three different types according to the way they are funded, namely local authority-led, multi-agency-led and PPPs. For more detail on this matter, see Kasey Treadwell Shine and Michelle Norris, *Regenerating Local Authority Housing Estates: Review of Policy and Practice* (Dublin, Centre for Housing Research 2006), Housing Policy Discussion Series 15–30.

15 The role of housing associations has also aided government efforts. Their role in CED would require further research which is outside the remit of this research.

16 PPPs were first introduced in Ireland on a pilot basis in June 1999. For more information on PPPs, see Rory Hearne, 'Origins, Development and Outcomes of Public-Private Partnerships in Ireland: The Case of PPPs in Social Housing Regeneration' (Combat Poverty Agency, November 2009) Working Paper Series 09/07; and Rory Hearne, *Public Private Partnerships in Ireland: Failed Experiment or the Way Forward?* (Manchester, Manchester University Press 2011).

17 See n 11 and Hearne, 'Origins' (n 16).

legal aid services from an exclusively legal perspective,[18] but rather from a much wider perspective aimed at combating poverty and social exclusion. Law would form part of a composite of legal, social policy and community development efforts that as a whole would interact to address issues of poverty and empower the local community, thus developing our understanding of CED law and lawyering.

Thus, Ballymun Community Law Centre (BCLC) was born out of a development/poverty agenda based on regeneration, particularly social regeneration,[19] and not directly as a result of access to justice calls – an agenda under which public interest lawyers reacted favourably to regeneration efforts by contributing to the creation of this independent community-based law centre, resulting in the formation of a collaborative practice that made lawyers part of the development process[20] rather than simple observers.[21] Moreover, BCLC would eventually facilitate the improvement of the socio-economic infrastructure and development of the community by using different legal approaches and techniques, such as the establishment of community legal education and the creation of mediation services,[22] as well as working in partnership with government.

Consequently, the creation of BCLC provided for the use and implementation of a strategic (and comprehensive) model of legal aid supported by the government, an approach which had been called for since the 1970s but had been ignored by the government until then.

This chapter therefore aims to discover how CED law and lawyering is practised in Ireland by examining the case of BCLC as an example of the interaction between public interest law and regeneration. The first part offers a brief overview of public interest law and CED in the US with a focus on disinvestment and redevelopment as a way of having some grounds for comparison. The second part offers a background as to the regeneration process in Ireland, including (with broad strokes) the influences of sustainable development policies in regeneration. The third part gives an overview of the regeneration process of Ballymun, thus providing the context for the case study. The fourth part offers BCLC as a case study of CED,

18 It could be argued that the Free Legal Aid Centres campaign for a strategic model of legal aid was always part of a general anti-poverty campaign, but it has always been viewed from a legal stance.

19 Interview with Evelyn Hanlon, Chair of the Board of Directors, BCLC Ltd (Dublin Civic Offices, 17 January 2012).

20 Because the lawyer can provide, for example, legal education, it helps with the understanding of the rights/obligations of the community.

21 The different origins of BCLC when compared to other community law centres in Ireland such as the Northside Community Law and Mediation Centre (NCL&MC) has important practical implications – for example, it places community law centres within a regeneration/sustainable development agenda.

22 Note, however, that community legal education and mediation services were part of legal approaches and techniques already used in Ireland by the NCL&MC and until 2002, it was the only community-based law centre existing in the country. More information about the NCL&MC can be accessed through its website www.nclc.ie accessed 18 January 2013.

arguing that CED law and lawyering exist in Ireland and that their use and practice can help with the strategic model of legal aid by expanding the role of law and the legal system in bringing about social change via the combination of law, social policy and community development, while at the same time changing lawyering attitudes through a re-balancing of power, thus achieving empowerment.

Origins of CED

Although CED as a movement started in the 1960s, its roots and genesis can be traced back to the pre-Civil Rights era and the disinvestment in American cities from the 1900s to the 1950s. The pre-Civil Rights era sought to aid the economic achievement and political power of the 'newly emancipated African American slaves'.[23] The views of community development espoused by Robert Owen and Charles Booth in the nineteenth century,[24] coupled with the ideologies of Booker T. Washington and W.E.B. DuBois in the early twentieth century and the lack of investment in the inner cities, also had an input in cementing these roots. Booker T. Washington sought to create black self-help and mutual assistance, developing and promoting black business ventures and economies,[25] as he felt that people were not ready for integration.[26] W.E.B. DuBois, for his part, promoted the education of black students to college level, as he saw education as the best way for advancing the development of African Americans.[27]

The disinvestment in American cities from the 1900s to the 1950s was mainly an urban problem that was rooted in a combination of political, economic and historical causes. The industrialization of the nineteenth and early twentieth centuries acted as an engine attracting people to the cities as there were plenty of jobs available. Immigration from 1880 to 1920 brought millions from Europe and, after 1920, a large number from Mexico.[28] In this climate of new people, there was still much segregation. According to Massey and Denton,[29] segregation was never as severe as with African Americans. Their pattern of internal migration meant people from the southern cities went to the northern cities in search of work and people from rural areas travelled to urban areas also looking for work. This shift occasioned a fast increase in population and within 40 years (1910s–1950s), the social landscape had changed forever. By the 1950s, the level of net-flow migration

23 Clay, Jr and Jones (n 5) 5.

24 Robert Halpern, *Rebuilding the Inner City: A History of Neighborhood Initiatives to Address Poverty in the United States* (New York, Columbia University Press 1995) 128.

25 Clay, Jr and Jones (n 5) 5.

26 Halpern (n 24) 128.

27 Clay, Jr and Jones (n 5) 5.

28 Douglas S Massey and Nancy A Denton, *American Apartheid: Segregation and the Making of the Underclass* (Cambridge, MA, Harvard University Press 1993) 18.

29 ibid 17–59.

from rural to urban had reached 1.5 million, with 1.4 million in the 1960s, further transforming the racial and class composition of American cities.[30]

These new arrivals to the cities settled where their predecessors lived, which in turn gave rise to overcrowding, a shortage of facilities and public services and a growth in the population size of the ghettos. Yet, despite the population growth during the 1950s and the 1960s, especially in the northern cities,[31] housing segregation was maintained.[32] From the 1950s to the 1970s, the percentage of African Americans in these cities doubled.[33] By then, the black migrant population had increased to 4.5 million.[34]

The segregation problem was also aided by the use of racially restrictive covenants which restricted the amount of housing available for African Americans, making segregation in urban communities even more acute. Many neighbourhood associations agreed not to sell to African Americans. This created an effective mechanism to keep 'people out' until the 1940s, when the Supreme Court ruled that racially restrictive covenants were unconstitutional.[35] Violence and private contracts also played their part, which were also sanctioned by the police by not recruiting people of colour until after the 1950s. Other mechanisms used to maintain and reinforce racial segregation within cities were also fostered, intentionally or unintentionally, by some of the policies of the federal government.[36]

Consequently, activists working in low-income communities in the 1960s wanted local residents to be part of the revitalization of their own communities,[37] as it was the input from the local population that could best address the issues of segregation, lack of services and disinvestment. Added to this, philanthropic responses to disinvestment, such as those promoted by the Ford Foundation in the early 1960s, as well as the creation of different government programmes that sought the participation of local communities under the auspices of the War on Poverty and beyond, further encouraged this approach, marking the start of the CED movement, a movement aimed at benefiting those neighbourhoods that on many occasions commercial development would not touch because of the social conflicts found within them.[38]

30 ibid 45.

31 ibid. The main cities that saw large increases of the population were Chicago in its south and west areas, Cleveland on its east side, Philadelphia on its north and west sides, and Newark, Detroit, Baltimore and Washington DC in their central areas.

32 ibid 46.

33 ibid 45.

34 ibid 46.

35 *Shelley v Kraemer* 334 US 1 (1948).

36 See later on in this chapter for a description of some of these policies.

37 Clay, Jr and Jones (n 5) 4.

38 ibid.

Philanthropic responses to disinvestment: the Gray Areas programme and Mobilization for Youth

In 1961, as a policy response to community disinvestment, the Ford Foundation funded two major neighbourhood-based initiatives: the Gray Areas programme (Gray Areas) and Mobilization for Youth (MFY).[39]

Gray Areas was a new institution which sought to leverage funds in the private sector to create projects in the public sector.[40] It also brought to the fore a discussion in terms of policy. By looking at low-income and inner-city communities from the inside out, it was felt that these communities could be fixed. It was designed to coordinate local institutional actors and focus on the growth of local areas. However, it failed, as its policy was not receptive to community participation. It did not emphasize the participation of the residents of the communities it was trying to fix[41] and ended up not doing what it said it would (i.e. fix communities from the inside out). However, it did not demolish or destroy the local communities it focused on. Instead, it informed policy to create the War on Poverty[42] by moving neighbourhood-based initiatives from the philanthropic sector to the federal government.

MFY, the second initiative, was aimed at tackling the gang problem in the inner cities.[43] It encouraged residents to define their own agenda, expanding the idea of community work to that of becoming an organizer, and, at the same time, organizers could receive a salary for their community work. It was much more militant, 'more activist and confrontational',[44] than Gray Areas. It offered leadership development within the inner city areas, a type of leadership that would play a bigger role in the late 1960s.[45] It also influenced the institutional reforms required in schools, welfare and housing departments, and community initiatives.[46]

Government programmes and participation of local communities

The Community Action Programme and the Community Action Agencies The Community Action Programme[47] (CAP) was one of the programmes of the War on Poverty of the Kennedy and Johnson administrations.[48] It was established under

39 Halpern (n 24) 89.

40 Gray Areas was different from redevelopment or urban renewal as it was a departure from these previous models.

41 Halpern (n 24) 92.

42 The War on Poverty set out in the Economic Opportunity Act 1964 had two main objectives: to prepare children, youths and 'to some extent' adults to take advantage of the economic opportunities created, and at the same time to enhance those opportunities: ibid 107.

43 ibid 101.

44 ibid 105.

45 ibid.

46 ibid.

47 Pub L 88-452, 20 August 1964, 78 Stat 508. Title II, Part A, Sec 202.

48 1961–69.

the Economic Opportunity Act 1964,[49] with the goal of utilizing and mobilizing resources (either in rural or urban areas or both), providing social services, assistance or other activities (such as 'developing employment opportunities, improving human performance, motivation, and productivity, or bettering the conditions under which people live, learn, and work')[50] that would in turn tackle poverty (including its cause or causes). The administration and coordination of CAP was performed by the Office of Economic Opportunity (OEO), an agency also established under the Act for this purpose.[51]

Under the CAP, financial assistance for these programmes would be provided through public and non-profit agencies eligible for funding. These agencies therefore came to be called Community Action Agencies (CAAs).[52] CAAs thus embodied 'the federal government's assumptions, intentions and specific programs'.[53] The CAP, through the CAAs, had the fiscal duty of administering two different types of funding: one for local initiatives and one for national emphasis programmes. The former had a budget allocation of 40 per cent, while the latter had 50 per cent. Legal aid projects (through the Legal Services Programme)[54] were to be funded by the national emphasis programmes, while community economic development was under the umbrella of local initiatives.[55]

In order to qualify for funding, the projects had to include participation from the residents of the locality where the funding was sought. However, 90 per cent of the project funding went to 'direct services', such as health, education and housing.[56]

However, the CAP, via the CAAs, was not successful as a twofold problem was created: on the one hand, there was never enough local participation, and on the other hand, the staff of the CAAs dominated the projects, while the CAA boards were sometimes unaccountable.[57] There were also further problems with the OEO[58] and, as a result, it was abolished in 1974.[59] Its grant-making power was

---

49 Pub L 88-452 (n 48).

50 Pub L 88-452 (n 48) Sec 202(a)2.

51 ibid Title VI, Part A.

52 Clay, Jr and Jones (n 5) 7.

53 Halpern (n 24) 107.

54 The Legal Services Programme was one of the programmes of the War on Poverty. For more information on the programme, see Lauren Breen, Louise Howells, Susan R Jones and Deborah S Kenn, 'An Annotated Bibliography of Affordable Housing and Community Economic Development Law' (2003) 13 J Affordable House & Cmty Dev L 334, 335.

55 Halpern (n 24) 108.

56 It is interesting to note that CAAs were meant to administer a variety of services, including 'community economic development'. See Simon (n 11) 386; and also Halpern (n 24) 108.

57 Simon (n 11) 386.

58 The OEO administered not only CAP but also the other programmes established under the Economic Opportunity Act.

59 Peter Edelman, 'The War on Poverty and Subsequent Federal Programs: What Worked, What Didn't Work, and Why? Lessons for Future Programs' (2006) Clearinghouse

later given to the Office of Community Service within the Department of Housing and Urban Development (HUD).

Thus, CAA organizations that had received funding prior to all these changes 'reinvented themselves as economic developers'[60] and those who survived played a role in the strengthening of the CED movement. This is because the organizations that had sought funding from CAP paved the way for the creation and nurturing of different affiliations, organizations and peoples who would otherwise never have come together. They all could enter into dialogue as to how the community could be improved from different angles and also gave poor people a voice as to some of the problems affecting their lives.[61] These dialogues could take place among 'single-issue coalitions, tenants' organizations, legal services, public interest law firms [and] various rights organizations'.[62] Furthermore, the government never really grasped the type of 'indigenous movement that was becoming the principal engine of development in inner-city communities', that is, the CED movement.[63]

From a policy perspective, the CAP, through the CAAs, was different from the 'Gray Areas' model of 1961, as it included, in its own way, community input. The federal government was learning from the urban renewal mistakes of the past.[64] This meant that community input or 'organizing' was moved into federal policy. However, the CAP also experienced problems as CAAs faced corruption, and their boards on many occasions were motivated by self-interest rather by the benefit of the community. CAAs also experienced lack of resources and issues of control. There were also critiques about the failure of CAAs to properly implement the requirement of 'maximum feasible participation'.[65] The concept of maximum feasible participation meant that local residents would take charge of their own 'problems' through playing a significant role in 'determining their priorities, resource priority and local activities of local "War on Poverty"'[66] by participating in the boards of CAAs – which meant that the whole community would work towards the same goal. However, not all the community was represented as people on the boards were not the 'most disfranchised' section of a community, but rather frequently represented only a fraction of them, usually family and friends of

---

Review Journal of Poverty Law and Policy 7, 10.

60 Simon (n 11) 387.

61 Halpern (n 24) 115–16.

62 ibid 115.

63 ibid 114. Halpern also says that the reasons for this, in the historical record, are not clear.

64 Although CAP was based on the Gray Areas model which incorporated its place-based approach, it modified some aspects as a response to what people thought the limits of the Gray Areas were.

65 In 1966 the government amended the 1964 Act requiring that one-third of the board be made up of 'representatives of the poor', but things did not change. See Halpern (n 24) 110–11.

66 Ibid 108.

specific interests.[67] In other words, board members often were not representative of the community.

Most importantly, however, members of Congress started to criticize CAAs as they noted that they were becoming vehicles for mobilizing communities in demanding reforms and local access to jobs, resources for schools, housing, etc.,[68] and because of this, they argued, local government might eventually lose control.[69] Thus, regional OEO administrators started to back down from prior commitments as to what they would fund.[70]

CAAs therefore made the city governments very uncomfortable as they were essentially organizing communities against their own cities through community action and participation. Although participation was viewed by the OEO as an end to the alienation of communities and thus as a way of strengthening democracy,[71] in practice, the reality was very different, as participation was used as 'a vehicle for political power'.[72]

The Model Cities Program The Model Cities Program[73] was a new federal measure against the threat of local mobilization created by the CAP.[74] It was the first federal programme of the HUD[75] and the last government effort by President Lyndon B. Johnson[76] and the War on Poverty to bring an end to crime in urban areas among other reasons. Funds for the Model Cities Program were channelled via the Demonstration Cities and Metropolitan Development Act 1966.[77]

The Model Cities Program was meant to change inner-city neighbourhoods through the coordination of federal and local efforts pertaining to 'professional planning, coordination of federal and local programs, concentration of resources

67 ibid 110.

68 ibid 110–14.

69 ibid 110–15.

70 ibid 116–17. Halpern cites an example of when local communities set their own priorities, such as the setting-up of a community school and a reading programme, they were told that these 'were not OEO priorities'.

71 The strengthening of democracy by way of participation of the individual within his or her community is also an important aspect of how CED lawyering developed in Ireland. See below, particularly the case study of BCLC and the concept of social regeneration and citizenship.

72 Halpern (n 24) 109.

73 42 USC §3301 et seq. See also CE Olken, 'Economic Development in the Model Cities Program' (1971) 36 Law & Contemp Probs 205.

74 Halpern (n 24) 118.

75 The HUD was created as a government department by the Department of Housing and Urban Development Act 1965 (Pub L 89-174). For a history of the HUD, see http://portal.hud.gov/portal/page/portal/HUD/about/hud_history accessed 18 January 2013.

76 1963–69.

77 Pub L 89-754, 3 November 1966, 80 Stat 1255 (42 USC 3301 et seq).

and innovation'. However, it lacked community input.[78] This lack of community input made the Program resemble the Gray Areas' view of how to tackle poverty,[79] silencing the voice of the community once more.

Because of the social unrest of the 1960s, the few businesses that had planned to relocate to the ghettos no longer did so, and the original funding for the Model Cities Program was reduced. Within two years, the budget of $500 million in funding to cover 75 cities became a budget of $300 million in funding to cover 150 cities.[80] Thus, the Program was ended in 1974.

The Use of Policy and Legislation Towards the Advancement of CED and the Emergence of CED Law

It is important to highlight that the 1960s was also a period of social unrest. There was social unrest due to the 'Ghetto riots'[81] which took place during the summers of 1963–68 and there were further riots occasioned by the assassination of Dr Martin Luther King Jr. in 1968. There was also the passage of the Civil Rights Act 1964[82] and of the Fair Housing Act 1968,[83] both of which were intended to put an end to discrimination. Moreover, there was an emergence of direct action strategies and a renewed interest in community development, as residents were tired of the segregation, disinvestment, lack of interest and investment by the government, and were inspired by the ideas of Saul Alinsky[84] – ideas that talked about those who have and those who have not.[85] By the end of the decade, people had seen the possibility of social change through community action and participation, which in turn had further influenced the viability of a number of government programmes,[86] adding to the growth of CED.

By the 1970s and the 1980s, neighbourhood activism exploded as community groups were formed in order to 'demand more and better services from city governments'.[87] The government responded by the formulation of policies and the updating and enactment of legislation that created institutions and enhanced community participation, involvement in land use and environmental process.

78 Halpern (n 24) 118.

79 ibid.

80 ibid 120–21.

81 ibid 119.

82 Pub L 88-352, 78 Stat 241, enacted 2 July 1964.

83 42 USCA §§ 3601–31.

84 Saul Alinsky was a community organizer and is considered to be the father of the modern community organizing movement. He also created the Industrial Areas Foundation (IAF) in the 1940s, a national community organizing network.

85 Halpern (n 24) 87.

86 This meant that the social and political landscape was very different from that of the beginning of the 1960s.

87 Simon (n 11) 388.

This allowed for the challenging of infrastructure developments in court.[88] The evolution of these policies also created trends which sought the decentralization of public administration on the one hand and the development of local markets along 'socially desirable paths' on the other.[89] As a result, the CED movement could direct these government efforts towards the tackling of poverty and the empowerment of communities.

What follows is therefore an explanation of the most important policies, legislation and tools relevant to CED, which in turn brought about the emergence of CED law and lawyering, particularly those relating to redevelopment and access to capital, with the understanding that some of the policies, legislation and tools pre-date those enacted by the War on Poverty, while others became highly technical or too complex to be understood by non-professionals in the field.[90]

Policies, legislation and tools

Redevelopment In short, the primary function of redevelopment (which is also known as urban renewal) is the removal of blighted areas by bringing revenue to these areas, while at the same time redirecting capital flow and enhancing accountability. But redevelopment may further represent two different functions or meanings. On the one hand, redevelopment may be equated with the changing of the physical infrastructure in a localized area. However, it may also refer to the legal process that brings about that change in the physical infrastructure.[91] For the purposes of this chapter, when referring to redevelopment, the latter meaning is preferred.

The redevelopment process, from a legal point of view, was created in the US in 1949 under the auspices of the National Housing Act 1949[92] and the Housing Act 1954,[93] which supported the local efforts to revitalize 'blighted' areas. It created structured negotiations and produced binding contracts to ensure that these renewal efforts could take place by providing federal funds to 'acquire slum properties, assemble them into large parcels, clear them of existing structures and prepared them for 'redevelopment'.[94] Redevelopment, however, was criticized as it created a process of removal that did not benefit the people it was supposed to. It

---

88 ibid.

89 ibid 378.

90 Clay, Jr and Jones (eds) (n 5); William B Fulton, *A Guide to California Planning* (Point Arena, CA, Solano Press Books 1999).

91 WH Simon refers to Redevelopment (with a capital R) as a 'term of art' which refers to a special legal process. See William H Simon, *The Community Economic Development Movement: Law, Business, and the New Social Policy* (2nd edn, Durham, NC, Duke University Press 2001) 7.

92 Title V of PL 81-171 (Title V of Public Law, approved 15 July 1949).

93 Massey and Denton (n 28) 55.

94 ibid.

caused injustices by giving a series of tax incentives to local areas in order to carry out development. It further subsidized 'the private participants through sweetheart land deals, cheap financing, tax breaks, and publicly provided infrastructure tailor[ed] to their investments'.[95]

Due to the negative impact that the redevelopment process had caused, the federal government ended some of the financial support allocated for redevelopment. Now, under the patronage of the Housing and Community Development Act 1974,[96] funding is granted in the form of Community Development Block Grants (CDBGs) instead.[97] Under this arrangement, each local government, rather than the federal government, could decide how to allocate the CDBG funds given to them.[98]

Statutory reform was also put in place to ensure that there was community participation in the redevelopment process. Federal laws applicable to federal and locally supported federal projects gave relocation rights to displaced tenants, home-owners and businesses. Some states, such as California, also enacted rights for projects that received state funding.[99]

However, the redevelopment process (before the 1974 Act) survived under the law of some states as the local tax revenue from properties was limited.[100] This meant that redevelopment could channel further income towards the coffers of the local government via the tax revenues produced by redevelopment. In California, this process became known as the 'fiscalization of land use' (the local government obtains income revenue from land use and development). The effects of this fiscalization of land use triggered the redevelopment of areas, even though these areas were not 'blighted', but they were nevertheless redeveloped, as local governments could collect the tax revenue.[101] As will be shown in a later section, redevelopment would become an important element in the further advancement of CED law and lawyering.

Redevelopment and its interaction with CED To further understand redevelopment and how it interacted with CED, it is also important to highlight that redevelopment was also influenced and shaped by other types of government

95 Simon (n 11) 381.

96 Pub L 93-383, as amended; 42 USC-5301 et seq.

97 For a current view on the distribution of CDBGs, see: http://portal.hud.gov/hudportal/HUD?src=/program_offices/comm_planning/communitydevelopment/programs/entitlement accessed 18 January 2013.

98 Simon (n 11) 381–82.

99 ibid 382–83. This also means that there are some good examples of redevelopment, such as the City of East Palo Alto in California and the Dudley Street Neighborhood Initiative (DSNI) in Boston. DSNI is a non-profit corporation that organizes locals around development planning, which, thanks to a Massachusetts Redevelopment Law, it has been given various powers, including Eminent Domain.

100 ibid 382 at note 7. Simon mentions Proposition 13 as one example in California.

101 This practice of using redevelopment to obtain income became very popular in the 1980s and 1990s.

policies, such as the Federal Housing Administration's loan programme, the urban renewal of 1949, the use of public housing, the auto industry and transportation, and the allocation of tax breaks for home-ownership, all of which are briefly described below.

The Federal Housing Administration and its Loan Programme The Federal Housing Administration (FHA) was created in 1934,[102] under the National Housing Act 1934,[103] in order to stimulate the construction industry. Its aim was to promote home-ownership, which had come to a halt after the Great Depression. However, in order to promote home-ownership, it also had to guarantee home loans. The effect produced by the FHA loan guarantee scheme meant the banks were free to make more loans, as the loans were low risk (because of the FHA guarantee). This process facilitated the purchase of homes in the suburbs, originating the 'white-flight' phenomenon. This was a move away from the overcrowded city dwellings to the idyllic suburban residence of single-family homes. One of the consequences of this subsidized move – which was originated by this government policy – was the creation of an exclusionary movement that did not provide finance for multi-family dwellings, leaving the poor in the overcrowded inner-city ghettos. In this way, the FHA loan programme added momentum to the development of CED.

The Urban Renewal of 1949 The urban renewal of 1949 helped in bringing infrastructure development to poor areas, but also exacerbated the redevelopment problem. First, there was an identification process which included condemnation areas[104] through the use of eminent domain. Second, private developers received federal government funding in the form of subsidies in order to redevelop those condemned areas. As a result, the development of luxury housing increased, while at the same time housing for low-income people decreased. This method of urban renewal had the effect of displacing the poor without replacing the housing destroyed in the process. Note that urban renewal was supposed to improve the cities and benefit the poor, not displace them. Again, the impact on CED was that it added momentum to the CED movement, as urban renewal was decreasing the amount of available housing for those less well-off.

Public Housing Although the idea of providing public housing for the poor had been around for decades, it was not until the 1930s that the idea of building public housing first emerged in poor neighbourhoods, as the building of public housing could increase the creation of jobs in the construction sector during the Great

---

102 Peter Dreier, Todd Swanstrom and John H Mollenkopf, *Place Matters: Metropolitics for the Twenty-First Century* (Lawrence, University Press of Kansas 2001) 108.

103 Pub L, 84-345, Stat 847.

104 Condemnation is the term used in the US to indicate that an area has been 'taken' by government for redevelopment, public use (such as for the widening of a road) or other purpose.

Depression.[105] The first urban public housing was carried out by the Public Works Administration, together with unions and non-profit organizations.[106] The public housing model first tried was in 1934, under the National Housing Act 1934 (the same Act that created the FHA), under which local housing authorities built and operated the housing units. Later, in 1937, a new National Housing Act[107] was passed,[108] which set the path for the massive public housing construction of the 1950s. It created subsidies for housing construction[109] in the form of 'low-cost loans to local and state governments'.[110]

However, in the 1950s, the selection of sites on which to build public housing was carried out by municipal planning departments, which in turn was dominated by private real estate and outside interests.[111] This meant that the construction of public housing was situated in low-income communities, most of which were located in areas adjacent to rivers and highways.[112] This oversight left the public housing residents with a lack of economic opportunity. The public housing areas had no economic base in which the residents could take part and, if they existed, the economic opportunities were very minimal, leaving the newly built public housing communities with no essential basis that could create viable communities.[113] The only feasible economic ventures to which residents could aspire were the creation of informal economies such as drug dealing.[114] At the time, one of the greatest housing projects built was 'Pico Aliso',[115] located in the City of Los Angeles. Pico Aliso was said to be 'socially optimum', but in time became a place that harboured criminals and criminality.[116]

Then, in the 1970s, rather than having the local authorities manage and build public housing, a new public housing model was tested, which tried to expand tenant choice and the availability of public housing. This programme was called

---

105 Halpern (n 24) 71.

106 ibid 72.

107 Pub L 75–412, 50 Stat 888.

108 The 1937 Act is also known as the Wagner-Steagall Act.

109 Massey and Denton (n 28) 52.

110 Halpern (n 24) 72.

111 ibid.

112 The location of the public housing construction was due, in part, to a flawed design.

113 The issue of public housing would also be a factor in the regeneration of Ballymun, as discussed later on in this chapter.

114 Halpern (n 24) 77.

115 http://articles.latimes.com/keyword/pico-aliso-housing-project accessed 18 January 2013.

116 Pico Aliso has now been demolished and replaced with more suitable housing focused on the 'new urbanism' theory. Demolition started in 1997 and was completed in 1999. For more information, see 'Demolition of Pico-Aliso Housing Project Begins' (8 August 1997) http://articles.latimes.com/1997/aug/08/local/me-20535 accessed 18 January 2013.

'Section 8', referring to the section of the Act in which it was found. Under s 8 of the Housing and Community Development Act 1974, certificates are given to people who meet means-tested criteria in order to help them pay the costs of rent. The rent charge can only be 30 per cent of the household income. Thus, the certificate given is intended to cover the difference between the market-based rent and the maximum rent payable by the tenant.[117]

The way in which 'Section 8' operated led to a change of approach by the first Bush and Clinton administrations[118] in two ways: by the issuance of vouchers, commonly known as 'voucherization', and by the provision of HUD programmes. Voucherization means that a tenant receives a flat amount of money in the form of a voucher to help with the costs of rent, but the amount is not related to the market value of a rented property. The tenant is therefore free to negotiate for a rental price that could come as close as possible to the value of the voucher. However, this voucher approach does not incentivize the building of new housing or tenant participation which goes against the development of CED.

In contrast, the provision of HUD programmes does help in the development of CED as the programmes favour a 'community building approach',[119] which encourages tenant participation. HUD programmes also promote home-ownership by encouraging the buying of government housing by the tenants, and by combining housing with financial assistance so that residents can achieve economic independence. One example of the HUD programmes is HOPE VI,[120] which is also a major participant in the building of public housing.[121]

The Auto Industry and Transportation The development of the auto industry and transportation at the federal level was similar to that of redevelopment. The federal highway programme under the Federal-Aid Highway Act 1956[122] displaced as many people as urban renewal (redevelopment) did.[123] Communities, particularly African-American and Latino communities, were displaced or broken apart in order to free up land for the construction of motorways. In Los Angeles, for example, the main Mexican-American neighbourhood, Boyle Heights, was fragmented by the construction of five highways running through the neighbourhood.[124] Ironically, the construction of motorways and the destruction of neighbourhoods stopped when funding for defence issues became a priority during the Cold-War.

117 Simon (n 11) 391–95.

118 1989–93 and 1993–97, respectively (Clinton was re-elected; his second term was 1997–2001).

119 Simon (n 11) 394.

120 ibid 395. HOPE stands for Housing Opportunities for People Everywhere.

121 This is described in more detail below.

122 Public Law 84-627. For a current view of the Federal Highway Administration, see: www.fhwa.dot.gov/index.html accessed 18 January 2013.

123 Halpern (n 24) 69.

124 ibid 70.

This meant that policies relating to transport, together with the auto industry, were breaking up long-established communities and creating exclusion, not to mention the lack of public transport facilities for those communities.

Tax Breaks for Home-Ownership Tax breaks for home-ownership gave a tax subsidy to home-owners but not to renters. This meant that there was a large federal involvement in the process, facilitating the white-flight phenomenon and the impoverishment of inner-city areas, while at the same time creating inequality.

Gentrification

The features of gentrification are usually the adaptation of physical infrastructures: there is a change in housing, new businesses enter an area at a disproportionate rate and more retail stores open. There is more public investment, new public infrastructure and extra financing from the private sector. There is also greater policing of low-income communities and a rise of landlord harassment towards tenants. Thus, gentrification is a controversial issue for low-income communities, as on the one hand, it improves neighbourhoods, but on the other, it also causes displacement. It is a force of private action and of public policy in which the public dimension also plays an important role as to how it is conducted.

Causes and consequences of gentrification

The causes and consequences of gentrification are the two sides of the currency of redevelopment. There is a government angle and a private angle, two different points of views that on many occasions work in unison, creating a ripple effect of causes and consequences. From a government point of view, gentrification plays an important part in the redevelopment process as it increases tax revenues by the issuance of the different licences and permits involved in the process. Eminent Domain[125] also plays a role as the land subject to the gentrification and redevelopment plans may need to be purchased. As a consequence, the more an area is gentrified, the higher the revenues for the local government.

From a private point of view, gentrification means that there are new business opportunities in which investors and speculators have a say. The earlier move from the city to the suburbs under the 'white-flight' phenomenon becomes a flight from the suburbs into the city, as people want to live near work and enjoy the lifestyle it offers and the ease of convenience of living within the city, not to mention the cultural amenities that exist within the city. This 'flight back' is therefore the ripple effect of further causes and consequences that feed gentrification.

But the obvious, yet forgotten, consequences of gentrification are the socio-economic changes it brings to the inhabitants of the gentrified areas. Many statistical comparisons conclude that there are no differences in the rate of exit of population from gentrified areas (i.e. the population level of people leaving the

125 In Ireland, its equivalent is the Compulsory Purchase Order.

area and moving into the area remains the same), yet the studies do not mention the reasons why people leave or migrate to a gentrified area. Sometimes the empirical evidence[126] does not show the true picture about displacement issues. For example, the statistical story could be accurate but displacement could still be occurring, as the dynamics of the neighbourhood become different, rather than the rate of people arriving and leaving.[127] Over time, there is a reduction of affordable housing as the housing stock dwindles, the displacement of small businesses by bigger chain-type businesses takes place, and there is a further impact on the homelessness population as they are forced to move out of the area as well.

Gentrification at the federal level: HOPE VI

The appearance of public housing in most of the US was, for many years, the physical high-rise 'suburb in the sky' style. Most people living in these suburbs were low-income people who also faced segregation as most of the public housing was located in central city areas and in low-income neighbourhoods. Poverty became encapsulated between tower blocks, leaving few employment prospects for its residents. This concentration of poverty fostered crime, especially in these types of suburbs in the sky.

Due to the poverty and crime situation, two different proposals were translated into policies that resulted in the Housing for People Everywhere (HOPE)[128] programme. First, there was a de-concentration in housing in the 1960s in Chicago, which led to a lengthy period of litigation, with its effects lasting for around 40 years.[129] Although it was a long fight, it formed a consensus that de-concentration was needed at the national level. And second, in the 1980s and the 1990s, the presidential commissions[130] focused on getting rid of public housing by

126 It is uncertain if there is a problem with the dataset of the studies conducted in certain gentrified areas.

127 More often than not, the homeless population is told to move out without offering alternatives to their homelessness. It is a 'not in my backyard' attitude that gets rid of the poorest of the poor.

128 http://portal.hud.gov/portal/page/portal/HUD/programdescription/hope1 accessed 18 January 2013. Please note that the link is to HOPE I, but is to refer to the meaning of the acronym, not HOPE VI itself.

129 In 1966, the American Civil Liberties Union (ACLU) initiated a class-action lawsuit against the Chicago Housing Authority, indicating that the policy of the housing authority to build social housing only in areas with high levels of poor people (including a high number of minorities) meant that there was a contravention of the 1964 Civil Rights Act (racial segregation). The aim was to have social housing built in white-neighbourhood areas. The case eventually ended up in the Supreme Court in 1976 as *Hills v Gautreaux* (425 US 284), as a result of which the Chicago Housing Authority was ordered to build housing in different areas.

130 These presidential commissions were held by President Reagan under the Commission on Housing 1982 and were later endorsed by President George HW Bush.

demolishing it. This, combined with the need of de-concentration of housing at a national level, led to HOPE VI.

HOPE VI was designed in 1992 as a way of revitalizing housing programmes, moving public housing into a new phase, which resulted in a slowdown of the gentrification process. The housing model was now moved from high density to low density and was dispersed among the mixed-income population. The physical structures that were built were also different, as they predicated the theory of 'New Urbanism'.[131] For the first few years, HOPE VI was implemented via housing proposals, and in 1998, there was the housing law reform which started to codify HOPE VI.

Viewed from a public policy angle, in theory, HOPE VI creates an emphasis on the participation by the private sector in the government gentrification process, as financing can be made available to the private developer, which in turn can be directed towards building public housing in areas that have been gentrified.[132] But in reality, this structure moves low-income residents away from their communities and replaces their homes with private housing. It is a double act that responds to gentrification and in turn facilitates gentrification. So, as a matter of policy, HOPE VI favours projects which have private funding, posing the question of whether the mixed financing model is a good model for public housing or not, as one of the concerns is that the private market displaces low-income housing.[133]

Redevelopment in California: gentrification at the local level

Although the federal government ended some of the support for redevelopment in 1974, redevelopment survived in the form of state law, as states could obtain revenue from the proceeds of land use and development. This fiscalization of land use in California, for example, gave rise to a number of legislative instruments,

---

131 New Urbanism is an urban design movement that 'focuses on building walkable, mixed use neighborhoods with a strong sense of place as an alternative to sprawling low-density, single-use, automobile dependent development'. Brian W Ohm and Robert J Sitkowski, 'Integrating New Urbanism and Affordable Housing Tools' (2004) 36 Urban Lawyer 857. For an interesting account of its development, see Jerry Frug, 'The Geography of Community' (1995) 48 Stanford Law Review 1047, particularly at 1089–94. For more information, including a Charter for new urbanism, see the Congress for the New Urbanism's website (they are the main promoters of new urbanism in the US): www.cnu.org accessed 18 January 2013.

132 See the earlier discussion of LIHTCs above for the mechanisms and involvement of private developers within government housing.

133 The consequences of HOPE VI are varied, depending on the location and the state at which it is used. A tracking study was undertaken in the 2000s. For example, there was little displacement in Washington DC and it was also discovered that there was not a lot targeted for the residents who were displaced, which was about 78 per cent. For a CED critique of HOPE VI, see Ngai Pindell, 'Is There Hope for HOPE VI?: Community Economic Development and Localism' (2002) 35 Connecticut Law Review 385, 395–408.

including the California Community Redevelopment Law,[134] and the creation of the California Redevelopment Association.[135] This organization provides a number of services to the community, such as legislative advocacy, professional development and public education, among others.[136]

For example, in Los Angeles to date, there are 32 redevelopment areas.[137] In 1999, the publication of a study[138] evaluating the 'commercial redevelopment activities in the 1990s'[139] of the Community Redevelopment Agency of the City of Los Angeles, 'the oldest and best-known economic development agency in the city'[140] concluded that there was a 'substantial amount of development activity in many low income areas … [but] the "return" of that investment … was mixed'.[141] Thus, the city needed to focus first on developing an 'economic development strategy',[142] as it lacked one, and second, on the quality of the jobs available and offered in these areas as a result of the development.[143] This meant that poverty lawyers had to expand their portfolios, thus using transactional law to alleviate poverty as well as allowing new economic justice groups to emerge, furthering the development of CED as a whole.

Added to this, the internal critique of CED posed by Cummings,[144] who argued that market-based CED was not helping communities to alleviate poverty,[145] together with changes in neighbourhood dynamics in the 1990s and the 2000s (brought about by the real estate market), altered the structure of what community-based organizations could do.[146] Now communities could have a say

---

134 California Health & Safety Code §§ 33000 et seq. Available at www.leginfo.ca.gov/cgi-bin/calawquery?codesection=hsc&codebody=&hits=20 accessed 18 January 2013.

135 www.calredevelop.org/CRA accessed 18 January 2013.

136 ibid.

137 There have also been an extra two proposed redevelopment areas to date. See www.crala.net/internet-site/Projects/index.cfm accessed 18 January 2013.

138 The study was carried out by the UCLA Center for Labor Research and Education and the School of Public Policy and Social Research of UCLA together with the Los Angeles Alliance for a New Economy (LAANE).

139 UCLA and LAANE, 'Who Benefits from Redevelopment in Los Angeles? An Evaluation of Commercial Redevelopment Activities in the 1990s' (1999). http://laane.org/downloads/WhoBenefitsStudy.pdf accessed 18 January 2013.

140 ibid.

141 ibid.

142 ibid.

143 ibid.

144 Cummings (n 8); see also Scott L Cummings, 'Mobilisation Lawyering: Community Economic Development in the Figueroa Corridor' in *Cause Lawyers and Social Movements* (Stanford, Stanford University Press 2006).

145 Cummings (n 8). Cummings argued that market-based CED was privileging localism, which impeded the promotion of broad-based economic reform through 'cross-neighborhood coalitions' that integrated legal advocacy and community organizing.

146 Scott L Cummings and Benjamin S Beach, 'Further Consideration: Community Benefits Agreements' in *Community Economic Development Law: A Text For Engaged*

in the development of their own communities, which is best exemplified through Community Benefit Agreements.

An example of redevelopment, public interest law and CED: Community Benefit Agreements and the empowerment of communities The 'hot real estate market' which characterized the period from the mid-1990s until the late 2000s, meant changes for neighbourhood dynamics as well as in the structure of what community-based organizations could do. Disadvantaged areas were now the subject of local development programmes that promoted city redevelopment rather than urban sprawl. In addition, the internal critiques of CED meant that some community groups sought for development to be accountable, thus ensuring that government subsidies received by developers to revitalize low-income communities truly benefited these communities.[147]

City redevelopment meant that poor communities were now in the plans of developers, private re-investment and speculators – all of which contributed to the rise in value of real estate, gentrification and the displacement of low-income residents. This also brought about changes in the structure of what community organizations could do.[148] Faced with this dilemma, community groups and residents had to decide how to best participate in local development decisions and ensure that affordable housing and living wage jobs benefited the residents (thus making local development accountable), which came in the form of Community Benefit Agreements (CBAs).[149]

CBAs are basically contracts between the community or different organizations representing the community, the local authority and the developer which impose a number of positive obligations on each party. For example, the developer agrees to provide public amenities, while the community agrees not to disrupt the development, and the local authority's role is to ensure that this takes place.[150]

CBAs emerged in Los Angeles around the late 1990s due to the many issues that had arisen because of gentrification.[151] Different community groups wanted to change the conditions of the local population by challenging outside investment and bringing benefits to the community, which was often overlooked during the gentrification process. As a movement, CED had an interest in having an impact

---

Learning (Durham, NC, Carolina Academic Press 2012) 322–23.

147 ibid 322–25. For a full internal critique of CED, see also Cummings (n 8).

148 Cummings and. Beach (n 146) 322–23; Cummings (n 144).

149 Cummings and. Beach (n 146) 325–26.

150 Cummings and Beach (n 146) 326–28. In Ireland, the equivalent may be some of the planning obligations under the Planning and Development Act 2000 (or s 106 of the English Town and Country Planning Act 1990). However, more research in Ireland would be needed to ensure that this assertion is correct.

151 At the time, Richard Riordan, a Republican, was the Los Angeles City Mayor (1993–2001) and under his policy, it was very easy to do business as there was no focus on job quality and the industries that supported the Mayor had low wage policies.

on job creation and ensuring that there were quality jobs in the gentrified areas. In the 1990s, there was no CED strategy to combat the issues of gentrification for the Los Angeles area. Therefore, when the development of the 'Staples Center' in the downtown area of Los Angeles threatened the displacement of many of its low-income residents and existing communities, the creation of CBAs was an attractive model for community groups and CED lawyers to pursue.[152]

Twenty-nine organizations came together, forming a coalition that focused on the development of the Staples Center, among which were those who opposed the agreement, those who supported the agreement conditionally and those who supported it fully.[153]

The Sructure and Mechanisms of the CBA The parties to the CBA were the coalition, the city and the private developer. They formed a triangle in which the coalition spoke to the other two parties. The city gave tax subsidies to the private developer and the coalition formed a cooperation agreement in order not to disrupt the developer (otherwise the coalition would have threatened disruption). There were also different ways to threaten disruption, such as lawsuits, strikes, the divestment of funding from political funds (no monetary support to politicians), etc., which enabled participants to use the CBA as leverage.[154] This leverage, rather than just litigation, was and is constantly used within CBAs.[155]

Although there were also other types of leverage available for community groups, such as the use of publicity (which could harm the project and repeat players such as developers need good publicity), the housing element, the Mello Act 1982,[156] Civil Rights law, door-to-door organizing (such as sending letters)

152 Note that the precursor of the Staples Center CBA was the Hollywood & Highland Complex. LAANE had agreed with the Los Angeles City and the developer to an agreement that would benefit the local residents.

153 Strategic Actions for a Just Economy (SAJE) and LAANE were the main players within the coalition. LAANE had a bigger agenda as its work related to the labour movement in Los Angeles. Also by this time, LAANE had grown in size and it had started to work on the improvement of business sectors under a 'sector to sector' approach. This meant that by the late 1990s, it was working on the creation of 'good jobs'.

154 For example, with regard to the environmental review process which the Staple Center had forgotten to carry out (or overlooked), the coalition could only push for the delay of the project until the environmental review process had taken place, but could not stop it. As the administration of the city was changing from Republican to Democrat and all of the approvals were at a specific stage (development agreement, subsidies, land), the developers had to give in to the requests as highlighted in the approvals, which would not have occurred before the political change had taken place.

155 Beach has also written about the CBA experience in Los Angeles. See Benjamin Beach, 'Strategies and Lessons from the Los Angeles Community Benefits Experience' (2007) 17 Journal of Affordable Housing 77–112.

156 The Mello Act of 1982 is California state law 'which seeks to preserve housing for persons and families with low and moderate incomes in California's Coastal Zone'.

and the influence of council members, the use of the CBA was the main leverage of all of them. Thus, in 2001, a CBA agreement was negotiated, which also became known as the 'Staples CBA' and which formed the basis for the creation of other CBAs around the country.

CBA Mechanisms in General – Lessons Learned for the Future The development agreement for the Staple Center, which contained the CBA, was subsequently changed, resulting in a modification to the inclusionary housing requirement. This issue raised the question of the enforceability of the CBA, as once the CBA was agreed and contained within the development agreement, the coalition could not challenge it. Thus, because of the lessons learned, subsequent CBAs have taken different forms, for example, by making the coalition a third-party beneficiary of the development agreement or by placing the CBA under statute.[157] Recently, scholarly research has also suggested that CBAs are seen not as a good idea in the long term because of 'their potential for misuse'.[158]

For example, CBAs in New York have unfortunately been the victims of the 'heavy-handed involvement of public officials',[159] which have used CBAs as a disguise in order to involve a single private entity among a community,[160] to receive public subsidies[161] and to organize a 'one-sided' three-member coalition which 'reportedly had no independent legal representation in the negotiations'.[162] This is why CED lawyers ensure there is, first, plenty of communication among all the coalition members, second, that there is a consensus on the non-negotiable points and, third, that as part of the strategy, disruption is to be kept as part of a leverage point rather than to be used for something else.

To date, a good number of CBAs have taken shape across the US.[163] Some other examples of successful CBAs are: FRESC for Good Jobs and Stronger

---

For more information, see the Los Angeles Housing Department's explanation of the Mello Act Procedures http://lahd.lacity.org/lahdinternet/Portals/0/Occupancy/LandUse/MelloProcedures.pdf accessed 18 January 2013.

157 In 2005, the city of Milwaukee was the first city within the US to enact a CBA under legislation. The CBA, also known as the Milwaukee Park East Redevelopment Compact (PERC), is mentioned here because it applied the CBA concept as created but modified it to suit its own situation, something that Ireland could also do. However, further research in this area would be needed to assess if CBAs could be accommodated within the Irish landscape. It is submitted that community groups, partnership bodies and others would also have to be consulted. For more information in relation to the PERC, see http://www.communitybenefits.org/article.php?id=1494 accessed 24 July 2012.

158 Julian Gross, 'Community Benefit Agreements' in Clay, Jr and Jones (eds) (n 5) 189.

159 ibid 198.

160 ibid.

161 ibid.

162 ibid.

163 Glover Blackwell indicates that CBAs have taken place in 'dozens of communities'. See Angela Glover Blackwell, 'Equitable Development' in Clay, Jr and Jones (eds) (n 5) 184.

Communities in Denver, Colorado; Georgia Stand up in Atlanta and the Connecticut Center for a New Economy in New Haven.[164] In 2009, the Community Benefits Law Center was also opened in San Francisco,[165] a project of the Partnership for Working Families.[166]

As such, CBAs effected innovation and the advancement of CED lawyering, widening the perception of how access to justice could take place. The use of law, community action and organizing also played an important role and, as such, these also offer an attractive option for the development of CED in Ireland.[167] Yet, the links between regeneration and public interest law in Ireland took place in a different manner, underpinned by the concept of sustainable development and the auspices of regeneration.[168]

Background to the Regeneration Process in Ireland

Because the issue of regeneration is a broad area that can be researched in many forms, such as part of housing policy,[169] geography,[170] sustainable development[171] and others,[172] it is important to highlight that for the purposes of this research, regeneration in Ireland will be discussed in very broad terms in order to place

164 Greg LeRoy, 'Making Economic Development Accountable' in Clay, Jr and Jones (eds) (n 5) 228.

165 http://www.communitybenefits.org/article.php?list=type&type=132 accessed 2 May 2012.

166 http://www.communitybenefits.org/index.php accessed 2 May 2012.

167 This offers further food for thought when comparing the redevelopment process of Ireland to that of the US and how CED law and lawyering can further benefit the community. However, due to the scope of this research, it is only mentioned in passing.

168 To date, there is no exact definition of regeneration; it could be argued that gentrification in the US means regeneration in Ireland.

169 See, for example, Treadwell Shine and Norris (n 14); Michelle Norris, 'Regenerating Run-Down Public Housing Estates: A Review of the Operation of the Remedial Works Scheme' (2001) 49 Administration 25–45.

170 See, for example, Andrew MacLaran (ed), *Making Space: Property Development and Urban Planning* (London, Edward Arnold Limited 2003); Peter Roberts and Hugh Sykes (eds), *Urban Regeneration: A Handbook* (London, Sage 2000).

171 Nessa Winston, 'From Boom to Bust? An Assessment of the Impact of Sustainable Development Policies on Housing in the Republic of Ireland' (2007) 12 Local Environment: The International Journal of Justice and Sustainability 57–71; Nessa Winston, 'Regeneration for Sustainable Communities? Barriers to Implementing Sustainable Housing in Urban Areas' [2009] Sustainable Development 319–30; Nessa Winston, 'Urban Regeneration for Sustainable Development: The Role of Sustainable Housing?' [2009] European Planning Studies 1781–96.

172 Andrea Colantonio and Tim Dixon, *Urban Regeneration and Social Sustainability: Best Practice from European Cities* (Hoboken, Wiley-Blackwell 2011); Tony Manzi, Karen Lucas, Tony Lloyd Jones and Judith Allen (eds), *Social Sustainability in Urban Areas:*

the regeneration of Ballymun into a CED context. As such, it was deemed appropriate to also emphasize the role that sustainable development[173] has played in regeneration efforts before introducing the subject of regeneration itself.

The Role of Sustainable Development

Sustainable development 'is a fundamental and overarching objective of the European Union, aiming to continuously improve the quality of life and wellbeing for present and future generations, *by linking economic development, protection of the environment and social justice*'.[174] If the achievement of sustainable development objectives[175] (as envisioned by the EU and Ireland) is measured by the outcomes of development investment, such as regeneration (better infrastructure, better housing and roads, more jobs, more green areas), then the question that comes to mind is how these current regeneration efforts that promote sustainable development goals have influenced and facilitated the development of CED law and lawyering in Ireland.

Communities, Connectivity and the Urban Fabric (Oxford, Earthscan 2010) particularly chs 9–11.

173 It is important to keep it mind that theories about development also affect the type of policies that are enacted towards its achievement. In an article discussing the issue, Davis and Trebilcock indicate that the theories about development are 'highly contested', and they place sustainable development under one of these theories. While they briefly carry out a survey of these theories, they indicate that a sustainable development perspective means the identification of 'specific relationships between the environment and health status' as well as the relationship between 'poverty alleviation and enhanced environmental quality'. As a result, the creation of legal institutions that support the role of development are needed as they also carry implications for a wide range of form of law, such as constitutional, administrative, civil procedure and property law. The other theories they discuss are: modernization theory, dependency theory, economic growth, welfarism and feminism. See Kevin E Davis and Michael J Trebilcock, 'Legal Reforms and Development' [2001] 22(1) Third World Quarterly 21–36. For more scholarly writings about law and economic development, see Hans-Bernard Schäfer and Angara V Raja (eds), *Law and Economic Development* (Cheltenham, Edward Elgar Publishing 2006). In Ireland, poverty alleviation has also played a role in determining how sustainable development is achieved, particularly when it comes to social inclusion. It is submitted that further research is needed in relation to this, but this topic is outside the scope of this research.

174 Eurostat, 'Sustainable Development in the European Union: 2009 Monitoring Report of the EU Sustainable Development Strategy – Executive Summary' (Luxembourg, Office for Official Publications of the European Communities 2009) 2, available at http://epp.eurostat.ec.europa.eu/cache/ITY_OFFPUB/865-EN/EN/865-EN-EN.PDF accessed 18 January 2013 (emphasis added).

175 For example, social inclusion or the promotion of a healthy economy.

Funding for infrastructure development and regeneration has changed the landscape for a number of cities and towns in Ireland,[176] yet regeneration and the creation of sustainable communities do not equate immediately to access to legal services. Social inclusion cannot be achieved in isolation or without a proper civil legal aid system.[177] Achieving social inclusion under the umbrella of sustainable development becomes an illusion. It can be argued that the need to translate the sustainable development idea (including social inclusion) into concrete examples, such as regeneration, has influenced and facilitated the evolution of CED lawyering in Ireland, thus widening the development of access to legal services. In other words, by using a sustainable development approach, legal services are taken out of the field of 'justice' and become part of the array of services that a community should have in order to be sustainable at a social, economic and environmental level. This approach, in turns, helps not only CED lawyering but also CED as a whole to evolve.[178]

Sustainable development at the EU level

Sustainable development has become one of the fundamental objectives of the European Union (EU) in relation to the development of the EU as a whole.[179] The

176 In Ireland, only Ballymun and Limerick are listed as part of the regeneration programme in terms of housing schemes under the Department of the Environment's website. However, there are also other areas which are or were regenerated under refurbishment schemes, such as Knocknaheeny in Cork or Cranmore in Sligo; see http://www.environ.ie/en/DevelopmentHousing/Housing/SocialHousingSupport/RegenerationSchemes accessed 21 November 2012. It is important to note that although the regeneration of the Docklands in Dublin also contained the building of affordable housing and the regeneration of certain areas, the regeneration process of the Docklands was carried out in a different manner, so it is not included in the regeneration programme of housing schemes. For a thorough understanding of the Dublin Docklands Regeneration, see Niamh Moore, *Dublin Docklands Reinvented: The Post-Industrial Regeneration of a European City Quarter* (Dublin, Four Courts Press 2008).

177 Social inclusion within the legal system is part and parcel of public interest law and is thus highly relevant if we are to create synergies and proper sustainable communities in which access to legal services is a vital component of the development discourse in order to meet the needs of the 'most vulnerable in society' as indicated by the EU SDS.

178 Although the impact of this approach would need further assessment in the future, the opening of the law centre in Limerick confirms this point; thus, they have been established under the auspices of the Limerick Regeneration Agencies.

179 In order to provide some background to the situation, the concept of sustainable development was first formulated in the Report of the Brundtland Commission (*Our Common Future*) in 1987 and was defined as 'development that meets the needs of the present without compromising the ability of future generations to meet their own needs'. In 1997, the EU incorporated the concept of sustainable development as a fundamental objective of the EU by incorporating it into the Treaty of Amsterdam, under art 2 (now art 3(3) of the Consolidated Treaty of Lisbon).

Preamble of the Treaty on European Union as amended by the Treaty of Lisbon[180] indicates that all of the signatories to the Treaty are:

> Determined to promote economic and social progress for their peoples, taking into account the principle of sustainable development and within the context of the accomplishment of the internal market and of reinforced cohesion and environmental protection, and to implement policies ensuring that advances in economic integration are accompanied by parallel progress in other fields.

The Treaty does not have a definition of what is meant by sustainable development, although it is mentioned throughout.

In June 2006, the European Council adopted a renewed strategy towards sustainable development for the EU. The EU Sustainable Development Strategy[181] (EU SDS) defined what sustainable development meant for the EU as a whole.[182] It indicated that:

> Sustainable development means that the needs of the present generation should be met without compromising the ability of future generations to meet their own needs. It [sustainable development] is an overarching objective of the European Union set out in the Treaty, governing all the Union's policies and activities. It is about safeguarding the earth's capacity to support life in all its diversity and is based on the principles of democracy, gender equality, solidarity, the rule of law and respect for fundamental rights, including freedom and equal opportunities for all. It aims at the continuous improvement of the quality of life and well-being on Earth for present and future generations. To that end it [sustainable development] promotes a dynamic economy with full employment and a high level of education, health protection, social and territorial cohesion and environmental protection in a peaceful and secure world, respecting cultural diversity.

Moreover, it indicated that if sustainable development were to be achieved, four key objectives had to be integrated into the process, namely: (i) economic

180 The Treaty of Lisbon 2009.

181 The overall aim of this renewed EU SDS is

> 'to identify and develop actions to enable the EU to achieve continuous improvement of quality of life both for current and for future generations, through the creation of sustainable communities able to manage and use resources efficiently and to tap the ecological and social innovation potential of the economy, ensuring prosperity, environmental protection and social cohesion'.

Council of the European Union, 'Note from the General Secretariat to Delegations on the Review of the EU Sustainable Development Strategy (EU SDS) – Renewed Strategy' of 9 June 2006 [2006] (10117/06), available at: http://register.consilium.europa.eu/pdf/en/06/st10/st10117.en06.pdf accessed 18 January 2013.

182 ibid.

prosperity; (ii) environmental protection; (iii) social equity and cohesion; and (iv) meeting the EU international responsibilities.

In 2009, upon reflecting on how sustainable development could be achieved in the future and in response to the economic crisis, a revised EU SDS strategy was agreed.[183] Thus, it was established that this strategy:

> could focus on the EU's long-term goals in crucial areas, notably by … *promoting social inclusion* [as it is] [t]he most vulnerable in society [who] are at risk of being the most badly hit by the economic crisis and its effects may linger longest for them *unless effective measures are provided.*[184]

The question therefore arises as to how to provide effective measures in order to promote social inclusion under the umbrella of sustainable development and in order to meet one of the EU's fundamental objectives (i.e. sustainable development). It can be argued that CED can indeed offer an answer to this dilemma as it can use its mixture of social policy, community development and legal tools for the benefit of local communities, creating a space for sustainable development to grow.

Sustainable development at a national level

At the turn of the century, the Sustainable Development Council[185] (Comhar)[186] published a series of principles for sustainable development which could be used to determine if existing or future Irish policies were 'likely to lead to sustainable development'.[187] Moreover, Comhar's members agreed that if Ireland were to meet the goal of sustainable development, then sustainable development had to include 'environmental protection, economic development, and social development in an integrated manner'.[188]

---

183 Commission of the European Communities, 'Mainstreaming Sustainable Development into EU Policies: 2009 Review of the European Union Strategy for Sustainable Development', July 2009, available at: http://eur-lex.europa.eu/LexUriserv/LexUriserv.do?uri=COM:2009:0400:FIN:EN:PDF accessed 18 January 2013.

184 ibid 15 (emphasis added).

185 On 10 October 2011, it was indicated that the Council will become part of the National Economic and Social Council (NESC) and the role of the Council will be discontinued. See http://www.comharsdc.ie/index.aspx accessed 14 December 2011.

186 Previously known as the National Sustainable Development Partnership, the Comhar Sustainable Development Council has multiple stakeholders. It is made up of 25 people drawn from five sectors: the state sector, the economic sector, environmental NGOs, social/community NGOs and the professional/academic sector. See http://www.comharsdc.ie/about/index.aspx accessed 4 February 2011.

187 Comhar, the National Sustainable Development Partnership, 'Principles for Sustainable Development' 2. Available at http://www.comharsdc.ie/about/index.aspx accessed 21 November 2012.

188 ibid.

The 12 principles[189] were brought together under a number of different groups or 'themes',[190] although Comhar recognized that separating these principles into themes was 'somewhat arbitrary because by definition, principles are inter-dependent' and that integration between the different themes and citizen participation was essential.[191] Among these themes was that of social equity, which acted as an 'umbrella theme' for two separate principles: 'social inclusion' (Principle 8) and 'co-operation and agreement between states' (Principle 9). Principle 8 indicated that 'social inclusion should be promoted to ensure an improved quality of life for all'.[192] Furthermore, it specified that the significance, meaning and justification of this principle of social inclusion was based on the achievement of:

> a quality of life which provides essential needs and offers dignity. There is [a] need for social inclusion and equality of outcomes, so that there is no discrimination through which some sectors of society are disadvantaged and therefore unable to meet their own needs … [a]t a very practical level, there cannot be long-term planning in a society in which poverty is rife … Without social cohesion, the implementation of long-term strategies is made very difficult. Everybody, as a human right, should have the opportunity to make a living and achieve a satisfactory quality of life. But there exist social and economic barriers to the achievement of such equity.[193]

---

189 The are 12 principles overall: (1) the use of non-renewable resources should be minimized; (2) the use of hazardous/polluting substances and waste created should be minimized and waste management should be environmentally sound; (3) renewable resources should be used within the capacity for regeneration; (4) the quality of soils and water resources should be maintained and improved; (5) the diversity of wildlife, habitats and species should be maintained and improved; (6) air and the atmosphere should be protected and human-induced effects on climate should be minimized; (7) the development of resource potential in one region should not compromise the ability of other regions to achieve their own potential; (8) *social inclusion should be promoted to ensure an improved quality of life for all*; (9) *sustainable development depends on co-operation and agreement between states* (emphasis added); (10) the quality of landscapes, the heritage of the man-made environment and historical and cultural resources should be maintained and improved; (11) decision-making should be devolved to the appropriate level; (12) stakeholder participation should be promoted at all levels of decision-making.

190 The seven themes are: satisfaction of human needs by the efficient use of resources (Principles 1 and 2); equity between generations (Principles 3 and 4); respect for ecological integrity and biodiversity (Principle 5); equity between countries and regions (Principles 6 and 7); social equity (Principles 8 and 9); respect for cultural heritage/diversity (Principle 10); good decision-making (Principles 11 and 12).

191 Comhar (n 187) 3.

192 ibid 5.

193 ibid 21.

Comhar indicated that within Ireland, examples of inequalities in wealth and quality of life existed in every town, whether rural or urban, and thus affected social cohesion. Moreover, Comhar indicated that 'Access to basic services and the ability to meet fundamental needs are accepted as essential to sustainable development',[194] and if the problems created by the inequalities are to be addressed, then 'a broad strategy is needed if Ireland is to achieve or come close to sustainability'.[195]

Access to basic services is therefore an important element in providing effective measures that promote social inclusion under the umbrella of sustainable development, which in turn meets one of the EU's fundamental objectives.[196] Although the description of the principle of social inclusion does not mention access to legal services as part of it, it is well known that social and economic barriers exist where access to legal services is concerned. Access to legal services, and particularly the practice of CED law and CED lawyering, does enable people and communities to have the opportunity to make a living and achieve a satisfactory quality of life.

Sustainable development and social inclusion

As observed, integrating social inclusion into sustainable development goals is not something new, yet the possibilities of research are still unfolding. For example, research that combines the social, economic and environmental aspects of sustainable development or addresses the social aspects is still relatively new.[197] Similarly, in Ireland, social inclusion seems to be a common theme on the policy/government agenda,[198] and research into the social aspects of sustainable development is progressing. For example, there is now an interactive option on Comhar's website that looks at a series of 20 sustainable development indicators which inform the country about 'broad strategic progress on sustainable development challenges'.[199] Social inclusion is one of these indicators and it is intrinsically linked to poverty rates. This in turn can inform policy using a series of interconnected factors to ensure that there is sustainable development.

194 ibid.

195 ibid.

196 It is important to highlight that since 2012, the sustainable development role previously performed by Comhar has been integrated into the NESC.

197 See, for example, Malcolm Eames with Maria Adebowale (eds), *Sustainable Development and Social Inclusion: Towards an Integrated Approach to Research* (York, Joseph Rowntree Foundation 2002); Colantonio and Dixon (n 172).

198 For example, the Department of Social Protection has under its umbrella a social inclusion division. See http://www.socialinclusion.ie accessed 21 November 2012; the Economic and Social Research Council (ESRI) also has an area of research focused on social inclusion and quality of life. See http://www.esri.ie/research/research_areas/social_cohesion_and_quality_of_life accessed 21 November 2012.

199 http://www.comharsustainableindicators.ie/explore-the-indicators/comhar-indicators.aspx accessed 21 November 2012.

Sustainable development and local empowerment

The issue of local empowerment is a part of sustainable development strategies and Comhar also sees local empowerment as essential. In 2007, Comhar carried out a review of Ireland's sustainable development strategy, in which it recognized that exclusion in relation to the decision-making process was still taking place and that Principle 8 (social inclusion) had been left in the back-burner. Moreover, under the 'Theme for Governance and Sustainable Development', Comhar indicated that local and community grassroots groups played a governance role via community action. But, to date, there is no mentioning of the role of legal services (or lack of it) in the empowerment of communities or how they can contribute to the advancement of sustainable development. It is submitted that CED lawyering (and public interest law) can help to fill this gap as it provides for community legal education not just to individuals but also to community groups.

Regeneration: A Background

Defining regeneration depends on the particular viewpoint of each person.[200] In Ireland to date, there has been no real definition of regeneration.[201] Moreover, there is no national regeneration agency underpinned by legislation. For example, in reviewing the policy and practice of regeneration of social housing in Ireland, Treadwell Shine and Norris concluded that the current social housing regeneration arrangements are fragmented and that much more work is needed if Ireland is to have a coherent and cohesive regeneration policy.[202] Moreover, their research also showed that there were three different approaches to the implementation of regeneration projects within social housing. Depending on the type of funding received, these regeneration schemes could be divided into local authority, multi-agency or public-private partnerships. Local authority-funded schemes could also be subdivided into local authority-led or by led by an independent urban development company set up by the local authority to specifically oversee the regeneration (Ballymun and Limerick Regeneration Agencies are examples of this).

Some other scholars, namely Colantonio and Dixon, have argued that regeneration could be categorized under some 'main thematic narratives' in order to facilitate its understanding. For example, in relation to area-based regeneration and renewal, regeneration could be divided into a 'property-led physical approach', a 'business-driven approach' and a 'health and well-being approach', among others.[203]

Thus, it can be asserted that regeneration can, on the one hand, be divided according to how it is funded (Treadwell and Norris) and, on the other hand,

200 Colantonio and Dixon (n 172) 7.

201 Albeit that urban renewal is mentioned on a number of acts directed towards the promotion of fiscal incentives for developers (which intrinsically includes regeneration), urban renewal is not defined either.

202 Treadwell Shine and Norris (n 14) particularly 51–52.

203 Colantonio and Dixon (n 172) 8.

according to the type of approach used (Colantonio and Dixon). In Ireland, one can find all of the above approaches existing either separately or in conjunction. For example, Ballymun falls under the local authority health and well-being approach,[204] and most of the well-known 'commercially focused' regeneration that has taken place in Dublin has been 'area-based', which includes the property-led physical approach.

Urban regeneration

Context The Irish Department of Environment, Community and Local Government defines the aim of regeneration as:

> to build sustainable communities through a combination of social, educational and economic initiatives and also by rejuvenating the built environment by a mixture of demolition, construction and refurbishment of dwellings having regard to urban design guidelines. In addition, *local authorities are also required to focus on a strategic multifaceted approach to address the range of social, educational and economic issues that may be evident.* Procurement may take a number of forms, using public monies or private funding through a Public-Private Partnership. It is a matter for the local authority to submit proposals for regeneration of an area.[205]

Significantly, 'the process which facilitates sustainable development at a community level' (also known as 'Local Agenda 21') is separated from the regeneration schemes (regeneration schemes are found under social housing support), giving the impression that development and housing relate to infrastructure and to the physical development of an area, and are not related to the concept of sustainable development or to the environment at all. However, regeneration, particularly from the point of view of communities, is linked to Local Agenda 21.[206] The Department indicates that Local Agenda 21 is:

> a process which facilitates sustainable development at community level. It is an approach, based on participation which respects the social, cultural, economic and environmental needs of the present and future citizens of a community in all its diversity and which relates that community and its future to the regional, national and international community of which it is a part.[207]

---

204 Studying the type of regeneration and how they fall under the different classifications would require further research that is outside the scope of this paper.

205 http://www.environ.ie/en/DevelopmentHousing/Housing/SocialHousingSupport/RegenerationSchemes/ accessed 11 February 2012 (emphasis added).

206 No changes, to date, have been seen in relation to the new government (Fina Gael-Labour Coalition 2011).

207 http://www.environ.ie/en/Environment/LocalAgenda21/ accessed 21 November 2012.

Similarly, the Sustainable Development Unit of the Department recognizes that sustainable development is a matter for all concerned and deals with the policy issues driving the sustainable development agenda.[208] This aim of regneration is to be 'underpinned' by four different goals. These are: (i) to promote awareness, knowledge and uptake of a wide range of statutory, voluntary and community services; (ii) to increase access to formal and informal educational, recreational and cultural development activities and resources; (iii) to increase peoples' work readiness and employment prospects; and (iv) to promote engagement with policy, practice and decision-making processes on matters affecting local communities.[209]

Consequently, it is argued that the policies which facilitate sustainable development and the synergies between sustainable development and urban regeneration could assist in the construction of community law centres and in the achievement of social inclusion. This, in turn, could influence the further role/development of CED and CED lawyering in empowering local communities – and Ballymun is a good example of this.[210]

Regeneration of social housing In 1997, the Department of the Environment published a document entitled *Sustainable Development: A Strategy for Ireland*,[211] which contained a planned strategy for the achievement of sustainable development under the concept of urban regeneration.[212] Under this concept, the document indicated that the policies for achieving 'sustainable urban regeneration' would have 'key elements', such as the integration of strategic economic and social planning.[213]

Although the regeneration of individual dwellings had started to take place in Ireland from 1981 under a programme that provided for 'new windows, heating systems, bathrooms and extensions to inadequate local authority dwellings',[214] the refurbishment of entire housing estates did not take place until 1985.

---

208 'While obviously this is an overarching issue, which concerns all sections of this Department, all other Government Departments and the whole of society': http://www.environ.ie/en/Environment/SustainableDevelopment/ accessed 21 November 2012.

209 ibid.

210 The sustainable development concept is also shaping the community legal services to be provided by the regeneration scheme in Limerick. See PILA, 'New Community Law and Mediation Centre to Open in Limerick', 12 December 2012, available at: http://www.pila.ie/bulletin/december-2012/12-december-2012/new-community-law-and-mediation-centre-to-open-in-limerick/ accessed 18 January 2013.

211 Department of the Environment, 'Sustainable Development: A Strategy for Ireland', 1997, available at: http://www.environ.ie/en/Environment/SustainableDevelopment/PublicationsDocuments/FileDownLoad,1825,en.pdf accessed 21 November 2012.

212 ibid foreword.

213 ibid 150.

214 Norris (n 169) 27.

Literature on urban regeneration and management of social housing in Ireland is increasing,[215] but it does not deal with access to legal services or with services overall. Nessa Winston, in writing about urban regeneration and sustainable development, states that:

> For schemes in disadvantaged areas, *social supports are crucial for the success of regeneration programmes*. Some progress in addressing social disadvantage may be made from the provision of high quality, affordable housing in attractive environment. However, *a whole range of local support services are also required* … These elements of community and neighbourhood regeneration *tend to be neglected in research,* despite an acknowledgement that physical regeneration alone is not sufficient.[216]

While there is some recent literature on urban regeneration and social sustainability,[217] there is nothing on urban regeneration and access to legal services.[218] Moreover, recent literature indicates that 'a comprehensive study of urban regeneration from a social-sustainability (i.e. the social dimension of sustainable development) perspective is still missing'.[219]

In relation to, on the one hand, housing law and policy and, on the other hand, social policy, there has also been a lack of in-depth research conducted into their influences on regeneration schemes in Ireland.[220] A study carried out in 2006 by Dr Rory Hearne in relation to the role of PPPs in social housing regeneration indicated that PPPs left residents worse off, displacing and breaking up communities.[221]

---

215 See, for example, ibid; Kasey Treadwell Shine, 'Regenerating Unpopular Social Housing Estates: Can Complexity Theory Help to Achieve Best Possible Solutions?' (2006) 23 Housing, Theory and Society 65–91; Winston, 'From Boom to Bust?' (n 171); Winston, 'Regeneration for Sustainable Communities?' (n 171); Winston, 'Urban Regeneration for Sustainable Development' (n 171); Treadwell Shine and Norris (n 14).

216 Winston, 'Urban Regeneration for Sustainable Development' (n 171) (emphasis added).

217 Colantonio and Dixon (n 172); Manzi et al (n 172).

218 Regeneration as part of urban studies/geography area seems to have advanced in Ireland, yet to date, nothing has been found from a legal angle.

219 Colantonio and Dixon (n 172) 9.

220 Email from Dr Padriac Kenna to the author, NUI Galway (15 December 2011).

221 Note that this type of relationship (between the private and the public) is what one often sees and perceives in relation to some housing estates in Ireland as well as some 'famous regeneration projects' abroad. For example, the regeneration experience of downtown Los Angeles and the creation of a new downtown displaced and broke up entire communities. Ballymun was fortunate as it was not regenerated under a PPP approach per se. Recently, however, a new type of housing policy is developing in Ireland which may leave the provision of social housing to the private market (Dr Padraic Kenna's Housing Law & Policy class, Ballymun, January 2012).

The concept of citizenship under the remit of social policy has also played an important role in ensuring that an array of social services are provided as part of regeneration schemes, including community legal services. This is best exemplified by the regeneration of Ballymun and the creation of BCLC, but again, this area is only mentioned in passing.

The Regeneration of Ballymun

Background

Ballymun was to be the 'housing estate of the future'. It comprised a set of seven high towers, all named after the leaders of the 1916 Irish Rebellion, as well as a number of spine blocks and two-storey housing units. The Ballymun housing estate was to house a large number of families following the collapse of a number of tenement buildings[222] and the subsequent evacuation of the rest of the tenements in Dublin City in 1963. Ballymun was officially 'opened' in 1969, with many of its new residents experiencing 'life' in high-rise buildings for the first time. It initially contained 2,820 flats, a number later increased by the addition of 1,600 two-storey public housing units, making it 'one of the largest public housing estates in Europe'.[223] By the 1980s, much had changed and the housing estate of the future with its seven towers had become a housing estate error of the past.[224] Ballymun was now home to a high level of unemployment, with a large number of single-parent families and poorly serviced communal areas. Nevertheless, the 1980s was also a 'breeding ground' for activism in Ballymun.[225]

Due to the costs associated with improving/refurbishing the existing stock of housing, together with the expense of remedying structural defects, it was determined that the tower blocks and spine blocks would be demolished 'progressively over eight years' and replaced by new housing:

> The redevelopment of the housing was to be the central element in an integrated strategic plan for the economic and social development of the area which would include arrangements for consultation with, and involvement of the local community in its implementation.[226]

---

222 In June 1963, four people died following the collapse of tenement buildings in Bolton Street and Fenian Street.

223 Aibhlín McCrann (ed), *Memories Milestones and New Horizons: Reflections on the Regeneration of Ballymun* (Belfast, Blackstaff Press 2008) Foreword.

224 However, when first built, the architecture was considered modern.

225 Local activist presentation by Áine Rooney from the Ballymun Welfare Rights Group to the NUI Galway student's day trip to Ballymun, 11 March 2011.

226 BRL, 'Ballymun Regeneration Limited Completion Report' (2008) 7.

Thus, in March 1997, the go-ahead was given for the redevelopment of Ballymun by the then Minister for the Environment and the Minister for Housing and Urban Renewal,[227] and following a consultation with the then Department of the Environment and Dublin Corporation[228] (now Dublin City Council), a company limited by guarantee with no share capital was established to oversee the redevelopment.[229] The company became known as Ballymun Regeneration Limited (BRL).[230]

The master plan for the regeneration/redevelopment of Ballymun took place 'in consultation and partnership' with the community[231] and adjacent areas.[232] It proposed a strategy for the regeneration of the social, economic and physical aspects of the community and not solely for the physical infrastructure. Among the recommendations made during the consultation process carried out on a 'Public Planning Day', it was indicated that the residents needed 'decentralised advice and welfare rights'[233] among others. This recommendation would become the seed of the start of a community civil legal aid centre.

The master plan contained a huge number of proposals and different points of views. To date, 5,000 housing units have been built, with 80 per cent of them owner-occupied and 10 per cent rented.

Equipped with the strategy of creating social, economic and physical regeneration, and with the view of the community that there was a need to have a decentralized advice and welfare rights service, the idea of a community legal centre for the local residents came to the fore. Providing legal services would fall within the remit of social regeneration, a concept that places the idea of citizenship at its core.

Moreover, BRL viewed the concept of citizenship as that which included rights and responsibilities; therefore, a place where legal services were provided would be fundamental to the regeneration scheme. By having a law centre, people could learn about their rights and responsibilities. For BRL, having rights

227 ibid.

228 Dublin Corporation was renamed Dublin City Council in 2002.

229 It was felt that because of the distrust that the local community felt in relation to the government, having an independent body would be more appropriate. Interview with Sheena McCambley, Senior Planner BRL (Ballymun, 11 March 2011).

230 See McCrann (n 223) particularly 1–43.

231 The community consultation group was comprised of different 'umbrella' groups, namely Ballymun Housing Task Force, Ballymun Partnership, Area Forums, the Design Group, focus groups, working groups and adjacent Resident Associations.

232 The then Managing Director of BRL indicated that over 2,000 local people became involved in designing 'their new town', a figure which increased to over 5,000 when the Draft Master Plan was launched. BRL, 'Masterplan for the New Ballymun', 1998 (Foreword).

233 The recommendation was placed under the umbrella of 'Advice, Support and Community Development'. This umbrella or theme was one out of six themes that BRL decided to establish in order to address six key social themes that required specific attention under the Masterplan. ibid 6.

and responsibilities meant participation and involvement in the community, so everyone (people and community institutions) could be accountable.[234] Thus, BRL became a significant funder and proponent of having a community law centre as it would provide a service where none existed before. Furthermore, the community law centre would also act as an agent of empowerment, both through raising awareness of the relevance of law in society and through its educational activities.[235]

Case Study – Ballymun Community Law Centre

Background

The aim of this case study is to argue that CED lawyering exists in Ireland and that its use and practice can help in the promotion and implementation of a strategic model of legal aid, as well as to argue that public interest law and regeneration efforts can be connected through the further development of CED. It is envisaged that by expanding the role of law and the legal system in bringing about social change via the combination of law, social policy and community development tools, public interest lawyers can further understand and develop this innovative area of law. Although there is some research describing how BCLC was established,[236] it is submitted that by exploring BCLC from a CED perspective and focusing on its ongoing community involvement as a way of bringing about social regeneration, such as the provision of community legal education, an Irish version of CED lawyering can come to the fore.

In operation since 2002 and serving a population of almost 20,000,[237] BCLC's creation and history arose out of Dublin's blueprint for the regeneration of a disadvantaged neighbourhood, rather than out of a demand for the establishment of a community law centre.[238] Ballymun could be replaced with 'a self-sustaining urban centre' for the people in the area and the redevelopment plan could also provide for 'consultation with, and involvement of, the local community in its

234 ibid.

235 Email from Sheena McCambley to the author (11 March 2011).

236 Gerry Whyte, 'Providing Effective Access to Legal Services: The Experience of the Ballymun Community Law Centre' in McCrann (n 223) 115–34.

237 Ursula Halpin, Sylvia Mooney, Katrin Todt and Bernadette Walsh, 'Ballymun Community Law Centre: Evaluation Report 2009' (BCLC 2009) 12. The evaluation report contains a series of social demographics as published in the 2006 Census. Data from the most recent census is not yet available.

238 Gerry Whyte explains that the FLAC, following the establishment of the then 'Coolock Law Centre', campaigned for the creation of a community law centre in Tallaght, but it was never developed by the government. See Gerry Whyte, *Social Inclusion and the Legal System: Public Interest Law in Ireland* (Dublin, Institute of Public Administration 2002) 311, note 143.

implementation'.[239] This is because the *Sustainable Development* document issued by the Department for the Environment indicated that 'sustainability in housing require[d] tenant participation and empowerment'.[240]Although the document did not mention the provision of a community law centre, it was government policy that the 'strategic economic and social planning' linked the measures and programmes for urban renewal on an integrated basis to address the physical, economic, social and environmental regeneration of urban areas.[241]

As such, it can be said that the regeneration of Ballymun and the subsequent birth of BCLC is the first example in Ireland of how the practice of CED as a whole (i.e. as a concept and as a lawyering strategy) has evolved with open support from the government. Moreover, and although the government may not have realized it,[242] it can be argued that the government approach of addressing the physical, economic, social and environmental needs of the community on an integrated basis firmly rooted the concept of CED within that of regeneration and sustainability on the one hand and public interest law on the other (via BCLC). Although it took a few years following the beginning of the regeneration process for BCLC to open its doors, it celebrated its 10-year anniversary in November 2012.

It is also important to highlight that because BCLC was part of the regeneration project, it also received government support from the Legal Aid Board (LAB) in addition to state funding via BRL. This process of collaboration between the LAB and BCLC – a government-run civil legal aid scheme on the one hand and an independent civil legal aid service (in the form of the law centre) on the other – would not have been possible before, despite the call made by the Free Legal Advice Centre (FLAC) for the establishment of local community centres as part of its 'National Advice and Legal Service Council' programme back in 1992.[243]

---

239 Department of the Environment (n 211) 156.

240 ibid.

241 ibid 150.

242 BRL called for community services to be set up within the newly regenerated area. The process relating to the establishment of BCLC is described below. See also, Whyte (n 238) 332, note 215.

243 A call for the establishment of community law centres had also been requested in its submission to the Pringle Committee and mentioned in the Pringle Report back in the 1970s. For more information on the Pringle Report, see Dennis A Pringle, *Report to Minister for Justice: Committee on Civil Legal Aid and Advice* (London, The Stationery Office 1977); and also Mel Cousins, 'Legal Aid in France and the Republic of Ireland in the 1990s' in *The Transformation of Legal Aid: Comparative and Historical Studies* (Oxford, Oxford University Press 1999) 162.

How the Law Centre Became Part of the Master Plan[244]

In relation to regeneration, it was felt that there should be representative groups and organizations which were resourced to channel concerns, instead of the traditional outlets of protest marches and public meetings, where feelings and positions became entrenched and nothing got resolved. The provision of an independent organization with professional legal advisors and representation meant that if the people experienced what they saw as injustice, they could resolve it as equals; people tended to use the media and the political system for larger issues and disputes, but individuals tended to use the law centre.

Following the public meeting, a number of public consultations took place and a committee to oversee its establishment also met regularly.[245] Thus, in 2000, a Feasibility Study Report indicated that despite the evidence of deprivation and marginalization found within Ballymun, there was a strong network of community groups and organizations which, until then, had arranged among themselves to meet the needs of the community.[246] The Report called for the need to develop information and advice services to meet the changes brought about by regeneration, such as rectifying the decades of neglect and deprivation experienced within Ballymun.

The Report further recognized there were already a huge range of information and advice services within Ballymun, but no proper legal services. The FLAC only operated a voluntary service twice a week.[247] Moreover, it was an 'advice

244 Special thanks to Evelyn Hanlon, the current Chair of the Board of Directors of BCLC, for her insights into the history of BCLC. This section is based on the findings of a long interview with her (n 19).

245 The consultative process had taken place under a series of meetings. It included: BRL, Coolock Community Law Centre, Ballymun Community Action Programme, Ballymun Welfare Rights Group, Men's Networking Resource Centre, FLAC, Youth Action Programme, Ballymun MABS, Eastern Health Board – Community Welfare Service, Gardai, Dublin Corporation (now Dublin City Council), Women's Resource Centre, Threshold, Ballymun Housing Task Force, Balcurris/Baltbutcher Lane Estate Forum, Poppintree Estate Forum, Ballymun Youth Reach, Linx Project and Ballymun Men's Centre. The Committee also heard the views from other interested groups and individuals. David Ellis Community Legal Resource, 'Ballymun Community Law Centre: Feasibility Study Report', January 2000, 4. Note that the Action Plan also mentions Ballymun Citizen Information Centre. See David Ellis Community Legal Resource, 'Ballymun Community Law Centre: Action Plan 2000', November 2000, 4.

246 David Ellis Community Legal Resource, 'Ballymun Community Law Centre: Feasibility Study Report' (n 245) 7. The author quotes the Gamma Report 1995 (to date, I have been unavailable to find the original source).

247 FLAC was set up in Ballymun around 1969–70 and was run by law students. The solicitor would advise the students as to how to advise the client, so the solicitor never meet the clients personally. 'History of FLAC in Ballymun' 15–16, written by Dennis Barror, found at BCLC, 'Ballymun Community Law Centre Annual Report 2006', 2006.

only service' and there were no private solicitors in the area.[248] Thus, establishing a community law centre could satisfy the unmet legal need of the community as well as that of community groups, as people were seeking legal advice from the existing support groups available at the time, but these groups could not offer such legal advice.[249] The Report also deemed that the development of the law centre should be based on a number of principles[250] and the services should be offered through a combination of different approaches, namely casework, community support groups, training, information/education programmes and law reform and social policy work.[251]

More importantly, for the purposes of this research, the feasibility study also contained a definition of what a community law centre was,[252] thus setting the standard as to what a community law centre was supposed to do. This definition indicated that a community law centre was:

> an independent and community-based service which provides free legal aid and advice to individuals and groups in marginalised areas. It provides court and tribunal representation and usually concentrates on areas of law such as housing, debt, employment law, welfare rights, equality issues, and family law. However, a community law centre does not confine its work to individual casework. It also recognises that local information/advice/support groups also need to use

248 David Ellis Community Legal Resource, 'Ballymun Community Law Centre: Action Plan 2000' (n 245) 8.

249 David Ellis Community Legal Resource, 'Ballymun Community Law Centre: Feasibility Study Report' (n 245). The consultation process had also indicated that local groups were looking for a 'back-up service' in relation to their case work and a place that could offer training in legal issues and expertise in making submissions for reform, hence a law centre was best suited in terms of satisfying all these requirements. David Ellis Community Legal Resource, 'Ballymun Community Law Centre: Action Plan 2000' (n 245) 8.

250 David Ellis Community Legal Resource, 'Ballymun Community Law Centre: Feasibility Study Report' (n 245) 9. The principles were to: provide a community-based legal service; work to protect and promote the constitutional, legal and social rights of marginalized individuals *and groups*; *work with existing community organizations to complement and support their work*; provide an independent, professional and confidential service; be committed to a consistently excellent standard of service; ensure that the service be based on respect for individuals and equality of treatment; ensure that the service would seek to empower *both* the individuals *and groups* it works with. One way in which BCLC pursues working with groups is via its legal education services to groups when needed. Thus, community groups are trained to service their clients (emphasis added).

251 David Ellis Community Legal Resource, 'Ballymun Community Law Centre: Action Plan 2000' (n 245) 9–10. The feasibility study further indicated that the law centre should also work closely with the then CCLC and create a formal mechanism for an exchange of ideas, cooperation and, 'when appropriate', a sharing of resources.

252 The earliest definition offered to the government as to what a community law centre was can be found in the Pringle Report. See Pringle (n 243).

> the legal resources available in the community law centre to assist them in their work. This strengthens the work of such groups and enables them to meet the needs of their users more effectively. In addition these groups may need legal service to meet their own requirements, for example, in relation to company formation, or drawing up contracts of employment. Again the community law centre model will provide this service.[253]

By indicating that the role of the law centre was also to service community groups which in turn would also help to strengthen their work so that the community groups could meet the requirement of their users,[254] the author of the Report, Dave Ellis, had unknowingly described part of the process of CED law and lawyering, and how it worked in action. This is partly because the vision of BCLC was the product of the many years of experience Ellis had spent working with the NCL&MC, but also because the establishment of BCLC included a very different approach when compared to how the NCL&MC was created. [255] For BCLC, regeneration and the government policy of working in an integrated manner played a key role in its development. As such, there was an explicit acknowledgement that the role of a law centre is to serve community groups.

Additionally, Ellis, drawing on his experiences with the NCL&MC and his desire to involve more community development into law and legal practice,[256] shaped and cemented his vision of how a law centre would look in theory and practice. Aided and inspired by the potentials of regeneration, the vision precipitated the creation of a law centre which could not only meet a legal need but could also provide for the social and economic development of the community.[257] In other words, regeneration sparked the blossoming of CED lawyering in Ireland, connecting public interest law and regeneration under the umbrella of BCLC while at the same time addressing the need for an integrated approach in the provision of information and advice services, as indicated in the Report.[258]

---

253 David Ellis Community Legal Resource, 'Ballymun Community Law Centre: Feasibility Study Report' (n 245) 6. The description of what a community law centre is also appears in the Action Plan. See David Ellis Community Legal Resource, 'Ballymun Community Law Centre: Action Plan 2000' (n 245) 6.

254 David Ellis Community Legal Resource, 'Ballymun Community Law Centre: Action Plan 2000' (n 245) 6.

255 This is in contrast to the NCL&MC, which was set up to meet unmet legal needs, but under an access to justice approach. This difference also explains the geographical focus of BCLC when compared with the NCL&MC. The NCL&MC services two electoral district areas with a population of about 140,000.

256 Conversation with Sarah Flynn, wife of the late David Ellis (International Community Development Conference, NUI Maynooth, 16 November 2011).

257 This vision of community development when compared to the NCL&MC presents some interesting views in relation to the impact of CED.

258 David Ellis Community Legal Resource, 'Ballymun Community Law Centre: Feasibility Study Report' (n 245) 16.

The Report also proposed to meet the needs for family law issues in conjunction with the LAB,[259] acknowledging this would 'break new ground', but it was important to realize that the regeneration of Ballymun necessitated all types of services, both statutory and non-statutory, and thus new forms of thinking and the validity and recognition of new approaches when delivering legal services.[260] This process of collaboration proved to be crucial as it also facilitated the delivery of a strategic model of legal aid in partnership with the government, which up to that point had been unattainable,[261] thus supporting the argument that CED could act as a link between public interest law and regeneration and, as such, that it could facilitate the practice of the strategic approach to legal aid.

Local Management and Control

The attainment of local management and control of BCLC by the community is an ongoing process and goal, as reflected in the development of its management structure. The Report originally proposed that the running of the centre could be performed by a company limited by guarantee with an elected board,[262] indicating that the board 'should be as representative of the people of the area as possible' so that it could be aware of the needs of the community.[263] This model reflected the existing arrangements of the other existing independent community law centres at the time.[264] However, its management board would be different as it would also contain nominees of statutory agencies and others.[265] The membership of BCLC Ltd was later addressed in the Action Plan indicating that it should represent the people of Ballymun in order for the law centre to be 'responsive to the needs of the community'.[266]

In reality, however, local management and control has worked rather differently. According to Frank Murphy, the Managing Solicitor of BCLC:

---

259 The Civil Legal Aid Board had also proposed to work with BCLC following an interview with *Morning Ireland* (unfortunately, the date of the interview was unobtainable).

260 David Ellis Community Legal Resource, 'Ballymun Community Law Centre: Feasibility Study Report' (n 245) 11.

261 The NCL&MC and FLAC have been unsuccessful in obtaining government support in relation to the practice of strategic legal aid, although they have received government funding by the Department of Social Protection and the Department of Justice respectively.

262 BCLC would be a limited company limited by guarantee and managed by a management board.

263 David Ellis Community Legal Resource, 'Ballymun Community Law Centre: Feasibility Study Report' (n 245) 17.

264 At the time, the only other independent community law centre was the NCL&MC.

265 David Ellis Community Legal Resource, 'Ballymun Community Law Centre: Action Plan 2000' (n 245) 19.

266 ibid 20.

> one cannot just present a law centre as a *fait accompli*. One has to grow it in the community with the community and for the community. In an area where there were no solicitors, one has to work with the community to develop the law centre and its management.[267]

Currently, the management board is composed of nine people, two of which represent the local community. BCLC hopes that in the future, more community representatives will become involved. In the words of Murphy:

> in order to build local management and control takes place, there is a lot of ground to cover first, to make up for people's distrust in the legal system. After all, there were no legal services facilities in the area since the foundation of the housing estate.[268]

This view of rebalancing of power, of understanding the background of people and the community has also required BCLC to become a facilitator and take a step back and offer legal help when required, thus changing lawyering attitudes in order to achieve empowerment. This process, in turn, acts as a further example of CED lawyering in action as the lawyer acts as a facilitator, and by using different legal tools and approaches, it empowers the community. CED lawyering can therefore help to further facilitate local management and control, but it might take much more time than originally anticipated.

One important element of how BCLC can achieve local management and control is the role played by the project officer, whose main aim is to look for projects within the community and assess how BCLC can contribute to or create further projects that are needed within the community. This position was not envisaged within the original management structure, but it has proven to be a crucial role. For example, at present, the project officer runs a series of projects targeting the local community[269] in which BCLC can make an impact. The project officer also looks for projects within the community under which BCLC can provide assistance, making the role an example as to how CED lawyering as a lawyering strategy is currently being practised.

Services Provided

The current services provided by BCLC vary. According to Frank Murphy, BCLC aims to provide integrated 'holistic' services and it has a strategic approach 'vision' as to how to achieve this. It also provides for advocacy and it is open to trying

267 Interview with Frank Murphy, Managing Solicitor of BCLC (Ballymun, 23 February 2011).

268 ibid.

269 For example, the project officer has established a 'restorative justice' project. Please see below for more information.

new things in order to achieve integrated holistic services. Otherwise, the law and the legal process become detached from reality, isolating the law from the other components of a person's life, such as their mental well-being and family-related problems.[270] The law needs to be available to people in a wholesome/holistic/all-encompassing approach.[271]

The lack of a test-case approach also shows the more collaborative approach that BCLC has taken, and although it has represented clients in court in very important cases, particularly those relating to housing issues, it is the client and not the law centre who gives the instructions as to how the case is to be handled. *Pro bono* services are also offered by barristers and solicitors either in the form of representation or in delivering courses or seminars. NUI Galway, Trinity College Dublin and Dublin City University also support the educational work of BCLC.[272]

In an evaluation report carried out in 2009, it was indicated that the aim of BCLC in relation to community legal education was to deliver 'innovative legal education programmes' by promoting 'understanding of the law and encourage [sic] disadvantaged communities to use the law and work with the legal profession'.[273] Currently, three courses have been delivered to the community.[274] One course that has proven particularly beneficial is the housing law and policy course, as it directly relates to the changes faced by the regeneration of Ballymun as well as delivering an innovative approach by creating 'community legal education without walls'.[275]

The Restorative Justice Project for primary schools began in 2008 and is delivered in six primary schools within Ballymun under the umbrella of 'peer-to-peer mediation'. It teaches the children how to manage conflict and thus provides

---

270 It is interesting to point out that J Michael Norwood and A Paterson wrote an article back in 2002 about how to provide holistic legal services. Although the article was based on the ABA Rules of Ethics and the example used was from the New Mexico Law School Child Advocacy Clinic, it offers great insight as to how holistic legal services can be offered under an approach referred to as Multidisciplinary Practice (MDP). See J Michael Norwood and Alan Paterson, 'Problem-Solving in a Multidisciplinary Environment? Must Ethics Get in the Way of Holistic Services?' [2002] 9 Clinical L Rev 337. Note that if the Legal Services Regulation Bill 2011 is passed, provision to establish partnerships with non-legal professionals will be allowed, thus making it easier for CLCs to provide holistic legal services, which in turn will make it easier for CED lawyers to partner with other professions for the benefit of the community. Part 7 of the Bill even includes the term 'Multidisciplinary Practices'. See http://www.oireachtas.ie/documents/bills28/bills/2011/5811/document2.pdf accessed 20 January 2013.

271 Interview with Frank Murphy (n 267).

272 Halpin et al (n 237) 50–51.

273 ibid 17.

274 Such as social welfare law, family law and mental health law. The most recent Housing Law and Policy course offered by Dr Kenna started in January 2013 (the last one was completed in March 2012).

275 At present, further research into this approach is being carried out by the author.

for a better way to go into secondary education.[276] At the secondary level, the project is run under the umbrella of 'the law club' and covers legal topic courses as well as trips to the courts, a mock trial and a placement in a solicitor's firm to obtain work experience.

BCLC also has a number of mediation projects, which act as an alternative to conflict resolution. The idea of having mediation services from the outset was due, in part, to the view that legal issues could be resolved by other means than recourse to the courts.[277] To date, there have been a number of different mediation services: peer mediation, community mediation, family mediation and a pilot mediation project run in conjunction with the courts services. BCLC also runs outreach clinics every week in different areas within Ballymun with the aim of bringing legal services to those who cannot or who are unable to make it to BCLC's offices.

Extensive training programmes have been put in place to support community groups and maximize the community understanding of the law. In 2010, for example, BCLC participated in the advisory group of the 'Telling Women's Stories Project', a project facilitated by Amnesty International as part of the International Women's Day celebration (the project which included a session on human rights)[278] and in the 'Young Ballymun Literacivic Project', a project aimed at civic literacy.[279]

Funding

BCLC is currently funded by BRL,[280] the Law Society and the Bar Council.[281] The role played by BRL has been crucial in this regard as without it, BCLC would not exist. Evelyn Hanlon[282] explains that initially the then Department of Social

---

276 For recent evaluation of the Peer Mediation Programme in primary schools, see Seamus Farrell, 'An Evaluation of Ballymun Community Law Centre's Pilot Peer Mediation Programme in National Primary Schools in Ballymun Community: Managing Relationships and Behaviour in Schools through Mediation and Restorative Practices', 2010, on file with the author.

277 The way in which funding for the law centre came about is also important. See interview with Evelyn Hanlon (n 19) in relation to the origins of the law centre.

278 BCLC (n 247) 10.

279 ibid. BCLC was part of the advisory group.

280 BRL took over the funding in late 2004, when a request was made to it to take over the Joseph Rowntree Charitable Trust, which had funded the first three years of BCLC. BRL gave funding for the next three years (2005–08). See BCLC, 'Ballymun Community Law Centre Annual Report 2004' 4.

281 Between 2005 and 2008, the then Department of Community Rural and Gaeltacht Affairs also gave some funding for the development and delivery of Further Education and Training Awards Council (FETAC) accredited courses on Employment Law and Corporate Governance. Pobal provided funding for Housing Advice and Advocacy and the pilot peer-to-peer training. And in 2007, the Irish Fund funded the Community Mediation Training.

282 Interview with Evelyn Hanlon (n 19).

Welfare[283] was approached, but it was very clear that it did not wish to provide any funding for the Ballymun project. The Department of Justice was also approached, but indicated that it already provided for the LAB.

Thus, because BRL is funded by the Department of the Environment, the Department has been responsible for the continued existence of the law centre in Ballymun. It undertakes this funding as part of its commitment to social sustainability and social regeneration. Initially, some politicians wanted assurances that the centre would not take any clients who wished to take a case against the regeneration company or the council. However, as indicated above, the whole purpose and point of establishing a community law centre was to provide access to the law, other than in respect of family and criminal law, for people who could not afford it, regardless of what the basis for their complaint was. However, both BRL and BCLC did strongly promote the idea of alternative dispute resolution and community mediation as alternatives to going to court in every instance.[284]

Yet the main issue with BCLC's current funding situation is not about being able to meet the targets set in its Action Plan (2000),[285] but rather in relation to financial sustainability. The question that continues to linger around concerns the financial sustainability of BCLC in the long term, as once the mandate of BRL is completed, BCLC would no longer have an umbrella organization to channel funding.

Conclusion

The goals of achieving empowerment and having better communities have become clichés or even part of the rhetoric of development in the past few decades.[286] Nonetheless, the role of law and lawyers in promoting social inclusion as part of a sustainable development strategy has not become part of the sustainable development discourse.[287] If we are to overcome economic downturns, create jobs and enhance local economies, then the practice of CED lawyering can become an important aspect of how answers and solutions could be created while at the same time promoting social inclusion. Although it could be argued that lawyers are not really needed to combat social inclusion, the fact that BRL sees access to

283 The Department of Social Welfare funds (among other donors) the NCL&MC.

284 Interview with Evelyn Hanlon (n 244).

285 The conclusion of the 2009 evaluation report indicated that the areas of service provided as set out in the 2000 Action Plan were all on target and that the legal education programmes have filled the information gap within the community, not to mention the use of technology in linking its housing course with NUI Galway, its engagement with schools and free lunch talks. Halpin et al (n 237) 51–55.

286 A quick Google scholar search for 'community empowerment' revealed over 530,000 articles.

287 Except when drafting contracts and the legal issues associated with regeneration, *but* these are *not* from a community perspective.

legal services as part of social regeneration as a way of ensuring real citizenship in which rights and responsibilities can be ascertained by the community as well as by government is an indication that lawyers are needed. Because CED lawyering acts as a facilitator, CED is best placed to join the dots between regeneration and public interest law, and this is why BCLC offers the best example of how CED has developed and how it can continue to do so.

If economic recovery means economic development, then the role and evolution of CED lawyering is influenced by the goal of sustainable development, which in turns creates a new vision as to how to enhance the provision of civil legal aid services among communities.

Although there is nothing linking access to legal services to sustainable development, providing access to basic services, such as civil legal aid, in regenerated areas has created this link in an unexpected way. The link has allowed for the creation of a community law centre under a regeneration framework. Moreover, it has facilitated the role of CED lawyering in promoting/implementing a strategic model of legal aid.

BCLC overcame the constraints posed by the Irish government in respect of funding legal aid as the project was seen as part of the regeneration project of the area, as part of a public issue and as part of government policy as to how to achieve sustainable development. By developing new and innovative ways as to what is meant by legal aid and access to civil legal aid services, which includes access to legal services by community groups, a new form of lawyering can ensue, making the practice of CED law a reality.

Furthermore, although CED lawyering does not equate with merely servicing community groups, the involvement of NGOs is an essential component of its practice[288] and the case study of Ballymun has highlighted this.

---

288 Dana A Thompson, 'The Role of Nonprofits in CED' in Clay, Jr and Jones (eds) (n 5) 57–82.

Chapter 9
From Individual to Collective Squat: Economic Theory and the Regulation of Squatting in England and France

Jane Ball

Introduction

Squatters have been observed to be outsiders to society and treated as morally deficient. For Foucault,[1] stigma is produced by a discourse evidencing weakness in a power relationship with society. This kind of stigmatization was underlined by recent English legislation designating all residential squatting as a criminal activity. Nonetheless, squatters have choices.

There is also the question as to why individuals choose to join a collective squat (as defined below) rather than seek a home to themselves. France has a stronger history of militant squatting than England,[2] and therefore comparative study might assist in developing a response to this question. This situation will then be examined using insider-outsider theory, an economic theory originally developed by Lindbeck and Snower,[3] and adapted to housing markets by Ball.[4] Essentially, this theory suggests that established residents can protect their position because of 'transaction costs', which are the financial costs in terms of time, effort and money which create barriers to access to housing, but which incidentally also create barriers to eviction. If these barriers/costs are excessively high, the result is the stigmatization and exclusion of outsiders, which can involve the eviction of squatters even from disused non-residential buildings.

1 Michel Foucault, *L'Ordre du Discours* (Paris, Gallimard 1971).

2 England must be discussed rather than the UK because there are significant differences in the laws governing Wales, Northern Ireland and particularly Scotland.

3 Assar Lindbeck and Dennis Snower, *The Insider-Outsider Theory of Employment and Unemployment* (Cambridge, MA, MIT Press 1988); Assar Lindbeck and Dennis Snower, 'The Insider-Outsider Theory: A Survey' (July 2002) IZA Discussion Paper No 534 http://ssrn.com/abstract_id=325323 accessed 14 August 2012.

4 Jane Ball, *Housing Disadvantaged People? Insiders and Outsiders in French Social Housing* (London, Routledge 2012).

The advantage of individual squatting is that such long-term adverse occupants can acquire ownership rights over the property by 'adverse possession'[5] in England and by *prescription acquisitive*[6] in France. These are similar legal claims with similar results, but with very different terminology. The popular word 'squatter' is common to England and France, and so it is overwhelmingly useful to speak of 'individual squatting' to obtain 'squatters' title'. Today, squatters' websites use the terminology themselves, tending to shift the word away from the derogatory.[7]

In England, there may be an increase in collective squatting in response to the increasing criminalization of individual residential squatting, shortages of affordable housing and the policy of stigmatization of the squatter. The 'collective squat' here means a mutually defensive position for a group of squatters, occupying a small home, perhaps for communitarian, socialist, political or practical reasons. Alternatively, a collective squat might involve larger shifting populations or larger spaces: whole blocks, offices or factories, as in the French experience.

This chapter avoids the well-trodden path of economic and moral debates about the usefulness of squatting in order to explore the effects of transaction costs on the regulatory procedures obstructing or assisting this activity. The strategies of squatters and of the public authorities are explored, first using theories of stigmatization and then in the light of insider-outsider theory. The prospects of obtaining individual squatters' title are outlined, a situation which contrasts with collective squats offering a series of advantages of mutual support and claims of moral legitimacy. Finally, the different effects of this theory of power are considered in the global context.

Introducing Squatters and Their Choices

Squatters find themselves in a difficult position as stigmatized outsiders. Individual and collective squatting offer different routes to redeeming or combatting the moral views held against them. This is a question of strategy in different regulatory conditions.

5 Section 15 of the Limitation Act 1980.

6 Title XXI of Book 3 of the Code Civil, particularly arts 2272 to 79.

7 The word was always derogatory in the past because it used to refer to the non-English practice of individuals squatting on their heels on the ground.

Squatters as Outsiders

Becker[8] and Bouillon[9] both describe the position of squatters as outsiders. Cohen[10] and Cooper[11] argue that all squatters can be stigmatized as 'folk devils' accused of criminality and deviancy. Becker[12] goes further in his deviancy argument, suggesting that social groups which break rules or norms are labelled as outsiders by more powerful groups, and that this amplifies their disadvantaged societal position by adding adverse moral meaning to this. Bouillon[13] illustrates this by observing that squatters are perceived as having cumulatively dangerous characteristics: immigrants, poor people, the young, drug-takers.[14] This stereotype also involves danger to neighbourhood property prices, damage to property, and criminal and anti-social behaviour.

The stigma exists despite the variations in types of squatter. Bouillon[15] interviewed squatters and those dealing with them in the poor quarters of Marseille in a qualitative participant-observation study of several groups in 2000–05. She found that the age, motivation and moral rectitude of squatters were extremely variable, with a wide variety of reasons for resorting to squatting.[16] Fox-O'Mahony and Cobb[17] suggested a diversity of motive and types of property squatted in England, including neighbours disputing boundaries. Squatters are just people, but they tend to be demonized or idealized without a space for ordinariness.

Foucault[18] described power relationships embodied in discourse which produce stigmatization. The example given by Foucault was that the role of the madman in a drama has a double function: in the first place, he normally represents a stigmatized and incoherent presence who is not listened to, yet in the second place the madman sometimes speaks up, conveying the 'masked truth'.[19] In some ways, the strategy of collective squats declaring the moral bankruptcy of society, could encompass

---

8 Howard S Becker, *Outsiders: Studies in the Sociology of Deviance* (New York, Simon & Schuster 1963).

9 Florence Bouillon, *Le Squat: Problème Social ou Lieu d'Emancipation* (Paris, Editions Rue d'Ulm 2011).

10 Stanley Cohen, *Folk Devils and Moral Panics* (London, Routledge 2002).

11 Charlie Cooper, 'Places, "Folk Devils" and Social Policy' in Nigel Sprigings and Peter Somerville (eds), *Housing and Social Policy, Contemporary Themes and Critical Perspectives* (London, Routledge 2005) 69–85.

12 Becker (n 8).

13 Bouillon (n 9) 23–35.

14 ibid 29.

15 ibid .

16 ibid 4, 42–50.

17 Lorna Fox-O'Mahony and Neil Cobb, 'Taxonomies of Squatting: Unlawful Occupation in a New Legal Order' (2008) 71(6) Modern Law Review 878, 882.

18 Foucault (n 1) 14.

19 ibid 3.

the second function of truth-speaker, although the stigmatization of individual squatters means the squatter often appears to fulfill the first.

A Choice of Strategy

Squatters can adopt two strategies to counter moral disapproval. The first involves the individual acquisition of squatters' title and the second is collective protest or other collective activity. These are not mutually exclusive, but there is often a choice to be made according to which is the easiest to achieve. This chapter concerns the effects of morality as a strategy rather than arguing for or against the content of the morality presented.

Squatters' title can be obtained by individual squatters whose status might flip from immoral outsider to the traditionally moral status of property owner by this means. Green suggested tension between the English law of adverse possession and the English landowner as ideal citizen rooted in a long rural history. This produced a moral stereotype – a white, male farmer leaning on his gate: 'a pillar of the community, the backbone of the country, the salt of the earth'. Anyone who did not fit this stereotype would be regarded as an 'outsider'.[20] Similarly, Guerrand[21] recounted a nineteenth-century French view of the moralizing qualities of property ownership – people acquiring ownership underwent a novitiate, a training for a religious order.

The moral impression made is critical to this 'rehabilitation', so that the prospect of squatters' title incentivizes their developing a good relationship with their neighbours. Bouillion found that some squatters had a strategy of befriending neighbours to avoid detection, a time-consuming but personally rewarding transaction costs in the form of effort rather than money. Conversely, where other squatters were a neighbourhood nuisance, this would tend to alert the police or owners to their presence. [22]

Medium-size collective squats often adopt a moral political position to counter the perceptions of immorality arising from their stigmatization (these squats are described as 'medium-sized' to distinguish them from large shanty towns outside cities such as Istanbul). Bouillon described a collective ethos where squats create a 'place of emancipation' through their social, political and artistic activities or perhaps by allowing social asylum or experiment. She observed two types of squatting: first, the 'housing 'squat or 'squat of necessity'[23] – 'necessity' here expresses the desperate choices of people in need of housing seeking shelter;

20 Kate Green, 'Citizens and Squatters: Under the Surfaces of Land Law' in Susan Bright and John Dewar (eds), *Land Law, Themes and Perspectives* (Oxford, OUP 1998) 242 and 231.

21 Roger-Henri Guerrand, *Les Origines du Logement Social en France 1850–1914* (Paris, 41 Editions Ouvrières 1966), Introduction.

22 Bouillon (n 9) 25.

23 ibid 7.

second, the 'squats of activity' or 'squats of conviction',[24] which were a matter of choice and were intended for the reception of artistic, cultural or militant projects, although these tended to have less success in sustaining their occupation in France. There is a continuum from collective residential squats to pure protest, but this chapter concerns housing squats.

Collective housing squats are conducted, for example, by *Droit au Logement*, the Right to Housing (DAL)[25] – a militant French squatting movement. This tradition goes back to 1911, when demonstrations and squats were led by Cochon, an anarchist carpet-maker and housing campaigner who founded a 100,000-strong tenants' organization before the First World War. [26] The 'right to housing'[27] campaigned for by DAL is seen as a collective right, a social and economic right often associated with the political left. It is the legal basis for both tenants' rights and for the rights of disadvantaged people to be housed by the state. DAL is an *association*,[28] a not-for-profit vehicle for voluntary or political activity, and this is seen as a collective voice.[29] Such an explicitly collective approach attracts media interest in exposing a housing crisis.

England has its own protests, even if collective action is not legally reinforced as strongly as in France.[30] Reeve[31] described the UK post-war squatter movements as not always agreeing whether to behave in an exemplary manner or to use the politics of social confrontation. This collective tradition continues. Last year, the 'Occupy London' movement camped by St Paul's Cathedral. The movement included groups for education and debate. Unlike the DAL squats, this camp was to protest about a variety of social causes, but whose housing need was not so obvious. The groups were ultimately evicted,[32] showing that this was one of Bouillon's less successful 'squats of activities'.

---

24 ibid.

25 DAL, *Le Logement un Droit pour Tous* (Paris, Le Cherche Midi Editeur 1996).

26 Now reformed as la Confédération Nationale du Logement with a similar number of members.

27 Although mentioned in statutes since 1990, this was declared to be of constitutional value by décision no 94-359DC, 19 janvier 1995C of the Constitutional Council, now including the right to sue the state to provide housing (Code de la Construction et de l'Habitation arts L300-1 toL300-2).

28 Under a statute of 1 July 1901.

29 The *association* is connected to the right of association and is intrinsically collective.

30 For an account of collective culture and representation in housing and elsewhere, see Ball (n 4).

31 Kesia Reeve, 'Squatting Since 1945: The Enduring Relevance of Material Need' in Sprigings and Somerville (n 11).

32 Ben Quinn and Dave Johnson, 'Occupy London: Police and Bailiffs Move in to Evict St. Paul's Protesters' *The Guardian* (London, 28 February 2012). Available at: http://www.guardian.co.uk/uk/2012/feb/28/occupy-london-camp-police-clearance accessed 2 August 2012.

Squatting in England is generally more covert. Tough enforcement of English eviction law could offer almost a complete explanation for this compared to overt collective squatting found elsewhere. Protest is, however, a frequent feature of collective housing squats and a different tactic from the private law approach.

Insider-Outsider Theory and Squatting

This section considers how the difficulties, costs and expenses suffered by squatters and, conversely, the difficulties faced by owners in removing them can change squatter strategies. It uses insider-outsider theory, which casts light on the cause, nature and consequences of this. Insider-outsider theory was originally a only labour market theory based on the effect of transaction costs. Consequently, it should be explained what these costs are, how they are used in labour market and housing market theory, and then how they can be applied to squatters.

Insider-Outsider Theory and Transaction Costs

Williamson[33] described how the costs of making transactions could be so high that this changed people's economic behaviour. Indeed, they might not contract at all in order to avoid having to pay costs, such as legal fees or taxes. Transaction costs are not just about financial loss of profit, but also the time, effort and general inconvenience of acting. This has an effect on the functioning of markets where such costs are widespread. Coase[34] developed the idea that this changed individuals' behaviour. In another substantial development, Lindbeck and Snower[35] observed how transaction costs affect labour markets to protect 'insiders', well-established employees, although this also disadvantaged unemployed labour market outsiders without a job.

Insider/outsider theory explains how employers lose profits because of the transaction costs of 'hiring and firing'[36] employees, described as insiders. These transaction costs give insider employees an inherent economic advantage, because employers are reluctant to incur loss of profits arising from removing them and recruiting new employees. These costs and difficulties include barriers to entry, such as requirements for trade union membership, or other limitations to access to jobs. They might include barriers to exit, such as loss of productivity when there is a vacancy, severance payments, legal costs and the personal difficulty of the situation.

33 Oliver E Williamson, 'The Economics of Organization: The Transaction Cost Approach' (1981) 87(3) American Journal of Sociology 548–77.

34 RH Coase 'The Nature of the Firm' (1931) 4(16) Economica 386–405.

35 Lindbeck and Snower, *The Insider-Outsider Theory of Employment and Unemployment* (n 3).

36 Lindbeck and Snower, 'The Insider-Outsider Theory: A Survey' (n 3) 8.

As a consequence, insider employees can bargain to increase these transaction costs, again increasing the costs of dismissal, increasing wages and adversely affecting outsiders – those unlikely to obtain jobs. The extent of employee protection is a question of balance, of what is acceptable in any given society, but it is clear that unemployed outsiders would have to offer much lower pay to compensate the employer for incurring these costs and the risks of an unknown candidate. A situation with very high barriers to access and exit from employment is described by Lindbeck and Snower as 'insiderness'.

Lindbeck and Snower[37] described the stigmatization of outsiders as the result of this *insiderness* in the labour market. Where there is *insiderness*, insider workers desperately hang on to their job because employers become reluctant to hire anyone except the most qualified because of the great difficulty in dismissing a bad choice of employee in an unbalanced labour market. For outsiders, the effect is that their qualification for jobs deteriorates with the passing of time as difficult access to jobs means they lose contacts, training or references, and this produces social exclusion. Lindbeck and Snower[38] describe outsiders thus: 'They often live in the underclass neighborhoods of large cities, with meager social services, poor schooling, and scant police protection. These are the real "outsiders" in society.'

This chapter explores more effects of this well-established labour market theory and applies it to housing, in this case, to squatting. As concerns labour, the theory has been tested variously by econometric and empirical labour market studies internationally.[39] An example is that the Organisation for Economic Cooperation and Development (OECD) has used this to recommend reforms to labour markets in France, where high transaction costs were identified as causing market problems, including difficulties in job creation.[40] Significantly, outsiders are in a position of economic weakness in the job market.[41]

Lindbeck and Snower[42] argue that insider-outsider theory could be applied sociologically to any situation where there are insiders and outsiders. It has been applied to housing markets by a number of authors, particularly to describe how the entrenched interests of established local residents can be favoured: Berry and Hall,[43]

37 ibid.

38 ibid 3.

39 There is a review of developments in the previous 25 years and proof of the theory since 1988 in ibid.

40 The more accurate economic term for this phenomenon is 'hysteresis', a delay before the market responds to stimuli such as increased demand.

41 A general theme in 'The Insider-Outsider Theory: A Survey' (n 3).

42 ibid 30.

43 Mike Berry and Jon Hall, 'Institutional Investment in Rental Housing in Australia: A Policy Framework and Two Models' (2005) 42(1) Urban Studies 91–111.

Malpezzi,[44] Dogge and Smeets,[45] and Lux.[46] These locals were insiders in a broad sense. Ball[47] conducted semi-structured interviews with French social housing actors in three regions of France in 2005–06, finding that there were high transaction costs for access to and exit from housing. There were related tendencies to exclude outsiders, who in this study were disadvantaged people.

Insider tenants can protect their position in similar ways to employees. Removing tenants will cause the landlord to suffer loss of profits due to the transaction costs of rent loss, eviction costs and recruitment costs. This means insider tenants have an inherent bargaining advantage with the landlord.[48] Negotiated transaction costs and barriers to access and exit might include requirements for rental guarantees, tenant insurance and high deposits,[49] lower rents for insider tenants and serious difficulties in evicting. Again, when there is *insiderness* in housing markets, outsiders would have to offer much higher rent to compensate the landlord for these costs and risks of taking on someone unknown.

Housing markets have some differences from employment markets. The position of tenants compared with outsiders is strengthened by the fact that they pay rent, the direct source of profit, unlike the position of a paid employee. This tenant advantage applies so long as they pay. Owner-occupiers are insiders in a broad sense because the transaction costs of access and exit from these homes are very high, a kind of *insiderness.* This must have some effect, even if this only means that their homes are unavailable to outsiders.

Housing campaigners commonly seek the reduction of barriers to access, but not barriers to exit by eviction. To some extent, one often depends on the other and there is an almost brutal even-handedness about the practicality of this. A major objective of housing policy and a dilemma must be to find ways to enhance the security of citizens without excluding outsiders in ways that threaten their future capacity for a full and productive life.

Applying Insider-Outsider Theory to Squatters

It is an additional step to apply the theory to squatting. But how can you have transaction costs when there is no market and no normal financial transaction? Even though squatters do not pay for their space, they still have transaction costs

44 Stephen Malpezzi, 'Housing Prices, Externalities and Regulation in US Metropolitan Areas' (1996) 7(2) Journal of Housing Research 209–41.

45 Patrick JC Dogge and Jos Smeets. 'Freedom of Choice on the Housing Market: The Case of Eindhoven' (ENHR conference, Rotterdam, June 2007).

46 Martin Lux, 'Housing Systems: Change on the Way to the EU. Similarities and Differences, Integration or Convergence' (ENHR conference, Ljubljana, 2006).

47 Ball (n 4).

48 ibid.

49 In France, often provided by social organizations (such as Action Logement) set up to collect funding from working people to assist the housing effort.

based on Williamson's description of difficulties of action. These include barriers to access, the deterrence of the law and unfavourable conditions of occupancy. The costs of eviction are weighed against its economic advantages of free accommodation or acquiring title. Squatters are outsiders directly affected by barriers to access in the normal housing market. These transaction costs mean the balance of advantage can lie in collective squatting rather than seeking individual squatters' title when the latter is seriously obstructed.

Once squatters are in place, the transaction costs of evicting squatters are central to this analysis and this occupation of space is their major advantage. Home-owners might be reluctant to incur these costs for a building which might be unused and not producing a profit anyway. The cost and difficulty of evicting squatters increase when they squat collectively. Few would dispute that access to buildings for squatting should be difficult. Both English and French law treat intrusion into occupied homes with criminal penalties.[50] However, long-term unoccupied property is often the target of squatting and the morality of evictions or legal penalties is more equivocal.

There are also incentives to squat and related transactions. Entering a home has some qualities of a financial transaction because squatters choose to act to acquire valuable living space, albeit without consent. There are other transactions. Partially acquired rights to squatters' title might in principle be sold or inherited in both France[51] and England,[52] and there may be subletting, even if this agreement has no legal force. Bouillon[53] records a young couple hiring a room in a squat to take drugs in an otherwise normal transaction. She said the French authorities had criminalized *traffic* in squatted property. In the very large settlements of Istanbul, there are multi-storey concrete flat blocks with squatter landlords letting to squatter tenants.[54] The economic exigencies of life still intrude into squatting.

Squatters might also prefer to squat because it could be preferable to transactions within the normal market. In France, for example, in a housing crisis, people might encounter *marchands de sommeil* (sleep sellers), landlords charging outrageous prices for inferior and illegal accommodation. They are reputed to force recovery of rent by violence or by driving vulnerable women into prostitution.[55] In such contexts, squatting might seem comparatively civilized.

---

50 For example, Code Pénal, art 226-4 in France and Criminal Law Act 1977, s 6(1), in England.

51 Code Civil, art 2265.

52 *Asher v Whitlock* (1865) LR 1 QB 1, modified for registered land by the Land Registration Act 2002, sch 6, para 11. This might be modified by criminalization of squatting; see below.

53 Bouillon (n 9) 18.

54 Jasemin Alkiser, 'The Impact of Legal Regulations on the Squatter Housing ("Gecekondu") Phenomenon in Turkey' (ENHR conference, Toulouse, 2011).

55 Ball (n 4) 228.

Squatters are particularly strongly affected by stigma and difficulty in access to housing, because of *insiderness*. Bouillon[56] described squatters as ashamed to admit their status. Ex-squatters are particularly unlikely to find the references and deposits required for access without help. The personal situation of a person without housing deteriorates rapidly.

Central to insider-outsider theory is that the insider occupies a position, whether a job or a housing space, and they act to advance their economic interests, whether individually or collectively. This is normal and not essentially a cause for blame, but within a democracy intended to represent everyone, it can become distorted if the voices of outsiders are not heard.

Individual Squatting

Squatters can act individually or collectively in occupying a home. This section looks first at the acquisition of title by individual squatters in England and France. Then, the advantages of acquiring squatters' title are considered from the point of view of public order, with an emphasis on the importance of possession. Next, it must be recounted how the prospects of acquiring squatters' title or even remaining in place have been cut down in civil and criminal law in England.

Individual Squatting and the Private Law

The process of obtaining squatters' title might support public order due to the fact that it rewards those acting peacefully, like a property owner[57]or a good neighbour. This is a low-cost alternative to eviction for governments. However, the transaction costs of acquiring title have become almost impossibly high. This has long been the case in France and is becoming so in England. Nonetheless, some continental legal views on this procedure support the idea that squatters' title might be valuable for wider reasons.

Obtaining squatters' title is a small-scale and personal process, because this requires physical possession of the land by or on behalf of named individuals making the claim. This requires open and unconcealed possession and control of land for a fixed period of time: 12 years in England[58] and 30 or 10 years in France (explicitly peaceful occupation).[59] English title is acquired through adverse

56 Bouillon (n 9) 49.

57 Acting like a property owner is a requirement of French squatters' title but is presumed: Code Civil, arts 2256 and 2261.

58 Occupation should be open, notorious and unconcealed: *Lord Advocate v Lord Lovat* (1880) 3 App Cas 273 at 291, 296.

59 Code Civil, art 2272. The French general requirements are that possession of the land by the squatter should be 'uninterrupted, peaceful, public and unequivocal, and as an owner' (art 2261, author's translation).

possession where s 15 of the Limitation Act 1980 cuts off the former owner's title, while French squatters obtain title through *prescription acquisitive*, a slow process of accretion of rights.

The transaction costs of squatting might include physical force to obtain possession (although this is discouraged in both countries) and then physical force to evict. *Usucapio*, is a Latin term for *presciption acquisitive* which came down from the Romans in different social circumstances.[60] In the wilder reaches of the Roman Empire, displaced owners still might be obliged to carry out their own evictions, or call in the army. Here, squatters' title allowed recognition of a state of semi-military possession and control. In French law, the physical act of eviction is still designated as *manu militaria* (by the military hand).

Physical possession is still an essential element of both ownership[61] and acquiring squatters' title in England and France.[62] Indeed, there have been long European philosophical debates about the legal role of possession in ownership. In the nineteenth century, Savigny asked how possession, without any regard to its own lawfulness, can be the basis for rights. In a debate with von Ihéring, two arguments were proposed to justify the protection of existing possessors of land. Gordley describes these arguments and their use by continental jurists:[63] 'One, for which they often cite Savigny, is to preserve public order. The other, for which they often cite von Ihéring,[64] is to provide a more complete protection for the true owner. These are almost the only explanations that French jurists give.'[65]

Public order in French law encompasses not just law and order enforced by police, but rather the smooth running of society.[66] Following Savigny, the French legal notion of *prescription extinctive* by possession protects existing owners.

The idea that property is proved by physical possession deals with a procedural problem known as the *preuve diabolique* (diabolical proof).[67] If ownership is proved only by title deeds, then the passing of time means this proof must constantly be

---

60 RW Lee, *Elements of Roman Law* (4th edn, London, Sweet and Maxwell 1956) 119–23.

61 In England, this means acquiring a freehold or leasehold estate (more exactly described in the Law of Property Act 1925, s 1(1)(a) and (b)) or *propriété* (ownership) in France (Code Civil, art 544).

62 For France, Code Civil, arts 2255 to 57 and 2278. For England, see Kevin Gray, and Susan Francis Gray, *Elements of Land Law* (5th edn, Oxford, OUP 2009) Part II, but particularly 106.

63 James Gordley, *Foundations of Public Law. Property, Tort, Contract, Unjust Enrichment* (Oxford, OUP 2006) 56, referring to FC von Savigny, *Das Recht des Besitzes* (1803).

64 Rudolf von Ihéring (1818–92), a noted German jurist.

65 Gordley (n 63) 53.

66 See Code des Communes, art L.131-2 for the mayor's duties in this respect.

67 Often known as *probatio diabolica*, described in Philippe Malaurie and Laurent Aynès, *Les Biens* (Paris, Défrenois 2010) 193–94; and François Terré and Philippe Simler, *Droit Civil, Les Biens* (5th edn, Paris, Editions Dalloz-Sirey 1998) para 515.

renewed. If deeds are lost or something cannot be documented, then clear proof of occupation allows the continuation of the legitimate owners' title. This means that the transaction costs of such proof must not be too high.

Given that land is notionally perpetual, this view of possession provides a protection for individuals against losses in public land registers or against corruption.[68] In the long run, the peaceful presence of people on land is the best evidence of legitimacy. This common European view that possession is the root of property ownership tends to be undermined by the English development of title being proved by registration.[69] What if, with the passage of the centuries, the government was no longer benign in registering titles based on long occupancy for whatever reason, such as unacknowledged bureaucratic errors or lost deeds? The idea of possession in French law is a procedural part of the protection of the individual against the state.

Reducing Access to Squatters' Title

Access to squatters' title in England and France is difficult. However, this was recently relaxed slightly. In France there is the possibility of interrupting or postponing the passing of time needed to give squatters the right to title for a series of practical reasons.[70] A recent statutory reform addressed the problem that these postponements and interruptions were too long and numerous and that the law was too complicated.[71] From 1804, the law had required good faith on entry to land.[72] Since 2008, there is an accelerated claim for squatters' title – 10 years as against 30.[73] This requires both 'fair title'[74] and good faith. Good faith is always necessary, but is presumed. This presumption can be disproved.[75] Traditionally, good faith requires that occupiers should believe their occupancy to be legally justified, even if this is mistaken.[76] Many squatters might thus face a period of 30 years to obtain title. French tenants remaining *in situ* after their tenancy ends are

---

68 Malaurie and Aynès (n 67).

69 Note 58 refers to the Law Commission's view of this.

70 According to Code Civil, arts 2227 to 2246, for example, time does not start to run until the owner could have known of the occupation (art 2227) or when an owner is unable to act because he or she is a minor (art 2234).

71 Philippe Malaurie, 'Exposé de Motifs' in P Catala (ed), *Avant-projet de Réforme du Droit des Obligations et de la Prescription* (Paris, La Documentation Française 2006) Third book, Title XX. Statutory interruptions to prescription tend to favour certain types of owner, such as minors, by Code Civil, arts 2233 to 2239 applied by virtue of art 2259, which has no real English equivalent.

72 Under the old Code Civil, art 2258.

73 ibid art 2272.

74 ibid art 2274.

75 ibid.

76 Malaurie and Aynès (n 67) 173.

expressly excluded from squatters' title.[77] Obtaining squatters' title is thus more possible, but is still very circumscribed.

In England, civil law barriers to obtaining title by adverse possession have become higher. English law does not require good faith in the French sense above, and proof includes factual occupation adverse to the owner (without their permission) and with an intention to possess.[78] Acts of ownership, such as putting up fences and looking after the property, can act as evidence of this possession.[79] Nonetheless, acquisition of title to registered land (now most land in the UK) has become substantially harder, because when adverse possessors seek to register the occupied land, notice must be given to the property owner to allow them to object.[80] Then, the grounds which allow possessors to override objections from property owners are limited, such as a mistake about ownership by the possessor[81] or that it would be unconscionable not to register.[82]

However, in both France and England, governments have sought to strengthen the criminal law against squatting. In France, an amended article 224-6 of the Code Pénal was intended to create an offence of occupying a home without the owner's or tenant's permission.[83] However, parts of the bill were held to be unconstitutional by the Constitutional Council because the sanctions were disproportionate.[84]

In England, s 144 of the Legal Aid, Sentencing and Punishment of Offenders Act 2012 created an offence where someone enters a residential building who knows or ought to know that they are trespassing,[85] and if they have the intention of living there.[86] This is punishable by up to six months in prison and a £5,000 fine.[87] For this type of offence, it would be relatively easy to justify arrest, such as for damage to property or lack of an address of the defendant.[88] The Criminal Law Act 1977, s. 7 already created an offence where the squatter displaced the owner or tenant once the latter had requested the squatter to leave a home and they did not.

77 Code Civil, art 2269.

78 *Powell v McFarlane* (1979) 38 P & CR 452.

79 *Seddon v Smith* (1877) 36 LT 168.

80 Land Registration Act 2002, sch 6, para. 2.

81 ibid para 5(4)(c).

82 ibid para 5(2)(a). If the estate owner fails to respond to the notice, then the squatter can re-apply after 12 years adverse possession to be the registered proprietor. See Fox-O'Mahony and Cobb (n 17).

83 By original art 32 *ter* of the bill, now statute no 2011-267 du 14 mars 2011.

84 Due to décision no. 2011-625DC du 10 Mars 2011. This judgement did not specifically refer to the amendment, but to the government database of legislation.

85 For the non-common law reader, essentially entering and staying without permission.

86 Legal Aid, Sentencing and Punishment of Offenders Act 2012 s 144(1). See also Neil Cobb, 'Property's Outlaws: Squatting, Land Use and Criminal Trespass' [2012] Crim LR 114.

87 ibid s 144(5).

88 Police and Criminal Evidence Act 1984, s 25.

It remains to be seen if the new English offence will be strictly enforced or if the homelessness which often drives squatting continues to do so. Indeed, following the French view above, this new offence might be seen as disproportionate. It involves imposing criminal sanctions on a squatter who might be in urgent need of shelter or who is a long-established resident, as compared to the damage caused or the need to protect empty property. Disproportionality can be a violation of human rights[89] applying in France, as in England through the Human Rights Act 1998. The offence could breach the European Convention for the Protection of Human Rights and Fundamental Freedoms:[90] Article 3 (against inhuman and degrading treatment), Article 8 (protecting the home and family life) or Article 6 (requiring fair procedure in both administration and criminal cases.

This reduction in squatters' title can be seen as the product of stigmatization, resulting in a hostile public environment to this activity. The English Law Commission referred to squatters' title as 'theft of land' when proposing changes to Land Registry rules.[91] These changes make registration of squatters' title more difficult. Fox O'Mahony and Cobb set out arguments for and against squatting to consider this, but said that the Commission's view 'has copper-fastened the portrayal of the squatter's actions as wrong (tantamount to criminal activity), with the dispossessed landowner as the "victim" of the piece'.[92]

There is a progression from stigmatization to criminalization. Someone in the course of acquiring title might still pay taxes, send their children to school and obey the law generally. This useful kind of public order is less likely for a squatter designated as a criminal, because 'open' occupation might get them arrested.

Such an approach leaves little scope for acquiring title to disused or mistakenly occupied homes. Even the sale or other transmission of squatters' rights is made difficult in practice by s 144(4) of the 2012 Act, which states: 'The fact that a person derives title from a trespasser, or has the permission of a trespasser, does not prevent the person from being a trespasser.' This could mean fresh opportunities to arrest heirs and purchasers. The law is also retrospective, applying to squatters entering a home before 1 September 2012.[93] Within the time limits for criminal prosecution, even property owners who have neglected to act to protect their property[94] can have established occupants removed and charged with an offence, instead of issuing proceedings to allow occupants to stay in

89 Dirk Van Zyl Smit and Andrew Ashworth, 'Disproportionate Sentences as Human Rights Violations' (2004) 67(4) Modern Law Review 541.

90 Council of Europe, 4 November 1950.

91 Law Commission, *Land Registration for the 21st Century: A Consultative Document* (Law Com No 254) (London, HMSO 1998) para 10.5; Fox-O'Mahony and Cobb (n 17) 879.

92 Fox-O'Mahony and Cobb (n 17) 879.

93 Legal Aid, Sentencing and Punishment of Offenders Act 2012, s 144.

94 Neglect by landowners is one of the traditional justifications of squatting; see Fox-O'Mahony and Cobb (n 17).

place until a civil hearing, an effective attack on adverse possession. This reflects a kind of *insiderness.*

The Collectivization of Squats

Due to the physical presence of squatters and the transaction costs involved in removing them, collective squatting can offer a better defence to this hostile regulatory environment for squatters than individual squatting, although such collective action might not appeal to everyone. This section concerns the effects of this. First, the observations about the effects of unionization by Lindbeck and Snower are considered, then how squatters can react collectively against *insiderness* to improve their position, and finally the high cost of suppression of this.

Lindbeck and Snower on Collectivization

The collectivization of squatters could be a response to insiders uniting against them (in a broad sense). Lindbeck and Snower[95] described collective action in the unionized workforce. They argued that trade unions increase the disruptive power of workers acting together, such as by striking to improve pay and conditions. In this way, unionization thus increases the transaction costs protecting insiders. This was the case even where employers were unionized as well (as in France).

Rueda[96] suggested that *insiderness* in labour markets means that the government listens more to insiders by the privileging of lobbies, formal or informal, with stigmatization attaching to the less well off. This collective lobbying has a formal form in France and an informal form in England for both the labour and housing markets.[97] Nonetheless, it has been seen that England also has strong exclusionary policies in the area of the criminalization of squatting. These are different areas of law so that *insiderness* can be judged by the extent of any kinds of barrier to access to housing as well as by evidence of social exclusion.

In housing markets in France, there are patterns of insider representation and exclusionary behaviour similar to those in the labour markets. There is formal collective representation of tenants and landowners, collective bargaining processes influencing housing administration and the aligned content of laws. This form of unionization is common for all societal interests, including disadvantaged people represented by *associations*. It must be said that the same system of

95 Lindbeck and Snower, *The Insider-Outsider Theory of Employment and Unemployment* (n 3) 5.

96 David Rueda, 'Insider-Outsider Politics in Industrialized Democracies: The Challenge to Social Democratic Parties' (2005) 99(1) American Political Science Review 61.

97 Detailed information about French collective representation and social housing allocation in housing is available in English in Ball (n 4).

representation is responsible for the creation and administration of the welfare state which benefits the most disadvantaged.

Despite the provision of welfare, there is a particular problem of French localism obstructing policies to house disadvantaged people. Local insiders (here, local representatives of tenants, workers and local people) were strongly represented in planning, construction and social housing allocation decisions. However, outsiders seeking housing had very little voice in these various fora. This resulted in the tendency for local representatives to severely limit or refuse access to social housing for the most disadvantaged. There were also difficulties of access to private rental housing.

An effect of *insiderness* leads to both more squatting, due to difficulty accessing ordinary housing, and at the same time reduced rights for squatters. This is the stigmatization and the result of collective influence that Lindbeck and Snower predicted. You would expect exceptional hardship to be met by society with the greater provision of welfare, but if the condition of being an outsider increases the stigma attached to them, the result is likely to be less welfare provision for greater need, not more. Squatters and other outsiders are somehow seen as automatically unworthy, whatever the cause of their condition.

Why Collective Squats?

Where there is no longer any usefulness in the open and peaceful occupation required for squatters' title to be acquired, there are several incentives to squat collectively. This is a radical response to stigmatization and exclusion from housing due to *insiderness*, due to the impossibly high transaction costs in obtaining such title, and to barriers to access to housing generally. There are a number of advantages inherent in collective squatting.

It has been seen that collective squatters can strategically take the moral high ground by espousing causes or social activities. In France, combining a demonstration with occupation has been a popular tactic. This has been the case ever since the supporters of Cochon before the First World War occupied high-profile public buildings to draw attention to housing problems.[98] Mass squats by people in need of housing can involve occupying buildings that are unsuitable for housing, such as factories, public buildings or offices. This unsuitability underlines their housing need. In 2001, for example, 200 people occupied buildings belonging to a hospital organization in Marseille,[99] and the local court delayed their eviction due to a lack of local housing.

Squatting in buildings that are not homes has not been a common feature in England. Nevertheless, in England, the Legal Aid, Sentencing and Punishment of Offenders Act 2012, only criminalizes residential occupation, and therefore

98 DAL (n 25).

99 Described in a law report: TGI de Marseille, 16 mars 2001, 'L'assistance publique-hôpitaux de Marseille' *Le Monde* (Paris, 20 March 2001, 20).

squatting in non-residential property becomes more likely. Already, there has been a case of squatting in a London public library by way of protest.[100]

For effective communication and publicity, squatters are assisted by digital networks. The fate of collective squats can be followed on international websites, such as the multilingual [Squat!net][101] containing news, information and activities. In England, after the criminalization of squatting, legal advice is already available for squatters in this position by a dedicated website (www.squatter.org.uk), whilst more secure occupancy is campaigned for by Squatters' Action for Secure Homes (SQUASH). Any squatter with a smartphone can access these sites.

Collective squatters can appeal over the heads of neighbours to a larger political struggle: seeking support locally by manning squatted social centres and nationally by promoting various causes and internationally appealing to squatters' movements, to movements against eviction (such as the International Alliance of Inhabitants) or to human rights organizations. The support of immediate neighbours still matters, but less so.

There are other practical gains from banding together. Squatters might work in shifts to occupy a home to reduce the risk of eviction, and this group continuity does not rely on particular individuals. Groups can provide mutual support or physical defence, or even cheap places for people passing through. These activities can attract people who do not need to squat, increasing the incidence of squatting. Most important of all, a group is harder to evict than a single person.

In this way, collective action has benefits compared to individual squatting. Coase[102] suggested that people in business choose to work together in a firm if that firm's internal transaction costs are low. In that case, collective activity becomes more rewarding than working separately – a matter of economic convenience. Similarly, people act separately if the costs of acting together are too high. Added into this equation is that squatters might need to work together defensively in the face of *insiderness*, such as criminalization, which is difficult to avoid.

High Public Cost

There are at least three kinds of public costs involved in enforcing the criminalization of residential squatting: the possible very high costs of trying to evict a collective squat in a glare of publicity; the policing, surveillance and enforcement costs of trying to stop more vulnerable but mobile individual squatters; and the impact on individuals evicted requiring public welfare support.

---

100 See BBC News, 'Squatters re-open Friern Barnet Library' online at http://www.bbc.co.uk/news/uk-england-london-19590224 (accessed 26 September 2013). This double protest about closure of the lending library and about criminalization of squatting succeeding in keeping the library open.

101 [Squat!net] online at http://planet.squat.net/ (accessed 26 September 2013). The square brackets are part of the name of the organisation.

102 Coase (n 34).

The authorities face numerous dilemmas: how to fulfil their human rights duties; how to support tenants or property owners; how to investigate criminal, illegal immigrant or radical occupants within the squat; and how to evict people appealing to public sympathy.

In litigation to recover land, protesting squatters seeking publicity may wait until the final physical eviction before leaving their homes. A normal tendency in eviction cases is for individuals to depart in the earlier stages of the case, as can be seen by comparing statistics in England and France.[103] An English example of a difficult late-stage eviction was that of the Dale Farm travellers in 2011. These were not actually squatters, but home-owners evicted for a persistent breach of planning rules. However, it was one of the few recent examples of a collective eviction by the state in England. The policing costs of the eviction were estimated at £18 million.[104] Indeed, the rather effective English eviction process has been disapproved of outside England. Hoonakker[105] regretted the absence of a code of conduct for English bailiffs[106] in a multi-authored European work comparing national eviction and debt procedures. However, the privatization of the bailiff service increases this bad impression, with as yet relatively few formal safeguards for the public, compared to France, where there are also possible long delays in eviction.[107] Whatever the system, the existence of collective squatting increases the costs of eviction and has the potential to undermine public trust in the process if the eviction is seen to be unfair.

In France, there is a tradition of militant squats staying until the last stage of an eviction to make a point before the watching media. Physical eviction is a *voie de fait*, meaning a process normally in breach of human rights, which can only be carried out by the central state and by the police. Members of the militant squatting organization DAL have often confronted the police. At Cachan, some 500 squatters were evicted from disused university residences. The squatters initially refused to be split up and some went on hunger strike.[108] Collective squats can sometimes muster a public demonstration when they are evicted, again increasing eviction costs.

The criminalization of squatting by itself involves public costs relating to investigation, removal and arrest, detention pending trial, the trial itself and

103 Agence Nationale d'Information pour le Logement (ANIL), 'Droit et pratique de l'expulsion: une comparaison Angleterre France' (Habitat Actualité, December 2004).

104 Alexandra Topping, 'Dale Farm Evictions Mean the End of the Traveller Lifestyle, Say Gypsies' *The Guardian* (London, 18 September 2011); Robert Home, 'Forced Eviction and Planning Enforcement: The Dale Farm Gypsies' (2012) 41(3) International Journal of Law in the Built Environment 178.

105 Philippe Hoonakker (ed), *L'Exécution Immobilière en Europe. Entre Tradition et Modernité, Quelle Saisie Immobilière pour Demain, Editions Juridiques et Techniques* (Paris, Editions Juridiques et Techniques 2005).

106 At the time of writing reform is proposed.

107 See Ball (n 4) 238.

108 Bertrand Bissuel, 'Deux anciens squatters en grève de la faim ont été hospitalisés' *Le Monde* (Paris, 4 October 2006).

imprisonment. Afterwards, squatters with a criminal record are unlikely to be viewed as an acceptable tenant anywhere and thus will need to squat again. Even if squatters are only briefly detained, as Lindbeck and Snower suggested, the situation of stigmatized outsiders will deteriorate, in this case, due to the loss of a home and perhaps also the related loss of employment or family-break-up.

If the public authorities take care of the evicted, there might be less of a problem, but SQUASH[109] published a study in 2012 showing that implementing the Legal Aid, Sentencing and Punishment of Offenders Act 2012 would cost between £319 million and £790 million over five years compared to the £25 million estimated by the government.[110] Government figures had not included increased housing benefit costs and housing demand for squatters following the loss of free accommodation, costs to the public services of rehabilitating street sleepers and the costs of training and guidance. SQUASH did not take into account the potential extra cost of mass evictions or the possibility that individuals might not be rehabilitated, turning to crime, or that the stress of eviction and continuing difficulty in finding an appropriate home or rough sleeping can cause permanent damage to health.

Collective squatting and the criminalization of residential squatting both involve high public costs for relatively small benefits to insiders. This could also create a disruptive class of outsiders when accompanied by a sense of procedural unfairness. The divisiveness of protest conducted in this way is a problem for public order.

Different Global Responses to Squatting

Collective squatting will always have the benefit of weight of numbers. Insider-outsider theory and the ideas of Foucault describe squatters as being in a weak position, but large numbers of them might make a difference to the balance of power. This section widens the enquiry about how squatters are excluded or not excluded in different ways in France, the Netherlands, Turkey and elsewhere.

The dynamics of squatting will be affected by transaction costs, but the result might differ because of a whole series of factors. In the mature economies of Europe and the US, the extent of squatting can depend on various factors: transient occupation by young people accustomed to international travel; immigrants experiencing housing difficulties; expensive accommodation in cities; the amount of housing stock; the extent of law enforcement and surveillance; and the extent of local welfare provision. Where emerging or growing economies result in rapid

109 SQUASH, 'The Case Against Section 144' (March 2013) http://www.squashcampaign.org/docs/SQUASH-Campaign-Case-Against-Section-144.pdf accessed 1 May 2013.

110 The report was supported by Professor Danny Dorling of the University of Sheffield.

urbanization and very large suburban squatter settlements, there will be additional problems in coping with the sheer number of squatters.

One alternative is that collective squatting in homes is suppressed, but if the basic problem is housing need, this will be simply displaced. It has been seen that French squatting has involved large-scale invasions of non-residential property, but there have also been shanty towns or camps.[111] Le Marchand[112] described squatters living in disused tanker lorries, and local tradesmen would carry out adaptations to these as if they were normal homes. These are a form of collective squat, although they have become more covert in modern times.

Developments in the Netherlands suggest that the number of squatters can make a difference to the toleration of squatting. In the 1980s there were battles between groups of 20,000 or more squatters and the police, followed by a policy of pacifying squatters. Their numbers are now approximately 4,000 and, in 2010, the Dutch government passed a severe anti-squatting law, banning squatting anywhere.[113] Another recent development is what the Dutch call 'anti-squatters', known as 'house-sitters' in English (derived from 'baby-sitters'). These people occupy buildings to deter squatters for little reward, while in return being allowed to live in the buildings they protect. Priemus estimated that there were around 20,000 anti-squatters in the Netherlands, but these were people who might otherwise be squatters themselves. There was concern about vulnerable anti-squatters occupying offices and factories that were unsuitable for habitation and who might be endangered if the building were to be entered mob-handed.

In contrast, the growing strength of very large-scale suburban squatting has meant, first, the rediscovery of the usefulness of endowing people with ownership as a matter of law and order, and, second, the emergence of a common global support for squatters based on their housing needs. Governments across the world have endowed some of the inhabitants of large squatter settlements with ownership by public decree.

This has happened to some extent around Istanbul, where there was rapid urbanization and where squatter settlements housed up to half of the urban population. A patchwork of policies included pardoning squatters, granting title or allowing squatters to exchange plots. Alkiser has pointed out that 'this approach creates many conflicts and contradictions about property/tenure rights, public benefits, unearned income (undeserved urban rent), environmental quality and the liveable environments for everyone'.[114] This approach was thus not

111 Ball (n 4).

112 Arnaud Le Marchand, 'Travail mobile et habitat non-ordinaire dans les villes portuaires' in Valérie LaFlamme, Claire Lévy-Vroelant, Douglas Roberson. and Jim Smyth (eds), *Le Logement Précaire en Europe. Aux Marges du Palais* (Paris, L'Harmattan 2007) 243.

113 Hugo Priemus, 'Squatters and Municipal Policies to Reduce Vacancy; Evidence from the Netherlands' (ENHR conference, Toulouse, 2011).

114 Alkiser (n 54).

without its problems. Granting titles by public decree could raise expectations, with uncontrolled squatter settlements moving out of the city suburbs towards the wooded hills that provided the city's water supply. A lack of regularization meant a problem of enforcement of decent housing conditions, in supplying services, in planning and the ability to tax squatters. This shows the dynamics of a power relationship and the practical difficulties of moving on squatters linked to economic change, law and order.

In the case of very large-scale squats, the law can sometimes come full circle from resisting to accommodating squatters. Title by decree may not have quite the same advantages for incentivizing neighbourly behaviour as adverse possession and *prescription acquisitive*. A middle way can be found in Brazil, where title can be obtained after three years' occupation. Article 183 of the Brazilian Constitution of 1988 states that 'those who are squatters in an urban area of up to 250,000 (m^2), for a continuous period of at least five (5) years, without claim for housing, will be able to have its domain unless he/she has another urban or rural property', assuming the property upon which they are squatting is not being otherwise utilized. This accelerated approach is not new; in the US, the Homesteads Act 1848 provided title after 18 months in some cases of adverse possession.

These squats might well be too large to share the ethos of a collective squat but occupying space brings some power in any event. The transaction costs involved in removing squatters would be impractically high, particularly since the labour force of these suburbs might support the economic life of the city. Endowing them with property rights is useful for public order, peace and regulation, in spite of the problems identified by Alkiser. Despite these highly variable situations, the rhetoric from large urban slums has fed into a common moral rhetoric for all squats. The International Alliance of Inhabitants (IAI) has 'zero evictions' days[115] as part of its international campaigns, a globalization of justification and support.

To propose that eviction should not be allowed at all is just as one-sided as barring the way to squatters' title or declaring all squatters to be criminals. There is a question of balance. The objectivity of insider-outsider theory can lead to a way forward for study that might temper extremes. This means observing transaction costs and their effects as an indicator of where the economic problems lie.

Towards Solutions

Policies towards squatters tend to follow international trends and although a policy may exist in one country, there is no guarantee that it works. Three jurisdictions – England, France and the Netherlands – have attempted to increase the criminalization of squatters, although this attempt has failed in France. Of course, criminalizing large urban squatter settlements in developing cities could

115 See IAI, 'Zero Evictions Campaign' (2012) http://www.habitants.org/campana_cero_desalojos accessed 14 August 2012.

be counter-productive, since these might contain a majority of citizens. How can insider/outsider policy help?

Rueda[116] used insider-outsider theory to suggest that there are economic advantages in supporting outsiders in need before constituencies of insiders who need less help. This can improve the functioning of the market generally. Insider-outsider theory suggests that high transaction costs ultimately produce housing market difficulties for everyone. This affects vulnerable people first, particularly squatters, and especially if they are criminalized in ways that are disproportionate in relation to the alleged offence committed. If squatters are suffering difficulties or their numbers increase because of high transaction costs, then this might provide an early warning of problems in the housing market and consequent social disruption. The fact that they cannot find a home becomes a question of general interest, since difficulties in relation to access to the housing market due to high transaction costs may often be used to explain why they became squatters in the first place.

It might be possible to lower transaction costs one at a time, but this is difficult if there is a dominance of insiders affecting public decision-making. Lindbeck and Snower[117] make the practical suggestion that the answer to *insiderness* is to create a more 'level playing field' between insiders and outsiders. This can be done by increasing the voice of outsiders, reducing the voice of insiders or improving access to housing by reducing transaction costs. This might mean reducing the voice of local insiders in relation to decisions to provide housing, because housing-disadvantaged outsiders might not be popular locally. An example of such a mechanism is the decision of the French Constitutional Council that the criminalization of squatting is disproportionate, because it gave an ear to outsiders, not just insiders. Other major approaches involve the improved representation of outsiders and policies specifically taking account of their circumstances.

Conclusion

Squatting is frequently a response to high transaction costs in accessing the housing market. Consequently, squatters are strongly affected by these market conditions and are witnesses to its problems. These costs and conditions will affect others who are not squatters, or not yet squatters. The prevalence of squatting often demonstrates where these policies are failing. Studying these costs and insider-outsider theory can help to produce practical solutions. This necessarily means being wary of stigma associated with squatting, except as a symptom of a loss of bargaining power, or indicating the presence of barriers in relation to access to housing. More controversially, barriers to exit from housing cannot be too high, in the sense that procuring eviction in an appropriate case should not be

116 Rueda (n 96).

117 Lindbeck and Snower, 'The Insider-Outsider Theory: A Survey' (n 3) 40.

too difficult. What is considered too difficult is often a national cultural matter. Insider-outsider theory is an established economic theory that is applicable to the labour and housing markets. Extending this theory to squatting is fairly new, but requires further empirical study.

The increases in barriers to access described here tend to result in a move from individual to collective squatting. If access to squatters' title is effectively cut off by a move from high transaction costs to near-impossibility, there is also the loss of an incentive to care for the property and have good relations with neighbours. Such squatting could reduce state welfare costs for formerly homeless occupants and can be a means of integration. Ownership is still based on long-term possession and if individuals cannot support their title by showing a long period of possession or 'squatting' (often essentially the same thing), this also threatens ordinary home-owners. These owners might suffer difficulties with the 'diabolical proof', because of the perpetual need for evidencing transmission of ownership.

In addition, criminalization in England makes squatting yet more difficult, but also adds very high public costs in terms of policing and dealing with its consequences. The provision for this seems to be inadequate and does not holistically consider its ramifications. Prison is expensive and may leave people with a criminal record and no way back into normal housing or a job. Civil law adjudication as to whether squatters might have squatters' title becomes unlikely, however strong an individual case. The benefits of the policy are as yet uncertain.

It is not surprising that squatters choose to adopt the defensive position of collective squatting. Whatever the political or moral nature of the collective squat, its members can provide mutual support and continuity. As a group, they are much more difficult and expensive to evict, particularly if they are very numerous, such as in very large squats in emerging economies.[118] There is a danger of wider social unrest.

A collective squat can also call on wider digital and international communities to support an ethos of protest. This might shift public perceptions of morality to opposing the public authorities. Connections to politics and human rights can add an extra dimension to the moral arguments for and against squatters' title. This moral competition is progressed by squatters' local social and artistic activities or campaigns against homelessness generally. Such activities can bring people into squats who are attracted to the ethos of protest rather than because of a housing need to squat. A clumsy mass eviction could cause the general public to lose faith in the fairness of the eviction system or indeed support the squatting protest.

Insider-outsider theory involves examining what barriers are faced by all home-seekers. This is particularly useful when the moral debate has become so adversarial. It can show the costs of exclusionary policies within a future cost-benefit analysis, including the high public and personal costs of criminalizing squatters. This approach can also lead to better understanding of what causes these

118 Alkiser (n 54) 28.

problems. The representation of outsiders would also lead to a more democratic system with an all-round view of the procedural issues.

Chapter 10

Housing Ladders and Snakes: An Examination of Changing Residential Tenure Trajectories in the Republic of Ireland

Joe Finnerty and Cathal O'Connell

Introduction

This chapter explores aspects of current and prospective residential tenure trajectories in the Irish housing system, drawing on the metaphor of housing ladders and snakes. In common with many other countries, home-ownership, commonly portrayed as the highest 'rung' of this ladder, has been widely pursued at a policy level for many decades. In addition, low-income households have historically been accommodated by the state through the provision of social housing which has provided them with long-term, affordable, secure housing and which also held out the potential for tenants to become owner-occupiers through exercising a 'right to buy' tenant purchase option.

Since the onset of economic recession in 2008 and in line with the dominance of a home-ownership discourse, policy and media attention has been focused on the unsustainable mortgages of many of the cohort of home-owners who had bought homes at the height of the Irish house price bubble, which peaked in 2006. This chapter addresses this dominant discourse and its focus on home-ownership in two ways: first, it explains the puzzling issue of why a widespread slide – via a repossessions 'snake' – *down* the Irish tenure ladder for distressed mortgage holders has thus far not occurred; and, second, argues that the long-term re-structuring of the ladder's *ascent* for low-income households requiring social housing support has not received a commensurate degree of policy or popular attention, despite the fact that it signifies a major reconfiguration of the role of the state as an actor in the Irish housing system, especially in relation to housing options for low-income households. Prior to exploring these issues in greater detail, there is a discussion of the uses of metaphors in housing discourse and research, followed by an analysis of established residential tenure trajectories in the Irish housing system.

Housing Metaphors: Ladders and Snakes

The use of symbolic language in housing discourse and research has received increasing scrutiny in recent years, partly under the increased influence of social constructionism in housing studies.[1] A particular concern of such a constructionist approach relates to the unexamined assumptions embodied in the use of metaphors. In the case of the 'ladder' metaphor, there is a danger that presenting owner-occupation as the highest rung of the ladder reproduces the biases of the current Irish and other tenure systems, and privileges owner-occupation above all other tenures. To avoid this assumption, this chapter places long-term social housing and owner-occupation jointly at the top rung of the ladder as alternative forms of what is termed permanent settled accommodation.

The tenure housing ladder depicts an upwards tenure trajectory of the household from a situation of housing insecurity and vulnerability to one of relative security and stability in the form of settled/permanent housing. Conversely, the repossessions 'snake' (to expand the metaphor to include the traditional children's board game of Snakes and Ladders) portrays an enforced downwards trajectory of the household from a situation of relative security and stability in the form of settled/permanent housing to lower steps on the tenure ladder. The work of Kendig, Paris and Anderton,[2] Elphicke[3] and Beer, Faulkner, Clower and Paris[4] is drawn upon here, as is the wider application of the model of trajectories of social inclusion and exclusion employed by Room.[5]

---

1 K Jacobs and T Manzi, 'Discourse and Policy Change: The Significance of Language for Housing Research' (1996) 11 Housing Studies 543; K Jacobs, J Kemeny and T Manzi, 'Introduction' in K Jacobs, J Kemeny and T Manzi, (eds), *Social Constructionism in Housing Research* (Aldershot, Ashgate 2004); R Fopp, 'Metaphors in Homelessness Discourse and Research: Exploring "Pathways", "Careers" and "Safety Nets"' (2009) 26(4) Housing, Theory and Society 271.

2 H Kendig, C Paris and N Anderton, *Towards Fair Shares in Australian Housing* (Canberra, National Committee of Non-Governmental Organisations, International Year for the Homeless 1987).

3 N Elphicke, 'The Impact of the Recession. Rising Home Repossessions in the UK' (Social Situation Observatory – Network on Income Distribution and Living Conditions, Seminar – Housing, Social Inclusion and the Economy, 21 April 2009) http://ec.europa.eu/social/main.jsp?catId=1049&langId=en&newsId=1877&moreDocuments=yes&tableName=news accessed 22 August 2013.

4 A Beer, D Faulkner, T Clower and C Paris, *Housing Transitions through The Life Course: Aspirations, Needs and Policy* (Bristol, Policy Press 2011).

5 G Room, 'Trajectories of Social Exclusion: The Wider Context for the Third and First Worlds' in D Gordon and P Townsend (eds), *Breadline Europe* (Bristol, Policy Press 2000).

Established Tenure Trajectories in the Irish Housing System

To set the context for addressing aspects of snakes and ladders in the current Irish housing system, some discussion of the nature of established household tenure trajectories is required. For the past five decades, households entering the housing system in Ireland could expect to follow a housing career which would ultimately lead to secure/permanent accommodation in either social housing rented from the state or owner-occupier housing funded by long-term mortgage borrowings.[6] Eligible low-income households could normally expect to secure a local authority dwelling after a period spent on the local authority waiting list, while middle to high-income groups could avail themselves of a plethora of incentives to become owner-occupiers.[7] Many households that began their housing careers as tenants in local authority housing also became home-owners by availing themselves of the long-standing right to buy option, known in Ireland as the tenant purchase scheme, through which tenants could acquire their local authority dwelling at a heavily discounted price. For many households, regardless of their final destination, a brief transitional period was spent in the private rented sector and this was frequently the first source of independent housing for newly formed households. Only for a very small minority was private renting a final tenure destination, partly because of the appeal of social housing and owner-occupation, and partly because of the weak regulation of the sector and the poor standards of accommodation, especially at its lower end.[8] As a result of these established trajectories, a particular tenure division came to dominate the Irish housing system until recently in which a large majority of households followed a pathway to home-ownership, a further proportion rented from the state, while private renting played a largely transitional role as an initial tenure and accommodated a very small permanent tenant population mainly comprised of elderly tenants who occupied rent-controlled dwellings on a lifetime basis.

The established tenure trajectory followed by Irish households involved a progression from the household formation stage through short-term occupancy in private renting and on to permanent settled housing either as a traditional local authority tenant or as an owner-occupier. For the majority of households, the rungs of the ladder were sufficiently close together to facilitate reasonably unproblematic progression towards permanent settled housing on the basis that there was an adequate supply of social housing for prospective tenants to rent from

---

6 J Finnerty, 'Homes for the Working Class? Irish Public House-Building Cycles, 1945–2001' (2002) 27 Saothar 65. See also C O'Connell, *The State and Housing in Ireland: Ideology, Policy and Practice* (New York, Nova 2007).

7 D Redmond and M Norris, 'Setting the Scene: Transformations in Irish Housing' in M Norris and D Redmond (eds), *Housing Contemporary Ireland* (Dublin, IPA 2005).

8 A Ryall, 'A Review of Housing Legislation Since 1992' in Threshold, *Private Rented Housing: Issues and Options* (Dublin, Threshold 1999). See also Y Galligan, 'The Irish Private Rented Sector' in Norris and Redmond (n 7). See also P Kenna, *Housing Rights, Law and Policy* (Dublin, Clarus 2011).

the state and access to housing capital, combined with a range of state-provided fiscal incentives for aspiring owner-occupiers to purchase a dwelling on the open market. Over the last two decades, however, the tenure distribution has changed, notably in terms of the contraction of owner-occupation and local authority housing, and the expansion of the private and housing association rental sectors. This suggests that a structural shift may be occurring, in part promoted by the increasing role played by both private for-profit and not-for-profit landlords, and the elimination of policy biases which historically favoured owner-occupation.[9] These issues will be covered later on in the chapter.

Tenure Trends in the Irish Housing System

In reviewing housing trends in the Irish housing system, a striking feature has been the historically high level of owner-occupation and the consequent overshadowing effect this has had on the other tenures – private renting and local authority/social housing. At its peak, owner-occupation accounted for almost 80 per cent of the total housing stock, although over the past two decades this figure has fallen to its present level of just below 70 per cent.[10] In terms of market share, local authority housing peaked in the early 1960s, when it accounted for approximately 18 per cent of the total stock due to large-scale slum clearance and new construction programmes in urban areas dating from the 1930s onwards. Despite extensive building during the 1970s and 1980s, its overall proportion has never reached such heights again, largely due to the impact of privatization through tenant purchase schemes and more recently to the absence of large-scale new building output.[11] Private renting was once the dominant tenure in cities and towns and it housed over 85 per cent of urban households up to the 1940s. However, from that time onwards, it experienced a persistent decline in its share of the stock.[12] This was due to two main factors: first, the impact of slum clearance programmes and social housing provision for low-income households; and, second, the departure of middle-income households to home-ownership as a result of improved access to capital and a range of direct and indirect incentives provided by the state. Thus, the traditional dominance of owner-occupation was the outcome of state-driven political tenure strategies which promoted it over other tenures through a range of direct and indirect incentives. Furthermore, the growth of rental tenures was constrained by various factors which further enhanced the appeal of owning. Barriers to social housing entry, such as means-testing, resulted in access being confined almost exclusively to low-income households. In the private rented sector,

9 O'Connell (n 6).

10 Central Statistics Office, Profile 4, *The Roof Over Our Heads – Housing in Ireland* (Cork and Dublin, CSO 2012).

11 Finnerty (n 6).

12 Galligan (n 8).

weak levels of tenant protection and lack of security of tenure, as well as under-developed governance structures, relegated its function to a short-term transitional housing option. Thus, it could be argued that the growth of owner-occupation was as much a reflection of tenure constraint as tenure choice for households entering the housing market, as the alternatives were inaccessible or unappealing as long-term destinations for the majority of households.[13]

Recent Changes in Irish Tenure Patterns

The long-term dominance of owner-occupation in the Irish housing system would appear to be waning. In each of the four census counts conducted since the early 1990s, the level of home-ownership has declined, and according to the census of 2011, this form of tenure now includes just below 70 per cent of Irish households.[14] In the same period, the proportion of households accommodated in the private rented sector has risen from 10 per cent to 19 per cent, while social housing experienced a continued though minor reduction in its overall share and now houses 11 per cent of households.

As stated above, the underlying driver behind the reduction in the extent of owner-occupation has been the elimination of bias in Irish housing policy. There has been a gradual shift towards policy neutrality as many of the long-standing incentives and policy measures aimed at promoting owner-occupation have been phased out, among them first-time house buyers' grants, mortgage interest relief and the absence of property taxes. In addition, since the mid-1990s, rising house prices, which peaked in 2006, have had the effect of deterring some households from accessing the sector. Paralleling these developments, there have been signs of improvements in the regulation and governance of the private rental sector, which has resulted in strengthened tenant protection and tenancy rights (though this process remains a work in progress).[15] The private rented sector has also grown over the past two decades as a result of tax incentive-based urban renewal programmes in cities and towns which were introduced by the state in the 1990s to boost the construction sector and improve run-down urban areas.[16] This had the effect of bringing on-stream large volumes of apartments, many of which were purchased by investors for letting as private rentals. Policy change in relation to social housing, notably in terms of reductions in the volume of new building and a shift towards long-term leasing from the private sector, will also be a likely contributor to changing tenure trends,[17] and the implications of these prospective changes to the social housing

13 O'Connell (n 6).

14 Central Statistics Office (n 10).

15 Kenna (n 8).

16 Commission on the Private Rented Residential Sector, *Report of the Commission on the Private Rented Residential Sector* (Dublin, The Stationery Office 2000).

17 J Finnerty, 'A New Model of Social Housing?' (2010) 42 Cornerstone Issue 11.

rungs of the housing ladder are discussed further under the heading 'Changes to Tenure Trajectories for Low-Income Households' below.

Ireland in Comparative Context

Though owner-occupation is growing in many European countries, there would still appear to be a more balanced distribution between the owning and renting rungs of the tenure ladder in these countries, with the exception of Southern European countries such as Italy, Spain and Portugal, where ownership rates match if not exceed those in Ireland.[18] In Northern European housing systems, the rate of ownership is much lower and renting is more common than in Ireland. The UK (67 per cent), the Netherlands (58 per cent), Germany (41 per cent), France (57 per cent), Denmark (46 per cent) and Sweden (41 per cent) all have ownership rates below those of Ireland (69 per cent),[19] while their rental sectors are more mature in terms of ownership structures, governance and regulation, and tenants' rights. Comparisons with former communist Eastern European countries are more tenuous as a result of the mass privatization of social housing since the 1990s.[20]

An Irish Housing Snake?

Trends in Mortgage Arrears, Repossessions and Homelessness

The collapse of the Irish housing market, with price falls estimated to be in the region of 60 per cent since the peak in 2006,[21] and the accompanying economic crisis have severely reduced the number of households ascending to owner-occupation. Furthermore, the conditions for an emerging owner-occupation housing snake in the form of the enforced displacement of households to a lower tenure rung are present in the form of growing mortgage arrears, which have arisen out of and are compounded by rising levels of unemployment and stagnant economic growth. There has been a clear upward trend in the numbers of mortgages falling into arrears.[22] For instance, by June 2013, of the 770,610 private residential mortgage

---

18 A Pittini and E Laino, *Housing Europe Review 2012: The Nuts and Bolts of European Housing Systems* (Brussels, CECODHAS 2011).

19 Central Statistics Office (n 10).

20 J Hegedus, M Lux and N Teller, *Social Housing in Transition Countries* (London, Routledge 2013).

21 Daft.ie, 'The Daft.ie House Price Report: An Analysis of Recent Trends in the Irish Residential Sales Market 2012 Q3' http://www.daft.ie/report/Daft-House-Price-Report-Q3-2012.pdf accessed 19 March 2013.

22 Central Bank of Ireland, 'Residential Mortgage Arrears, and Repossession Statistics Q2 2013' http://www.centralbank.ie/press-area/press-releases/

accounts for principal dwellings held in the state, 97,874 or 12.7 per cent were in arrears of more than 3 months – up from 10.6 per cent in June 2012.[23] The question which arises from this trend is whether such arrears levels are generating 'snakes' in the housing system, as measured by key indicators such as house repossessions and rising levels of homelessness.

With regard to house repossessions, the evidence to date suggests that the snake has not taken hold. Despite the scale of arrears, the extent of repossessions is modest and in comparative international terms is extremely low. In the period from January 2012 to June 2013, a cumulative total of 1,050 residential units were repossessed from their occupants by lenders.[24] With regard to trends in homelessness, the Irish homeless population remains low and relatively stable.[25] While there has been an increase in the Dublin and Cork rough sleeper population in the latter half of 2012,[26] there is no evidence of the influence of structural mechanisms such as mortgage distress on the size or composition of the homeless population; individual or meso-level mechanisms such as mental health and addictions issues continue to predominate.

Banishing the Irish Snake? Policy Levers and Safety Nets

If the conditions for a snake are present in the Irish housing system, a puzzling issue is why has it not materialized in the form of mass repossessions? There are two primary explanations for the absence of a repossessions snake. First, there are the effects of public policy levers on the behaviour of financial institutions which have mediated the interactions between lenders and borrowers, and, second, there is evidence of effectively functioning social policy safety nets within the housing system. The primary public policy levers have taken the form of a code of conduct on mortgage arrears whereby mortgage lenders are legally bound to adhere to a Mortgage Arrears Resolution Process, which includes a moratorium on repossession proceedings against households that fall into arrears. This was imposed by the Irish state on banks and financial institutions which were the beneficiaries of the 2008 financial bailout. Under the terms of the bailout, the bad debts and defaulting loans (mainly those issued by Irish banks to developers

---

PagesMortgageArrearsandRepossessionStatisticsQ22013.aspx accessed 02 July 2013.

23 ibid.

24 ibid.

25 J Finnerty, 'Housing Exclusion and Homelessness in Ireland', Research Seminar: Housing, Social Affairs and Inclusion http://ec.europa.eu/social/main.jsp?langId=en&catId=1049&newsId=1877&furtherNews=yes accessed 26 August 2013.

26 Dublin Region Homeless Executive 2012, 'Number of People Sleeping Rough in Dublin in November 2012 at 87 Persons' http://www.homelessagency.ie/Media/2012-News/Number-of-People-Sleeping-Rough-in-Dublin-in-Novem.aspx accessed 19 March 2013. Eoin English 'Trebling in numbers sleeping rough as funds fall' *Irish Examiner*, (19 July 2013) http://www.irishexaminer.com/ireland/cwmhqlmhauid/rss2/ accessed 20 July 2013.

at the height of the property boom) were acquired by the state through a special purpose vehicle known as the National Asset Management Agency at an average discount of 57 per cent. In a gesture to distressed mortgage holders, a condition of participation in the bank rescue scheme was that the banks concerned could not initiate repossession proceedings for at least two years against households that fell into loan arrears. As a result, the repossession figures which have been recorded are comprised almost exclusively of foreign lenders who were not party to the state bailout, subprime lenders who lent money at very high interest rates to borrowers deemed to be too risky by mainstream banks, and mainstream bailed-out banks where the terms of existing agreements have not been adhered to by borrowers. Arising from the moratorium, financial institutions have been exhorted to be more proactive in dealing with borrowers and this has resulted in a greater level of engagement when repayment difficulties arise or mortgages are vulnerable to going into arrears. Most evidently, this appears in the form of the numbers of loans which have been re-structured. In the period from June 2011 to August 2012, this has grown from 66,000 to almost 82,000 mortgages, entailing a variety of re-structuring arrangements between lenders and borrowers including interest-only repayments, reduced instalments, loan term extensions, arrears capitalization, payment moratoria and deferred interest arrangements.[27] An implicit concern on the part of the banks that full acknowledgment of the extent of defaulting mortgages might necessitate either widespread debt write-downs or large-scale repossessions, with unwelcome financial and political consequences, has also played a role.

One obvious question which arises is what will happen when the moratorium period expires and banks are permitted to initiate repossession proceedings against mortgage holders who have fallen into arrears? According to observers, the most likely scenario to emerge will be one in which proposed personal insolvency legislation will have been enacted and settlements on mortgage debt will occur under its auspices. It is also likely that a graduated approach will be adopted by the lenders in pursuing arrears, with repossession of family homes acting as a last resort in favour of rental agreements which will allow households to remain *in situ*. Repossession of 'buy to let' rental properties which have arrears outstanding is far more likely to occur once a legal impediment in the Land and Conveyancing Law Reform Act 2009 relating to mortgages created before December 2009 and precluding banks from seeking possession has been eliminated.

The second part of the explanation for the absence of a snake in the Irish housing system relates to the effectiveness of existing social policy safety nets to support vulnerable households. The most prominent of these is known as the Mortgage Interest Supplement (MIS). This provision was introduced in the 1980s by the Department of Social Welfare (now known as the Department of Social

27 Central Bank of Ireland, 'Residential Mortgage Arrears, and Repossession Statistics Q3 2012' http://www.centralbank.ie/press-area/press-releases/Pages/MortgageArrearsandRepossessionStatisticsQ32012.aspx accessed 3 March 2013.

Protection) and is administered by community welfare officers. It is a part of the supplementary welfare scheme which offers temporary support to borrowers who need assistance to meet the interest element of mortgage repayments. Though historically an under-utilized provision, in recent years it has been availed of to a much greater extent as increasing numbers of home-owners encounter difficulties in meeting their mortgage repayments. Until the economic crash, the number of households availing themselves of MIS was modest and stable. However, since 2008, coinciding with the onset of the economic crisis, this number has grown significantly and had risen to approximately 19,000 by the end of 2011, with an expenditure of €67.8 million.[28]

This part of the discussion has explained why the threat of enforced tenure displacement facing some households at the top rung of the tenure ladder (those in the owner-occupied tenure with distressed mortgages) has not materialized, largely as a result of the effects of policy levers and social policy safety nets. However, as more households encounter difficulties in servicing their housing debts, it is likely that these policy levers and safety nets, in Ireland as elsewhere, will come under increasing strain, within the wider context of continuing economic stagnation, rising unemployment and government-imposed austerity policies.[29] Additionally, a restriction of MIS to borrowers in arrears for more than 12 months was introduced in June 2012, with the stated reason being to encourage lenders to engage more proactively in the mortgage arrears process.

Changes to Tenure Trajectories for Low-Income Households

The understandable focus on the difficulties of the cohort at the uppermost rung of the tenure ladder has resulted in a neglect of the longer-term public policy issue of how the reality of tenure trajectories has and will increasingly diverge from the policy and popular discourse of housing ladder ascent – the ideal of permanent settled accommodation – for Irish households.[30] While factors such as uncertainties around income, employment and house prices, and restrictions on mortgage credit have widened the rungs of the ladder for middle-income households, the focus in this section of the discussion turns to the ascent of the housing ladder by low-income households and specifically examines what is happening to the traditional tenure trajectory of low-income households towards permanent settled accommodation in local authority housing, with the scope for owner-occupation via tenant purchase. Continuing to employ the ladder as a housing metaphor, we

28 Department of Social Protection, *Annual Social Welfare Services Statistical Report – 2011* (Dublin, DOSP 2012) http://www.welfare.ie/en/downloads/ar2011.pdf accessed 3 March 2013.

29 A Wallace, D Quilgars and J Ford, *Exiting Unsustainable Home Ownership* (York, Centre for Housing Policy 2011).

30 Finnerty (n 17).

ask: (i) has the housing ladder changed for low-income households; and (ii) if so, what is the nature and impact of such change, especially for newly formed low-income households?

Changes to the Tenure Ladder

Drawing on an analysis of recent policy changes in relation to provision for low-income households, evident changes have occurred to the tenure ladder, mainly arising out of a reconfiguration of the relationship between private renting and social housing. The former is assuming a new policy significance while the latter appears to be falling out of favour and is being replaced by new arrangements which entail short-term and long-term leasing schemes for sourcing social housing in the private market. Table 10.1 below illustrates how direct provision by local authorities has been falling in recent years, while there has been a parallel growth in provision through the Rental Accommodation Scheme and the Long-Term Leasing Scheme, both of which draw heavily on the private rental sector as a source of accommodation and on the supplementary welfare rent allowance scheme as a source of funding.

Table 10.1 Sources of social housing provision 2006–11

Year	Direct Provision by Local Authorities	Direct Provision by Voluntary Landlords	Rental Accommodation Scheme	Long-Term Lease Scheme
2006	5,121	1,240	828	N/a
2007	6,988	1,685	2,077	N/a
2008	5,692	1,896	3,012	N/a
2009	4,089	2,011	1,990	N/a
2010	2,178	285	3,642	1,223
2011	810	140	6,337	1,193

Source: DECLG various years

The Role of Supplementary Welfare Rent Supplement

As stated earlier, until recently, private renting was viewed as a transitional tenure for many low-income households and as a permanent destination for a very small minority. Because they were low-income households, many private renters qualified for social housing but required financial assistance to meet the gap between their income and the rents demanded by landlords while they were on the waiting list. This gap was covered by a social welfare payment known as the rent supplement. Similar to the MIS for home-owners, the rent supplement is a welfare payment which is meant to be a temporary support until households are in a position to become self-sufficient in meeting rent payments.[31] Over time, a number of developments have occurred which show that private renting in Ireland is changing from a transitional to a longer-term housing destination for increasing numbers of low-income households. First, the rent supplement has unintentionally become a permanent housing support as many low-income households rely on it on an ongoing basis. This is evident from the growth in the number of claimants over the past decade, from 45,000 in 2001 to 100,000 in 2011, and amounted to an annual expenditure of €500 million in the latter year. Furthermore, a large proportion of these claims now extend beyond one year in duration.[32] In parallel with this, as the figures in Table 10.1 above illustrate, there has been a clear shift in emphasis in social housing policy in recent years away from direct housing output by local authorities towards rental and leasing schemes in the private market. In 2012 the state directly funded a total of 800 units, of which half were built by local authorities and the remainder by voluntary bodies, with most of these being allocated to 'special needs' rather than general needs households.[33] The shift away from direct provision towards market-based sources has been gradual and has been signalled for some time.[34] For instance in 2009 the then Housing Minister Michael Finneran TD stated that:

> We can no longer rely on the traditional acquisition and construction approach to meeting social housing needs. We must embrace every opportunity for delivering additional supply through market based mechanisms.[35]

This process is now well advanced and has been given added impetus in the most recent government *Housing Policy Statement* published in June 2011, which envisaged:

> A restructuring of the social housing investment programme to allow for the delivery of new social housing through more flexible funding models will provide key sources of delivery in the period ahead. The social housing leasing initiative

---

31 Department of Social and Family Affairs, *Report of the Social Partners' Group on Rent Supplement* (Dublin, DoSFA 2004).

32 Department of Social Protection (n 28).

33 Department of Environment Community and Local Government, 'Housing Minister Jan O'Sullivan Announces Funding of Over €250m to LAs from a Total Budget of €691m' *Development/Housing News* (20 March 2012) www.environ.ie/en/DevelopmentHousing/Housing/News/MainBody,29654,en.htm accessed 3 March 2013.

34 D Coates and D Silke, *The Rental Accommodation Scheme – An Overview of Financial Management and Control Systems* (Dublin, Centre for Housing Research 2006).

35 M Finneran, Ministerial Address (2009) http://icsh.ie/content/events/2009-national-social-housing-conference accessed 26 August 2013.

> and, in particular, the Rental Accommodation Scheme (RAS) will each play their part as long-term social housing supports. The Government also recognises that rent supplement – intended as a short-term income support – has become a de facto social housing support with many thousands of households reliant on the supplement to support accommodation costs for longer periods. This is not in the interests of the households receiving the support, local authorities or the Exchequer. The Government will rectify this by transferring responsibility for providing for the housing needs of long-term rent supplement recipients to housing authorities on a phased basis.[36]

The use of private renting to meet the housing needs of low-income groups has been recently reiterated by the government in terms of further reforms of how that sector is regulated. Under the auspices of injecting more 'tenure neutrality' into the housing system, there is a clear inference that this is being pursued in order to strengthen the capacity of private renting to fill a gap due to lower output from local authorities and social housing organizations. According to the Minister for Housing and Planning, Jan O'Sullivan TD:

> The challenge for government is to support the transition to a mixed tenure market that does not prioritise one housing tenure over another, that recognises that households housing needs will change over time and that provides a safety net to assist the most vulnerable to find housing solutions that meet their needs at a point in time.[37]

To the critical observer, the claim of tenure neutrality can be interpreted as favouring market-based solutions over direct provision funded by central government and delivered by local authorities. In practice some local authorities appear to view this as an opportunity to redefine their responsibilities from provision to procurement. In the face of severe reductions in capital building budgets, many local authorities have begun to revise their criteria for allocating social housing by classifying long-term rent allowance recipients as having their housing needs adequately met. In effect, this formalizes the status of such households as long-term residents of the private rental sector through rental and leasing arrangements with private landlords.[38] The shift to relying on the private market to meet long-term social

---

36 Department of Environment, Heritage and Local Government, 'Housing Policy Statement' 2011 http://www.environ.ie/en/DevelopmentHousing/Housing/PublicationsDocuments/FileDownLoad,26867,en.pdf accessed 26 August 2013.

37 Jan O'Sullivan, 'Putting Houses in Order' *Irish Examiner* (Lapps Quay, 14 January 2013) http://www.irishexaminer.com/weekend/putting-houses-in-order-219479.html accessed 19 March 2013.

38 Fingal County Council, 'Housing Strategy 2011–2017' (2011) http://www.fingalcoco.ie/Publications/Housing/Draft%20Housing%20Strategy%202011%20to%202017.pdf accessed 3 March 2013.

housing needs has not occurred as a result of a planned policy process. In reality, it amounts to the formalization of a de facto situation which has evolved over a long period. In that respect, it is not untypical of many aspects of Irish social policy where ad hoc responses which occur on an unplanned and uncoordinated manner are eventually reconstituted as new policy departures.[39]

Wider Rungs and Bigger Gaps

A number of implications arise from the move away from direct provision of social housing to procurement in the private market. For the majority of new social housing applicants, it signals the end of the traditional role played by social housing as a source of permanent settled accommodation.[40] The distinctions between local authority tenancies and private tenancies reveal how the former can be considered effectively a lifetime guarantee of settled permanent accommodation, while the latter is much more tenuous in terms of security and continuity. While local authority tenants and landlords may unilaterally terminate a tenancy under s 62 of the 1966 Housing Act, in practice this rarely occurs and qualitatively such a provision has no practical impact. The other mechanism by which a local authority can terminate a tenancy is by using the provisions of the 1997 Housing Act in relation to anti-social behaviour. However, in practice this is a convoluted and deeply contested route to adopt, and only occurs in extreme instances of anti-social behaviour. In contrast, private rental tenancies are regulated by the Residential Tenancies Act 2004, which provides a series of grounds for landlords to terminate a tenancy and the timeframes under which this can occur. Under the 2004 Act, the grounds for terminating a tenancy are set out systematically and clearly. Thus, while a tenancy cannot be terminated without reason, there are many grounds which a landlord can invoke and it is clear that the legislation weighs in their rather than the tenant's favour.[41]

There is also the question of what longer-term gain accrues to the state. Under long-term rental and leasing arrangements, dwellings revert to the possession of private landlords at the end of the stipulated rental or lease period regardless of the outlay of the state in rent payments. Thus, at the end of an extended and potentially expensive leasing period, the state is left with no capital interest in the dwelling. There are also issues in relation to continuity of supply as there is no guarantee that leases will be renewed by landlords, thus giving rise to implications for the housing stability and security of the tenants concerned. In certain circumstances, such as in competitive urban housing markets, where demand outstrips supply, landlords may prefer to let their units on the open market on the basis that higher

39 O'Connell (n 6). See also Department of Social and Family Affairs (n 31).
40 Finnerty (n 17); Kenna (n 8).
41 Kenna (n 8).

rents can be secured there, as opposed to renewing social housing leases where rents are capped below market rates.[42]

Rental accommodation and leasing schemes effectively categorize the social housing population into different classes of tenants based on their access to permanent settled accommodation. None of the types of tenancy now on offer to social housing applicants as a result of the shift towards sourcing social housing in the private market reach the bar of permanent settled accommodation set by traditional social housing. Existing tenants of local authorities occupy the top rung of the ladder in terms of secure settled accommodation, with the added benefit of being able to acquire their dwellings through the tenant purchase scheme. These are followed closely by tenants of voluntary and social housing landlords, who now have a variant of the 'right to buy' conferred on them under an incremental purchase scheme and are also protected from the vagaries of the free market with what are effectively lifetime tenancies. In contrast, tenants living in leased units are vulnerable to a range of factors outside their control that will influence how secure and settled their accommodation will be. In the best-case scenario, a household will be allocated accommodation under a long-term lease arrangement agreed between a social landlord and a property owner for a period of between 10 and 20 years. Under such an arrangement, a tenancy may be terminated by a landlord under the terms of the Private Rented Tenancies Act 2004 and a dwelling may be re-let on the open market at the end of the agreed lease period. However, of most concern is the situation faced by vulnerable low-income households that will continue to occupy mainstream private rented tenancies and have a portion of their rent paid under the state rent supplement scheme. Such tenancies can be terminated by landlords through a range of grounds provided for under the 2004 legislation. Such tenants also have a far lower threshold of continuity of accommodation and security compared to those in long-term leases and so must be considered very vulnerable to disruptions in their housing security. These vulnerabilities are faced by low-income tenants across the housing system; however, they are especially acute for those trying to access accommodation in competitive rental markets in large cities, where rental accommodation is much sought-after and where landlords can afford to be very selective about lettings in terms of tenant profile and duration.

The impact of these policy shifts is that the private rental sector as a terminal destination of low-income households will become formalized. The most recent official assessment of housing need recorded that the largest category of households who qualified for social housing were those in the private rented sector who were deemed to be 'unable to meet cost of their current accommodation'.[43] Traditionally this signalled entitlement to and allocation of conventional social housing. However, in the new policy environment, such households will be deemed

42 Finnerty (n 17). See also J Finnerty and C O'Connell, 'Return to Social Housing Preferable' *The Irish Times* (Dublin, 29 July 2004) 14.

43 Department of Social Protection (n 28).

to have their housing needs satisfied if they are in receipt of rent allowance for 18 months or more, or if the landlord they are renting from opts to join one of the long-term leasing schemes.

Conclusion

This chapter has examined two aspects of recent household tenure trajectories in the Irish housing system through the widely used metaphor of the housing 'ladder'. First, it has explored whether there is evidence of a snake in the Irish housing ladder which is leading to higher incidences of tenure displacement. Second, it has examined structural changes to the housing ladder itself and has analysed whether recent policy changes will make a trajectory towards permanent settled housing less likely for low-income households.

Current available evidence does not signal the emergence of a snake in the form of mass repossessions, largely due to the influence of public policy levers and the effectiveness of social policy interventions. However, this conclusion is subject to qualification as both of these factors will come under increasing strain if the public policy levers, especially in relation to conditions imposed on lenders, are relaxed or if social policy fiscal supports are curtailed as a result of the imposition of deepening austerity measures.

A broader issue, and arguably one more structurally significant in terms of housing policy, concerns the experiences of low-income households that have traditionally been housed directly by the state through local authority provision. It is clear that the housing ladder has changed for them and these changes are significant. Low-income households that enter the housing system are now almost certainly destined to be accommodated in a hybrid form of social housing which is predominantly owned by private landlords and leased temporarily by the state, which is manifestly not as secure as state-provided social housing.[44] Beyond the immediate experiences of households losing out on access to permanent settled accommodation is the underlying re-structuring of Irish social housing policy as we witness the end of large-scale direct provision by local authorities and the privatization of a key aspect of Irish social policy delivery. While the role of social housing has been much contested in academic and policy quarters in the UK, such as by Hills[45] and King,[46] no comparable conversation has occurred

44 For further discussion on issues relating to notions of security and well-being related to tenure, see R Hiscock, A Kearns, S Macintyre and A Ellaway, 'Ontological Security and Psychosocial Benefits from the Home: Qualitative Evidence on Issues of Tenure' (2001) 18(1–2) Housing, Theory and Society 50.

45 J Hills, *Ends and Means: The Future Roles of Social Housing in England* (London, CASE 2007).

46 P King, 'No Choice: Reforming Social Housing in England' (2008) 28(2) Economic Affairs 37.

in Ireland, despite the structural implications for the sector arising from current policy developments.

Index

References to figures are shown in *italics*. References to tables are shown in **bold**. References to footnotes consist of the page number followed by the letter 'n' followed by the number of the footnote, e.g. 26n106 refers to note no. 106 on page 26.

FSC
www.fsc.org
MIX
Papier | Fördert gute Waldnutzung
FSC® C083411

Kolibri 360 GmbH
Ferdinand-Jühlke-Straße 7
99095 Erfurt, Deutschland
produktsicherheit@kolibri360.de